DATE DUE

Deliver
THE Vote

Deliver the Vote

THE Vote

A HISTORY OF ELECTION
FRAUD, AN AMERICAN POLITICAL
TRADITION—1742–2004

Tracy Campbell

CARROLL & GRAF PUBLISHERS
NEW YORK

DELIVER THE VOTE
A History of Election Fraud, an American Political Tradition—1742–2004

Carroll & Graf Publishers
An Imprint of Avalon Publishing Group Inc.
245 West 17th Street
11th Floor
New York, NY 10011

AVALON
publishing group incorporated

First Carroll & Graf edition 2005

Library of Congress Cataloging-in-Publication Data is available.

ISBN-13: 978-0-78671-591-6
ISBN-10: 0-7867-1591-X

9 8 7 6 5 4 3 2 1

Interior Design by Maria Elias
Printed in the United States of America
Distributed by Publishers Group West

To Leslie, Alex, and Drew

Contents

"The one pervading evil of democracy is the tyranny of the majority, or rather of that party, not always the majority, that succeeds, by force or fraud, in carrying elections."

—Lord Acton

Deliver THE Vote

"The Inclination to Injustice"

I n 1887, Edgar Levey was a New York City poll official who possessed a trait that made him stand out among many of his peers:
He was horrified by the brazen manner in which votes were routinely
bought and stolen. Before the polls even opened in Levey's precinct,
long lines of illegal "colonizers" were waiting to cast their votes—votes
that had already been purchased, often by the very officials whom
Levey worked alongside. When the voting commenced, Levey was
further dismayed as ward heelers distributed five-dollar bills to
arriving voters with "no effort at concealment." He noted, sadly, "This
was my first introduction to 'practical politics.'"

When Levey confronted the vote buyers, things only grew worse.
He was soon surrounded by angry ward captains, whose taunts and
threats had a consistent theme—they were outraged that "a dude with
a clean collar had come to deprive them of an honest living." Levey
wondered: "How large a proportion of voters understands the practical
workings of our election methods?" That day, Levey learned a painful
truth: "Democracy is a failure."

That jarring assessment did not reflect the common views that the
republic stood as a "shining city upon a hill," whose elections were free
and fair contests that objectively measured the "consent of the governed."
Indeed, the American experiment seemed to represent a substantial

progression in how political power was earned. For centuries, power had rested with the descendants of a specifically ordained family, whose legitimacy to rule was grounded in the sanctity of their blood ties. Or, an even easier approach was one where military leaders acquired power by the benefit of an army. The fact that citizens would select their leaders by casting ballots rather than by using guns was the realization of a democratic dream.

Yet what Levey saw on Election Day was not limited to his precinct, to New York City, or even to his generation. Buying votes, stuffing or destroying ballots, moving polling locations, transposing results, importing illegal voters from other towns or states, suppressing, disfranchising, and sometimes killing voters comprises a long, sordid tradition in American political culture. In retrospect, it would be innocent to assume differently.

Unfortunately, one of the innocent people was me. Even after writing a book on a New Dealer who had been convicted of stuffing ballot boxes, I still assumed that Boss Tweed had been the first to take the bite from the corrupt apple in the Garden of Eden, only to discover that the corruption was there long before Tweed or the rise of Tammany Hall. What had begun as a small book on recent fraud quickly grew. My research took me back much farther than I ever expected, back to the early days of the republic. Indeed, I found so much fraud involving hundreds of local, state, and national elections, that I was soon staggering under the weight of so much evidence.

Imagine my dismay, then, on the evening of November 7, 2000, as I watched the presidential election returns. Part of that dismay stemmed from the fact that my already-onerous research agenda was now significantly compounded. Yet I was able to draw some solace because by that time, I had come to know something about American politics that most people were not prepared to accept as an ongoing reality: namely, that the process itself was deeply corrupted and had been so for over two hundred years.

As the 2000 recount played itself out, I knew I had seen many of the unfolding conditions before. When election fraud had surfaced in the past, even in presidential contests, people would get outraged for a short time, but then it would soon pass away. Partisans on the losing end might warn of dire consequences, but calm was quickly restored, and the indignant cries that a crime was going unpunished were silenced. Consequently, what we know as historical memory is not the outrage, but the passing away; not the flaw at the heart of the political culture, but that the flaw would be quickly corrected.

The end result is that when things like Florida occur from time to time, they are not perceived as part of a deeply entrenched tradition, but as a bizarre anomaly to be corrected by improved technology. Scholars and pundits of American elections generally conclude that we are not to worry about these episodes since they are not enough to change any but perhaps a few contests.* Plus, there was probably enough fraud on both sides in any given race to equal itself out. As the defense goes, any fraud that may have existed in bygone city machines or corrupt rural fiefdoms had long ago been eradicated. A contradiction appears in all of this: As the American people are forced to see themselves as increasingly remote from the process of selecting their leaders and influencing policy, they become resigned to their fate at the very moment they are told they have nothing to be resigned about. This book necessarily lives within that contradiction.

Despite all the changes in the mechanics of voting and the apparent safeguards, how has fraud—flagrant and subtle—persisted? The answer, I suggest, is a deeply embedded culture within American politics that considers cheating fully justifiable. Those contributing to this culture, which I will call the culture of corruption, have not been limited

* I use "fraud" to describe any systematic attempt to deliberately alter the election process for unfair advantage. This can be done through a variety of means and does not need to necessarily change the final results. The important issue is that the democratic integrity of the election is compromised as honest votes are diluted in the aggregate.

to cigar-chomping party bosses. Precinct captains, poll officials, and police officers were involved, as well as teachers, lawyers, and clergy. What makes this culture so enduring is that the participants did not perceive their deeds to be assaults on the democratic process. Rather, they internalized a powerful rationale that considered cheating part of a game that one has to practice in order to counteract one's equally corrupt competitors. Over the course of time, as the political and economic stakes increased, so did the corruption. In all, the history of election fraud has demonstrated an unwelcome civics lesson: Election fraud is a crime that usually pays.

This book does not attempt to provide an encyclopedic accounting of every conceivable stolen or contested election, or to utilize an array of statistics or formulae. The task at hand is to use selected examples from various eras and locales to describe how this culture has developed and survived over the years. These elections demonstrate how the results we study with such precision were often fashioned. Some of the elections may be familiar, others obscure. Some cases are remarkable for their sheer audacity, others for their naked brutality.

Not all elections, of course, are characterized by fraud, and not all politicians or insiders practice the art. In fact, many politicians, judges, activists, and reformers have spent a good part of their careers exposing the layers of electoral corruption in local, state, and national elections. Unfortunately, their attempts to "purify the ballot" have not been altogether successful. Contemporary reformers need to know the challenges and outcomes of these earlier episodes in order to understand the complexity of our current predicament.

At bottom, this is a book about the very roots of democracy. Elections are the lifeblood of the republic, and we know much about strategies and candidates, polling data and campaign finance. Yet the realities of Election Day itself remain shadowy. This book is my attempt to bring into the light the process whereby political power is conceived. It also seeks to reconcile Edgar Levey's bleak appraisal from over a century ago with the modern challenges facing an increasingly demoralized electorate. As such, it recognizes the dual nature of the democratic tradition best described by Reinhold Niebuhr: "Man's capacity for justice makes democracy possible; but his inclination to injustice makes democracy necessary."

PART ONE

The Failure of a Democratic Experiment

CHAPTER ONE

"I Never Saw Such Havock"

"The ballots didn't make the outcome,
the counters did."

B efore Philadelphia was known as the cradle of the republic, colonial elections took place at the State House (now Independence Hall). The milieu surrounding these early experiments in local democracy would be found deplorable by modern voters. The thick crowds on Election Day were often drunk and unruly, and many Philadelphians became accustomed to fights and brawls outside the venerable hall. When a voter could make his way past the throng, he placed his paper ballot through a nine-inch-square window and into a makeshift ballot box. At other times, a more straightforward approach was used. At the appointed time, election inspectors called out the name of a candidate, and voters made their selections known literally by standing by their man.

In such an environment, it was not surprising that Philadelphia elections often descended into open vote fraud and bloodshed. In 1742, when rumors swirled that illegal German immigrants were being imported to the city to swell vote totals, more than fifty sailors attacked Quakers and Germans attempting to vote. One sailor was not impressed by pleas to allow the election to proceed without violence. "We came to fight . . . and by God we will," he said. The resulting bloody riot exceeded the level of violence many had come to expect as routine when arriving at the polls. In all, over fifty people were arrested for election violence. One witness claimed, "I never saw such havock in my Life before."

The "havock" was not limited to Philadelphia. Part of the unruly nature of voting was a result of the disparate ways each city and state conducted elections. While paper ballots were used in a few elections, the preferred manner throughout the colonies was to simply express one's choice by voicing it in public, a process termed *viva voce*. This uncomplicated method struck a certain chord in the democratic ethos of nascent town-hall democracy, where a citizen could stand up and state his opinions to his fellow townsmen. It also made the process of voting vulnerable to manipulation and intimidation. To allow voters to cast their choice without fear of reprisal, South Carolina, North Carolina, Pennsylvania, and Connecticut experimented with secret ballots in some elections, but the general trend was to look unfavorably upon confidential voting. The effort to bring secrecy to New York elections failed in the State Assembly in 1770 on grounds that ignorant or illiterate voters would become the pawns of powerful political interests. New Jersey even required lists of how people voted to be published after each election.

A "CORRUPTING INFLUENCE"

Despite their nostalgic reputation, colonial elections were not the pristine exercises they appeared. Some notable figures, in fact, engaged in "electioneering" tactics that became a standard component of colonial culture. In running for the Virginia House of Burgesses in 1758, George Washington spent nearly 40 pounds—a considerable sum for the day—for gallons of rum, wine, brandy, and beer, all used to win over the votes of his neighbors. Washington's manager, Colonel James Wood, had worked feverishly to see his candidate defeat an opponent who had easily outpolled Washington in a previous election, and providing liquor was something ambitious candidates knew was a necessary part of winning over voters. While it may have been considered beneath the dignity of a candidate to openly solicit votes by campaign speeches, it was not beneath his dignity to lubricate the thirsty throats of prospective voters who may have trudged many miles to make it to the polls, a custom that colonists termed "treating."

As Washington awaited the election's end, he did not lament how obtaining a Burgess seat required competing in a vote-buying market. Instead, he feared that Wood had "spent with too sparing a hand." The future revolutionary general and president, in order to avoid charges of bribery, simply hoped "no exception were taken to any that voted against me but that all were treated alike," and added that he also hoped "all had enough." Apparently they had: Washington won.

Not long after Washington's victory, the House of Burgesses passed a law disqualifying any member of the House who, "before his election, either himself or by any other person or persons on his behalf and at his charge," had provided "any money, meat, drink, entertainment or provision . . . in order to get elected." Another member of the House of Burgesses, Thomas Jefferson, was also not above dispensing liquor on Election Day. Jefferson claimed such practices were not outright examples of vote-buying, rather mere rewards for travelers taking the time and expense to exercise their franchise. Yet another Virginian, James Madison, refused to provide liquor in his 1777 race, calling the practice of "swilling the planters with bumbo" a "corrupting influence." Evidence of how influential the "bumbo" could be was on full display when Madison lost his race. Even among the young nation's elite, the understanding existed early on that more was necessary to win an election than popular ideology or soaring rhetoric. It often required a liquid incentive.

In general, only white, property-owning men could vote in colonial America. Beside the usual paternalistic and racist justifications for limiting suffrage, even white men on the bottom of the economic ladder were considered unfit to vote. If propertyless men voted, asserted John Adams, "an immediate revolution would ensue." Strict rules on owning real property could alleviate that worry, but even property qualifications produced opportunities for corruption. In many local elections, office-seekers and their supporters often purchased freeholds for landless men in return for their vote, a process termed "fagot voting." After the election, the land was simply returned to the original owner. This form of early vote-buying was used frequently in colonial Virginia, New Jersey, New York, Rhode Island, and Connecticut. While seemingly "legal" in that the voters on Election Day all owned their own land, the underlying reality was far from what the property requirement had originally intended. In addition, election officials sometimes looked the other way when landless men attempted to vote if they were confident the votes would go a certain way. Difficulties in determining exact property lists and land values made the property qualification even more suspect. In 1760, Rhode Island gave the Assembly power to scrutinize the names of freeholders and to reject anyone whose land ownership was questionable.

Even determining the precise definition of "resident" proved a formidable task because of the transient nature of the colonial population as well as the sheer difficulty of proving legal residency. Consequently, some states allowed aliens to vote in local elections. The South Carolina Assembly passed a law in 1704 that allowed voting by aliens, even after an election three years earlier that had been termed "a scene of riot, intemperance, and confusion" because of voting by non-residents.

It was not a giant step to go from dispensing alcohol or contriving land titles to simply buying votes outright. Rationalized as a mere compensation for the effort taken to cast a vote, vote-buying was also dismissed as harmless electioneering, where the buyers claimed that purchased votes would probably have been cast in like manner without any inducements. The practice became so well known in Rhode Island in the mid-1700s that "Rhode Islandism" became a pejorative term for vote-buying. During an especially tough campaign, the Browns of Providence underwrote the buying of illegal voters as well as a practice not usually associated with vote-buying: paying some prospective voters *not* to vote. This was an especially effective way of vote-buying that ensured no suspicious activity around the polls on Election Day that could incriminate the vote buyer. On one occasion, Rev. Ezra Stiles (the future president of Yale) claimed that one third of the electorate in Newport, Rhode Island, stayed away from the polls, "silenced by connexions." Another form of intimidation occurred in Virginia in 1736, where one defeated candidate retaliated against some men he knew had not supported him by calling in loans they owed him. Many of these men lost their property and even ended up in debtor's prison, a not-so-subtle method of de facto voter intimidation that would be repeated in countless other colonial contests.

Because of the lack of uniformity or oversight in voting procedures, the individual charged with supervising the election at the local level, usually the sheriff, thus exercised enormous power over the election process. Not surprisingly, sheriffs were among the most skilled practitioners of the culture of corruption in colonial America. A frequent method sheriffs used in influencing an election involved moving or closing the voting location at the last minute to confuse and discourage voters. Sheriffs could not only manipulate poll locations, voting times, and voter qualifications, they could also simply change election results unilaterally and intimidate various voters. Sometimes sheriffs even punished voters by placing them on jury duty. Sheriffs and other local officials did not worry about the legality of their actions, for a simple reason: Up until 1725, for example, all manner of election fraud went unpunished in New Jersey because no laws existed which prohibited such conduct, not that the mere passage of legislation would have been able to curtail the corruption.

THE RISE OF PARTIES

Although political parties are not usually associated with colonial America, the class and economic divisions that had emerged in the colonies by the 1740s produced a precursor to the party system in the form of numerous interest groups, or "factions," that sought office by appealing to a particular set of voters. In New York, voters called for assembly elections to protect themselves against entrenched power, and were adamant on the importance of the secret ballot, while various elite groups vied for the support of the middle and lower classes. Some New Yorkers, similar to colonists everywhere, castigated such narrow appeals and stated that politics should serve only one "Publick Good"; others claimed that parties "are a check upon one another, and by keeping the ambition of one another within Bounds, serve to maintain the public liberty."

With the outbreak of the Revolutionary War, simmering political divisions necessarily arose between those siding with the revolutionaries or those remaining loyal to the king (Whigs and Tories, respectively), and later between those who supported a strong central government and those who wanted to allow more power to the states (Federalists and Anti-Federalists). As these divisions grew more acute, the disputes often carried over to local elections. With the rise of local "political clubs" in New York City, its elections quickly became more heated, violent, and corrupt, and an investigation of some municipal elections uncovered that women, transients, and even children had voted. Not all New Yorkers tolerated this state of affairs, and they argued that the only way to end the open corruption made possible by voice voting was to utilize the secret ballot. These reformers understood that fair elections were fundamental to some larger democratic impulses growing throughout the colonies, and consequently held their meetings under the revolutionary symbol of the Liberty Pole.

In some states, the degree to which election fraud was on the minds of the revolutionary generation was visible shortly after declaring independence. The Pennsylvania constitution of 1776 set certain punishments for bribery at the polls, and the next year the North Carolina state assembly passed a statute prohibiting bribery, ballot-box stuffing, and multiple voting. By 1784, New Hampshire made conviction of bribery at the polls a disqualification for holding office. After the passage of a series of laws in the 1790s prohibiting the presence of armed groups around the polls, the assembly passed another law in 1801 outlawing treating. Yet the treating law had virtually no impact on the widespread dissemination and consumption of liquor on Election Day, and by the early 1820s the New Hampshire assembly tried in vain to minimize treating by shortening the length of the election from three days to one.

Perhaps no elections in colonial America had more import than those that ratified state constitutions. In ratifying the basic structure of state government and the role of slavery or religion within the states, such elections would have profound implications. Yet these referenda displayed the paradox of a people striving to break off colonial tyranny but willing to use less-than-democratic means to enact a new political structure. In Massachusetts, the state constitution of 1780, the world's oldest functioning constitution and written by John Adams, was submitted to the people of Massachusetts for the required two-thirds majority. In Massachusetts, there was no uniform method of voting on the constitution, although the constitutional convention asked towns "to state their objections distinctly" on the ballots they submitted.

In 1916, the Harvard historian Samuel Eliot Morison examined

those ballots and found that "the two thirds majority was manufactured" by the convention. In carefully perusing the returns on two
selected amendments, Morison found votes affirming the amendments of 8,885 to 6,225, and 6,338 to 5,221, far short of the required
majority, yet both passed nonetheless. Morison concluded, "The Convention deliberately juggled the returns in order to make it appear"
that the two-thirds majority had been reached, and asked "whether the
constitution of Massachusetts, now in force almost 137 years, was ever
legally ratified?"

"THE PIVOT ON WHICH TURNS THE FIRST WHEEL"

As the framers of the federal Constitution struggled over the complex
details of creating a government, their concept of voting was rather
limited. The Constitutional Convention in Philadelphia was wary
about allowing white, propertied men, otherwise known as "The
People," to elect any branch of government directly, other than members of the U.S. House of Representatives. The Senate would be
chosen by state legislatures, and an Electoral College from the states
would select the president; the president, in turn, would nominate
members of the federal judiciary pursuant to Senate confirmation,
without any elections to complicate the process. The result proved a
rather limited idea of where power in the American republic drew its
initial source. From the very beginning, voting in the colonies was not
conceived as a natural or inalienable right, but as an earned and limited privilege.

Years later, in his inaugural address, President Washington elabo-
rated on the new machinery of American elections. "The election of
the different branches of Congress," Washington proclaimed, "is the
pivot on which turns the first wheel of the government—a wheel
which communicates motion to all the rest." Washington also praised

the apparent lack of corruption of American elections: "The exercise of this right of election seems to be so regulated as to afford less opportunity for corruption and influence; and for more stability and system than has usually been incident of popular governments."

During the first years of the Republic, Washington's claims concerning the purity of American elections were weakened upon closer examination. Whether he was aware of the culture that existed just below the visible layer of political activity is not clear, although his own history should have informed him of its persistence. Just determining who was eligible to vote in a given district remained a sticky issue, as many colonies did not even require voters to be naturalized citizens in their respective locales in order to vote. An example was provided in Connecticut, where Federalists enacted a Stand Up Law, which required voters in local elections to literally stand up when their votes were being polled. Under the guise of "reform," Federalists argued that this would streamline elections from the more cumbersome paper ballots, although the fact that it would allow Federalists to identify and punish Republicans was clear to all observers. How far other candidates and their supporters were willing to go to win had already been formed in a political culture that not only didn't trust the mass of the people to choose their own government, but also saw nothing particularly disturbing in intimidating prospective voters or in plying them with rum.

Yet the very structure of Congressional apportionment and presidential elections raised serious questions about the inherent unfairness created by the federal Constitution. In the infamous "three-fifths compromise," the framers counted every five slaves as three people. Thus, the South gained fourteen more Congressional seats and electoral votes due to its slave population that could not vote. Thomas Jefferson's Virginia alone had six additional "slave" votes, giving slave-owners there more electoral clout than non-slaveowners in northern states. Considering that Jefferson and Aaron Burr received just eight more electoral votes than the incumbent, John Adams, in the election of 1800, many discounted the Democrats' claim that the election was the "second American Revolution" or that it even represented the will of the people. Leonard Richards concluded that "Many historians, celebrating the virtues of the master of Monticello, forgot this fact; New England Federalists never did." This basic electoral advantage was crucial to Southern political aims until the Civil War.

While the structure of early American elections left most adult citizens out of the equation, the struggle to expand the electorate slowly won some victories. By the 1820s, property qualification began to disappear as Delaware, Maryland, Massachusetts, and New York abolished such requirements to vote. While some areas had briefly experimented with allowing women to vote, the electorate was still an all-male enclave. Yet new barriers to universal male suffrage arose. At the same time that property rules were ending, taxpaying requirements

The spirit of *viva voce* elections is captured in this 1852 painting by George Caleb Bingham, as well as the numerous opportunities for buying and stealing votes. Alcohol is distributed on the left, and one thoroughly intoxicated voter is held up awaiting his turn. The sign that hangs over the process reads: "The Will of the People." Credit: The Saint Louis Art Museum

were initiated in Connecticut, Delaware, Massachusetts, and New York, as well as in such western states as Ohio and Louisiana.

While the debate raged as to who should be allowed to vote, national politics took on a new light with the presidential election of 1824. That election had several leading candidates with vast political experience, such as Henry Clay and John Quincy Adams. Andrew Jackson, on the other hand, represented a different type of presidential candidate, who was precisely the kind of political leader the framers were worried about when constructing the Electoral College. Uneducated and gruff, Jackson possessed a violent temper and relied on his popular appeal rather than his intellect or political experience. When the votes were counted, Jackson commanded a plurality of the popular vote and had won more electoral votes than any of his competitors. However, since the Constitution required a majority of the electoral vote, the House of Representatives had to decide the next chief executive. Jackson assumed that the "people's house" would honor the clear preference expressed by the voters and make him president, but the House selected Adams. As Jackson fumed, the party tensions escalated, and in the 1828 election, Jackson's supporters turned out in record numbers to defeat Adams (Jackson's 647,286 votes in 1828 nearly doubled the entire electorate of just four years earlier).

Besides expanding the "spoils system" that would soon dominate American politics, Jackson's party-driven policies also created new tensions that made Election Day even more important. The national divisions that hinged on such matters as nullification, the Bank War, and the protective tariff drove deep political wedges within the electorate. Desperate partisans, anxious to win or retain offices that held vast patronage powers, were willing to do what was necessary to claim victory at the polls, especially if they felt cheated by their opponents. Within a very short time after the Revolution, the unity President Washington had hoped would oversee American politics had dissolved, and national, state, and local elections became bitter contests, often settled in ways that had little to do with the "consent of the governed."

"Let Dogs Be Registered!"

Like many other states, Kentucky had a chronic problem of illegal aliens who claimed residency for voting purposes. Although the state constitution required one year's residency for voting purposes, the inherent difficulty in defining and tracking residency made discounting illegal voters nearly impossible. By 1840, reformers in the state called for a registry law, whereby all who wished to vote registered in the county or city where they resided. Such reforms appealed to a number of Kentuckians, one of whom noted that elections by the 1840s witnessed "much corruption and fraud." In Louisville, one resident said the problem was especially widespread. "There are to be found at all times a floating population of several hundred," who on Election Day "come forth from their haunts of pollution to claim the rights of citizenship." A registry law, in another voter's opinion, "will purge corruption, preserve purity in our elections, and secure the rights of suffrage to every citizen."

While some supporters of a registry system expressed their concerns out of a heartfelt wish to "preserve purity," most undertook their work out of a desire to preserve partisan advantages under the guise of electoral reform. Whigs were especially supportive of registry laws, since they felt Democrats resorted to importing voters in a large number of elections. One loyal Whig confided to the newspaperman and party leader Thurlow Weed that "If we can pass a good Registry law to protect us from fraud, we are safe for all time to come." Loyal Democrats, on the other hand, felt the reform excluded citizens who had just recently moved to a new residence. Additionally, Democrats argued that voter registration was an unwarranted intrusion into the act of voting that might prohibit a number of otherwise legal voters from participating, particularly if it were accompanied by a registry tax.

Registration, like the act of voting itself, varied from state to state and was also ripe for opportunities for fraud. In the 1857 Iowa constitutional convention, one delegate named Price objected to a proposal to require a three-month residency requirement within a specific county. "What are these county lines and what are these counties politically?" Price asked. "They are mere organizations for carrying on the business of the State at large." For Price, the answer was simple: "Let any man vote anywhere where a ballot box is," since, in his estimation, "corruption will exist." In a clear testimonial of the persistence of the culture of corruption, Price added: "Provide your laws as you will, you cannot entirely prevent it."

In the Maryland constitutional convention, one of the delegates, William A. Spencer, essentially agreed with Price's views, claiming that a six-month residency requirement would solve nothing in his state's elections. To Spencer, the only answer was to exact harsher punishments for illegal voting. Efforts to enact registry laws subsequently failed in Iowa, Indiana, and New York, where Democrats opposed Whig and Republican attempts to enact a registry law because it would shut off the naturalization "mills" in which so many immigrants were added to the rolls in the days leading up to an election. Democrats in New York even paraded the streets with banners testifying to the latent corruption that accompanied the lax registration: "Let Dogs Be Registered!" Yet when registry laws were enacted, partisans found unique ways to circumvent the rules. In Saginaw City, Michigan, a registry law actually helped Republicans steal a local township election from the Democrats. The law established a registry board in each ward. Republicans headed each ward's registry board, and subsequently disfranchised scores of Democrats who had not legally registered, but allowed Republicans to vote, registered or not.

The essential arguments about registering voters boiled down to a debate between two members of the 1850 Ohio Constitutional Convention, G. Volney Dorsey and Rufus P. Ranney. The two sparred over whether the state should create guidelines for establishing residency in order to vote. Dorsey was the most ardent defender of the state's transient voters, saying "We have a large population on the canals of our State who reside only on boats; and which would be the greater wrong—to allow them to vote where they are, or to disfranchise them altogether?" Ranney countered, "In what county would you allow such a citizen to vote?" "In the county where he is on the day of the election," Dorsey replied, adding, "he must have a residence somewhere; and where it is he should have the right to vote." Throughout the country, similar debates occurred which sought to define residence requirements before registration could work adequately. Underneath these arguments ran a less notable claim that centered on which party felt most assured of getting their vote out, legal or otherwise.

"WE OUGHT TO BE THE LAST PEOPLE AFRAID TO VOTE"

Beyond questions of registration, the transformation to paper ballots proved troublesome. At first, paper ballots were usually printed by the party and often given to the voter well in advance of the election, and some required the voter to write in the name of his choice. Numerous elections saw a wide range of names and spellings for a particular candidate, all of which called into question the legality of those votes. To counter these problems, parties then resorted to printing ballots of a specific size or color, which allowed illiterates to instantly recognize their preferred party candidates. Such methods, however, also made detecting how one had voted relatively easy. Standing near the polls, partisans could distinguish by the color or shape of the ballot whether a specific voter had been supportive or not. Enterprising partisans could also use a number of election tricks, such as purposely printing a ballot to resemble the ballot of a contender in areas where they knew illiteracy was high and the opposing party was popular. Everyone from tenant farmers to small shopkeepers knew inherently that their votes were being closely watched by landlords, bankers, and powerful officials. A "wrong" vote could mean the loss of employment or the foreclosure of a loan. In Massachusetts, a Whig newspaper published names of those seen voting Democratic "so that the enemies may be known."

By 1788, New York and New Jersey had instituted ballot voting, and by 1796 Georgia, Pennsylvania, South Carolina, Vermont, and Tennessee had followed suit. Not all states prohibited voice voting, even up to the mid 1800s. In a constitutional convention in Kentucky, delegates discussed the continuing reliance upon *viva voce*, but decided to resist paper ballots. One delegate, a Mr. Turner, stated that "fearless independence" existed among Kentuckians, and therefore "no man cares who knows how he votes." Another skeptical delegate, a Mr. Hardin, stated that no doubt there were some unscrupulous landowners who intimidated their tenants, and in some urban areas "where there are large manufacturing establishments, and where a man can control the votes of a thousand operatives, it may be necessary to protect them." Yet in the end, Hardin was not convinced that voice voting should be eliminated, offering rather blandly, "In this country, above all others in the world, we ought to be the last people afraid to vote." *Viva voce* remained part of the new constitution, and Kentucky, along with Virginia, remained the only states adhering to voice voting at the time of the Civil War.

In Massachusetts, Whig leaders wanted to make certain no one confused the ballot with secrecy, and in 1839 passed a law requiring that all paper ballots be submitted unsealed and unfolded. Although this was repealed twelve years later, other enterprising pols knew that even sealed envelopes presented no hindrance to stealing votes. In

Williamstown, Connecticut, Democrats designed an envelope that was similar in color to the Whig ballot. Illiterate Whig voters unknowingly found themselves using some of these envelopes and casting their own votes inside. Canvassers subsequently threw out a large number of Whig ballots because they officially contained two different votes—one on the ballot and one placed by Democrats on the envelope.

In New York, Whigs used less-subtle techniques, including importing nearly two hundred thugs from Philadelphia to intimidate New York City Democrats in the 1838 election. The "toughs" each received $22 for their services, while "repeaters" (those who voted more than once in any given precinct) received $5 if they also distributed false Democratic ballots to unwitting voters. Police officers loyal to the Whigs freed inmates in order to cast their votes for the Whig ticket. Such methods were ultimately successful in electing William Seward to the New York governorship over William Marcy by 20,179 to 19,377, thus elevating Seward to national prominence that would culminate in his appointment as Lincoln's Secretary of State twenty-two years later.

TAMMANY HALL

Like so many other American cities in the nineteenth century, New York underwent another significant development in antebellum politics: the rise of the city machine. In fact, the very location of this machine produced a term that became synonymous with boss rule and election fraud—Tammany Hall. Few places better understood the dynamics of the culture of corruption. The source of Tammany's power, and later of that of its legendary leader William M. "Boss" Tweed, was located in its ability to corral armies of immigrants into quick naturalization mills and then the voting booths. Tammany also used political gangs, sometimes called "shoulder hitters," whose intimidating tactics kept scores of anti-Tammany voters away from the polls. Yet Tammany did not always have to resort to fraud to maintain their power. Often the rewards of cooperating with the machine were enough to persuade enough people to keep the machine in power on Election Day. Yet not wishing to take any chances and with considerable opposition, machines always had an assortment of election tricks at their disposal.

Tammany employed the full spectrum of election fraud. In addition to repeaters, "thugs" intimidated voters; "floaters" voted several times, usually going from one precinct to another; or "colonizers," illegal voters residing in another city or state who could swell the registration rolls at the last minute and easily sway a close election, were used. Before an election, Tammany agents scoured the city looking for aliens, who were brought to party headquarters, where blank applications were promptly filled out. The aliens were prompted in how to properly answer a judge's questions concerning their residency. Witnesses were also crucial to the process, and paid witnesses were coached into remembering the aliens' names and their addresses. Squads of these aliens were then taken to Superior Court or the Court of Common Pleas, where they were brought before a judge. Answering the judge's questions correctly (if they were asked at all), the witnesses would do their duty (usually swearing to the legitimacy of scores of aliens at a time), and the judge would sign the necessary documents to make the alien a proper citizen, who would then be able to vote for Tammany candidates at the next election. It was not unusual for a judge to process eight hundred such aliens in one day.

In an 1843 election, Tammany's men imported inmates from the Blackwell's Island Penitentiary to vote in Democratic wards. Tammany also employed paupers from the city almshouse, giving them clean clothing, money, and tickets for grog after they had cast their vote for Tammany candidates. The use of gangs, violence, and other methods of wholesale fraud practiced by Tammany Hall stalwarts only grew in intensity throughout the nineteenth century. For Tweed, who plundered the city's treasury, elections were just another component of the machine's overall tactics. The crucial element on Election Day, Tweed knew, involved far more than just "getting out the vote" or winning over skeptics with powerful oratory. "The ballots didn't make the outcome," Tweed admitted, "the counters did."

As the Tammany gangs demonstrated, another effective technique involved hiring "rowdies" to go into certain precincts and threaten, push, or assault prospective voters. New York City had been long known for the use of "rowdies" in its city elections. As early as 1769, Peter Livingston wrote a friend that if his political adversaries used force on Election Day, "we have by far the best part of the Brusers [sic] on our side who are determined to use force if they use foul play." Sometimes that force involved stuffing ballot boxes. In an 1844 election, 55,000 votes were recorded in New York City, although only 41,000 were legally eligible to vote—an impressive turnout of 135 percent. Observers commented that the city's dogs and cats must have been affected by an unusual dose of civic pride.

In 1851, thugs known as "Short Boys" descended upon a district in the Eighth Ward and violently drove out the election inspectors and inserted "ballots by the handful." In an Irish district, hired rowdies started a fight at around noon on Election Day that caused a terrible commotion. Police were called in but could not contain the fight, and one police captain had his jaw fractured. Later that day, election inspectors considered the election in that ward to be illegal and refused to sign the official return, which, of course, was precisely one of the primary purposes of those who had originally hired the rowdies. By 1854, a municipal reform committee critical of Tammany Hall proclaimed, "In some wards it has become as much as a man's life is worth to vote at all, unless he votes as ordered." The committee also understood the cumulative effect of these hired thugs on legal voters: "The respectable citizens of both parties have retired from all primaries in disgust and abandoned them entirely to bullies."

In the 1852 general election, New York City witnessed a new and even bolder form of intimidation. A committee of Democrats led by Peter Cooper decided to mail ballots to every home in the city, even Whig ones. This move was an overt attempt to bypass Tammany Hall, which prohibited distributing votes in areas it felt were hostile. At the city post office, a gang led by Tammany's Daniel Sickles demanded the ballots. When he was refused, Sickles and his men attacked the officials guarding the boxes, and made off with 36,000 of the 80,000 or so ballots. Sickles then returned to Tammany Hall, where he was warmly received, and boasted of his exploits.

Tammany's clout, like the machines in so many other cities, rested with its control of the city's police force. Since the mayors and other local elected officials usually appointed the police chief, the job of the chief and those who worked for him were on the line on Election Day. Tammany leaders also required all members of the police force to contribute to an "Election Fund." Those refusing to do so were summarily punished by losing their jobs or by being forced to work twenty-four-hour shifts. Consequently, the fund reached $10,000 for any given election in the 1850s. On Election Day, some of this money was used to pay those very same officers who took the day off to "electioneer" for Tammany candidates. These off-duty officers, even in plain clothes, could threaten or bribe voters with blatant impunity. On-duty officers looked the other way as Tammany men brought axes and pistols to the polling places to destroy ballot boxes and threaten voters.

In the 1856 general election, a scene of intense violence, a conservative estimate placed the number of fraudulent votes in New York City at 10,000, which provided the necessary margin of victory for Tammany candidates. Utilizing the police as an active agent to steal votes or intimidate voters, New York City's political machine provided a model for a number of other city machines to emulate. Reformers all over the country devoted a great deal of time over the next century attempting to remove the police from the control of the mayor and place it in the hands of a commission or other non-partisan board.

"THE EMBODIMENT OF ALL THAT IS FRAUDULENT"

Violence was not just relegated to cities on the eastern seaboard. In the West, voters understood that going to the polls was often a dangerous task. One St. Louis voter lamented in 1840: "Cannot something be done by this enlightened city to make the passage to the polls safe, and free from terror?" Besides the usual problems of waiting for well over two hours to cast his vote, this individual also noted that he was subjected to various threats and physical assaults throughout the day. "Must we approach [the polls] at the price of loss of apparel, life, or limb?"

Throughout the 1850s, as the sectional crisis worsened, more and more episodes of election fraud began to appear in the pages of local newspapers. Although many of these papers had a particular partisan bent that could offer a convenient and misleading excuse to account for an election defeat, competing partisan papers also kept close tabs on the election methods of their rivals. In New Orleans, the 1852 elections were the subject of scrutiny from both the *Commercial Bulletin* and the *Bee*. Most of their attention was devoted to the Plaquemines Parish of Louisiana, from where observers noticed that a large number of illegal voters were imported to New Orleans on steamboats. Plaquemines became one of the focal points of the culture of corruption well into the twentieth century. The term "plaquemining," according to the *Bulletin*, referred to:

> The embodiment of all that is fraudulent in elections—of all that tends
> to degrade the ballot box, and make it instead of being the medium
> through which freemen may honestly express their preferences, the

means whereby moneyed demagogues may purchase their way to place
and power, to say nothing of the winning of wagers.

"If the Whig Party did not keep both eyes wide open and steadily
fixed," the *Bee* claimed, the Democrats might "convert all the alligators
and oysters in Plaquemines into legal voters." It had been customary
since the mid-1840s for voters from Plaquemines to be ferried to New
Orleans in order to swell the ranks of the electorate. The tactic was
becoming all too common throughout the nation. In New York City,
the term was known as "pipe-laying," which referred to the practice of
importing voters from outlying areas into the city under the pretense
of laying pipe for the city's aqueduct. This practice, which dated to the
late 1830s, had only one purpose: to swell the number of illegal voters.
After the election, the "pipe-layers" simply went back home. In an
1840 Illinois election, illegal voters were ferried up the Wabash River
where they served as "repeaters" in riverfront towns. The allegations
even invoked a reaction in the state house, where Representative
Abraham Lincoln offered a resolution condemning the frauds, proposing "to provide any punishment within the bounds of humanity, for
those who could abuse such a right."

In New Orleans, the recipient of Plaquemines's electoral bounties,
abusing such a right became an exercise in audacity. A yellow-fever
epidemic that hit the city shortly before the 1853 election took over
20,000 lives. Although no more than 10,500 votes had ever been cast
in the city before, over 13,000 votes were cast in 1853. Responding to
swelling Democratic numbers after the contagion had wrecked the
city, party leaders pathetically claimed that the epidemic simply spared
the lives of their partisans. A thoroughly disgusted local newspaper
editorialized that newcomers to the city should take notice of Providence's leanings when voting. One outraged observer noted: "The
demon of fraud himself could not, therefore, on this occasion, have the
supernatural effrontery of denying his intervention in human affairs!"

A general rule about election fraud is a rather simple one: The smaller the election, the easier it is to steal. Local elections are easier to corrupt than state elections; state elections are easier to corrupt than national ones. Yet even presidential elections presented opportunities for larceny. In 1844, James K. Polk, the Democrat, narrowly defeated Henry Clay, the Whig, by 38,367 votes out of 2,700,560 cast nationwide. Polk's victory in the Electoral College was wider, 170 to 105. Yet within some of the states that Polk carried, the margins were very narrow, and suspicious.

In New York, whose electoral votes alone had been enough to swing the balance (if New York's 36 votes had gone to Clay, Clay would have won the election, 141–134), Polk won by just 5,106 votes. Whigs contended that the election had been stolen. The charges were not new: padding voter lists with illegal immigrants; buying votes with liquor or cash; and stuffing ballot boxes with impunity. One Whig wrote from New York City that "we feel here the whole result has been changed by the foreign votes in this city." Over 5,500 immigrants had been naturalized in the three months preceding the election in New York City, and twice that amount throughout the state in the same period. On election eve alone, 497 new voters had been naturalized in New York City. These votes, everyone understood, were cast for Polk. Similar charges came from Cincinnati, Pittsburgh, and Baltimore.

In Louisiana, Clay had even more reason to feel cheated. One Louisiana voter consoled the Whig leader: "You have lost this state by the most unprecedented frauds and rascality." Polk officially won Louisiana by just 699 votes. In New Orleans, where Polk racked up a majority of 414 votes, John Slidell had organized the Democratic vote effort by bringing in voters from other parishes. The methods Slidell used in New Orleans were varied: "Parishes giving more votes or as many as there are white inhabitants of all sexes and ages being in them. Steamboats chartered to convey voters in the same day at different Polls, and every other species of fraud that could be imagined."

While Democrats cried "poor loser" at such charges, it was obvious that Louisiana was carried by Polk because of Plaquemines Parish, where total votes had jumped from 250 in 1840 to 1,007 Democratic votes alone in 1844, although the 1840 Census indicated only 538 white males over twenty years old lived there. Polk's fictitious 990-vote margin in Plaquemines essentially won him Louisiana's six electoral votes.

Twenty years after the tumultuous 1824 election had seen the House give the presidency to John Quincy Adams, now a president had been installed by fraud. Yet Polk's ascension did not produce angry crowds or calls for President Clay to assume his rightful office. Instead, Whigs concluded that registry laws were necessary to prevent more fraud in future elections, while Democrats casually dismissed claims of a stolen election. Despite the collective resignation, no one could deny that the methods used in New York and Louisiana to hijack the election for Polk had enormous consequences for the young nation. After President Polk went to war with Mexico, the methods that brought him to power took on an even more profound meaning.

DEFINING THE PROBLEM

How widespread was fraud in the early republic? Scholars have engaged in an extended debate concerning the extent of election fraud in early American elections. While a few have suggested that fraud may have affected five percent of the vote in every election, others dismiss these claims. Complicating the matter was the ubiquitous cry of "fraud" by the losers of a given election or partisan newspapers to explain why their views did not win over a majority of the electorate. One scholar states that illegal voting in antebellum America "was neither widespread nor significant" since even the best-known examples of fraud constituted less than five percent of the electorate. To prove widespread fraud, a rather strict standard is utilized: "The turnouts in virtually *every* county for *every* election must reflect substantial fraud." In other words, the only real proof of fraud is to see unusual shifts in voting, such as when a Whig, say, received 10,000 votes in one election and 20,000 the very next year. By focusing solely on returns and other raw data, these studies neglect the social realities of American elections, and how statistically small numbers can have huge consequences on Election Day.

Such standards, for example, cannot measure the role of violence in frightening away voters, or the role of bribing voters not to vote, or in simply measuring how a corrupt election judge could transpose a figure or award votes for candidate X to candidate Y's column. It also ignores the fraud that can occur regularly, such as when candidate X buys ten percent of the vote in successive years and thus, under scholarly analysis, there would be no fraud since there were no variations in the aggregate. Fraud certainly did not play a significant role in every antebellum American election. Yet claiming that fraud did not occur in every local race and is, therefore, minimized nationally, understates the corrosive nature of the problem. Simply put, inflating voter rolls, intimidating voters, buying votes, and stuffing ballot boxes was a part of the game one necessarily played in American politics. In some races, these methods gave the election to the wrong candidate. In others, these practices did not determine the winner, but over time produced some cumulative results that did not bode well for the republic.

Playing that game sometimes took bizarre turns. In an 1855 New Mexico election, a suspended Catholic priest, Padre Gallegos, ran against Don Miguel Otero, for a seat as a delegate to Congress. In the official returns, Gallegos won by 99 votes. Upon closer inspection, it was evident that the voting had been unorthodox in the extreme. In one locality, one hundred more votes were cast than there were legally registered voters. In the town of Socorro, Gallegos allegedly rounded up nearly two dozen underage boys to vote, and admonished them to swear they were of age. If they did so, Father Gallegos promised the boys he would absolve them of the sin of false swearing.

An even more revealing episode occurred in Rhode Island, where Whigs and Temperance forces were waging a bitter struggle for a town council seat against a pro-rum slate. Near the end of the day, a wagonload of voters appeared, all demanding to vote and all clearly drunk. One of the Whigs present promised the inebriated voters that if they voted for the Whig-Temperance candidates, each would receive a gallon of gin. They quickly agreed and voted accordingly. In such a way, the "Rum Cabal" was turned out of office.

FREEDOM OR SLAVERY

By the 1850s, the culture of corruption had become such a major component of American political life that a new party was formed whose hallmark was a fierce desire to combat this culture, if necessary, with violence. A nativist, anti-Catholic party known as the "Know-Nothings," or the "American" party, had a determined approach: "Americanism against foreigners—the people against the government." The party itself sprang from elements within the Whigs who felt that their elections had been thoroughly corrupted by fraudulent immigrant votes. Fired by almost a religious zealotry, the Know-Nothings were convinced that they should fight fire with fire.

In Louisville, the party hit fertile soil. Over half of the foreign-born population in Kentucky in 1850 resided in Louisville, particularly German and Irish immigrants. Native Louisvillians deeply resented the presence of these populations, and were obsessed with keeping such "undesirables" from the polls. In Louisville elections in May 1855, Know-Nothings used widespread violence to capture City Hall. Due to their newly-won power, the Know-Nothings oversaw the appointment of election officials. Of the 68 election judges in Louisville,

64 were Know-Nothings. These judges required each voter to read his
vote aloud, and marked the vote opposite the candidate's name in a
book. This technique was skillfully employed to spot and reject the
votes of immigrants, many of whom could not read English or spoke
with a heavy accent. If that were not enough, violence was always an
effective Know-Nothing tool.

As another Louisville election, in August 1855, approached, the
Know-Nothings worked to ensure that none of the undesirables cast
their vote at all. The City Council, dominated by the nativists, ruled
that in the heavily immigrant First Ward, only one voting booth would
be established. One local Democratic paper claimed that such a move
essentially disfranchised nearly a thousand voters and concluded: "The
election of Napoleon in France and Santa Anna in Mexico was no
more farcical than the election in Louisville is to be next Monday." A
German-oriented paper published in Louisville meanwhile claimed
that "The day of decision is not far away, and it brings us either
freedom or slavery."

A former Whig and outspoken Know-Nothing editor, George D.
Prentice, whipped the nativist flames in the weeks leading up to the
election with highly suggestive rhetoric. "Our friends must so
organize," Prentice wrote, to "exclude every fraudulent voter, no matter
who he may be and under what pretext his vote may be offered."
Before the polls opened on Election Day, the Know-Nothings forcibly
took control of each of Louisville's eight wards, and allowed only those
who openly displayed yellow ballots (distributed by the party) to vote.
Immigrants had to bring their citizenship papers and often waited
hours in the hot August sun to vote, usually with no success, while
officials allowed those with yellow tickets in the back door. In the First
Ward, where the voters had just one polling place, only ten percent of
the potential electorate cast votes, disfranchising hundreds of voters,
just as the Democrats had predicted.

By midday, gunfire had erupted. By late afternoon, the city was in the midst of a full-scale riot, and a German brewery was set on fire by a nativist mob, killing ten. By evening, the mob had spread to some of the city's tenement houses, where fifteen homes were burned. When the polls closed, the Know-Nothings scored major victories, while the city had trouble totaling the number of casualties. All together, probably two dozen people died and many more were wounded, while the property damage was estimated in the hundreds of thousands of dollars. The election was the culmination of a half-decade of anti-immigrant rage and resulted in an election where violence and murder ruled. As the German *Louisville Anzieger* declared after the election, Louisville "should decide if it may still count itself among the well-mannered and civilized cities of the world."

In New Orleans, the Know-Nothings suspected that Democrats would use armies of repeaters to steal a March 1854 city election. The nativists deployed dozens of armed men to watch suspicious voters at selected precincts. Before long, fights broke out and the polls were subsequently closed in order to stave off a city-wide riot. In November 1855, the violence in New Orleans increased, as more nativist thugs from Mobile and Memphis intimidated voters, stole ballot boxes, and shot and killed one Irishman. The following year, the nativists in New Orleans used even more heavy-handed methods. In one precinct where a Democratic challenger was bayoneted to death, the final tally in that precinct was 90–0 in favor of the nativists, a typical result in many Know-Nothing strongholds. The governor of Louisiana estimated that between 1854 and 1856, one third of all legal New Orleans voters were denied their right to vote due to nativist intimidation. The culture of New Orleans elections—as part of a growing national trend—was becoming increasingly brutal.

The Know-Nothings were certainly not a party that has received widespread acclaim, either from their contemporaries or from historians. This is not surprising. They were bigoted and violent, and represented many of the uglier undercurrents of American politics. Yet the Know-Nothings' zealotry was fired, in part, by the understanding that the nation's election system was essentially broken. They saw various "undesirables" helping corrupt politicians to steal elections, and felt completely justified in using force to fight their righteous war at the polls. The perception that they were taking election fraud to new heights did not bother them—they rationalized that they were simply playing the game that Democrats and Whigs had started, and they were right about that point.

Once a political group or party feels a government is illegitimate, revolutionary methods immediately become legitimate. In a sense, considering the manner in which voting was conducted in early America, it was not surprising that a party such as the Know-Nothings responded in the way it did. Their ominous emergence spoke loudly to the latent frustrations many Americans were experiencing in seeing elections stolen on a regular basis. The surfacing of guns tragically underscored what a short distance the young nation had come since the days of monarchy.

CHAPTER TWO

The Limits of Popular Sovereignty

"We are playing for a mighty stake and the game must be played boldly."

When Alexis de Tocqueville traveled throughout the United States in 1831, he commented on the character of American elections: "I may here be met by an objection derived from election-eering intrigues, the meanness of candidates, and the calumnies of their opponents." These "evils," Tocqueville noted, are "doubtless great, but they are transient." To this French observer, the "desire of being elected may lead some men for a time to violent hostility; but this same desire leads all men in the long run to support each other." The ability of elections to bring enemies together, at least to Tocqueville, was profound—"if it happens that an election accidentally severs two friends, the electoral system brings a multitude of citizens permanently together who would otherwise always have remained unknown to one another." In time, a series of elections in the Midwest Territories would put Tocqueville's faith that elections could solve a wrenching national crisis to the test.

By the 1850s, the country struggled mightily over how to resolve the festering sectional division over slavery. Every possible answer offered by Northerner or Southerner, abolitionist or slaveholder, was greeted with immediate suspicion by the other. While even many abolitionists were content to allow slavery to remain (for the time being) where it was already entrenched in the deep South, the question of the Territories was another matter. The Compromise of 1820 had drawn a geographical line within the Louisiana Purchase that declared the territory north of the 36-30 parallel "forever free." Yet the line could not resolve the widening gulf that separated various factions migrating to the territories. Steadfast slaveholders objected to any infringement on their perceived "rights" to bring their "property" into another state and wanted the compromise repealed, while "free-soilers" opposed allowing any possible expansion of slavery at all.

At this crucial moment, the need was greater than ever to find some satisfactory answer to the issue of slavery in the territories. Short of taking up arms, the ballot box was seized upon by a number of politicians as the only legitimate way to determine the future course of slavery. Unfortunately, elections in Kansas would only serve to increase the sectional hostility and exacerbate the crisis. In time, hundreds of native Kansans discovered they had thousands of neighbors they had never known before, neighbors who had never stepped foot in the territory except to intimidate those who opposed slavery, stuff ballot boxes, kill a few people, and rig a new state constitution.

KANSAS DIRT

For some members of Congress, the easiest and fairest way to deal with the "impending crisis" was by allowing elections to determine the will of those residing in the territories. Illinois Senator Stephen Douglas had espoused this very notion, "popular sovereignty," as the only fair and democratic way to settle whether a territory would be slave or free. To Douglas, popular sovereignty embodied the very ideal of local control, whereby "the people of every separate political community have an inalienable right to govern themselves in respect to their internal polity." With the introduction of the Kansas–Nebraska Act in 1854, he sought to make it national policy. If successful, Douglas hoped to ride popular sovereignty to the White House. After President Franklin Pierce signed it into law on May 30, all eyes quickly turned to the approaching elections in Kansas to observe whether popular sovereignty could work.

The rightful inhabitants of the territory, as the notion held, would decide for themselves whether to allow or prohibit slavery. If a majority of the residents of the territory voted to prohibit slavery, it would be codified in the state constitution and be respected by Northerner and Southerner alike. Yet even this seemingly democratic referendum proved problematic. How would such an election be conducted? By what standard would a resident of a territory be determined? Would they vote on slavery per se, or on members to a constitutional convention who would then take up the issue? What would happen in the near future when more residents came to the area, and perhaps, a new majority was ready to overturn the original election results? Already, popular sovereignty was not as easy a proposition as it seemed.

The first test case came in November 1854, in an election to determine a delegate to Congress. Kansas was soon flooded with groups whose only expressed wish was to increase their numbers at any cost, regardless of whether these people would ever live a day in Kansas. From the northeast, bands of men opposed to slavery, "free-staters," came to the Kansas Territory. Many of these men belonged to the Emigrant Aid Society, which had sponsors such as William Cullen Bryant and John Carter Brown.

The very notion of Northern outsiders flocking to the territory in order to prohibit slavery angered pro-Southerners, including a large number living in Missouri. Resenting the possibility that Kansas might outlaw slavery, these Missourians formed secret societies with names such as the "Sons of the South" and the "Blue Lodge." In ways that would resemble the Ku Klux Klan after the Civil War, these groups had secret handshakes and passwords, and were oath-bound to protect each other's identities. Their avowed purpose was to protect slavery, by force if necessary, and their immediate aim was to rig the elections in Kansas. In the village of Douglas large companies of men on horseback came across the border on the day before the election, surrounded the polls, and threatened anyone with death who dared challenge them. "Damn the abolitionists," they cried. "Kill them!" Although there were only 35 registered names on the official poll books, 261 votes were cast, all but 26 votes for the pro-slavery candidate, John M. Whitfield. Similar episodes occurred in various other wards in Kansas, but none were quite as brazen as the Seventh District, located about 75 miles from the Missouri border. Although the Seventh District had only 53 qualified voters, 604 voted in the election, all but seven for Whitfield.

Although Whitfield defeated his nearest opponent by almost 2,000 votes, the numbers of illegal voters was daunting. Out of 2,833 votes, 1,729, or 61 percent, were fraudulent votes. A Congressional committee found that the election was "a crime of great magnitude. Its immediate effect was to further excite the people of the northern States, and exasperate the actual settlers against their neighbors in Missouri." After conducting a survey of Kansas, the committee further concluded that "in the present condition of the Territory a fair election could not be held." The House voted to vacate the seat.

The outcry against the tactics of the Missourians provoked Kansas Governor Andrew Reeder to order a census of the territory, which determined that 2,905 eligible voters lived in a population of 8,601 residents. Yet Kansas permitted any "resident" male to vote, and that term was loosely defined. Pro-slavery Missourians were more than ready to stretch that term to any limits. "The pro-slavery party generally contended that if a man was here but half an hour he was entitled to vote," commented one Leavenworth resident, adding that Missourians considered their "mere presence here made them voters."

Upon completion of the census, Reeder ordered another election for March 1855 to determine the members of the legislative assembly. In this contest, the same dynamics occurred. The Emigrant Aid Company helped more emigrants find their way to Kansas, while "border ruffians"—pro-slavery zealots from Missouri—reacted to this development by pouring across the border to vote illegally in Kansas, and drew their pistols on any election judge who dared challenge their credentials. The ruffians were lead by ex-Senator David R. Atchison, who had publicly proclaimed his desire to protect Kansas for pro-slavery forces. According to one observer, Atchison stated he and his followers were going to vote, or else they "would kill every God damned abolitionist in the district."

When George Dietzler, a citizen of Lawrence, spoke to some of the Missouri men before the election about their residency, one took off his shoe to show Dietzler the dirt in his socks was Kansas dirt, which in his mind was all the proof of residency he needed. Beyond such episodes, there was no masking the sheer terror created by the Missourians. One Kansan, J. N. Mace, described an encounter he had with some Missourians in Lawrence when he attempted to vote:

I stepped forward, put my hand inside the window, and gave my name; when, at a word from one of the two men who stood one on each side of the window, I was seized by the people in the crowd, and dragged from the polls through the entire crowd. They made shouts of "Kill the nigger-thief," "Cut his throat," and many cries of that kind. I saw revolvers cocked and bowie knives drawn, all around me at that time. After I had been dragged out of the crowd

I regained my feet. I had a small American flag under my arm. When I got to my feet, I unfurled it and held it over my head. I told them we had no law to protect us, and I sought protection under the American flag.

Mace's life was spared, but he was not allowed to vote.

One of the men who had traveled from Missouri to the Bloomington district of Kansas was S. J. Jones, who candidly admitted to locals he had just arrived in Kansas and fully intended to vote in order to make it a slave state. Jones added that he and his men would vote, and "that if they could not vote by fair means, they would by foul." When election judges at first refused to allow Jones and his men to vote, another pro-slavery Missourian threatened to fire a hundred shots into the room and kill everyone there. Soon, the marauders stole the ballot box by force, all with a "Hurrah! For Missouri!"

The final election tally revealed the scope of the fraud: the pro-slavery forces won in an election where the total vote was 6,307, with nearly 5,000 of those votes being clearly illegal. Atchison boasted of the results to Senator R. M. T. Hunter of Virginia, although he exaggerated the extent of the fraud: "We had at least 7,000 [Missouri] men in the territory on the day of election," wrote Atchison, adding candidly the reason behind the cooked numbers: "We are playing for a mighty stake and the game must be played boldly." The historian David M. Potter concluded that what the pro-slavery forces had done "was steal an election." The audacity of the fraud stung many observers. Had a free and fair vote been taken of legal voters, a Congressional committee concluded that free-staters would have won a majority of seats. The committee also concluded: "This invasion is the first and only one in the history of our government, by which an organized force from one State has elected a legislature for another."

The free-staters, repulsed by the methods used in the election, simply refused to recognize the legitimacy of the new government and formed their own. The pro-slavery legislature passed laws to rig future elections and formed a territorial militia that vowed to attack any free-state "revolutionaries." In May 1856, the pro-slavery militia "sacked" the town of Lawrence, burning the free-state governor's residence, and looting numerous stores. In retaliation, anti-slavery zealots like John Brown went to Kansas and with his sons brutally murdered five pro-slavery supporters. The bloodshed in Kansas, which served as a kind of opening of the Civil War, was grounded in the fact that no territorial government existed that had the legitimacy of power conferred on it by a democratic election. Popular sovereignty could not work if free and fair elections did not exist.

FEDERAL COMPLICITY

When word of the massive fraud reached Governor Reeder, he sought the support of President Franklin Pierce, who refused to intercede. Pierce's reaction gave cues to the Territories that, for all intents and purposes, the legality of elections really did not matter and that popular sovereignty was an irrelevant policy. Considering the methods used by the 1850s to pad registration lists or steal votes, the actions of the border ruffians were not unexpected. But the federal government essentially looked the other way and rubber-stamped the methods of the ruffians in ways that had far more significance. After all, the federal government had complete authority to determine the validity of elections in the Territories. With the passivity of President Pierce, the federal government abdicated its responsibilities in Kansas. This was precisely what Senator Charles Sumner had in mind in May 1856 when he proclaimed that Pierce's actions constituted the real "crime against Kansas."

The new pro-slavery legislature met in Shawnee Mission, near the Missouri border, and put through the laws of Missouri without

changing hardly a word. Free-soilers disparaged the "bogus" legislature, held their own elections, and chose a free-state governor and legislature. The two governments simultaneously claimed legitimacy,
decried the tactics of their opponents, and prepared for more bloodshed. The historian Kenneth M. Stampp aptly concludes that the
Kansas government was "a travesty of Douglas's 'great principle' of
popular sovereignty."

In the early 1850s, even as the Know-Nothing movement flared, a
new party emerged that combined segments of the Whigs with some
disgruntled northern Democrats. Calling themselves Republicans, the
new party soon grew to be the main competitor of the Democratic
party. Its essential ideology was contained in the phrase, "Free soil, free
labor, free men." Republicans were staunchly opposed to the spread of
slavery and to the notion of popular sovereignty, since it allowed voters
in the territories to conceivably enact and legalize slavery. To Republicans, the matter of slavery was too significant to be left to local control, and the elections in Kansas had revealed the latent fraud behind
popular sovereignty. Ironically, what Senator Douglas had hoped
would ease sectional divisions and smooth the way for his presidency
suddenly became a rallying cry for those who opposed him. The
sudden strength of the Republicans and the threat they posed gave
Democrats—especially Southerners—a new rationale for stealing
elections.

The fact that the Kansas elections had nothing to do with popular
will pervaded national discussion of the Territories. In his inaugural
address in 1857, President James Buchanan, a Democrat, highlighted
the vote fraud in Kansas, and stated "the imperative and indispensable
duty of the Government of the United States was to secure to every
resident inhabitant the free and independent expression of his opinion
by his vote." In the capital of Lecompton, Kansas Governor John W.
Geary urged the fraudulently elected legislature to adopt strict residency requirements for voting and severe penalties for "false voting" in

an effort to bring legitimacy to future elections. His efforts failed; rather, the legislature passed statutes protecting slavery and made even the act of publicly denying the legality of slavery in Kansas a felony.

In Washington, President Buchanan was at a loss as to what to do in Kansas. He weakly reiterated the bankrupt notion of popular sovereignty, but now both sides of the slavery issue were reluctant to submit to such a plan considering the widespread election fraud. Buchanan chose Robert Walker to be the new governor of Kansas, and upon his arrival in the territory Walker proclaimed that the upcoming constitutional election would be free from fraud and violence, although how this would be achieved he did not say.

In June 1857, another election took place in "Bleeding Kansas" for delegates to a constitutional convention. Anti-slavery forces in Kansas were so thoroughly convinced that a free and fair election was impossible that they boycotted the election altogether. Pro-slavery stalwarts did not even register voters, since having a fair election was not their intent. The counties that bordered Missouri, which were loaded with pro-slavery zealots from both states, ended up with two thirds of the delegates to the convention. Four months later, another election was held in Kansas, this time to determine a new territorial legislature. Governor Walker appealed to Washington to protect the state from Missourians by dispatching two thousand troops to the territory. Yet Buchanan, like his predecessor, was unwilling to support free elections. In a bizarre move, the president deferred the decision to his cabinet, which was composed mostly of members wishing to admit Kansas as a slave state. The cabinet refused to supply troops, and the rout was on.

The methods used by the pro-slavery forces in the area had not changed. In the Oxford precinct, which bordered Missouri and was little more than a village of six houses, the pro-slavery forces received 1,625 votes. Citizens of Oxford later claimed that no more than ninety votes were cast from their area. When inspectors examined poll books from the Kickapoo precinct, they found that voters had signed their names "William H. Seward, Horace Greeley, John C. Fremont, and Millard Fillmore." In McGee County, although only fourteen votes had been cast in an election just months before, 1,200 votes were now cast. One Kansan, John C. Vaughn, testified that the scenes around the polls were alarming: "men and boys violently drunk, armed with dirks and clubs . . . double voting was barefaced." Walker summarily threw out the results and certified the elections of free-state candidates. An election won "by frauds so monstrous," Walker stated, "would be more fatal to our party than any defeat, however disastrous."

Although he won acclaim from many corners of the American political landscape, Walker's actions were not well received in the Deep South, where he was loudly criticized as having usurped his proper authority. Yet one border-state newspaper understood Walker's actions in a different context. "Southern honor," wrote the Louisville *Democrat,* "would not permit it to denounce a man for exposing fraud, for the corruption of the ballot box was infinitely more dangerous than the slavery question ever was." In Kansas, at least, the two items combined in a politically potent way. Without a free election to determine who could rightfully decide on the slavery issue in the Territories, the sectional debate over slavery, as well as the tariff dilemma and judicial appointments, reached a point of crisis that Buchanan decided to let stand. One Northern newspaper wrote in prescient terms: "Heaven only knows the end of the civil war thus righteously begun?"

After hoping his cabinet could settle the issue, all President Buchanan could do was meekly utter: "It is to be regretted that all the qualified electors had not registered themselves and voted under its provisions." To those on the ground in Kansas, Buchanan's words belied the reality of the election. Responding to the president's statement, one observer, M. McCaslin, wrote: "In 14 or 15 counties no sheriff nor any officer made any appearance to take the registration of the voters. Whether there was no sheriff or whether they refused to act, I don't know." But McCaslin understood one essential fact that escaped the president: "Those people were disfranchised. The failure of them to vote was not their fault; the failure of them to register was not their fault. They couldn't, even if they had wanted to." McCaslin also knew the larger implications of the Kansas situation. If the fraud were allowed to stand, McCaslin wrote, "It will present the brilliant spectacle of a Democratic Congress cramming a constitution down the throats of a large unwilling majority with the point of a bayonet."

For President Buchanan, the dynamics of Kansas were symptomatic of the national crisis and his own role in sanctioning election fraud. Flagrantly fraudulent elections had produced a pro-slavery legislature that called a constitutional convention in Lecompton, which had been elected by just a fraction of the Kansas electorate because free-staters boycotted the election. The convention, in turn, wrote slavery into its handiwork and refused to submit the final document to the people of the state. The Lecompton constitution claimed that "The right of property is before and higher than any constitutional sanction, and the right of the owner of a slave to such slave and its issue is the same and as inviolable as the right of the owner of any property."

Additionally, the new constitution forbade any amendments that would "affect the rights of property in the ownership of slaves." All the while, Buchanan well knew that if the democratic process had actually been in place, Kansas would have prohibited slavery, yet he placed his support behind the Lecompton constitution nonetheless. Buchanan and his cabinet had no trouble in extending slavery into Kansas and saw this as a blow to the Republicans.

Events in Kansas were nothing less than an open and crass repudiation of the sacred principle of popular sovereignty and an open invitation to hasten the culture of corruption on Election Day. When the president endorsed the Lecompton Constitution, wholesale election fraud had scored a spectacular victory for pro-slavery stalwarts. Even after the elections had been exposed as a veritable hijacking of the democratic process, the president and the federal government used their powers to verify the sad reality that the Kansas elections did not matter. Stephen A. Douglas, who had opened the fissure in Kansas with his act in 1854, came out in opposition to what he termed the "Lecompton swindle," primarily because it violated the essential principles of popular sovereignty.

At an infamous White House showdown between Buchanan and Douglas over Lecompton, the president was said to have made veiled threats concerning the future of a Democratic senator who opposed a Democratic president. Douglas was thoroughly unimpressed and responded: "Mr. President, I wish you to remember that General Jackson is dead." Although Buchanan may have had the necessary votes in the Senate, he did not enjoy that advantage in the House. The president's promises of lucrative contracts and patronage could not win the day.

Congress finally permitted a new Kansas election on the entire constitution, and in the first fair election held in the territory, the sovereign voters summarily rejected Lecompton and its defense of slavery by 11,300 to 1,788, as free-staters won over 86 percent of the vote. By virtue of these results, the enormity of the fraud in the earlier elections was finally revealed.

The defeat of the Lecompton Constitution exposed Buchanan as an incompetent and possibly corrupt chief executive, and Douglas's notion of popular sovereignty as a sham. Perhaps more than anything else, the ideal of free and fair elections had been utterly repudiated, either as a way to solve the slavery issue or even as a way to determine the popular will, considering the partisan rivalries that now existed. The stench of the Kansas "elections" and the president's defense of the Lecompton Constitution burdened Northern Democrats. That autumn, Republicans scored major gains in the House, where they now held a three-to-one majority. With presidents such as Pierce and Buchanan countenancing election fraud, the confidence Americans could place in their ballots declined to ever lower depths.

The elections in Kansas provoked even more passionate sectional and political animosities. Yet it was all avoidable. The federal government refused to address the culture that permeated the entire process of popular sovereignty and gave further license to vote thieves. The elections also demonstrated the ultimate consequences of fraud, which was not just limited to the blood that flowed in Kansas. By 1858, the issues surrounding the Kansas elections had become a dividing line within the Democratic party so that in the next presidential election, the party was irrevocably split. When a system that cannot be trusted to register the popular will goes unchecked, the results can be devastating.

"WHAT IS POPULAR GOVERNMENT WORTH?"

While the events in Kansas took election fraud to new and more dangerous levels, other areas of the country found that elections had little validity for measuring the people's will. In 1855, a gubernatorial election in Wisconsin displayed how a statewide election could be stolen. While the president and Congress ignored the fraud in Kansas, a courageous court in Wisconsin took dramatic actions that demonstrated how fraud did not have to be acknowledged and could even be remedied.

On Election Day, the incumbent Governor William A. Barstow defeated the Republican challenger, Coles Bashford, by a mere 157 votes out of over 72,000 cast. The election itself was relatively quiet. The real action took place afterwards. In Waupaca Falls, for example, observers noted that 612 votes had been cast, all but 59 for Governor Barstow, yet the town had a total population of only two hundred citizens. A Republican newspaper congratulated the town for getting out "*all* the voters, women, boys, babies and all." When investigators looked into the supplemental returns from the town of Spring Creek, which gave Barstow a 91-vote majority, they were shocked to discover that no such town existed in Wisconsin. Similarly, in Bridge Creek, which gave Barstow a 76-vote majority, investigators learned that no one lived there or was even eligible to vote. In Gilbert's Mills, Wisconsin, the supervising poll worker also happened to own the mill, and swore that he never opened the precinct and had no idea how Barstow obtained a 39-vote majority from his district. Why did Gilbert refuse to open the polls? Because he had learned that his workers were all Bashford men. In all, investigators discovered hundreds of supplemental votes cast from fictitious locales for Barstow, and that if all fraudulent votes had been duly thrown out by the state canvassers, Bashford would have won with over a thousand-vote majority.

As Governor Barstow assumed office for another term, Republicans took the case to the state Supreme Court. In early 1856, the conclusive evidence was found. In scrutinizing the returns from Spring Creek and Bridge Creek, which were supposed to be sixty miles apart, the official sheets were not only from the same type of paper, but were from the same sheet, which had been torn in half when the forged returns were submitted. When the two sheets fit neatly together and proved obvious fraud, the Barstow administration was plainly in trouble.

The Wisconsin state government waited for the state's high court to hear the case and rule on the validity of the election. By late March, the details of the election were well known and the pressure was growing on Governor Barstow to resign. In his closing statement, the lead attorney for Bashford spoke in dramatic language of the political culture that surrounded the previous election:

> What is popular government worth if these things are to be? What is the condition of public morals in this state if such things are tolerated? It is a grievous reproach upon the whole state—a bitter and terrible reproach—that any man could be found to claim the meanest and lowest office—even that of fence viewer or dog killer—on such frauds as these. I can conceive to what lengths polit-

ical madness may carry a man, but I cannot conceive how men can consent to roll in such corruption as this.

The court apparently agreed with this conclusion, and summarily overturned the results of the election, proclaiming that the Barstow government was guilty of "gross mal-administration." An unrepentant William Barstow resigned, saying he did so in order to save the state from civil strife, and Coles Bashford was quickly sworn in as governor. By giving the voters of Wisconsin the man who had actually won a majority of the votes, even four months after the election, the state Supreme Court exercised considerable political courage. Yet the court's action had far larger ramifications. By carefully perusing the evidence, and ignoring the Barstow cries that too much time had elapsed since the election, the Wisconsin Supreme Court displayed how an independent judiciary can play a vital constitutional role in overseeing contested elections and can resolve them without regard to partisan motivations. In the process, the Wisconsin justices validated popular sovereignty and democracy itself. Unfortunately, no one outside Wisconsin heeded the message.

The eastern seaboard and even the Midwest Territories were not the only areas to witness rampant fraud. In San Francisco, investigators looking into a local election found an ingenious device that, no doubt, swayed many races. Ballot boxes deployed throughout the city used secret compartments that contained sliding doors. After conducting an otherwise legal election, election judges could then merely slide open a secret door and deposit hundreds of fake ballots and hide the real ballots. Democrats in San Francisco had grown so accustomed to hired thugs smashing ballot boxes that they deployed steel boilers in some precincts to serve as ballot boxes. One election supervisor, James P. Casey, had mysteriously won an election to the Board of Supervisors even though he had never even been a candidate for the office and his name was not on the ticket.

Angry recriminations arose over the methods people like Casey used to win elections, but the lid blew off in 1856, when a former election inspector, James "Yankee" Sullivan (who had learned his trade in Tammany Hall), confessed to participating in widespread election fraud in San Francisco. After being paid $100 to switch votes for one candidate, Sullivan noted he had been approached by a representative of the opposing candidate at a saloon. After agreeing upon an increased fee, Sullivan decided to use his skills in stealing votes for his new client. After reading of Sullivan's exposé, thousands of angry San Franciscans joined the Vigilance Committee to protect the ballot box as a "husband would the honor of his wife."

REGULATING THE ELECTION

There was no mistaking the fact that by the late 1850s, election fraud and violence had reached new levels in America. The events in Louisville and "Bleeding Kansas" reappeared with a vengeance in Washington, D.C. in the summer of 1857, where the Know-Nothings made their last stand. To defeat a slate of Democrats vying for offices such as surveyor, collector, and city alderman, the Know-Nothings hired approximately fifty "plug-uglies" from Baltimore to intimidate and severely disrupt the Democratic vote. The thugs from Maryland had considerable experience, since election riots had become commonplace events in Baltimore. Know-Nothings had brought tubs of bloody water to selected Baltimore precincts to dunk Irish voters in during the presidential election of 1856. In an election where one was killed and dozens injured, Know-Nothings had no trouble capturing all of Baltimore's wards and electing a mayor and a majority of the city council. They were well prepared to take their methods to the nation's capital.

On June 1, 1857, the trains arrived in the D.C. depot carrying the first assortment of the vote thugs with the self-described purpose of "regulating the election." One Washington newspaper, whose investigative sources obviously had little connection to the social world of local elections, confidently predicted that morning that "The municipal election today will not, we apprehend, be conducted in other than a quiet and proper manner, such as becomes intelligent freemen to observe." Shortly after the polls opened, that optimism proved short-lived. Fighting broke out in the First Precinct of the Fourth Ward, where long lines of Irish and German voters proved an easy target. After unsuccessfully trying to bully their way through the line, the men from Baltimore retreated, to return soon thereafter with brickbats and revolvers. Shooting erupted and the violence quickly spread. One Irish voter was so badly mutilated that he could not be identified. After a morning of riots, Washington's Mayor J. B. Magruder wrote a desperate letter to President Buchanan:

> Upon the representation of credible citizens that a band of lawless persons, most of them not residents of this city, have attacked one of the polls . . . and after maiming some 20 good and peaceable citizens, have driven the remainder from the polls, have dispersed the commissioners of the election, and threaten further violence . . . I respectfully request you order out the company of United States Marines now in this city to maintain the peace.

Knowing that this was not some faraway territory such as Kansas, the president responded by dispatching 110 Marines with fixed bayonets to the Northern markethouse, where the border thugs were located. Upon seeing the detachment of Marines, the "plug-uglies" obtained a cannon and were prepared to fire on the troops when an army general named Henderson, still dressed in civilian clothes, placed himself in front of the muzzle and implored: "Men, you had best think twice before you fire this piece at the Marines." After exchanging gunfire, the Marines then quickly seized the cannon, and the ruffians from Baltimore quickly left for their home city, one of them saying they could "whip the police, but when it came to United States troops they weren't thar." In just one day, at least eight had died and nearly two dozen were wounded. That evening, Know-Nothing leaders in D.C. deplored the actions of the president and the Marines as a "cruel, cowardly, and bloody massacre of the innocent." Election thieves, it seems, were not accustomed to federal intervention.

The Baltimore *Sun* editorialized about the election riot in Washington by noting how such Election Day violence had become all too common:

> It cannot have escaped our readers that the violent proceedings in which these disturbances commenced have become an ordinary feature in the election of our principal towns. So little attention has been attracted to their significance that men have suffered them to pass almost without comment, while we have been excited, as a whole people, on hearing of similar outrages in Kansas . . . all that has passed in Kansas can scarce parallel the outrages which marked the history of the last municipal election in the capital of the United States.

On the eve of the Civil War, the practice of importing armed gangs to "regulate" an election had indeed become so commonly utilized that it simply did not draw much attention outside the borders of the city in which it was used. Although Democrats and Know-Nothings had been in the vanguard of fraud and violence in the antebellum era, the newly created Republican party was not above reproach. In Goodhue County, Minnesota, for example, Republicans racked up remarkable victories in the November 1857 general election. Yet the election displayed some troubling anomalies. In 1856, the county had had 499 Democrats and 471 Republicans. The next year, Democrats had 705, but the Republicans had swelled to 1,223. With a census that spring that showed only 1,652 voters in the entire county, it was obvious the Republicans had been busy registering false names. At the precinct level, the fraud was too obvious. In the Kenyon Precinct, for example, there were only 33 voters—yet the final count resulted in the Republicans winning, 68–6.

1860

By the time of the secession crisis in the winter of 1860, the young nation had seen its fair share of bought voters, intimidation, violence, and outright forgery. Fraud had routinely occurred in elections ranging from local sheriff to the presidency. As the events in the Territories revealed, without free and fair elections, the notion of popular sovereignty as a means to defuse the slavery debate was nothing more than a hollow shell. It also demonstrated the impact of the federal government's legitimizing fraudulent tactics and results by looking the other way.

With the threat of secession and war in the air, there was one last election that might help ease the tension, the presidential race to replace Buchanan in 1860. Yet just as the Kansas elections had only deepened the sectional anger and mistrust, the 1860 election would prove again that elections were incapable of stopping the national hemorrhaging.

During the nominating conventions, the sectional and political divisions ruptured to near the breaking point. The Democrats, after quickly rejecting any notion of renominating the hapless Buchanan, were so divided over slavery in the aftermath of "Bleeding Kansas" that they broke into three factions—Stephen Douglas representing the northern wing of the party, John C. Breckinridge the southern wing, and John Bell, who lead a last rallying of old Whigs and Unionists, now christened the Constitutional Unionists. After rejecting such well-known anti-slavery leaders as William Seward of New York, the Republicans nominated a relative moderate, Abraham Lincoln of Illinois. After existing as a party for less than a decade, the Republicans seemed poised to claim the White House.

As evidenced in Kansas, by 1860 the national divisions were so profound that the desire by all parties to win at any cost presaged an unprecedented degree of fraud in the upcoming presidential election. Southern slaveholders were particularly repulsed by Lincoln's anti-slavery sentiments. After Douglas had discredited himself with Southerners over his apparent ambivalence concerning the Dred Scott decision and stubbornly held on to the weary principle of popular sovereignty, Southerners threw their support behind Breckinridge of Kentucky.

Yet Southern Democrats did not need to resort to the usual kinds of fraud to defeat Lincoln. They had already taken care of that in the most effective way: Lincoln was denied even a place on the ballot in ten Southern states. In the north, where fusion tickets of Douglas and Breckinridge were employed in New York, New Jersey, Pennsylvania, and Rhode Island, fraud surfaced. In the Twelfth Ward of New York City alone, 500 of the 3,500 registered names were fictitious. Tammany Hall, in firm opposition to Lincoln and the Republicans, registered nearly a thousand false names in the Ninth Ward. Not surprisingly, Lincoln lost New York City by nearly 30,000 votes. But Tammany was unable to deliver the state for the Democrats, as Lincoln won the Empire State and its critical 35 electoral votes. In all, although he did not receive even a single vote in ten Southern states, Lincoln won the popular vote by over a half million, and beat his closest rival in the Electoral College, Breckinridge, by 180 to 72. Shortly after his inauguration, as the cannons began shelling Fort Sumter on April 12, the failure of popular sovereignty was obvious.

CHAPTER THREE

"Can You Hold Your State?"

"Dead or alive, they would all cast a good vote."

I n 1880, Henry Adams wrote a novel, ironically titled *Democracy*, in which a venerable Illinois senator named Silas Ratcliffe candidly recalled why he had helped steal a state election during the Civil War:

> In the worst days of the war there was almost a certainty that my State would be carried by the peace party, by fraud, as we thought, although, fraud or not, we were bound to save it. Had Illinois been lost then, we should certainly have lost the Presidential election, and with it probably the Union. At any rate, I believed the fate of the war to depend on the result. I was then Governor, and upon me the responsibility rested. We had entire control of the northern counties and of their returns. We ordered the returning officers in a certain number of counties to make no returns until they heard from us, and when we received the votes of all the southern counties and learned the precise number of votes we needed to give us a majority,

we telegraphed to our northern returning officers to make the vote
of their districts such and such, thereby overbalancing the adverse
returns and giving the State to us.

The senator concluded, "I am not proud of the transaction, but I
would do it again."

Although Adams's account was fictional, Ratcliffe's justification of
election fraud was all too real. As the nation turned to bullets over ballots to settle its bitter political divisions, the methods that Silas Ratcliffe defended would help define American politics during the Civil
War and Reconstruction.

"WITHOUT RESTRAINT OR REGULATION"

With the outbreak of war in April 1861, the question of whether any
elections would be held during the conflict seemed obvious. When
President Lincoln suspended the writ of habeas corpus, would elections be next? Other issues complicated the matter further. Since many
state constitutions explicitly fixed the location of voting to be confined
within the states, could soldiers even vote and would they cast their
vote from the frontlines? How would an already broken electoral
system cope with the demands of war?

In 1862, a report from a select committee of the New York City
Board of Aldermen described the conditions that had dominated the
recent city elections. From the outset, it sounded as if the report could
have been written in 1842 or 1822. The polls were "notoriously and
proverbially the scenes of the most disgraceful fraud, chicanery, and
violence," the report claimed. "They are without legal restraint or regulation," adding that "peaceable and orderly citizens" held the elections
in contempt.

The 1862 elections were the first national contests conducted during the Civil War. Selecting members of Congress, who could then vote for military appropriations or impeach the commander-in-chief, allowed citizens a chance to voice their support of or opposition to the war effort. Additionally, whether soldiers could participate in these elections was a matter of considerable debate. Most state constitutions stated that voters could still cast a vote outside their local precinct if they were away from home conducting business for the U. S. government or the state. Yet soldiers were considered excluded from this rule. The first state to allow soldiers to cast their vote in the field was Wisconsin, which legalized absentee voting in 1862. Eventually, nineteen states enacted laws allowing soldiers the right to vote by absentee ballot.

Democrats, however, objected to soldiers voting because they suspected loyal soldiers would vote for the party of Lincoln. In Lincoln's home state of Illinois, a soldiers' voting bill was defeated in 1863 when Democrats held a legislative majority, yet the same bill passed in 1865 when Republicans held a majority. In New York, Maryland, Wisconsin, Indiana, Michigan, and New Hampshire, support for allowing soldiers to vote fell along the same party lines. New York's governor and future Democratic presidential candidate Horatio Seymour opposed soldier voting, using a rationale that belied his obvious partisan anxieties: "It would be worse than mockery to allow those secluded in camps or upon ships to vote, if they are not permitted to receive letters and papers from their friends, or if they have not had the same freedom in reading public journals."

The mechanics of soldier voting varied from state to state. Some states allowed soldiers to vote by proxy, in which a soldier recorded his vote on a piece of paper and sent it to a friend or family member, who would then vote in the soldier's place at the prescribed precinct—theoretically, the friend would cast the vote as the soldier wished. In others, soldiers placed their ballots into a box just like they would have at home. The votes of the soldiers would then be thrown in with those of civilians in order that no one could determine how the military vote went. In New York, a Soldiers Voting Law said that if a soldier's name was not on the registry list, a resident of the district could swear that he knew the soldier and attest to his residency in order for the soldier to be registered.

Some areas saw authorities bend over backward to include the soldier vote, sometimes in ways that opened new opportunities for fraud. Since officers distributed and counted the ballots, intimidation and false counts were possible. The worry that officers could manipulate returns caused Iowa to appoint election commissioners for each regiment. Connecticut went so far as to have commissioners assume all election duties and excluded officers from all voting-related procedures. Some officers sabotaged these efforts by moving their troops closer to the front lines, well beyond the range of safety for civilian commissioners. Yet in some remarkable moments, soldiers voted. Members of the 76th Pennsylvania Company E reported that Confederate troops stopped firing on Election Day under the mistaken impression that the Union troops would vote for Democratic candidates.

"YOU CAN FILL THEM UP AS WELL AS WE CAN HERE"

Holding a presidential election in the middle of a civil war was evidence that the Constitution could not be postponed. Yet the 1864 election was also a referendum on Lincoln's handling of the war effort and presented the possibility of a new policy toward the Confederacy. If a Democrat could defeat Lincoln, the new president could sue for peace, and negotiations for official recognition of the Confederate States of America could occur. On the other hand, if Lincoln were reelected, the chances of a Union victory seemed likely. When Democrats nominated General George McClellan, the soldier vote took on new meaning. Some Congressional Democrats were worried about how the troops might use force to ensure a Republican victory.

This drawing by Thomas Nast appeared in *Harper's Weekly* one week before the 1864 election. It warned how "peace Democrats" would obtain their fraudulent votes to defeat Lincoln by registering the dead. Credit: *Harper's Weekly*

Rep. Lazarus Powell of Kentucky complained that a Colonel Gilbert, commanding a regiment of federal troops, had forcefully dispersed a summer meeting of the Kentucky Democratic Party, and he soon introduced legislation that would prohibit the Army from interfering with the conduct of the election. With such tensions running high, there was much to be worried about as the nation prepared for the 1864 presidential vote.

With so much on the line, the temptation to resort to fraud was strong. The most conspicuous example occurred, not surprisingly, in New York, where Governor Seymour appointed nearly sixty agents to collect only Democratic votes from the state's soldiers. In late October 1864, seven of these agents were arrested for impersonating military officers who had forged names and signatures of soldiers for the purpose of illegally recording their votes in the upcoming general election. One of those arrested, Edward J. Donahue, Jr., had written to a leading state Democratic official, saying:

> I send with this note a number of ballots for your county. I made out
> a number from the list you sent me . . . I guess you have enough.

Fearing that you may not I enclose envelopes and powers of attorney sworn to. You can fill them up for Columbia, or any other county. You can fill them up as well as we can here.

A roll of four hundred patients in the Jarvis Hospital in Baltimore was also included, and another witness testified, "Dead or alive, they would all cast a good vote." Donahue and another accomplice were found guilty, and were given a severe sentence approved by President Lincoln that was rare in the annals of American vote fraud: life imprisonment.

Republicans, wary of the massive illegal registration in the 1860 election, found countless false names in an investigation of the New York City registry rolls, and the absentee soldier vote was a vulnerable point for corruption. Thousands of forged registration papers had been filed for soldiers, officers' certificates had been forged, and numerous sick, disabled, and dead soldiers had been illegally registered. With rumors of Confederate agents just across the Canadian border conspiring to steal the New York vote, President Lincoln dispatched General Benjamin F. Butler to New York City along with artillery and six thousand troops, just before the election. Butler established a civilian surveillance system of the election, to report possible fraud to him directly. With his troops just outside the city, Tammany Hall was thoroughly intimidated, and the city saw one of the quietest elections in memory. Yet the *New York Times* pointed out that even with Butler's presence, fraud still occurred in heavily Democratic areas: "It was only necessary for a man to proclaim himself for 'Little Mac,' " the paper reported, "to have his vote accepted without regard to his residence or qualifications for suffrage."

In Albany, a different sort of intimidation occurred when a Democratic election inspector appointed a number of local butchers as "special constables" to patrol the election and maintain order. Their real purpose was to frighten away Republican votes by forming wedges every time a prospective voter approached with a ticket indicative of the party of

Lincoln. Like those who had participated in the bloody New York City draft riots of 1863, the butchers' contempt for Republicans originated with Lincoln championing the cause of emancipation rather than preservation of the Union. When one voter attempted to sneak a Republican ticket inside a Democratic ticket, he was discovered and, fearing for his life, went away without voting at all. The butchers maintained their vigilant presence all day against anyone who dared endorse the Emancipation Proclamation and "black Republicans."

While Indiana allowed no soldiers to vote in the field, a number of suspicious soldier votes surfaced in a crucial October 1864 gubernatorial election. Troops from the 60th Massachusetts Regiment took advantage of the lax restrictions in Indianapolis, and many soldiers voted a dozen times each, and some claimed they had done so twenty-five times for the Republican candidate. In the border state of Kentucky, a Madison County election judge was approached by Union officers with a list of seventy men who should not be allowed to vote. If they did so, the officers claimed, the voters would be shot. In other Kentucky counties, soldiers stood by with their rifles and bayonets, openly cursing and threatening Democratic voters. Although these tactics did not swing enough votes to change the election, the image of soldiers standing by the polls and intimidating voters should not be surprising, considering how the war overwhelmed even the usual fierce partisanship accompanying a typical presidential election.

Lincoln won rather easily, with an Electoral College margin of 212 to 21. Among his soldiers, Lincoln won 78 percent of the ballots. In those states that allowed soldiers to vote in the field, the total soldier vote was barely over 150,000. No doubt the exigencies of war prevented many from casting a vote, but the political opposition to allowing soldiers the franchise played a significant role as well. An early student of soldier voting estimated that over 1.3 million Union soldiers were effectively disfranchised when they entered the Army.

BLACK SUFFRAGE

When the war ended in 1865, no development was as revolutionary as black suffrage. For former slaves and freed blacks, the promise of equality was empty if not followed by the right to vote. By 1870, that "right" was apparently guaranteed through the ratification of the 15th Amendment, which read: "The right of citizens of the United States to vote shall not be denied or abridged by the United States or by any State on account of race, color, or previous condition of servitude."

With the power of the ballot, it seemed American politics would be changed forever, and the survival of the Democratic Party, particularly in the South, was in peril. On the face of it, Democrats had much to fear. In 1867, black turnout for a constitutional referendum in Georgia reached nearly 70 percent, while that figure approached 90 percent for a vote in Virginia. Without control of local or state governments to stop it, Southerners used a well-worn tactic to stop the black vote: terror.

The Ku Klux Klan emerged on the heels of the war as a vigilante group determined to reestablish antebellum race relations. It opposed black education, black economic and social equality, and black suffrage. Consequently, the KKK was a frequent presence surrounding Election Day during Reconstruction. In Tennessee, where the Klan was born, the pattern was soon set: Freedmen attempting to vote would be whipped, shot at, and threatened with death, while Republican officeholders—white or black—were similarly threatened if they remained in office. In suppressing the black vote, the Klan became an operating arm of the Democratic party throughout the South. Until more "legal" forms of vote suppression could be utilized, flagrant fraud was the only way Southern whites could ward off the agency of African-Americans exercising their franchise.

In Camilla, Georgia, vigilantes killed nine African-Americans shortly before the 1868 election. Their message was heeded. Only two courageous Republicans dared to cast a vote on Election Day. In Americus,

Georgia, only 137 African-Americans voted out of 1,500 eligible freedmen, and most of them were bribed to vote for Democrats. "The whole affair was such a farce and everything connected with it so illegal," the agent concluded, "I don't see how it is possible it could stand as a legal vote or showing the sentiments of this county."

When African-Americans attempted to vote in Mississippi's constitutional referendum in 1868, they were driven away by armed gangs. Eleven illiterate freedmen from Duck Hill put their marks to a sworn statement that they had voted Democratic, but were "radicals" at heart, and were told if they voted for the constitution they would be forced to leave the state. The Grand Cyclops of the KKK issued the following warning to any blacks thinking of voting for the constitution: "The trying hour is at hand! Beware! Your steps are marked! The eye of the dark chief is upon you. First he warns; then the avenging dagger flashes in the moonlight." The presiding military officer in the area, Major General Alvan C. Gillum, refused to investigate such outrages.

During Reconstruction, African-Americans faced fraud and worse if they went to the polls. This drawing was titled "One Vote Less." Credit: *Harper's Weekly*

Due to such tactics, it probably was not surprising that the constitution lost by 7,600 votes. Former slaves in Mississippi, in a free and
fair election, would have overwhelmingly supported a new state constitution that prevented former confederates from holding office.
Freedman Thomas W. Stringer doubted whether "as many as 25 colored men would be found in the State to vote against" the constitution. Democratic Judge William L. Sharkey disagreed, claiming that
no frauds had occurred in Mississippi, and that the reason was that
freedmen really wanted to vote with their Democratic brethren. "A
great many of them belonged to Democratic masters," Sharkey reasoned, "and they imbibed the principle of democracy."

"WE INTEND TO SUCCEED BY INTIMIDATION"

The presidential election of 1868 was the first one conducted after the
Civil War. In the former Confederacy, the election was of particular
significance. The way in which the contest was held in Louisiana displayed how free and fair elections were little more than a farce in the
Deep South. In St. Landry Parish, after three leading Democrats
caned a Republican editor, riots soon broke out along partisan and
racial lines. For weeks, armed groups of whites roamed the parish,
inflicting terror on blacks. One New Orleans newspaper reported that
over a hundred freedmen were killed during the riots, while a state
investigation claimed over two hundred deaths.

The violence produced the desired results on Election Day.
Although a Republican gubernatorial candidate had received over
2,500 votes seven months before, Republican presidential candidate
Ulysses S. Grant did not receive a single vote from St. Landry Parish.
The registration supervisor put it in chilling terms: "I am fully convinced that no man could have voted any other than the Democratic
ticket and not been killed inside of twenty-four hours."

Throughout other parishes, threats of similar violence were heard in the days leading up to the election. In Bossier Parish, according to the state investigation, riots killed 162 people. In Caddo Parish, estimates of the number of African-Americans murdered during the 1868 election ranged from 185 to 300. Between the Civil War and the end of Reconstruction, more African-Americans were murdered in Caddo Parish for Election Day activities than for any other reason. Throughout Louisiana, state workers were threatened with losing their jobs if they did not vote for the Democratic presidential candidate, Horatio Seymour, while African-Americans needed "protection papers" saying that they belonged to a Democratic club. Even with federal troops on guard, three freedmen were murdered near Monroe. Through such intimidation, the results were predictable. Seymour carried Louisiana, 80,225 to 33,225. Considering that the Republicans had won more than 69,000 votes in the April 1868 governor's race, violence and intimidation had obviously stolen the state race for Seymour. Ulysses S. Grant, a Republican, received just one vote in Bossier Parish, although two thousand Republicans were registered. In New Orleans, a Congressional committee found that the vigilante violence was so severe that the city was consumed in a "state of anarchy." A sobering assessment came from an anonymous member of the White League, who claimed, "It has been charged that the white man's party intends to achieve success by intimidation. This is strictly true. We intend to succeed by intimidation." Succeed they did. In the six months preceding the election, over a thousand African-Americans were killed in Louisiana. In that same period, Democratic vote totals more than doubled.

When a joint committee of the Louisiana general assembly investigated the election, it found that "the so-called election in parishes which were in a state of anarchy was no election, and that the so-called returns from those parishes are null and void." The state's electoral vote was thrown out, a foreshadowing of how Louisiana elections would fare for some time to come.

Georgia provided another warning of the state of elections in the former Confederacy. Although there were over 27,000 "colored" voters registered throughout the state, Grant received just over 3,500 votes for president. Those figures became even more troubling upon closer inspection. In Columbia and Randolph counties, although there were 3,047 registered African-American voters, Grant received only two votes. In Newton County, over four hundred black voters were frightened away from the polls by the Ku Klux Klan.

When terror was not used, more subtle tactics worked. Democratic poll officials repeatedly challenged black voters to pay poll taxes (although the governor had declared in late October that one's ability to vote could not be challenged on the grounds of non-payment of taxes). White voters, meanwhile, who had paid no such tax, were allowed to vote. In Pike County, a notary public named Joseph Youngblood related that "when a colored voter offered to vote, and his ticket was folded, it was opened, and if for Seymour (the Democratic candidate), it was put into the ballot box." If the vote was for Grant, Youngblood related, "his tax receipt was called for, and if voter could not show a receipt his vote was refused." Youngblood understood the consequences of such brazen fraud upon the course of Reconstruction: "If something is not done for the protection of loyal men they will be forced to abandon the ballot box."

The problems with the 1868 election were not just confined to the former Confederacy. In New York, Tammany Hall's well-known naturalization mills worked feverishly before the 1868 election. In October 1868 alone, over 65,000 people were naturalized in the courtrooms controlled by Tammany. William M. Tweed himself acknowledged that in 1868 "a great many persons were naturalized" in order to vote. Was the election fair? Tweed later admitted that "I don't think there was ever a fair and honest election in New York City."

The naturalizations were just the beginning. Gangs of repeaters

Thomas Nast's image of William "Boss" Tweed and the source of his political power in New York City. "As long as I count the votes," Nast quotes Tweed, "what are you going to do about it?"
Credit: *Harper's Weekly*

were also used to fraudulently register themselves. The repeaters met at a prescribed location run by a party representative. There they received a scrap of paper with a fictitious name and address. The repeater would go to the place of registry, assume the name and address, and be registered accordingly. The repeater would then return to the party representative, who would repeat the process, with another fictitious name and address, usually at a different precinct.

One of the largest repeating centers was located at the corner of Second Avenue and 32nd Street, and was run by Sheriff James O'Brien. On the night before the 1868 election, over three hundred repeaters were housed in this building. In his official capacity, O'Brien hired more than two thousand deputies for the election, whose job was to "arrest anyone who interfered with the voting." Not surprisingly, no Democratic repeaters were arrested by O'Brien's deputies, but scores of Republican poll officials and challengers were. Some tipped-off election inspectors, in plainclothes, watched as men ordered by William "Reddy the Blacksmith" Varley registered in various locales on the same day. When the inspectors raided Varley's office, they found a book that detailed where the men had registered and under what names and addresses. In one day, eight of Varley's men had registered a total of 161 times.

Seymour carried New York state by exactly 10,000 votes, and a later House investigation concluded that the Democrats in New York had committed "every known crime against the elective franchise." Tweed later admitted that the machine went one step further. In order to control the timing of the New York City returns to overcome the upstate totals, "one thing we did was take possession of the wires, so as to keep them employed." The machine telegraphed portions of the Bible to delay election returns until the appropriate time.

Despite the fraud used in Seymour's behalf, it was not nearly enough to overcome the popular support for the former commander of the Union Army. Grant garnered over 300,000 votes more than Seymour nationally, and won the presidency by an Electoral College 214 to 80. The story that unfolded in this contest foretold a chilling vision of future elections in the Deep South, where Democrats saw winning—by any means—necessary to ensure racial control in the wake of emancipation.

In the face of this assault on the democratic process, voters did not sit by idly and accept the state of affairs that accompanied the polling place. In New York City, anti-Tammany organizations tried to restore fairness to the election process. A "Vigilance Committee of New York City" held mass meetings to challenge widespread election fraud. This organization was just one of many urban reform groups that arose after the war, all of which met with little success. In December 1869, the committee charged that New York voters "had been robbed by Tammany Hall of the privilege of voting, and their candidates cheated of their rights by unparalleled swindles and enormous frauds." After receiving the usual rejections from city courts and state party leaders to their calls for justice, indignant committee leaders tried another tactic, asking Congress for a "uniform election law" that would guarantee the "free right of voting." Upon passage of this act, the committee concluded, all would be well in the republic: "Our free and glorious institutions will be saved from otherwise unavoidable destruction." The purple language could not hide the futility of their cause.

Another device used by anti-Tammany reformers to curtail fraud was the old call to enact registry laws. A new city registry system enacted in 1866 demonstrated the ineffectiveness of this tactic. Since the poll lists of previous years served as the basis of the new lists, the false registrants before the war were now legal. In examining the registry rolls in 1866, New York City police discovered that more than 15,000 fraudulently registered names had been added to the lists, which underscored how Tammany could adjust to such reforms with relative ease.

To counter the tactics of Southern Democrats, the Republican majority in Congress responded in 1870 with the Enforcement Acts, which prohibited intimidation and violence at the polls, as well as prohibiting racially biased election laws (the Ku Klux Klan Act gave the president authority to deploy troops to protect elections). Election supervisors were appointed to watch for election irregularities; for the next seven years, on average, seven hundred cases of violations of the Enforcement Acts were prosecuted by the Justice Department each year.

In Arkansas, a Congressional election in 1870 demonstrated why these laws were necessary. In the Third Congressional District, John Edwards was proclaimed victorious by Governor Powell Clayton. A grand jury then indicted Gov. Clayton for violating the Enforcement Act by giving the election to a man who had not actually won the race. Testimony before the grand jury revealed that Edwards's opponent, Thomas Boles, received between 800 and 2,130 more votes than Edwards; yet, with rampant ballot-box stuffing and massive false registration, the governor was satisfied to certify the election for Edwards.

A Congressional investigation eventually found that the evidence for fraud was so overwhelming that Edwards was removed from his seat and replaced by the rightful winner, Boles.

THE THEFTS OF 1876

Few American elections have drawn as much intense scrutiny as the presidential election of 1876. While the story of how the contest was decided in the weeks and months after the votes were cast has been exhaustively covered, the role of fraud in the election itself has tended to be obscured. When viewed within the context of what had transpired since 1865, the events of 1876 do not appear so unusual.

After two rather lackluster and corruption-filled terms of President Grant, who had announced his decision not to seek a third term, the major parties feverishly sought to nominate candidates who could claim the White House. Adding to the drama was an economic depression that had started in 1873; the nation's economy was still contracting three years later. In addition to these concerns, the fates of Reconstruction and millions of freedmen hung in the balance. The Republicans settled on a candidate who had managed to avoid offending major elements of the party, Governor Rutherford B. Hayes of Ohio. Upon accepting his party's nomination, Hayes told anxious Southerners that the time of military occupation was over and that "honest and capable local self-government" would be allowed to grow in his administration.

The Democrats, meanwhile, nominated New York's Governor Samuel Tilden, whose reputation was founded on his role in helping to topple the Tweed Ring in New York City five years earlier. Although the Democrats seemed handicapped by the memories of the Civil War and their prior defense of slavery, the twin issues of corruption and depression spelled trouble for the Republicans.

As the election approached, political observers assumed Tilden would win virtually all of the Southern states, while Hayes would most likely take thirteen Northern states. The election, then, hinged on key "swing" states such as Indiana, Ohio, and Tilden's own New York. Not surprisingly, the Republican *New York Times* carried ominous reports of Democratic repeaters invading Indiana and Ohio weeks before the election. In New York City alone, Tammany was busy registering thousands to vote for Tilden in numbers that far exceeded previous registrations. (Despite his role in uncovering the magnitude of the corruption of Boss Tweed, Tammany's Democratic allegiances to the state governor were still paramount.) In Brooklyn, registration figures reached 98,307 in late October, compared to just 73,651 the previous year.

In Mississippi, whites interpreted the upcoming election as nothing less than a crusade. "To lose the election this fall would entail upon us such a canvass and such scenes in the fall of 1877 as no well-wisher of the State would like to see," said the Aberdeen *Examiner.* After Democrats scored their inevitable victory, the paper proclaimed:

> God gave the victory to a people who were contending for liberation from the basest thralldom ever endured by a civilized race, and who would have been justified in swinging up their oppressors as food for the buzzards to the boughs of our forest trees.

On Election Day in Smithville, Mississippi, a white Republican came to the polls to distribute tickets, only to find an ominous spectacle: In front of the polls voters found a freshly dug grave, and a sign next to the makeshift coffin read: "Death to any man that votes the radical ticket here today." It was no surprise that only one Republican vote was cast in Smithville, and that hearty soul, Minor Tubbs, had to run for his life for over four miles. Sheriff Lee had over a thousand affidavits of men who had been driven away from the polls in Monroe County by force and threats. This was the same district that had given Grant a 2,343-vote majority just four years earlier.

In Florida, the rhetoric surrounding the vote grew more heated as the election approached. The Republican governor, Marcellus Stearns, warned African-Americans in his state that a Democratic victory meant war, and all black schools "would be abolished because the whites did not want to educate them with their tax money." One Republican leader in Alachua County advised the blacks in his county to "carry their guns on election day." Beyond these flourishes were some economic threats. Planters in Jefferson County established a "priority system" for granting credit and divvying up farmable land. First preference, according to one historian, "would go to those voting Democratic, second to those not voting at all, while those voting Republican would be considered last." In Monticello, town leaders, including landlords and doctors, vowed that they would charge their clients suspected of voting for Republicans a surcharge of twenty-five percent. A less subtle means was used by the Florida Central Railroad Company, which distributed Democratic ballots to its workers in Nassau and Duval counties, and maintained a careful list of those employees who brought back a ballot on Election Day; any who did not would be fired on the spot.

A worried Hayes confided in his diary just weeks before the election: "Another danger is imminent: a contested result." Hayes was prepared for Democratic corruption at the polls, particularly in the South, but he was more concerned with the structural means of electing a president in the United States:

> And we have no such means for its decision as ought to be provided by law. This must be attended to hereafter. We should not allow another Presidential election to occur before a means for settling a contest is provided. If a contest comes now it may lead to a conflict of arms.

Perhaps not even the most prescient observer could have predicted just how close this election would be, at least in terms of the Electoral

College. On election night, Tilden appeared in the lead in both the popular and electoral count. In fact, Hayes himself went to bed that night believing he had lost. Tilden held a lead in the popular vote of more than a quarter million votes, and after New York's electoral votes were put in Tilden's column, the Republicans seemingly had little hope. Having won Indiana, Connecticut, and New Jersey, and assuming that Tilden had carried the South, Democrats were confident of winning over two hundred electoral votes. But Republicans also knew that they controlled the returning boards in Louisiana, South Carolina, and Florida, and word was sent to delay returning their counts. In one of the most famous telegrams in American political history, Republican party chairman Zach Chandler alerted party leaders in those states: "Hayes is elected if we have carried South Carolina, Florida and Louisiana. Can you hold your state?"

To Republicans in those critical states, they knew that "hold your state" meant to cook the numbers, in whatever manner necessary, to secure a Hayes victory. Republicans conceded that Tilden had won 184 electoral votes; but that was one vote shy of the Constitutional requisite for winning the election. Hayes had won 166 electoral votes, and his aides obviously had their eyes on nineteen "disputed" votes in South Carolina, Florida, and Louisiana. Since Appomattox, those three states had all seen their fair share of voter intimidation and Klan violence, as well as outright election fraud.

In Louisiana, the decades of open warfare on Republican voters had their intended effect. In East Feliciana Parish alone, there had been over fifty separate occurrences of political violence by vigilante groups toward Republicans. Although there were 2,127 registered Republicans in the parish, Hayes did not receive one single vote. Even worse, in Ouachita and Morehouse parishes in the northeastern part of the state, two noted black Republicans had been murdered the month preceding the election. By Election Day, it was not surprising that reports from all over the state indicated a rather "quiet" day. The damage had already been done, but Democratic patrols reinforced the message to any lingering black voters. In East Baton Rouge, East and West Feliciana, Morehouse, and Ouachita parishes, in just two years a Republican electoral majority of 3,979 votes had been turned into a Democratic majority of 3,493.

In Mississippi, a state that did not even figure in the election controversy, stories from various locales there were consistent with other Deep South states regarding Democratic intimidation of black voters. One resident explained how the election proceeded in Jackson. When one poll official took Republican tickets handed him by black voters, he threw them on the floor and substituted Democratic tickets for them, which he then placed in the ballot box. "Such plain stealing was noticed by everybody present," wrote the anonymous black voter, "but nobody dared to say anything, as it would have resulted in the arrest and murder of the complainants." In Ebenezer Precinct, an armed gang killed the Republican official responsible for distributing the election tickets for his party. Scores of African-Americans reported that they had been told "to vote Democrat or die." The *New York Times* understood that the implications of the election fraud extended much farther than whether Tilden or Hayes won the White House. The point of the fraud had far-reaching effects on Reconstruction policy and the state's African-American population: "There is nothing in store for them but complete subjugation to the old slave-master, or extermination."

The election margin was razor-thin in Florida, where official returns had Hayes leading 24,327 to 24,287, a 40-vote lead. In a pattern that would again be played out in 2000, there were widespread reports of spoiled ballots and otherwise legal voters being illegally purged. In Alachua County, Democrats charged that Tilden had been cheated out of over two hundred votes, which was verified by one conscientious citizen of one precinct, who stayed at the polls all day, duly writing down every individual who arrived to vote. In his total, 319 total votes should have been recorded in his precinct, yet the official returns indicated 563 votes had been cast in the precinct, providing Hayes with a false majority of over two hundred votes. In Jefferson County, some Democratic precincts were removed or abolished altogether, while in another precinct fifty more votes were counted than existed on the registration lists. In many other counties throughout the state, similar problems with both Democratic and Republican votes arose, and begged the question as to how the Florida tallies should be counted, as well as who should do the counting.

As the parties fought over how to settle the dispute, it was not surprising that overtones of yet another civil war were frequently heard. When a train carrying some Republican couriers was wrecked in Florida shortly after the election, charges came from the state house that the train had been "ku kluxed," and President Grant dispatched troops to the state to maintain order. "Tilden or Blood" was an often-heard cry from Democrats, as the St. Louis publisher Joseph Pulitzer said that a hundred thousand men should come to Washington "fully armed and ready for business." Speaking before an "immense mob" in Indianapolis, George W. Julian claimed that "millions of men will be found ready to offer their lives as hostages to the sacredness of the ballots as the palladium of our liberties."

President Grant reacted to such threats on Washington, D.C., with his own threat of martial law. Congressional Democrats responded by threatening to impeach Grant for misusing the military to intimidate voters. Yet Grant was not intimidated, and he also warned his generals to be on the lookout for any potential fraud. "Should there be any grounds of suspicion of fraudulent counting on either side," Grant warned, "it should be reported and denounced at once. "No man worthy of the office of President," Grant wrote, would be "willing to hold the office if counted in, placed there by fraud." The question remained whether either candidate, under the existing circumstances, *could* govern if his minions could manage to scrape together 185 electoral votes.

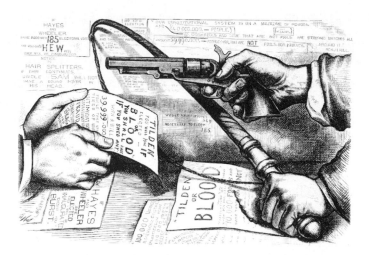

The dual image of bullets and ballots is seen here in Nast's infamous "Tilden or Blood" cartoon from 1877. Credit: *Harper's Weekly*

WHO DECIDES?

The year 1876 provides another laboratory for studying how contested presidential elections can play out. When the vote totals are so close—even based on thoroughly illegitimate numbers—and the charges of fraud are so intense on both sides, who has the final authority to determine the winner in a way that the country will recognize? The Constitution offered little real guidance in how to proceed when so many disputed votes remained. The votes were to be opened before a joint session of Congress, and if no one received a majority of the entire Electoral College count, the House of Representatives would then be given the election. Yet there were divisive partisan dynamics present that were not anticipated by the Founding Fathers. Since Republicans controlled the Senate, Democrats were wary of that body deciding which contested returns from the three states in question should be counted, while Republicans were not about to see the Democratic-controlled House get the election. With such an impasse, could a winner be determined in a way that would not damage the presidency and the Constitution?

Both parties, in the meantime, felt cheated. Republicans claimed that if a peaceful election had been held, Hayes would have carried more Southern states, and that the party of the "bloody shirt" was attempting to steal the presidency by force. One partisan from Louisiana was thoroughly disgusted at the Democratic bullying of black voters, and described Election Day atrocities in the state as similar to "the most terrible stories of the Spanish Inquisition." Democrats countered that their man had won the popular vote and was on the verge of being cheated out of office by Republican office-holders at the state level and in Congress.

The two candidates and their parties adopted differing stances as the turmoil ensued. Tilden retreated to his New York home in December and ruminated over the legal issues concerning the counting of electoral votes and made no public claims on the presidency. After prematurely conceding that Tilden had been elected, Hayes took a more aggressive stance, claiming victory and approving of Republican attempts to negotiate with South Carolina and Louisiana Democrats, all the while assuring them that a Hayes administration would treat the South far differently than Grant had. Republican Senator Roscoe Conkling admitted privately that he thought the Democrats had won, and was puzzled by Tilden's quiet response. Conkling wondered whether Tilden and his supporters meant "to act upon the *good boy* principle of submission, or whether we mean to have it understood that Tilden has been elected and, by the Eternal, he shall be inaugurated."

While the events in Florida before and on Election Day were corrupted by the Democrats in order to diminish the African-American vote, the events in the Sunshine State after Election Day were corrupted by Republicans, who controlled the canvassing boards and were on the lookout for any suspicious activity that could warrant throwing out Democratic vote totals. In a Key West precinct, which gave Tilden a 342-vote margin of victory, the canvassing board threw out the results entirely on the grounds that election inspectors had adjourned before properly completing the canvass and had the count moved to the following day without public notification. In the interim, the ballot box was out of public view, which, to Republican canvassers, presented the possibility of fraud, the results were summarily thrown out. Despite Democratic protestations, in such ways the official vote would be recorded as a Hayes victory.

Although on Election Day Louisiana electors for Tilden had a majority of at least 6,300 votes, outraged Republicans claimed that that majority was built on fraud and intimidation. The returning boards, dominated by Republicans, heard allegations of fraud in a number of parishes. One Republican newspaper reported that in some selected parishes, the state of affairs in the months leading up to the election was nothing less than "a state of war": "with hostile camps, roving patrols of five companies, acknowledging no law except their own will and the directions of the Democratic State Committee." In East and West Feliciana, East Baton Rouge, More-house, and Ouachita parishes, the paper claimed, "the unarmed Negroes are virtually prisoners of war, and as completely under the control of the Democratic guerrillas as the prisoners of Andersonville and Salisbury were." In East Baton Rouge Parish, the tactics used to intimidate voters in the Third Ward were not atypical. After seizing a room that adjoined the election commissioners, the "bulldozers" brandished rifles and shotguns, and in this open display, "these champions of 'free, full and fair elections' succeeded in carrying the poll unanimously for the Democrats." In West Feliciana Parish, self-styled "regulators" stood near the polls and carefully recorded the names of all Republican voters, threatening them with a visit in the dark of the night for their disloyalty. Ohio's Republican Senator John Sherman wrote to a friend in Louisiana of his "repugnance to the scenes of violence in some of the parishes in Louisiana." He was not alone in his revulsion. On December 5, 1876, the board officially threw out the returns from Grant and East Feliciana parishes, and in the process rejected approximately 15,000 votes, most of which were Democratic votes, thereby giving Hayes a statewide majority of several thousand.

The question then became: Which returns should be certified? With a deadlock looming, a compromise was brokered in Congress whereby an Electoral Commission would decide the outcome of the Hayes–Tilden race. The makeup of that commission, obviously, was a matter of deep interest to both parties. The law establishing the commission settled on fifteen members—ten from Congress equally divided between the parties, and five members of the Supreme Court. The justices appointed to the commission would consist of two Democrats and two Republicans who would then be allowed to name the final member of the commission. Unless partisan politics were left out of the equation, which possibility only the most naïve observer would have considered, this last pick would undoubtedly be the swing vote that would effectively select the next president of the United States.

Most observers assumed Justice David Davis would be the choice, a Republican who nonetheless was rumored to be willing to give Tilden at least one of the disputed states and, consequently, the presidency. Yet when Democratic legislators in Illinois conspired to elect Davis to the U.S. Senate (the only Supreme Court justice ever to leave the bench for the Senate), his appointment to the commission was now greatly in doubt. Had the Democrats done this in token appreciation for what they hoped would be Davis's concurrence that Tilden should be president? Or had Machiavellian interests deep within the Republican Party secretly allowed this in order to deny Davis's selection for the Electoral Commission?

In any event, Davis promptly resigned his position on the commission, and Justice Joseph Bradley, a Republican, took his place. Meanwhile, bribes in the range of $200,000 (the equivalent of roughly $4 million today) were supposedly offered to members of the returning boards in

Louisiana. Congressman Abram Hewitt, Tilden's campaign manager and one of his closest aides, later claimed that a "less scrupulous" Democrat had actually agreed to carry out the bribe on Tilden's behalf, but that the governor himself, upon learning of the prospective deal, had intervened to stop it. With Justice Bradley adhering to party lines, a series of 8–7 votes denying all Democratic claims subsequently gave the disputed nineteen electoral votes to Hayes, who officially won in the Electoral College by a margin of 185–184. Angry Democrats were left to question the new president's legitimacy, and referred to him as "*Rutherfraud* Hayes" and "His Fraudulency."

Despite his "victory" in the national popular vote, Tilden had lost. While there would not be a second civil war or violence surrounding the inauguration, some embittered Democrats refused to accept Hayes as the legitimate chief executive, while others reluctantly accepted the new president as long as all federal troops were removed from the South. Hewitt declined to have any dealings with the new president, adding that Hayes felt that his position "had been secured by frauds which ought to have led him to resign his high place and to appeal to the people in a new election for such decision as the sense of public justice might require." Of course, Hewitt would not have advised a President Tilden to submit to such a special election had the results of the Electoral Commission been different. But the central point was that Hayes was president, and despite any lingering sense of "public justice," the lessons were rather clear: Once in office, assume power as if the vote had been unanimous, and leave any notions of unfulfilled "justice" to the embittered losers.

All that was really certain was that the winners and losers in this election would not be determined by voters casting their conscience in a free election. When the players also act as referees and there are essentially no rules, questions of legitimacy extended well beyond the persona of Rutherford B. Hayes to the republic itself. Perhaps it was best said by Congressman and former Amherst College president

Julius Seelye, who noted: "No facts were ever proved more conclusively than the fraud and corruption charged on the one side and cruelty charged on the other. Which of the two sides went further it would be very hard to say. The corruption of the one side seems as heinous as the cruelty of the other side is horrible." The memory of the election, at least among white Floridians, was one that sounded very similar to Henry Adams's Senator Ratcliffe. The Florida *Times-Union* proclaimed in 1899 that in the pivotal election of 1876, white men "violated the sanctity of the ballot box" in order to save the state "from shame and [their] community from destruction."

Who actually won? Some of the most distinguished American historians have reached varying conclusions, yet the majority opinion seems to suggest that Tilden was robbed. Earlier writers put either Florida or Louisiana in Tilden's column, giving him enough electoral votes for victory. In Louisiana alone, Tilden's early lead ranged between 6,000 and 9,000 votes, enough to seemingly withstand any amount of cooking the numbers and, with it, enough to give Tilden the presidency. In the 1950s, C. Vann Woodward agreed with his contemporaries that Florida should have gone to Tilden and he therefore should have won by an electoral count of 188 to 181. More recently, Eric Foner concludes that "it is probably impossible to say who 'really' won the election of 1876," but he argues that had the election been free and fair, Hayes would have carried the Deep South states on the basis of the black vote for the Republicans.

The real story of 1876 goes beyond these immediate concerns. It was the culmination of over a decade's worth of election corruption where both parties saw each other as deliberately stealing elections. The point had been reached long before where honest accounts of the popular will were the farthest things from anyone's mind. To Southern Democrats, the Republican effort to extend the franchise to former slaves was a fundamental corruption of the electoral system—and they were on solid ground in claiming that many of the

Republican efforts behind black suffrage were grounded in the desire to obtain more Republican votes, rather than as an issue of civil rights. Republicans, on the other hand, saw the wholesale violence and blatant manipulation in such places as Louisiana, Florida, and Mississippi, and understood that black voters were targeted because they would vote Republican. Both parties justified their actions as merely responding to the other's fraud. Was anybody really expecting an *election* in 1876, other than the one to see who could better manipulate the count?

The 1876 election should thus not be seen as an anomaly, very different from so many that had preceded it. It demonstrated how systemic fraud delegitimized the registry lists, the casting and counting of votes, and the governments that would follow. In the end, a system so thoroughly infused with the culture of corruption can result in electoral crises such as 1876. For a government that had looked the other way at the elections in Kansas twenty years before, no one should have been surprised at what occurred in 1876.

THE GREATEST DANGER TO FREE GOVERNMENT

In the immediate aftermath of the election recount, the disgust with election practices was widespread; yet in too many cases, the apparent outrage was defined along partisan lines. Democrats may have fumed over 1876, but their indignation was expressed mostly in the ways the recount favored Republicans rather than a preoccupation with the erosion of democratic principles. From various quarters, certain predictable reforms were suggested as antidotes to a rotting system. From Constitutional amendments ending the Electoral College to specific laws concerning how presidential votes would be counted in the Senate, these were the typical reactions from an electorate reeling from an embarrassing election. One Congressional committee proposed distributing electoral votes pro rata based on the popular vote. Yet these calls for reform, like those that would follow other closely contested presidential elections, quickly dissipated.

Congress called for investigations of the election, headed by Representative Clarkson Potter, a Democrat of New York. The decision whether to even hold these hearings turned, naturally, on partisan concerns. Potter and the Democrats wanted the hearings in order to inquire into the "alleged fraudulent canvass." Republicans, wincing at the word "fraudulent," objected on the lines that Potter's inquiry would implicitly harm the country by opening old political wounds. Treasury Secretary John Sherman, a major figure in the Louisiana recount, dismissed Potter's committee as nothing more than "manufacturing ammunition for the fall campaign." The Republican Congressional Committee went further, saying the Democrats were attempting to institute "anarchy and Mexicanize the government by throwing doubts upon the legitimacy of the title of the President." The *New York Times* editorialized that the committee's work might even threaten the "business confidence" of the country. Potter responded in equally dramatic words:

> When a large portion, if not a large majority, of the people believe that the last Presidential election was secured by organized fraud, surely an inquiry to ascertain the facts ought to be had. . . To throw out the votes of one side and keep in the votes of the other without cause, to invent pretexts for such wrongs, to permit figures to be altered, returns to be forged, frauds to be perfected, and generally every means by which the will of the people may be frustrated and the popular voice stifled, then becomes possible and there may be thus a condition of things absolutely destructive of free government.

Potter won the argument, and his committee struck paydirt, when one of the election canvassers in Florida revealed some of the machinations that had occurred in his state. Since his inauguration, Hayes had given plum jobs to those who had served him well in Florida and Louisiana, including a Cabinet post and several ambassadorships. He also nominated Samuel B. McLin to the Supreme Court of New Mexico. McLin, a former editor of the Tallahassee *Sentinel* and a member of the state canvassing board, had been beaten with a cane on the streets of Tallahassee by a Democratic member of the canvassing board. When the Senate rejected McLin's nomination, he soon grew ill and swore to a deposition in the spring of 1878. In it, McLin claimed that he understood his role as a canvasser was not to be an objective observer dedicated to reporting a free and fair vote, but rather it was his "privilege and duty, in a political sense, to give the benefit of every doubt in favor of the Republican party." In retrospect, McLin admitted that he had feared for the country if a Democrat were to win the White House and that a "combination of influences" had compelled him "most powerfully in blinding his judgment and swaying his actions."

Like others involved in the election crisis, McLin's role was not as objective referee dedicated to ascertaining the will of the voters; his role was as advocate for his party, a role that seems pervasive in such accounts. A thoroughly nonplussed *Nation,* in reporting these "Florida confessions," nonetheless defended the legitimacy of Hayes's presidency: "No honorable man could accept the Presidency if before accepting it he was bound to satisfy himself that in every state in which he had a majority, the vote had been lawfully cast and the count honestly made." Such was the descriptive terminology employed even by a progressive journal to justify election fraud, and added to a culture that saw lawful voting and honest counts secondary to the legitimacy of an executive who was to their liking.

The Potter Committee's findings revealed to a cynical electorate what many had already expected, that Tilden and not Hayes was the "real choice" of those who had been permitted to participate in the

1876 election. "For the first time in the history of the government," the report read, "electoral votes challenged as fraudulent and false were, nevertheless, received and counted, and did, in fact, change the results of the election." The report was particularly clear in describing the election in Louisiana:

> Here, then, was disclosed a new danger. A discretionary power over the result of an election in a State by one of the parties, to be exercised with the aid of external influence and patronage, and with the protection of Federal troops, is, of all conceivable things, the greatest mockery in the way of an election and the greatest danger to free government.

It was also obvious that partisans working to deliver the vote in Louisiana, South Carolina, and Florida to Hayes received considerable benefits for their service well out of proportion to partisans working in other states or areas. No proof was brought to bear that Hayes or his advisers had made promises of jobs in return for the disputed votes; but in the inner world of power politics, no such promises need to be made. With the presidency in the balance and all that went with it, those working to secure those precious disputed electoral votes could expect a grateful president to reward them accordingly. The Potter Committee also uncovered evidence of Democratic attempts to bribe electors, which diminished Democratic cries of a "stolen election." It was not that the Democrats were innocent victims who had a free and fair election stolen from under their noses; rather, they did not have the muscle or the skill of their Republican counterparts when and where it mattered most.

Clearly, what the first eight decades of the nineteenth century demonstrated was that the fledgling nation had become a playground of Election Day bribery, thievery, and violence. Whether the corruption emanated from New York City or Florida, there was a ready explanation that it would be somehow corrected. Yet for former slaves, whose voting rights had been nullified by the Democratic party, the admonitions that better days were fast approaching rang hollow.

CHAPTER FOUR

"The Holiest Institution of the American People"

"We have ruled by force, we have ruled by fraud, but we want to rule by law."

A s the country emerged from Reconstruction and in 1877 inaugurated a new chief executive elected in a tainted contest, worries over the legitimacy of elections themselves came to the fore. By the late 1880s, reformers of virtually every persuasion felt the excesses could be eradicated by the secret ballot or the growing faith in technology. The *New York Times* expressed it best when it described a new Belgian mechanism that its inventor labeled the "Perfected Voting Machine," as "a device for registering voters without possibility of fraud." White Southerners, on the other hand, felt that the crimes of Reconstruction could be solved by another electoral reform called black disfranchisement.

SELF-PRESERVATION

The leading voices of Southern society—ministers, teachers, and editors, to name a few—considered their efforts to eradicate the African-

American vote a patriotic duty. The *Selma Times* noted that it did not "believe it is any harm to rob the vote of an illiterate Negro." Considering that black suffrage had been forced upon the South by "bayonets," the newspaper claimed "The first law of nature, self-preservation, gives us the right to do anything to keep our race and our civilization from being wiped off the face of the earth." Sen. John Tyler Morgan of Alabama bluntly concluded that fraud was a "necessary measure" because of the "outrage" of "Negro domination."

Southern political machines, every bit as effective as the Northern city versions, had elected a coterie of Democrats to state houses and Congress, where they steadily gained seniority and power. To see how members of the "Solid South" came to power, the Tillman brothers of South Carolina provide a good example. In 1880, Rep. George D. Tillman ran for reelection against Robert Smalls. Smalls was everything Tillman detested—he was an African-American and he was a Republican. Tillman beat Smalls by over 5,400 votes, but Smalls contested the election. When a House committee came to South Carolina to investigate, it found that Tillman's district was "controlled by violence and intimidation on the part of organized and armed bodies of white men, directed entirely against the colored voters." The number of votes for Tillman in every county in his district exceeded the total number of eligible white males. As the majority of the committee concluded, "if [Tillman] received all the white vote he must also have received more colored votes than [Smalls], and in most cases more colored votes than white votes." The committee threw out the entire results in Edgefield County, part of Aiken County, and several precincts in other counties in the district. (Edgefield has a certain prominence in South Carolina politics, producing ten governors and Senator Strom Thurmond, a Dixiecrat. It also produced George Tillman's son, James, who was South Carolina's lieutenant governor and best known for murdering one of the state's leading newspaper editors.) The House agreed with the committee's findings and voted to seat Smalls instead. But the House's action hardly impeded Tillman and his followers. In 1882, using the same tactics he used in 1880, Tillman regained the seat over Smalls and never lost again.

While Tillman left his mark in the House, his better-known brother became a power in the Senate. "Pitchfork Ben" Tillman was elected South Carolina's governor in 1890, and from 1895 to 1918 served in the U. S. Senate. Ben Tillman had learned his politics as a Democratic manager of a poll in Edgefield County, where in the election in 1876 he drew pistols on black Republicans. The wholesale fraud and intimidation allowed Democrats to carry Tillman's precinct 211 to 2. The votes from Edgefield County were thrown out, and before long the presidential election crisis of 1876–77 ensued. In time, Ben Tillman became one of the country's most racist demagogues, once comparing African-Americans to monkeys. "To hell with the Constitution," Tillman said, if it dared interfere with lynching.

This 1880 cartoon depicts the reality of voting in the South. Democratic Speaker of the House Samuel J. Randall introduces the "Great Democratic Moral Show," while behind the curtain awaits an armed former Confederate who will make certain the votes are cast correctly. The placard on the left reads: "A Full Vote, A Free Ballot, and a Fair Count." The Democratic creed underneath says: "As for the negroes, let them amuse themselves, if they will, by voting the Radical ticket. We have the count." Credit: *Harper's Weekly*

Tillman's four consecutive elections to the Senate, and his rise to seniority within the upper chamber, were built on tactics that had helped
catapult his brother to victory. South Carolina's Republican voters,
white and black, had no way to prevent his ascendancy. Yet the state's,
and the nation's, African-Americans had to live in a nation governed
by lawmakers like Pitchfork Ben.

Shaving Moustaches

Big Tim Sullivan, a veteran of Tammany Hall, understood some of the
more detailed nuances of repeat voting. The key, according to Sullivan,
was having the hired repeater grow a full beard before the election.
"When you've voted them with their whiskers on, you take them to a
barber and scrape off the chin fringe," said Sullivan. After voting a
second time, Sullivan would have more facial hair removed, vote them
for a third time, and then have the mustache shaved. "If that ain't
enough and the box can stand a few more ballots," Sullivan boasted,
"clean off the mustache and vote them plain face. That makes one of
them good for four votes."

In 1884, in the middle of an era known as Gilded Age, the audacity
of people like Big Tim was not confined to Tammany Hall. In a New
Mexico House race, Tranquilino Luna beat Francisco Manzanares.
When a House committee examined the results that came from
Valencia County, they were horrified to see that Luna had won, 4,259
to 0. The vote from Valencia had never exceeded 2,200. Investigators
also found massive alphabetical voting—where ballots were cast by
voters who happened to correspond exactly to the alphabetical registry
list—and cases where the entire returns from various precincts were
fictitious. The audacity of the theft was simply too much for even
those accustomed to some amounts of election chicanery. The seat was
awarded to Manzanares.

Contesting elections was serious business, and those black Republicans who dared to report an election violation understood that the terror was not limited to registration or Election Day. In Florida, African-Americans who testified in federal court about election fraud in Madison County were lynched by white mobs—a clear message of what constituted normal cultural practices and what was perceived to be violations of those norms by Southern whites. In an 1890 House race in Arkansas, Republican John Clayton lost to incumbent Democrat Clifton Breckinridge by 846 votes. Clayton contested the results and personally visited the small town of Plumerville where a ballot box had been stolen. In the course of obtaining testimony from local participants, Clayton was murdered. Local newspapers dubbed the murder a "political assassination" aimed at crushing any close look into the election methods in rural Arkansas. The House committee concurred, and concluded that the theft of the Plumerville box alone had cost Clayton over four hundred votes, before vacating the seat entirely. At the next election, however, Breckinridge won with no difficulty. The lessons were abundantly clear: Challenging Southern election methods was a cause only for those willing to die in the process.

SOCIAL DARWINISM AND ELECTIONS

The culture of corruption of the Gilded Age did not exist in a vacuum. In many ways, it fed off of larger economic and political forces. The Industrial Revolution that exploded in the United States after the Civil War caused the tectonic plates of the country's political structure to shift, and the ways candidates and parties approached elections adjusted as well. Social Darwinism ruled Wall Street, and this ethos filtered down to the nation's schools, churches, and elections. A society that celebrated ruthlessness in business could find election fraud even more justifiable, especially considering the profound questions of tariffs, government subsidies, and land policy that were all on the line. As David Callahan notes, cheating was at the heart of the new ethos: "These titans of industry cheated each other, they cheated and destroyed their smaller competitors, and they cheated consumers."

The Industrial Revolution had another consequence that brought a certain justification to election fraud. As more and more impoverished Americans felt the political system was rigged against them, their alienation from politics made manipulating elections even easier. If social Darwinists were right, and some people were born to rule, many vote buyers and unscrupulous poll officials reasoned that it was perfectly acceptable to steal votes from the uneducated and uncivilized masses on behalf of the "right" candidate or party.

CHALLENGES

By the late 1800s, the two-party system that dominates to this day was in place. The parties protected themselves against any third-party challenges by outspending their opponents, using demagogy to dismiss them into oblivion, and simply keeping them off the ballot when necessary. When third parties managed to overcome these considerable impediments and work their way onto the ballot, the major parties had other effective weapons at their disposal—namely, intimidation and fraud—and they used these skillfully.

An illustrative example occurred in Mississippi shortly after the end of Reconstruction. When Greenbackers ran for office in 1878 in Lowndes County, Democrats used some well-worn tricks to quash the insurgent vote, such as firing a cannon every half hour on Election Day. Throughout the First District, Democrats printed up false ballots that suggested that the Greenback candidate for Congress had withdrawn from the race. To make certain that Greenbackers could not spread the message that the election was still on, Democrats tore down telegraph wires. After losing the race, Greenbackers contested the results, but no witnesses could be located willing to testify in public about Democratic methods.

In 1880, Mississippi Democratic election officials were as blatant as ever in ensuring that no fusionist efforts (Republicans combined with Greenbackers) would unseat a Democrat. While some poll officials refused to open the boxes in public, in Clay County three young men were tried for stuffing ballot boxes. After a four-day trial, they were convicted and given stiff fines of $250.00 each. Yet the young men were greeted as heroes when they returned home, and a poem was composed in their honor:

> *Our welcome, gallant trio,*
> *Clay County's free-born sons!*
> *Convicted of true manhood*
> *Thrice welcome honored ones.*

Any sense of corrupting democratic forms was overcome by the emotion that the young ballot stuffers, in keeping a party composed of blacks and radical farmers out of power, had displayed "true manhood" and would be held in a place of honor in the hearts of their fellow citizens who, no doubt, were "free-born" as well. This was a vivid example of the power that the culture of corruption held in the deep South. As a token of the esteem with which the young men were held by their peers, a concert was held that raised funds sufficient to pay their fines.

In areas outside the South, election fraud sometimes triggered some violent reactions. Chicago ward heelers of various political persuasions had long bribed voters with alcohol or intimidated them with fists and drawn pistols, stuffed ballots, and used creative counting procedures to ensure that their candidate won. For third-party candidates, the chances of a fair election in the city were dim, especially for socialists and anarchists. In 1880, after losing a race for alderman, the Socialist candidate, Frank Stauber, sued, and a local court uncovered stories of excessive fraud. Stauber eventually regained his seat, yet the jury refused to convict the poll workers, saying that the workers had acted in "good faith." *The Alarm,* a Chicago-based Socialist weekly, was equally indignant, saying that Chicago election practices demonstrated that "Practical politics means the control of the propertied classes." As George Schilling, a prominent member of the Chicago Socialist movement, observed, the Stauber episode "did more, perhaps, than all the other things combined to destroy the faith of the Socialists of Chicago in the efficiency of the ballot." A Chicago German newspaper expressed the feeling among many of its readers: "The holiest institution of the American people, the right to vote, has been desecrated and become a miserable farce and a lie."

The anger among the German population in Chicago was not new. For years, many of them had felt that Irish Democrats practiced a variety of illegal means to steal elections. The Germans who belonged to the Socialist Labor Party in the 1870s had endured Irish police officers beating Germans, and had seen the polls moved the night before an election. By the 1880s, the Socialist Labor Party had essentially given up hope of winning a free and fair election in Chicago. One of them, Albert Parsons, was later executed as one of the principal figures in the Haymarket affair. Parsons claimed that the Stauber affair and the accumulated evidence that stolen elections were so culturally accepted led him to reject the very notion of achieving political change through elections. Parsons wrote that he realized "the hopeless task of political reformation" could never occur through the usual means accorded at the polls, and that he simply lost "faith in the in the potency of the ballot." Others came to Parsons's conclusions as well, and their collective outrage finally vented itself in the streets of Haymarket.

In May 1886, anarchists affiliated with the International Working People's Association went on strike demanding an eight-hour day. Chicago police confronted the strikers and when a bomb was thrown into a group of police, seven eventually died. Four of the anarchists were later executed. One of the causes that directly led to the Haymarket tragedy was election fraud, along with the anarchists' subsequent frustration that authentic civic life had all but vanished in Chicago.

"MEN OF THE STRICTEST INTEGRITY"

The presidential election of 1884 was another blot on the nation's electoral reputation. The Democrats nominated Grover Cleveland of New York to run against the Republican James G. Blaine of Maine. Cleveland won yet another close race, edging Blaine in the Electoral College by a margin of 219–182. All eyes, before and after the election, were on Cleveland's home state of New York, which gave him the presidency by less than a thousand votes. Blaine and his supporters claimed that imported voters and other illegal votes had cost him New York and, consequently, the White House, but he refused to challenge the results. New York election returns were always suspect to the loser, and for some good reasons. Four years earlier, one observer in New York found that over twenty percent of the vote in one precinct was purchased, with prices ranging from $2.00 to $5.00. What struck this observer was the casual nature of the vote-buying, and who participated in it.

> Men of the strictest integrity, who would scorn a dishonorable action in any business or social matter, do not hesitate to take an active part in open bribery, and they do not lose caste in the community by so doing. Their action is considered a necessary part of "practical politics," and to be applauded in proportion to their success—i.e., to the number of votes they secure by outbidding their opponents.

In the South, Republicans understood that the methods used by the Democrats in the "Solid South" had not vanished following the 1876 election. Poll workers in one Mississippi county accepted ballots through a slit in a wall, whereby the official casually counted all Democratic votes and discounted as many Republicans as he desired. In Florida, Democrats used election-day threats to frighten away black voters, and stole several ballot boxes. In Mississippi, Georgia, and South Carolina, Democrats carried 98 counties with black majorities, indicating the extent to which the black right to vote was quickly disappearing. In Loreauville, Louisiana, eighteen blacks died in rioting in the three days leading up to Election Day in 1884. The parish, which had supported Republicans before the riots, quickly became a Democratic enclave. In a sense, with one portion of the country so thoroughly intimidated that Republicans could never expect a fair return, could *any* presidential race in this era be excluded from the list of elections where fraud was rampant and influential?

Republicans noted the utter duplicity of Southern elections and moved to restore some semblance of fairness at the polls. A bill, introduced by Rep. Henry Cabot Lodge of Massachusetts, sought to extend federal supervision of local elections. It provided that federal officials would be empowered to inspect registration lists, certify the count, and, if necessary, overturn the results of an election. The House version gave the president the authority to dispatch troops to ensure the fairness of a particular contest, which is why the bill came to be known as the "Lodge force bill." In proposing the legislation, Lodge noted: "When half the states almost are so controlled that they cheat in the count," he wrote, the GOP "struggle to carry the country is hedged with difficulties." The essential logic behind the Lodge bill was reiterated in the 1888 Republican platform: "The present Administration and the Democratic majority owe their existence to the suppression of the ballot by a criminal nullification of the Constitution and the laws of the United States."

Southern Democrats, of course, saw the bill as a threat to white supremacy. The bill brought back images of Northern aggression as well as passionate defenses of states' rights and Southern liberties. While the bill was aimed only at federal elections, the same races often saw contests for state and local offices, and the idea of close federal supervision of those races naturally rankled many whites in Dixie. One thoroughly disgusted Mississippian noted the obvious hypocrisy of his brethren: "Well, now, 'liberty' is a grand subject. And yet we hear an appeal in the name of 'Liberty' for the right to stuff a ballot box and make fraudulent returns."

The bill generated passionate debate in the House, where it passed without a single Democratic vote. The bill stalled, like so many other reform measures, in the Senate, where a 33-day Democratic filibuster killed it. Southern senators understood what a force bill could mean to their very power base. These men, such as Mississippi's James George, South Carolina's Ben Tillman and North Carolina's Furnifold Simmons, who held their power because of a electoral system rigged to give them an advantage at the expense of blacks and the Republican party, were not about to slit their own political throats. The Lodge bill's death, coupled with further Congressional assaults on the right to vote in the 1890s, ended for seven decades any real federal move to assure that Southern elections would be free and fair.

Although the Fifteenth Amendment supposedly protected black voting rights, a series of Supreme Court decisions effectively nullified the amendment. In 1876, in *U.S. v. Reese,* the Court came to the remarkable conclusion that the Amendment did not bestow on blacks the right to vote, it only prohibited the exclusion of someone from voting on account of their race. Using *Reese* as a pretext, other lesser courts essentially invalidated the amendment, making disfranchisement Constitutional. Yet in 1884, in a case that received relatively little attention, the Court unanimously affirmed the federal government's right to punish someone for obstructing another's right to vote. In *ex parte*

Yarbrough, the Court upheld the conviction of members of the Ku Klux Klan who had forcefully obstructed a black man from voting. Justice Samuel F. Miller, writing for the Court, dismissed arguments that the federal government had no power to protect elections from fraud:

> That a government whose essential character is republican, whose executive head and legislative body are both elective, whose numerous and powerful branch of the legislature is elected by the people directly, has no power by appropriate laws to secure this election from the influence of violence, of corruption, and of fraud, is a proposition so startling as to arrest attention and demand the gravest consideration.

The Court recognized that "the temptation to control these elections by violence and by corruption is a constant source of danger." Yet in 1903, in a similar case involving a Congressional race in western Kentucky, the Court essentially reversed itself from the *Yarbrough* decision, arguing that "Congress has no power to punish bribery at all elections." For those hoping the Supreme Court would be an ally in protecting minority voting rights from bribery, violence, or fraud, they would be sorely disappointed.

APPROACHING THE GATES OF THE PENITENTIARY

The 1888 election proved a watershed in the federal approach to election methods. In fact, the 1888 presidential contest was one of the most corrupt in American history, a comment on how little reform had come since the tainted election of 1876. President Cleveland was pitted against the Republican Benjamin Harrison in a contest in which the returns were odd on several fronts. Harrison won an Electoral College majority, but lost the popular count by over 60,000 votes.

Had Cleveland been robbed? Again, a perspective is necessary in examining these results. In ways that had not changed since 1876, any Democratic successes in the South were grounded in fraud. Had African-Americans been allowed to vote, Harrison would have won several of those states, and accumulated a much broader majority in the Electoral College and a considerable majority in the popular vote as well. In West Virginia, Cleveland won by a mere 500 votes out of more than 159,000 cast, although 12,000 more voted than were eligible to do so. In New York, Democrats were put in the ironic position of charging the Republicans with illegally importing "colonizers." The stench from the New York election alone led GOP chairman Matt Quay to the famous remark that Harrison never knew "how close a number of men were compelled to approach the gates of the penitentiary to make him President."

Yet the most explosive charges of the election originated in Harrison's home state of Indiana. Out of over a half million votes, Harrison won by just 2,376. By the late 1880s, Indiana had acquired a notorious reputation in the annals of electoral corruption, being primarily a regional center for colonizers to neighboring states. In fact, it was known widely as "Venal Indiana." The election in Indiana would have attracted plenty of attention as it was, yet a letter from a key GOP leader revealed not only the techniques that would be employed in winning Indiana, but the culture that now pervaded American elections in general. The letter was written by William W. Dudley, the national treasurer of the Republican national committee, who instructed GOP workers in Indiana to:

> Divide the floaters into blocks of five and put a trusted man with necessary funds in charge of these five and make him responsible that none get away and that all vote our ticket.

Commentators have long since debated whether these instructions were literally true. One historian dismissed the whole affair and declared that the 1888 election in Indiana was "the cleanest in years." Yet a contemporary, R. H. Dabney, was convinced that the "floater" vote had a profound impact. He found that in Monroe, Indiana, although the town had a voting population of 700, he estimated that floaters constituted 85 percent of these votes. He watched as Republicans brought these voters into town on election eve and had sentries guard them through the night. Dabney also knew that charges that only blacks did such things were absurd: "The Hoosier floater is but too frequently neither Negro nor foreigner, but your genuine free-born American sovereign."

In the aftermath of the the Lodge bill's defeat, reformers sought answers to the overwhelming problem of election fraud. Calls were loud for tighter restrictions on registration systems, yet even this was a double-edged sword. Stricter registration laws that required a set term for residency usually worked against the working class, who moved frequently. Democrats complained that landlords might evict residents close to an election in order to disfranchise them. Republicans countered that without some verification of the registry lists, fraud would continue to be rampant. Meanwhile, third-party leaders understood that registry laws were "practically of no avail. The count of the vote may be guarded," the *National Economist* editorialized, "but false registration will effect the ends of rascality." Throughout, everyone knew that partisan politics played into the equation. When it came to fraud, the parties each pursued tactics that would necessarily hurt their opponents' base while helping their own.

VOTING IN SECRET

Following the 1888 election and the "blocks of five" revelations, the sheer speed with which the nation adopted a new voting method was breathtaking. The *Nation* commented just days after the 1888 election that drastic changes in the way men voted needed to occur in order to restore confidence in the structure of American democracy. "If the act of voting were performed in secret," the paper predicted, "no bribed voter could or would be trusted to carry out his bargain when left to himself." The obvious answer seemed the "Australian" ballot—a uniform ballot printed by the state to be cast in private. The new ballot would list the party nominees and voters would mark their preference in secrecy and submit the ballots into a box without any distinguishing marks that might indicate their vote. The drive to secure what would become the standard practice of all American elections began in Louisville, Kentucky (the process of how the secret ballot came to Louisville is covered in Chapter Five). The first state to adopt the new ballot was Massachusetts in 1888, and soon thereafter even Grover Cleveland supported its passage nationwide.

State legislators jumped over each other to enact the secret ballot, but not out of a righteous effort to rid the system of fraud. The parties understood that the new system would save them the expenses of printing ballots, would hamper split tickets, and would make third-party challenges even more difficult. As the historian Peter H. Argersinger writes, with the advent of the Australian ballot, "Those who controlled the state thus gained the power to structure the system in their own behalf." While the rules of the game may have changed somewhat, the purpose of the game certainly had not. If the advent of the new ballot had been enough to drastically alter the playing field, the parties would have approached the secret ballot with considerable caution. Yet by the time the 1892 election came, three quarters of the states in the Union had adopted it, and by the early 1900s only three states were left that did not have some provisions of the Australian system. Rarely has such an overhaul in such sweeping terms occurred, and the notion now that men could freely vote their conscience and would, therefore, return the nation to its more democratic foundations was widespread. When voter turnout began to

A satirical sketch of the new Australian ballot. A ward heeler brings an illiterate voter to the professor, asking him to teach the student three words: "Dem, Rep, and Prohib." The heeler then notes "It's meself as kin attend to the rest of the taichin." Credit: *Harper's Weekly*

decrease, observers casually dismissed the declining numbers as little more than decreased fraud at the polls.

But the evidence is abundantly clear—the Australian ballot did not decrease the extent of fraud. It only changed the way the fraud occurred. Likewise, the secret ballot served as an effective tool to disfranchise poor whites, illiterate immigrants, and Southern blacks, and made it more difficult for third parties to gain a foothold within the electorate. Southern whites were especially receptive to the new voting method, and did not bother to hide their reasons for supporting it. The Democratic *Memphis Daily Avalanche* editorialized that "It is certain that many years will elapse before the bulk of the Negroes will reawaken to an interest in elections, if relegated to their proper sphere, the corn and cotton fields, by some election law which will adopt the principle of the Australian ballot." After the bill was first drafted in Tennessee, the Democratic party leadership added, as an afterthought, that the bill would also "stop the cry of fraud," but not the fraud itself.

The first laws establishing the new voting methods were, of course, passed by state legislatures comprising Democrats and Republicans who were not interested in an objective exercise to make balloting fairer and free from intimidation. Where possible, they wanted laws that would ensure their parties' success at the polls. In Vermont, for example, Republicans were successful in keeping the secret ballot confined to the larger, urban areas, where they assumed the Democrats controlled the immigrant populations that might have difficulty reading a ballot. In other areas, Democrats won the ability to "assist" voters in the polls, which opened a wave of methods that could bypass the whole point behind the secret ballot. As with so many other "reforms" passed under the ostensible heading of anti-fraud measures, the secret ballot was mired in a partisan effort to secure advantage over the opponent at the polls.

If the secret ballot were not enough, another reform aimed at curtailing fraud was first used in an 1892 election in Lockport, New York. Rather than using paper ballots, the Myers Automatic Booth lever voting machine utilized a mechanical device to record votes without any paper. The machine's inventor, Jacob H. Myers, said the device would "protect mechanically the voter from rascaldom, and make the process of casting a ballot perfectly plain, simple, and secret." This was no simple invention. The Meyers machine utilized hundreds of moving parts that recorded a vote once a lever was pulled beside a candidate's name. The machine returned the lever to the starting position after the vote was cast, and the machine was designed to block a voter from voting more than once. Befitting the Industrial Revolution, the voting machine seemed to herald a new day in which technology would finally bring an end to the widespread fraud that characterized so many American elections.

"THE PEOPLE ARE DEMORALIZED"

There is no better example of how the secret ballot had no impact on curtailing vote fraud than what happened to the People's party, or Populists, in the 1890s. The 1892 party platform underscored the prevailing notions about voting in America: "Corruption dominates the ballot box . . . the People are demoralized." These agrarian activists commented on the recent movement to secure passage of the Australian ballot: "Many of the States have been compelled to isolate the voters at the polling places in order to prevent universal intimidation or bribery." Yet the passage of the Australian ballot did not bode well for third-party challengers. Since the state was responsible for printing official ballots, and the rules for gaining a place on that ballot were written by members of the major parties, third parties were in trouble from the start. Coupled with new laws that allowed voters to vote a "straight" party ticket by checking a box at the top of the page, the new ballots discouraged voters from "split" votes for third parties.

In the South, the People's party ran straight into the fortress that protected white supremacy—the Democratic party. The political culture that permeated Democratic circles was on guard for any challenges, and knew what to do once they were spotted. A Louisiana newspaper put it best: "It is the religious duty of Democrats to rob Populists and Republicans of their votes whenever and wherever the opportunity presents itself and any failure to do so will be a violation of true Louisiana Democratic teaching." The "teaching," or in other words, the received culture of Deep South politics in the 1890s, had little use for true democratic forms of any kind.

In 1894, Populists throughout the South were treated to a wide assortment of election tactics. In Alabama, the race for governor pitted Populist Reuben Kolb against Democrat William Oates. Oates had defended the practice of stuffing ballot boxes to keep black Republican voters from swaying state politics, and to those Democrats who felt a pang of conscience, Oates reassured them that "The recording angel will shed no tear in blotting these acts from the record of the final account." Oates received 57 percent of the vote, although the number of black voters threatened before the election is unknown. Kolb protested and simply declared that he considered himself the newly elected governor. "We here in Alabama white and colored," proclaimed a Kolb supporter, "feel that we are but slaves to a despotism of fraud and political serfdom."

After the Alabama legislature refused to intervene, a bizarre and possibly frightening scene developed on Inauguration Day, as both Kolb and Oates arrived in Montgomery expecting to be sworn in as the new governor. A local judge sympathetic to Kolb administered him the oath, and Kolb then marched down Dexter Avenue to the capitol with his supporters. They were met by armed troops, and when he was denied permission to speak on the capitol grounds, Kolb went to a nearby street to declare that he was the legitimate governor of Alabama. One Kolb supporter then proudly proclaimed that if being an opponent to "ballot box thieves" made one an anarchist, then he was an anarchist. Yet the displays of protest had no bearing on the state house, where Gov. Oates was in power. The group then dispersed, with a bitter Kolb vowing to one day win "redress" for the wrongs done to him through election fraud.

In 1896, in Robertson County, Texas, several of the candidates on a Republican–Populist ticket were African-Americans. On Election Day, Democrats stole ballot boxes and paraded around predominantly black precincts with their pistols prominently displayed. Unsure that these tactics suppressed the black vote sufficiently, party leaders sent word to Democratic County Judge O. D. Cannon to hold his precinct. Cannon did, literally: he went down to the polls and stayed there with his pistol. Cannon proudly boasted of having threatened at least a thousand African-American voters away from the polls. As a result, he added, "Not a Negro voted," that day, or afterward. When the returns were opened, an African-American Populist seemed to have won a seat in the Texas legislature. Election officials quickly counted him out. The outraged candidate threatened to contest the election, which was all Judge Cannon needed to hear before he reached for his gun and shot the man in the arm. Cannon later admitted that "I only shot when I thought I had to. I know God pulled me through." When one African-American Populist candidate for county commissioner was actually declared the winner of his race, he declined the office because of the organized violence he had witnessed. With the swearing in of his Democratic opponent, the historian Gregg Cantrell writes, "White supremacy returned to Robertson County."

"WE HAVE TAKEN A CITY. TO GOD BE THE PRAISE"

By the late 1890s, the People's party was finished as a legitimate threat to the Southern Democratic party. Yet the threat had been real, and needed to be addressed structurally. The leading state in the movement to accomplish legally what fraud had done for so many years was Mississippi. In fact, the methods chosen by Mississippi's constitutional framers were adopted by so many of the other Southern states that it acquired a name: the Mississippi plan. Making the poll tax, property qualifications, and literacy tests the bedrock of state law, Mississippi accomplished in 1890 what "redeemers" had been hoping for since the passage of the Fifteenth Amendment: a "legal" way to disfranchise African-Americans. The need for these measures rested in the accumulated outrage at the election fraud that had become so endemic to Southern elections. "Fourteen years of fraud excited nausea," the president of the Mississippi convention proclaimed. The time had come for Democrats to use their control of state governments to make white supremacy permanent.

In the Alabama constitutional convention, in a strange logical twist,

Democrats noted that legalizing black disfranchisement was necessary so whites would not have to sully their hands in election fraud. On one hand, the convention president, John Knox, said election fraud was a necessary tool in the white supremacist battle, one that was deeply ingrained in the very fabric of the nation. Stealing votes, according to Knox, was simply part of the Jeffersonian notion of the "right to revolution." Knox explained that stuffing ballot boxes was "a revolutionary measure, justified upon that ground." After submitting the new constitution to the voters, defenders of the document claimed that by ratifying it, whites would no longer have to resort to such means; cleaner elections would prevail. A newspaper in Clanton claimed that "the old constitution makes force or fraud in many localities essential to the proposition of white supremacy." If the new constitution were adopted, then it was clear that it would allow "a sure path to honest elections in the future."

In Louisiana, a Democratic newspaper noted that "It is true that we win these elections, but at a heavy cost, and by the use of methods repugnant to our idea of political honesty." Louisiana had become, in the estimation of the New Orleans *Times-Democrat*, "the head center of ballot box stuffing." After Mississippi's lead in 1890, other states undertook similar developments either during the height of the Populist revolt or afterward, and their intent was to do far more than disfranchise Republican-leaning blacks.

Consequently, what violence and fraud had accomplished before became codified in a slew of new Southern state constitutions in the 1890s. Poor whites would be severely affected by poll taxes and literacy tests; and although some states instituted "grandfather clauses" ostensibly to protect these voters, and parties often paid the poll taxes of voters they felt would support them, thousands of whites had lost the right to vote by the turn of the century. "Conservatives of neighboring states," wrote C. Vann Woodward, "grappling with powerful Populist opposition, eyed the results of the Mississippi plan enviously." By

1901, Louisiana, South Carolina, North Carolina, and Alabama had adopted such codes into their own constitutions, and the overall impact was startling. In Louisiana alone, the figures for those registered to vote—immediately before and after the disenfranchising elements were adopted into the new constitution—show how successful the framers were in disposing of threats to the Democratic party:

	WHITES	BLACKS	TOTAL
REGISTERED, 1897	164,088	130,344	294,432
REGISTERED, 1900	125,437	5,320	130,757

Those eligible to vote had been cut by more than half. Ninety-six percent of the state's black voters were legally disfranchised, while over twenty-three percent of white voters, most of whom were the poor whites who had been attracted to the People's party, lost the franchise as well.

The *Nation* understood that election fraud was originally "started by whites that wanted to defraud blacks of their votes. As was inevitable, it has been extended in its range until one faction of whites cheats another." No one was more blunt than Alabama's former governor Oates, who told his state's constitutional convention, "I told them to go to it boys, count them out," a direct admission of how the black vote was handled. But Oates lamented an obvious byproduct of the fraud that gripped the region: "White men have gotten to cheating each other until we don't have any honest elections." Populism certainly had something to do with this development, but critics such as the *Nation* did not understand that fraud had been a part of the American republic from the very beginning, and its more recent manifestations, as bad as they were, were symptomatic of the culture deeply embedded in American politics.

No state provides a better example of white reaction to African-American and white populist electoral strength than North Carolina.

In 1894, a Fusionist party of Populists and Republicans won the governorship, a majority in the General Assembly, and a host of local offices throughout the state. These triumphs were too much for white supremacists to bear. The real problem reactionaries faced in the Tarheel State, according to Glenda E. Gilmore, "was the practice of democracy," where Fusionists restored the "home rule" to local offices, rather than allowing state officials to appoint them. African-Americans and Populists consequently won posts previously held by Democrats.

North Carolina Democrats corrected the situation in 1898. Using intimidation and blatant election fraud, the Democrats recaptured five of the state's nine Congressional seats in that year's election. More than anything else, what occurred in Wilmington provided a clear lesson to all who dared challenge white supremacy. Days before the election, former congressman and Confederate veteran Alfred Moore Waddell told a mass meeting of whites in Wilmington, "Go to the polls tomorrow, and if you find the negro out voting, tell him to leave the polls, and if he refuses, kill him." The threat of racial violence and unchecked fraud changed a Republican majority in Wilmington of 5,000 in 1896 to a Democratic majority of 6,000 just twenty-four months later. Yet controlling the polls in Wilmington was not enough. After the election, whites essentially declared war on the city's African-Americans.

Led by Waddell, a mob of four hundred men attacked a black newspaper office, then went on a killing spree in the black districts. The extent of the slaughter is unknown, but the most conservative figure lists seven dead, while other sources estimate as many as three hundred. After several days, Waddell assumed the mayor's office, and a local minister proclaimed "We have taken a city. To God be the praise." Once the sanctioned riot in Wilmington was over, writes Joel Williamson, "there was no need for it to happen elsewhere." After Wilmington, white Democrats elected Charles Aycock governor in 1900 and amended the constitution to disfranchise African-Americans. In his inaugural speech in

1901, Aycock stated that until the moment blacks received the franchise, "the fairness of our elections was never questioned." With black suffrage, according to the new governor, elections were "a farce and a fraud." He later altered his appraisals of the Democrats' methods to achieve white supremacy: "We have ruled by force, we have ruled by fraud, but we want to rule by law."

THE AGENTS OF DEMOCRACY

The "coup d'etat" in North Carolina was rivaled by one in Kentucky. In 1899, the Democrat William Goebel ran for governor against the Republican William S. Taylor and a third-party candidate who had bolted from the Democrats, former governor John Y. Brown. Goebel was a ruthless man who had even been indicted for murder after allegedly killing a political opponent in 1895. After his acquittal, Goebel used his seat in the state senate to secure a new election bill he introduced in 1898 that would forever be known as the Goebel Election Law. It gave broad powers to a three-member Board of Elections, which would be the final arbiter in certifying all elections and in settling all election disputes.

Opponents of the bill called it a "force" bill, recognizing the stigma associated with that term. The *Courier-Journal*'s editor, Henry Watterson, saw the bill as a naked grab for power by Goebel. When the law was enacted, the legislature appointed two Democrats and one Republican to the new board, ensuring that the Democrats would ostensibly control future elections, such as the governor's race in 1899. Brown warned that he had heard too many Democrats say "We care not what be the vote; we will do the counting." There were dire predictions of bloodshed on Election Day, and Governor William Bradley called out the state militia to keep down any violence in Louisville. To the Cincinnati *Enquirer*, "the contest here will scarcely deserve to be classified as a battle of ballots." Rather, the newspaper argued, that it would be a struggle "between the forces of organized fraud, seeking to defeat the will of the voters," and the "agents of Democracy," bound to prevent the fraud.

Election Day itself went rather peacefully, a poor foreshadowing of events to come. The election results were not definitive. Although Taylor was in front by approximately 2,000 votes out of over 400,000 cast, Goebel's supporters contended that Taylor's lead was based on illegal and fraudulent votes. Goebel also contended that in four other counties, tissue paper ballots (where false ballots made of tissue were inserted inside legal ballots) gave Taylor 3,251 more votes than Goebel. To settle the contested returns, of course, was the same board Goebel had helped create the previous year.

Both sides insisted the other was trying to steal the election, and local papers dueled over the returns. The *Courier-Journal* reported a Goebel majority, but the *Evening Post* claimed that his rival used "fake returns" to change Taylor's victory of 3,500 to 4,000 votes to a defeat of several thousand. Governor Bradley, fearing a possible "revolution," asked for federal troops from President McKinley, who declined the request.

In early December 1899, the election board began its proceedings, but they did so under great tension. Hundreds of mountain Republicans arrived in Frankfort by train, brandishing weapons and warning of violence if Goebel were declared governor. Democrats countered that this was armed intimidation to a lawfully comprised proceeding. When the board issued its ruling, it was another stunning development. By a 2–1 margin, the board decided in favor of Taylor, claiming that the law did not allow them authority to go behind a county return. Three days after the board's decision, Taylor was inaugurated as governor of the Commonwealth of Kentucky.

For Democrats who held a considerable majority in the state legislature, there was one last move: Goebel could contest the results to the legislature. Amid charges of bribes being offered for legislators' votes, Goebel claimed that fraud in forty counties had deprived him of his office. By the end of January 1900, as the contest hearings were under way, the GOP had brought in over a thousand armed mountaineers to the capital city. Democrats, meanwhile, vowed to fight force with force.

On the morning of January 30, as Goebel was walking to the hearings, a shot rang out. Goebel was hit with a single bullet to the chest. Witnesses claimed the shot had come from a window in a building adjacent to the capitol, a window that was located in the office of Secretary of State Caleb Powers, a Republican and an outspoken Goebel critic. Goebel was taken to a local hotel, and as the news spread, angry Democrats were readying for more gunfights and vowing revenge. Goebel's condition was grave, and as he fought for his life, the contest committee of the legislature met once again. On a partisan vote, the committee recommended that Goebel be declared governor. An astonished Taylor, realizing how dangerous the situation was becoming, announced that the General Assembly should meet in London, a Republican stronghold approximately a hundred miles to the south. Taylor remained in Frankfort, guarded by five hundred militia. As the legislators met the next day, Republicans fled to London, while Democrats, challenging Taylor's right to remove the capital, remained defiantly in Frankfort. That afternoon, the Democrats called a quorum, and declared Goebel governor. The Chief Justice of the Court of Appeals quickly made his way to Goebel's hotel room and swore in the dying man as governor. For a time, the state had two governors, and two legislatures meeting in separate cities.

It was a dangerous condition indeed. Both sides claimed rightful and lawful ownership to the governor's chair; both sides claimed the other had acted unlawfully and vowed to fight for their man to the very end; both had their contingent of armed men ready for war in the quiet streets of Frankfort. It was yet another result of an electoral system that was essentially broken, one where people did not trust the results of an election. "Governor" Goebel's condition worsened, and on February 3, 1900, only three days after being sworn in, Goebel died, the only governor in United States history to die while in office as a result of an assassination (the peculiar circumstances of the events caused the tortured wording of the claim). Democratic Lieutenant Governor J. C. W. Beckham was sworn in as governor of Kentucky, a situation no voter would have imagined three months earlier.

Taylor feared for his life if he did not resign and again asked President McKinley for help. But the president refused to send federal troops to a situation that *Harper's Weekly* called the "the greatest political crisis in any state" since Reconstruction. The *Outlook* described to its readers the state of "anarchy" that existed in Kentucky. Who would decide the election? Would the result be respected? Taylor agreed that the courts should have the final say and decided to submit the ultimate question to a body that was seemingly above politics. The state's highest court, the Court of Appeals, sided with the Democrats in April, and Taylor's hold on the governorship rested on an appeal to the U.S. Supreme Court. Meanwhile, some Republican officials had taken their case to the U.S. Court of Appeals in Cincinnati, asking for an injunction against the State Contest Board in some other election issues. Judge (and future president) William Howard Taft threw out the case, claiming there was no ground for federal interference with a state election, and that the state courts would be the final arbiter. The Republican case seemed weak, at best, as it headed for the Supreme Court.

When the nation's highest court handed down its decision, on May 21, 1900, it agreed with Judge Taft's assessment that the states, not federal courts, should decide the election, thereby upholding the Kentucky court's decision. Taylor, with no options left and under indictment as an accessory, fled the governor's mansion and the state, and lived the remainder of his life (twenty-eight years) in Indianapolis. The partisan bitterness over the election remained for generations, as

Republicans felt that the properly elected governor had been cheated out of office, while Democrats felt that the GOP had resorted to cold-blooded murder.

Sadly, both sides were right. As the twentieth century dawned, partisans had ample reason to believe they would be cheated at the next election unless they were willing to resort to disfranchisement or stuffing ballot boxes. If that did not work, of course, more extreme measures were always available. This was a dangerous situation that was not confined to Wilmington, North Carolina, or Frankfort, Kentucky. The culture of corruption thrived everywhere. The utter contempt the parties displayed for each other reinforced the latent disdain they each had developed for the democratic process.

PART TWO

The Struggle to Reclaim Democracy

CHAPTER FIVE

How to Steal an Election

"God damn the law, we're Democrats."

I n 1907, the Kentucky Court of Appeals, an institution not known for its radicalism, threw out the entire results of a Louisville municipal election from two years earlier. In the ruling, the court concluded,

> No people can be said to govern themselves whose elections are controlled by force, fear, or fraud. And the people who do not govern themselves are slaves.

The events that led the court to take such action, and to use such language, were indicative of the election practices in so many other American cities. Yet scholars examining Gilded Age elections would never use the term slavery to depict the civic life of early twentieth-century America. Instead, there exists a mind-numbing array of statistical analyses that seek to provide the comforting scientific appraisal that election fraud was a marginal influence throughout the land. Yet for the people of Louisville, such statistical abstractions provided little comfort and fail to adequately describe the on-the-ground reality of what they faced when they went to the polls.

Louisville is not a location that one normally thinks of as a cesspool of corruption. Quite the contrary, as the city that pioneered the Australian ballot, it is usually seen as progressive and mostly immune from the problems that plagued so many other areas. Louisville's location—a border city in a border state—places it at a certain crossroads of the country. Neither too northern nor too southern, neither too large a metropolis nor too small a budding town or hamlet, it is an ideal location to examine how one election was stolen.

"THE POLITICAL FILTH OF LOUISVILLE"

After Reconstruction, Louisville was Kentucky's largest city and the eighteenth largest in the nation. Between 1880 and 1900, the city's population increased from 123,758 to 204,731. The city relied heavily on Ohio River commerce for its economic base and had a cosmopolitan mixture that included Democratic Irish Catholics and Republican African-Americans. Politically, the Democratic party effectively controlled the city as the memories of the Civil War persisted, and the winner of the city's Democratic primaries was effectively the winner of the general election in November.

Throughout the 1880s, Louisville had experienced a series of fraudulent city elections. To correct the problem of repeaters, a Louisville representative, Albert Stoll, introduced a bill in the Kentucky legislature calling for mandatory registration in Louisville. Stoll told the assembly that "repeating and fraudulent voting are so common" in Louisville that "a law for the registration of voters would remove the greatest part of the evil." His bill became law in 1884, but it had no effect on reforming the process. Three years later, in a blatantly corrupt mayoral race, a plot was uncovered whereby the names of the candidates on the poll books were purposely situated so close together that corrupt clerks could place a mark in the wrong column without being easily detected. One insider understood that "you must be sure and get the clerks 'fixed,' that's half the battle." A self-appointed committee called the Commonwealth Club overseeing the 1887 municipal election stated it was "thoroughly disgusted" with the methods used to manipulate and steal votes. Henry Watterson, publisher of the local newspaper the *Courier-Journal,* concluded that the election "was without parallel in the history of Louisville for fraud and corruption."

One of the members of the 1887 committee was Arthur Wallace, a Louisville state representative. After reading an article on the new secret ballot system used in Australia, Wallace approached some area judges to see whether a law mandating such a system could pass constitutional muster in Kentucky. Wallace's bill could not be applied to the entire state without amending the state constitution, so it affected Louisville's municipal contests only. When the "Wallace Election Bill" quietly became law in February 1888, Louisville became the first municipality in the nation to adopt the new voting method. At its inaugural municipal election in December 1888, the *Courier-Journal* proclaimed proudly "the election was a quiet one, and the Wallace law stood its first test very fairly." A Louisvillian writing in the *Nation* claimed that the election "was the first municipal election I have ever known which was not bought outright." Yet not everyone was so convinced. The *Courier-Journal* noted that vote-selling was still practiced, even with the new ballot. "As to vote buying, there seems to be no solution," the paper claimed. "The best of men weep over it and wipe their eyes and write a subscription to the election fund."

By the 1890s, John Whallen, a young burlesque theater owner, became the acknowledged king of Louisville's Democratic party. Known as "Napoleon" by some of his cronies, a teenage Whallen had served as courier to Confederate General John Hunt Morgan and had moved to Louisville after the war to co-manage the Metropolitan Theater. In 1880, Whallen and his brother Jim opened the Buckingham Theater, which soon became widely known for its bawdy performances. Described glowingly by one supporter as one who "has gathered about him a large and formidable following," that "he controls with extraordinary skill and ability," Whallen understood that the real source of political power rested in controlling elections. In a discreet understatement, the supporter also noted Whallen's forces are "powerful at the polls," and that Whallen "understands right well how to station them to the best advantage." The Buckingham was also a well-known center of community support in times of economic crises or natural disasters, which, of course, was one of the foundations of Whallen's popular appeal. Following one especially hard winter storm, Whallen opened a commissary next to his theater where a reported $25,000 in groceries and coal were distributed gratis to needy Louisvillians. Whallen once boasted that his burlesque theater was the real center of the city's political apparatus, a place that he once described candidly as "the political sewer through which the political filth of Louisville runs."

In his memoirs, Arthur Krock, a Louisville native, recalled that in most political meetings held by Whallen, "it was customary that the Louisville police be represented," because, according to Krock, the police "had to know the nominating and electing game plan . . . and put it into operation. This often required documentary knowledge of the peccadilloes and worse of the aspiring politicians, especially those who were Republicans." This knowledge, Krock understood, "was more powerful than their night[sticks]."

"WE WERE CHEATED ON EVERY SIDE"

Whallen ensured his control over the city's election machinery in ways that made him unique among American political bosses. In 1892, for

example, when Whallen was confident that his handpicked candidate
for city chancellor would lose in a party primary, he urged the party to
adopt a rather unorthodox method of voting. These primaries, which
were exempt from many election laws and the secret ballot, were especially ripe for fraud. Whallen's new method involved a house-to-house
canvass, which Whallen proudly claimed was "superior to all other
forms of primary elections." His plan required all voters to be at home
on one of two nights for a three-hour period. To Whallen, this method
would "remove the crowding of voters into small spaces where liquor,
money, and bullying can get in their work." In effect, the maneuver disfranchised nearly five thousand of the city's 13,108 eligible Democratic
voters due to residence changes or to the fact that they simply could not
be located or were not at home at the appointed times. Even more,
door-to-door canvassing had the intended effect of properly ensuring
that a bought vote was appropriately cast, and the threat of losing a city
job or services certainly permeated the exchange. A critical newspaper
was appalled by Whallen's hubris, charging that he had "gone a step farther than he ever went before." If party members wished to participate
in "a conspiracy as far reaching as it is shameless, they deserve to be
walked upon and spat upon by such men as Whallen."

After temporarily losing control of city government in the mid
1890s, Whallen reappeared, helping his hand-picked candidate win
the mayor's race, due in large part to a new method employed by followers of Whallen: police intimidation of African-American voters.
When a prominent African-American attorney attempted to vote, he
was confronted by a police officer who told him, "I have worn out four
billies and I will wear this one out on you." Less violent means, such as
clerks slowly checking registration lists, meant those wishing to vote in
the heavily African-American Ninth and Tenth wards often waited
hours to cast a ballot. Of course, many found that before they had
reached the front of the line, the polls had closed. In one precinct, the
polls were not opened until after noon. (The *Courier-Journal*, never one
to question allegations of Democratic wrongdoing, blamed a drunk

Republican election officer.) The losing mayoral candidate concluded he had lost nearly 4,500 votes in these wards alone and concluded "we were cheated on every side." Without the strong arm of the police, Whallen's machine could not have controlled Louisville's elections.

Whallen's cronies used other methods to fight the Republican turnout among African-Americans. By 1900, the 28,651 African-Americans living in Louisville comprised nearly fourteen percent of the city's population. Although Democrats had not legally disfranchised African-Americans in Kentucky as they had throughout the Deep South, electoral intimidation and fraud remained potent tools in the hands of people such as Whallen. The historian George C. Wright wrote that Whallen hired black "shadies" to form Negro Democratic Clubs, which were little more than instruments of organized intimidation of African-American voters, and concluded that "Negro thugs, as much as anything else, kept many blacks from viewing the Democrats as a respectable party." When that tactic failed, Whallen resorted to the well-tested strategy of appealing to white supremacy and the fears of what Republican victories might bring to Louisville's racial climate.

Whallen's forces in the Democratic primary of 1899 employed a daring technique to keep the opposition vote down. Pat Grimes, a saloon owner and Whallen crony, installed a "portable voting place" in a train car near the convergence of the 11th and 12th wards. The Whallen forces feared a heavy turnout from this area for an anti-Whallen candidate. So, as Grimes considered it, a particularly skillful way to diminish these votes would be to simply move the car away when long lines of voters developed.

Yet when it became clear that his candidates were trailing, Whallen resorted to an even more audacious tactic on the afternoon of the election. Acting under the auspices of the Democratic party's central committee, Whallen simply annulled the primary election results altogether. Following this election, one local blacksmith claimed that a member of the self-described "Honest Election League" had given him cash to buy votes. Within the office of the League, according to the blacksmith, were tables full of stacks of money. The man who was doling out the funds was Arthur Wallace, the author of Louisville's Australian ballot bill eleven years earlier.

By the early 1900s, then, John Whallen directed the Democratic machine in Louisville. But he was not without his opponents among the city's Republican stalwarts, as well as a number of Democrats who resented Whallen using the city's political apparatus to increase his personal wealth and political power. The city's GOP also grew increasingly frustrated with Democratic electoral practices. An election in 1903 contained more than its usual share of moved precincts and falsely registered voters, excluded duly chosen election officers replaced by Whallen cronies, and stuffed ballot boxes. Eighteen strong Republican precincts were also moved on Election Day. Not surprisingly, these precincts returned Democratic majorities such as 243 to 5. In the Sixth Ward, a Democratic challenger questioned the credentials of nearly twenty-five African-American men waiting in line. He was soon approached by one police officer who told him "You damn fool, those niggers you're throwing out isn't Republicans; they're our own repeaters!" Although some members of the Democratic party had hoped to "put Whallen out of business" with this election, their efforts failed. A thoroughly disgusted *Evening Post* concluded that the "audacity of the steal is its most astonishing feature."

With the 1903 election fresh in their minds, disenchanted Democrats joined with angry Republicans to form a Fusionist party which, with its combined strength, hoped to defeat the Democratic mayoral candidate, Paul Barth, in the upcoming 1905 election. The Fusionists' objective was simple: "to destroy the system or political machine which has brought such evil to our City, and the perpetuation of which is so fraught with menace for the future." The Fusionists struggled for a candidate of their own. In their canvass, Joseph T. O'Neal was the front-runner. During the Fusion convention, O'Neal's nomination apparently was defeated 111–109, but the convention's chairman, Alfred Seligman, announced that O'Neal was affirmed 119–111, simply giving him an additional ten votes. According to Robert W. Bingham, several newspapers and former mayor George Todd "threatened to expose the fraud underlying the whole thing" but decided to remain quiet. With their combined strength, the Fusionists posed a significant threat to Whallen's hold on the city.

Nothing Short of Revolutionary Tactics

Election Day fraud can begin with fraud on registration day. Someone registered illegally can then vote "legally." The Whallen machine employed area criminals to intimidate African-Americans from registering, and understood that the illegal registration of "repeaters" had a dual effect: It could potentially crowd off from the rolls many legal voters, thus making the job of controlling the election that much easier. The machine also used its control of the police on registration day. When challenges were made by Fusionists to some questionable Democratic attempts to register, a Louisville police officer named Roman Leachman threatened the challengers on several occasions. Leachman shouted that if an official "refuses to register another man, I will smash him in the head and kill him and I will come and throw his carcass into the street; he doesn't amount to anything." One official meekly inquired if Leachman was overstepping his bounds, and in revealing language Leachman underscored the reason for the police presence at the registration booths: "To hell with you. This means nothing to your crowd, and means four years for me, and of course I am going to look out for my own interests." The next day, Fusion workers were simply thrown out of their polling places and Democratic officials seized registration books and completed them in private. Papers in St. Louis warned the citizens of Louisville that eighty "practical politicians" were doing their work, repeatedly registering under false names. The paper stated that the repeaters "would work wonders increasing the population of Louisville." By padding the rolls with thousands of illegal voters, the machine was now prepared to "get out the vote" in November.

Roman Leachman was not the only policeman working during the registration period to steal the election. When the Fusionist Arthur D. Allen complained of irregularities in one precinct, Officer Jack McAuliffe knocked him unconscious and threw him in jail. A thoroughly unsympathetic Kentucky *Irish-American* alleged that Allen had "made a movement as if to draw a weapon," whereupon Officer McAuliffe gallantly "hit Allen with his club rather than shooting him." Later that day, Allen was convicted of disorderly conduct. In considering how to counter police intimidation, a member of one of the city's leading families suggested "nothing short of revolutionary tactics in Louisville will accomplish the purpose." He favored taking a dozen or so men to the polls on Election Day, armed with "concealed weapons or shotguns."

In the Tenth Ward, a Fusionist registration officer named William O'Mara discovered the extent to which the Democrats would go to corrupt the registration process. O'Mara claimed that John Keane, a Democratic committeeman for the Tenth Ward and a saloon owner, offered O'Mara a glass of lemonade on registration day. Seconds after the first sip, O'Mara recalled "I found myself whirling around and I thought the house was falling in." After being led to a chair, O'Mara finally understood what had happened. He had been drugged to make it easier to steal his registration records. After several minutes of dazed confusion, O'Mara was then taken outside where he was assaulted and his records taken. When he saw the "official" roll printed in the newspaper, O'Mara discovered that over sixty-five names had been added to his registration lists.

Charles Schuff, the county sheriff, knew that the key to neutralizing the Republican vote was in keeping large numbers of African-American voters away on Election Day. Schuff revealed that over 2,500 African-American registration certificates had been bought and were tucked away in a safe where, in Schuff's words, "we can control them." The money could also be used to purchase someone's non-participation. One African-American resident, William Moore, later testified that he was offered $2.00 to not register. Reducing the turnout was as critical to stealing the election as was intimidating voters and stuffing ballots boxes.

The 1905 election also revealed the dynamics behind those election officers who were charged with being neutral referees of the city's electoral process. Of 356 election officers in Louisville's twelve wards, 89, or one quarter, either worked for the city or county, or were listed as having relatives who did so. Another 48 workers, or 13 percent, were listed as "gamblers" or "bartenders." Fusionists understood that if those responsible for ensuring the legality of the election had a vested interest in the election's outcome, or owned saloons where much of the electioneering occurred, chances of another stolen election loomed high.

"ALL ELECTIONS REQUIRE MONEY"

In order for all of the corrupt figures in the Louisville election to do their jobs properly, money was a necessity. The 1905 Louisville mayoral race provides a rare opportunity to see how much money was used in a Gilded Age municipal election. Bank records revealed that the Democratic Campaign Fund had deposits of over $69,000 between August 31, 1905, and Election Day in early November, nearly three times the amount of the Fusionist fund. Furthermore, those records show that during registration week in early October, $22,290 was withdrawn, and on Election Day, another $23,360 was removed from the account. By the end of November, all of the $72,612.50 which had been in the campaign fund had been depleted.

Fred R. Bishop, treasurer of the Democratic campaign fund, later described how he went about raising these funds. Candidates for various city offices were to contribute ten percent of their current city salary, while police officers contributed according to their rank: The police chief gave $125; lieutenants, $50; and patrolmen, $32. Other city employees were expected to give five percent of their earnings to the fund. Bishop added that no threats were necessary to secure these sums and dismissed suggestions that his efforts served to corrupt the system. "All elections require money," Bishop claimed. "You can't have an election without it."

The manner in which the campaign fund was spent was instructive. The fund actually had nothing to do with printing campaign buttons or distributing placards, and everything to do with manipulating votes. The Campaign Committee instructed Bishop on how much to give each ward on the night preceding registration day. Bishop was well versed in the nuances of conducting elections. Was there a verbal understanding as to how to disburse the money? "No," said Bishop, "it was not necessary to have an understanding at an election," adding that spending large sums "has to be done." Bishop gave one ward captain nearly $2,500 on election eve. When Bishop was asked why that particular amount, he casually replied because that ward had "very near 7,000 votes." The larger the ward, the larger the amount given to each ward captain.

On Election Day itself, ward and precinct captains would return periodically for more cash. The method by which the money was distributed was not done with exacting accounting precision. Bishop simply related that whenever a captain came in, "whatever they say they have to have, I give it to them." What they did with the money was not Bishop's concern. In fact, he never even recorded in his ledger how much he distributed. Afterward, Bishop simply burned all of his election records entirely because, in his understated words, "election business is not good stuff to have laying around."

After acquiring the money from Bishop, the ward captains knew what to do with it. They spent part of their money paying city police officers and firefighters to take the day off to perform various chores in helping the Democrats. More than twenty percent of the city's firefighters claimed they were sick on Election Day and were put to use on behalf of the Democratic campaign. The *Evening Post* understood the degree to which the police force was an arm of the machine. Each officer, the paper revealed, was required to register from his residence three to seven "phantom" voters. All told, 313 illegally registered voters came from the houses of police or firemen. Officer John Quinn boasted that he had personally purchased over two hundred registration certificates from the Tenth Ward. When The Rev. W. A. Jones went to the 14th Precinct in the Fifth Ward to replace a Fusion election officer who had taken a leave for lunch, he was told by the Democratic challenger to leave immediately. Jones refused, and he was attacked by Police Officer Willis Allen. Even though Jones had three witnesses to the beating, none would corroborate his account. When Fusionists placed men with cameras in various precincts, for example, an angry Police Chief Sebastian Gunther ordered his men to "drive every son of a bitch off the street that has a camera."

"THE WAGON THAT STOLE OUR RIGHTS"

On election eve, an estimated 10,000 people gathered at the courthouse to support the Fusionist candidates. At the gathering, the theme of the various speakers was consistent: Be alert for election fraud by the Democrats. During the meeting, some angry police officers— obviously in the pocket of the Democrats—waded through the crowd, writing down the names of those in attendance as visibly as they could. The Democrats held a simultaneous rally, yet only a handful of voters attended.

When the polls opened, voters in several wards could not vote because of an insufficient supply of ballots. In the Tenth Ward, voters in the 31st Precinct could not vote until shortly before noon because the election commissioners had not arrived. In other areas, legal voters were denied their franchise in apparently "legal" terms. Lucius Alexander, an African-American in the Fifth Ward, tried to vote, but when he approached the poll, "they said the name had done voted, and I couldn't vote." Had he been able to do so, Alexander said he would have voted Fusionist, and added: "I never voted no other kind of ticket but the straight Republican ticket ever since I have been able to vote." More blatant examples existed as well. In the 38th Precinct of the Third Ward, three armed men simply took the ballot box at gunpoint, loaded it on a wagon and carried it away. Afterward, one African-American resident of the precinct saw the wagon the culprits used in carrying the box and remarked, in words that poignantly underscored what had occurred, "that looks like the wagon that stole our rights."

In the Sixth Ward, Police Officer John Enright refused to allow a number of properly registered African-Americans to vote because they lived in a "disreputable place." When their landlord came to vouch for them, Enright switched to a different line of reasoning, admitting frankly "these Negroes ought to be disfranchised." He then did just that by refusing them entry to the polls. Others told Enright that as an officer of the court, he was pledged to uphold the law, to which Enright sneered: "To hell with the law, what do I care for the law?" and proclaimed that no African-Americans were allowed to vote on his watch: "None of their damn color shall vote here." When pressed that he was exceeding his authority, Enright replied: "By God, I have been through this thing before; I know what I am doing."

In the Tenth Ward, Police Officers Lee Speed and James J. Tierney allowed elderly voters brought to the polls on omnibuses from the Little Sister of the Poor Home to vote immediately, at the expense of other voters patiently waiting in line. When some of these voters took ten minutes each to cast their vote, others who had been waiting since shortly before 6:00 A.M. simply left. One observer counted between twenty-five and thirty men who left before voting, because they had to get to their jobs. When Tierney was questioned about allowing the elderly voters in ahead of many who had been waiting for nearly four hours, he angrily raised his club and threatened anyone challenging the vote. B. M. Rivers, a Republican challenger in the Fifth Ward, was shocked when he challenged a voter's qualifications and was summarily ignored by Democratic election officers. Rivers turned to his statute books to cite his legal authority in election challenges. Pat Hartnett, the Democratic challenger, expressed nothing short of outright contempt for the statute books in a language that underscored the events of the day: "God damn the law, we are Democrats!"

In the Twelfth Ward, a former member of the fire department and devout Whallenite, John Barry, pulled a pistol on an election worker and demanded the ballot books. With the help of three policemen, Barry took the books to another location, swore in his own election workers, and proceeded to stuff ballot boxes with hundreds of his own votes. Another Republican challenger in the Twelfth Ward, Henry Fundstine, took a more charitable approach to the matter of allowing "repeaters" to vote. When one of his friends named Kinney came in and attempted to vote under the name of "Burns," Fundstine asked how Kinney spelled his last name. Kinney winked and said "some people spell it 'B-Y-R-N-E-S.' To which all Fundstine could do was allow Kinney to go in and vote. "Kinney needed the money and I didn't want to beat him out of it," Fundstine remarked, adding "I knew he needed it. He is a man that can't work hard and I let him go on and get the $2.00. It did him more good than it would do me for him not to vote."

Throughout the day, John Whallen kept a low profile, though he ventured from the Buckingham on at least one occasion. When the Republican challenger, Tony Giuliano, went to his precinct in the Sixth Ward, he was met by several men, including Whallen, who asked Giuliano to check on another challenger's whereabouts. Upon Giuliano's return, Whallen informed him "we have done swore a man in your place and another man in the other man's place." Giuliano protested, but Whallen simply told him "the best thing for you to do is to get out of here." One of the new election officers Whallen had summarily installed that morning was Roman Leachman, the police officer who had so conspicuously intimidated prospective voters on registration day.

"FRAUDS OPEN AND BRAZEN"

While Fusionists were outraged at the blatant theft, the Democratic *Courier-Journal* glowingly reported the official results of the election the following day: Barth had beaten O'Neal by 19,645 to 16,557 (a margin that eventually expanded to 4,826 votes). A humble Barth stated he could not attribute the victory to himself, but gave thanks "to the loyal support of the unswerving Democrats of this city." The election was not without its share of election problems, according to the paper, noting that Fusionists were allegedly armed with clubs and ax handles and were committing outrageous acts of violence upon unsuspecting and innocent Democrats. The following day, the *Courier-Journal* editorialized on the results of the election with prose that marks the end of many stolen elections:

> All things considered [the election] was as free of disturbances as could be expected . . . that the beaten party should cry "fraud" has become a matter of course; the fairest among them, however, and the manlier—conscious of their own shortcomings and seeing both sides of the record—have been disposed to take their medicine and abide by the result.

The Fusionists refused to go away. Calling themselves the "Committee of One Hundred," they organized to raise the necessary funds to contest the election and "take the police out of politics." Leading the Fusionist campaign was Helm Bruce, a Louisville attorney, who, along with James P. Helm, Alex Barrett, and William Marshall Bullitt, began deposing hundreds of witnesses in preparing their case before the Jefferson Chancery Court. Had it not been for Bruce, the 1905 Louisville election would have quickly faded away as another anecdotal episode of some "alleged election irregularities" in an obscure city election where frauds on both sides cancelled each other out. But because of his efforts, the inner workings of the 1905 race were exposed in graphic detail.

At the beginning of the investigation, a review of the city's registration lists revealed some of the full extent of the fraud. At least 790 illegal registrants had voted in the mayoral election. The open vote-buying was not done discreetly. Thomas J. Godfrey, who owned a tenement house on East Jefferson Street in the First Ward, told investigators he had been approached shortly before registration day by four men who offered him $45 to swear that five men lived in the house whom Godfrey had never seen. The going rate, it seems, for illegal registrations was $9 per person. One poll official, Walter Peoples, testified he had been offered $100 in the 15th Precinct of the Eleventh Ward by a Democratic sheriff, Enos Huff. Huff's offer was to give Peoples $75, keep $25 for himself, and for Peoples to give the Democrats a one-vote margin in the heavily African-American and Republican precinct. In the Twelfth Ward alone, 830 properly registered voters had tried to vote but were unable because no ballots had been supplied.

The Republican *Evening-Post* wrote lyrically of the breadth of the fraud in Barth's election. There was evidence of:

> frauds perpetrated by repeaters; frauds due to conspiracies; frauds in the count; frauds consummated only by violence; frauds open and brazen; frauds subtle and silent; frauds in the third, frauds in the

tenth; frauds in respectable parts of town and frauds such as one might expect in the Red Light District.

In March 1907, the Jefferson Chancery Court ruled on the election contest. By a 2–1 margin, Judges Shackleford Miller and Samuel B. Kirby refused to overturn the election, saying that fraud was undoubtedly a major factor in the Democratic victories, but that such corruption affected only nine percent of the vote, not enough to invalidate the results entirely. Judges Miller and Kirby concluded that in the Twelfth Ward, "many of the Democrats behaved very badly, but the place to deal with them is in the criminal and not in the civil courts." The decision did not lack for political machinations. Whallen had supported Judge Miller in his first election to the Chancery Court in 1897. Miller returned the favor the following year by deciding a case for Whallen that allowed the city to purchase land from Whallen for a courthouse annex. Not surprisingly, Whallen firmly supported Miller in his reelection bid in 1903.

The court's decision was not surprising to thoughtful observers of Louisville's court system. In the previous three years, of eighty-seven election cases brought before the Jefferson County Circuit Court, only one resulted in a conviction, an African-American who was given a six-month sentence in the workhouse for violating election laws. In some of these cases, police officers involved in the 1905 election, such as Roman Leachman and Martin Donahue, had their charges dismissed. Bruce and his partners appealed the Chancellors' ruling to the Kentucky Court of Appeals, the state's highest court, which was composed of five Democrats and one Republican. Throughout it all, Mayor Barth and his cohorts ran the city with little regard for the contest appeal. As the months and years went by, the realistic chances of undoing the results of the 1905 election grew increasingly slim.

The court's actions only verified what some saw as a thoroughly corrupt political system. "We have the best election laws and the worst

possible elections in Louisville," said Lafon Allen of the Municipal
Voters' League. "Such a thing as an honest election is unknown in
Louisville," Allen concluded, adding that part of the problem was that
"it is impossible in our city to have a man convicted for stealing an
election. We have no confidence in our judges."

THE TRIUMPH OF DEMOCRACY

In April 1907, seventeen months after the election, Kentucky's high
court finally heard the case. Arguing for overturning the election,
William M. Bullitt asked the court, "Are elections to be carried that
way? If we cannot get relief in this case, can you conceive of any election where a court of equity could give relief?" Bullitt concluded:

> When the Apostle Paul was scourged by the Roman Captain
> without a trial, he made that Captain quake with fear with the
> magic words "I am a Roman Citizen." The citizens of Louisville ask
> this high tribunal that they should make the word "citizen" in Ken-
> tucky as sacred as it was in the days of the Roman Empire . . . and
> they ask that you say once and for all that the policemen have no
> greater right than a Captain of the Roman government had, and
> that policemen shall be taught once and for all that they are not
> excused from wrongdoings.

Bullitt presented the court with a chart he titled "The Rape of the
Ballot." In it, he concluded that 6,296 voters had been disfranchised.
He was countered by Joe C. Dodd, representing the Democrats, who
told the court that the Fusionist campaign had been "designed in
fraud, backed up by vilification and abuse." When the court
adjourned, Whallenites who had traveled to Frankfort made some
"muttered threats" against Bullitt. Yet the "real bosses," according to

the *Evening Post*, "realize that any act of violence at this time would have disastrous results."

On May 22, 1907, the Court of Appeals issued a stunning ruling. By a 4–2 vote, the court agreed with the Fusionists that the election had been marked by overwhelming evidence of illegal registrations, destroyed ballots, stolen ballot boxes, alphabetical voting, and police violence. Central to the court's ruling was overturning the Chancery Court's finding that not enough ballots had been stolen to affect the outcome of the election. The majority opinion, written by Judge John B. Lassing, stated:

> The force and violence used by the partisans under the protection of the police; the pernicious activity of the police themselves in and about the polling places, coupled with the large number of illegal votes shown to have been cast, we are led to the inevitable conclusion that a "free and fair" election . . . was not held.

The Court of Appeals went a further step, and agreed with Bullitt that 6,292 voters had been disfranchised in the election, more than enough to overturn the election's results. The court thundered:

> We cannot feel that our duty in this case is fully performed without insisting that it is absolutely necessary for the preservation of a democratic form of government, that the right of suffrage should be free and untrammeled. No people can be said to govern themselves whose elections are controlled by force, fear, or fraud. And the people who do not govern themselves are slaves.

Finding that the methods used by the Democrats were "abhorrent to the spirit of our civilization and our Government," the court summarily overturned the results of the 1905 city election and ordered all Louisville municipal offices vacated immediately. Governor J. C. W. Beckham was given authority to name an interim mayor and other city

Following the decision by the Kentucky Court of Appeals that overturned the 1905 Louisville election, this cartoon depicts a disappointed Democratic machine that echoed "Casey at the Bat." One angry member of the crowd says "Kill the umpire." Credit: *Louisville Evening Post.*

officeholders until a new election could be held in November 1907. A delirious *Evening Post* claimed that with such a "triumph of democracy," the ruling restored "self government to Louisville." *Outlook* commented that the ruling would "put heart into those everywhere who are fighting against the tyranny of political corruption."

Governor Beckham quickly appointed Robert W. Bingham to fill the mayor's post. Bingham, coincidentally, had been elected county attorney in 1905 and was one of those removed by the Court of Appeals' ruling. In his brief tenure, Bingham worked to expose some of the machine's corruption within city government. With the Fusion movement gone and the polls under close watch, the Democratic mayoral nominee, Owen Tyler, lost to Republican James F. Grinstead in a relatively quiet election in November 1907 to complete Barth's original term. Yet the real test of whether Whallen still controlled the city and its elections would come in the next regular election in November 1909.

A CITY OF WHITE PEOPLE

With the Court of Appeals' decision fresh in the minds of the city's
voters, Whallen could not depend on the usual methods to ensure victory for his partisans in the 1909 mayor's race. Rather, Whallen
reverted to white supremacy for his drive to win back the mayor's
office. The day before the election, the *Courier-Journal* ran on its front
page a letter supposedly written by an local African-American named
"Pinky" to other members of a fictitious group called the "Young
Men's Colored Republican Club." In the letter, "Pinky" wrote "if the
republican party wins this fall we will have everything" and vowed that
after a Republican victory "people of our color will be on an equality
with any dam [*sic*] white person." It was an obvious forgery, but such
blatant race-baiting worked. The Kentucky *Irish-American*, an instrument of the Whallen machine, posed the case plainly for its readers:
"Do you want Negro domination or do you want Louisville to remain
a city of white people, for the white people, and governed by white
people?" Campaigning for mayor, William O. Head told a crowd of
white German-Americans that he had seen a black man in charge of
some white workers on a city street. "A negro was bossing them around
and was cussing one of the men." Head implored, "Do you want that
condition of affairs to continue in this city?"

The following day, Whallen's candidate won by 2,316 votes, with a
majority of nearly 1,700 votes in the Twelfth Ward accounting for a
good part of his victory. On election night, a very satisfied Whallen
said: "I went into this fight to win . . . and the good people of
Louisville rallied to our support with unswerving devotion." The jubilant new mayor told Whallen, "The people were with us in this fight
and your work has been wonderful." Then, Whallen and Judge
Shackleford Miller, who had decided for the Democrats in 1905,
shook hands in victory. Whallen had another reason to smile. He and
his brother won almost $10,000 in election wagers. A thoroughly dis-
gusted Bingham reflected that with the return of the "old corrupt and

vicious Democratic ring," that "conditions here now are as bad, if not worse, than they have ever been."

For African-Americans living in Louisville, the 1909 vote taught them everything they needed to know about elections. The state's highest court may have invalidated election theft in the 1905 race, but race-baiting in 1909 accomplished what stolen ballots could not do. After winning the mayor's office, Head and the Democrats kept African-Americans off the city's payroll and even extended segregation to the city's jail.

The return to power of the Whallenites also had one tangible affect on the city's police force. By 1908, of fifty-two officers who had been implicated in some form of election fraud, twenty-four had been dismissed from the force, and eight more had resigned, among them Roman Leachman. One local newspaper declared that the police themselves were particularly pleased with the new dynamics in city politics since they would no longer have to contribute money to Democratic coffers, or "do humiliating deeds for the *Courier-Journal*'s crowd." In November 1909, shortly after the Whallenites returned to power, six of the fired officers were suddenly reappointed to their duties. Some, like Frank Buddell, went on to lengthy careers and later received their city pensions. Others suffered no penalties at all for their activities. Officer Steve Wickham, in fact, had been promoted to captain in July 1907. The alliance between Louisville's corrupt political machine and the city's police force, which served as a powerful instrument of fraud on Election Day, remained intact.

"LOUISVILLE IS NOT A HARDENED SINNER"

The 1905 election and its aftermath was not an isolated incident in Louisville's electoral history. In 1923 and 1925, the same dynamics played out, complete with stories of "concentration camps" where repeaters—the "Go Get 'Em Boys"— were taught their trade by party officials, and with the Court of Appeals later throwing out city governments based on blatantly fraudulent elections. With the third rebuke of its elections in two decades, the *New York Evening World* concluded, "No city with any self-respect can indefinitely stand such reflections on its civic integrity." The *Courier-Journal* disagreed: "Louisville is not a hardened sinner, and neither defends nor condones what took place." Unlike other cities, the paper noted, at least Louisville could boast "that the crooks don't always get away with it."

Considering all that had happened, the Louisville story offers the distressing conclusion that the crooks mostly did get away with it. Whallen grew rich, and never spent a day in jail or paid one cent for his election crimes. When he died in 1913, his funeral procession included over a hundred carriages of mourners, one of the largest in the history of the city. His place as city boss was assumed by his brother Jim, who carried on the family tradition. When Jim died in 1930, one of his pallbearers was none other than the Australian ballot reformer, Arthur Wallace.

CHAPTER SIX

"The Lowest Layer
of Corruption"

*"I know it isn't right, but this has been going
on for so long that we no longer looked upon it
as a crime."*

I n 1905, the muckraker Lincoln Steffens described the ways in
which Rhode Island was essentially "a state for sale." Steffens portrayed the state as one intimately tied to big business, whose politics
were "grounded on the lowest layer of corruption that I have found
thus far—the bribery of voters with cash at the polls." Steffens quoted
Governor Lucius F. C. Garvin, who said in 1903:

> That bribery exists to a great extent in the elections of this state is a
> matter of common knowledge. No general election passes without,
> in some sections of this state, the purchase of votes by one or both of
> the great political parties. It is true that the results of the election
> may not often be changed, so far as the candidates on the state ticket
> are concerned, but many assemblymen occupy the seats they do by
> means of purchased votes.
>
> In a considerable number of our towns bribery is so common and

has existed for so many years that the awful nature of the crime has ceased to impress.

As many of his colonial forbears would have understood, Garvin knew that vote-buying was not perceived within the state's political culture as the purchase of the franchise, but rather as "compensation" for time lost in visiting the polls.

Many reformers assumed structural changes in the way votes were cast could finally fix a broken system. After the widespread usage of the Australian ballot had come into vogue—without essentially changing the extent of fraud—another possible answer to the paper ballot presented itself with the introduction of voting machines. Many states began turning to the new mechanical devices after the turn of the century. New Jersey, for example, used over 350 machines statewide by 1908. Yet problems quickly arose. Splitting tickets was made cumbersome with the machines, and write-in candidates seemed doomed. Others worried that skilled election handlers would still know how one voted, while anxiety was prevalent that there was no way to tell if one's vote was accurately recorded. The New Jersey legislature put the question of voting machines before the voters in a 1908 referendum. Out of 335 election districts, a majority of voters in a staggering 321 districts rejected the new machines and voted to return to paper ballots.

One way to get around the thorny problem posed by secrecy was the chain ballot. This system was designed to ensure the reliability of the purchased vote. The vote buyer began the process early in the morning. He would go the poll and receive a ballot. Instead of depositing the ballot in the box, he would slip a blank piece of paper in the box and carry the real ballot outside. When a prospective vote seller arrived, the buyer would mark the ballot and give it to voter to take inside. The voter would deposit the marked ballot in the box, bring a fresh, unmarked ballot to the vote buyer, who would then pay the voter. When the next vote seller appeared, the process was repeated.

States also extended the use of absentee ballots to other itinerant voters besides soldiers, such as mail carriers and railroad workers. By the end of World War I, nearly every state allowed soldiers to vote, while twenty states provided absentee ballots for work-related absences. While the desire to extend the suffrage to all qualified voters who could not be home on Election Day was strong, taking the ballots themselves away from the polls opened new opportunities for vote buying and intimidation. The irony was that absentee voting compromised a system that had just placed newfound importance on secrecy.

HEARST

Not even the wealthiest of candidates were immune to having votes, and elections, stolen out from under them. In fact, William Randolph Hearst, one of the richest and most powerful newspaper publishers of the era, found this to be the case when he ran for mayor of New York City in 1905—coincidentally the same year of the Louisville mayoral race.

Hearst would seem an unlikely victim of election fraud. He was, after all, one of the giant figures of American politics. Hearst's father had made a fortune in mining and parlayed that into a U.S. Senate seat from California. William inherited his father's fortune and turned his ambitions to the newspaper business, and by the 1890s Hearst owned several leading papers that became linked with "yellow journalism." While Hearst served two terms in the U.S. House, it did not satisfy his ultimate ambition, which was entertained by a few delegates to the 1904 Democratic national convention who hoped Hearst would receive the presidential nomination. In 1905, Hearst ran for mayor of New York on a third-party platform that opposed Tammany Hall, and here he saw how election fraud could be skillfully utilized against even someone of his considerable journalistic and political clout.

Unlike modern elections where candidates announce for office years in advance, Hearst did not declare for the mayor's office until just a month before the election. After unsuccessfully looking for someone to run against the incumbent mayor and Tammany favorite George McClellan, the son of the Civil War general and presidential candidate in 1864, and the Republican William Ivins, Hearst announced he would run himself on the Municipal Ownership League ticket. Throughout October, Hearst spoke before numerous crowds, exhorting them to reject Tammany Hall and bolt the major parties. His message caught on with the city's working class, and by early November Hearst seemed to have a real chance of winning. The threat he posed could be measured by Tammany's desperate diatribes, which called Hearst an anarchist, a socialist, and even implied that he had played a role in William McKinley's assassination. The *New York Times* went so far as to implore its readers to abandon the Republican candidate and vote for McClellan to stave off a potential Hearst victory.

Although the role of money in American elections has seemingly been covered from every angle, one corrupting influence has not received serious attention from scholars: Elections in the early twentieth century were a prime target for gamblers. Days before each election, newspapers reported the amounts wagered and the odds on specific candidates, and gamblers used these posted odds in a variety of ways. Conceivably, if a bettor felt confident about a candidate's chances, he would place a wager in that candidate's name and, of course, receive a return if his man won. Yet the bets could have different motivations entirely. If a candidate was a long shot and, if elected, would bring a higher return, the temptation to coerce votes or stuff ballots increased. The open practice of wagering on elections produced many complications that added to the prevailing culture of corruption.

New York bookmakers reported that election wagering favored

McClellan generally by 2 to 1. After public utility stocks went suddenly higher, McClellan's odds even went up to 2½ to 1, a clear sign that the some of the city's economic stalwarts felt comfortable with McClellan's chances, as well as an indication that Tammany was ready to do what was necessary. Others inside the bookmakers' offices openly wondered why so little money was being placed on Hearst. Perhaps insiders understood the significance of Elections Supervisor George W. Morgan's assertion that same day that more cases of false registrations and plots of vote floaters had been uncovered in 1905 than in any previous year in New York City.

One city newspaper reported afterward that the November 1905 election was "the most extraordinary election ever witnessed," a remarkable distinction if true. Throughout the day, Tammany's minions ensured that McClellan would win. Poll watchers were intimidated, ballot boxes mysteriously disappeared or were delivered to the wrong address, and scores of people reported seeing floaters and repeaters moving around the city throughout the day. Police officers casually stood by and observed as Hearst's poll watchers were beaten and shot at. Several Tammany precincts held back their returns after the polls closed, knowing these returns might provide the margin of victory for McClellan. Hearst's campaign even sent over some men during the election to pose as "tramps" to see if Tammany men would bribe them to vote for McClellan. Three such men were offered various bribes, including a gold watch. After suspicion arose that the men were decoys, the Tammany thugs beat them and chased them away.

By night's end, as Tammany gauged the final results, its handiwork was apparent. The election returns showed that McClellan had beaten Hearst by 222,795 to 219,708, with Ivins finishing a distant third. While McClellan's forces claimed victory, Hearst vowed he would go to court to fight against the massive vote fraud which he felt had cost him the election. "We have won the election," Hearst claimed, "all Tammany's intimidation and violence, all Tammany's false registration, illegal voting and dishonest count have not been able to overcome a great popular majority." The *New York Times* dismissed Hearst's claims of fraud and reveled in McClellan's victory, saying it "spared the city the humiliation, the trials, and the dangers of four years' management of its affairs by a peculiarly reckless, unschooled, and unsteady group of experimenters and adventurers." Had Hearst been elected, the *Times* warned, his assumption to power "would have sent a shiver of apprehension over the entire Union."

Undaunted, Hearst asked that a recount be undertaken. While his attorneys filed suit, Hearst claimed his fight was to reclaim "the dignity of the franchise." With investors fearful of the pending litigation, city utility stocks took a nosedive. The prolonged election contest drew new wagers, and this time the smart money was being placed on Hearst. Considering that he could hire armies of attorneys to fight Tammany and use his papers to expose its fraudulent practices, even the most cynical observers were willing to place a wager on Hearst. One anxious bettor wanted to place $10,000 on Hearst's contest even before the election wagering market opened, hoping to get even better odds than later, when he assumed so much money would be placed on Hearst as to drive down the odds.

The following day, Hearst's challenge was bolstered when an unsealed ballot box, full of uncounted ballots, was found in a barber shop located in the 21st Assembly District. The discovery of the box directly contradicted the receipts held by the city police showing that all boxes had been delivered to the Board of Elections. Two more boxes were located in a tailor's shop, one with mutilated ballots, the other empty. Hearst was so confident that he boasted he would not need a recount to be declared mayor, considering that his aides had already located over 8,000 spoiled ballots where voters had placed an additional "X" on the Hearst party box as well as the one for the candidate.

An unusual voice was added to the New York drama by John L. McLaurin, a former Democratic senator from South Carolina who witnessed the city election. In discussing the recent election, McLaurin compared what he had just seen in New York to the practices in South Carolina: "I was never more disgusted in my life," stated McLaurin, adding that the treatment afforded Southern black voters "even in the heat of politics is a paradise compared to what I saw some of the Hearst voters get in New York." Despite his party affiliation, McLaurin said he would have supported Hearst considering what the local Democratic party had done.

McClellan's supporters vowed to fight any recount, and as an indication of the heavy hitters behind McClellan's cause, Alton B. Parker, who had been the Democratic nominee for president of the United States just the previous year, headed McClellan's legal team that argued his case before the state Supreme Court.

On November 27, 1905, the New York Supreme Court ordered that ballot boxes in five election districts be opened and recounted. In a pattern that would be repeated nearly a century later by Al Gore, Hearst's forces decided to demand a recount in just a few, selected precincts, which his opponents charged would be an "entering wedge for a more preposterous one, involving the opening of every ballot box in the city." As the process began, Hearst picked up seventeen votes from the first few days of the recount. With seven hundred more boxes awaiting, the Hearst forces were confident of victory nearly a full month after the election.

Yet Hearst's confidence was short-lived. In early December, the New York Court of Appeals ruled that under existing law, Hearst had no right to demand a reopening of the ballot boxes. The Hearst lawyers hoped the state legislature might intervene to pass an act authorizing the recount, a move that was quickly rejected in Albany. On December 27, almost two months after the election, McClellan was officially declared mayor of New York by a plurality of 3,472 votes.

For the next two years, while McClellan worked at his desk as mayor, courtroom battles continued as more stories of the election abuses at the hand of the Tammany machine were revealed. Yet the allegations had no effect on the administration of city government, or on the public perception of McClellan's right to govern. Once again, as another recount began in May 1908, the public was treated to a daily dose of Hearst's apparent gains in the 1905 race. By the end of the month, the recount was finished, and Hearst's official total netted less than a thousand more votes in all, still giving McClellan a margin of over 2,900 votes. Hearst's lawyers argued, at too late a date, that the recount proved that in certain districts more votes were cast than were recorded in the poll books. By this time, the New York Supreme Court had had enough, and ruled that McClellan had won the recount and directed that he be found to have been legally elected in 1905. After claiming he would be declared mayor and serve out McClellan's term, Hearst reversed course and said he was "satisfied" with the court's decision and that all along, all he was really interested in pursuing was an "honest count of the votes."

In the end, Hearst's deep pockets and the power of his newspapers and the persuasion of his attorneys could not overcome a political machine that knew how to win. The power of Tammany Hall's tricks once again was too much to overcome, even for one of the richest men in the world.

"IT'S JUST A CONDITION DOWN THERE"

From cases such as Louisville and New York, it would be easy to assume that election fraud was primarily an urban concern in the early 1900s. Yet the countryside was infected with the same political culture. Few examples better illustrated how vote-buying had become a way of life than Adams County, Ohio. It also brings to light an issue that has infused election fraud from the very beginning. Who is the real culprit in buying votes? The politicians, or the voters themselves?

Vote-buying had a long history in Adams County, located near Cincinnati in southern Ohio. The price of a vote in the 1910 election ranged from a drink of whiskey to a whopping $25, although estimates placed the average at $8—still a considerable sum for the day. Since the 1890s, reformers in the county had tried unsuccessfully to curb the open purchasing of votes. Yet when party leaders vowed to sign agreements refusing to participate in vote-buying, some outraged voters objected and vowed they would vote against the first party that dared to sign the agreement. To these voters, Election Day was an economic opportunity. Struggling to make ends meet, these rural citizens saw for themselves little to gain in the outcome of an election, no matter who won.

While Adams County may have been similar to hundreds of other rural American counties, it had one major difference from the rest of the country: It had Judge Albion Z. Blair on the local bench. Blair was a hard-nosed jurist who not only refused to look the other way at the rampant corruption in his midst, he aggressively went after those who sold their votes. Judge Blair had been on the lookout since 1906, when a group of approximately a hundred local vote sellers informed him that they had committed no transgressions, since officeholders earned substantial pay from their service. For Judge Blair, it was an eye-opening exhibition of the entrenched corruption that flourished in his county. He resolved that at the appropriate time, he would use his power to fight the graft at the polls.

Blair found that opportunity in the November 1910 election, and he impaneled a grand jury to investigate the allegations of election fraud. In his opening charge, Blair warned that if no jury in the county were willing to bring indictments of fraud, then nothing less than a state of "anarchy" ruled the county. But before the case could proceed, the court struggled with whom to indict: the one who bought the vote, or the one who sold his vote?

Blair's remedy was to pursue indictments against the vote sellers and then compel them to testify against the vote buyers. His decision brought immediate rebuke from the local clergy, who claimed that the vote buyer was the real culprit, and Ohio's Governor Judson Harmon agreed. Yet Blair remained steadfast, and even defended his methods along blatantly class lines. Since vote buyers were usually composed of some of the leading business and political leaders of the county, Blair reasoned, the sellers tended to come from the poorer elements of the local population. Blair concluded that indicting those "who furnished prosperity" to the county would cause greater suffering to the entire community. Blair went even further: The vote buyer was the less guilty of the pair since he only sought party gain, while the vote seller was out entirely for himself.

Throughout the first half of 1911, a parade of witnesses appeared in Judge Blair's court, testifying to the extent of vote-buying in Adams County. From the banks that provided the large amounts of cash during election season, to the party committees and then the precincts, it seemed as if the entire county was involved in one way or another. By summer, hundreds of indictments had been returned, and 328 people pled guilty. Blair intimidated many more into coming to court and confessing their crimes rather than going to trial, where the fines and other penalties would be much harsher.

Yet beyond fines ranging from $5 to $25, Judge Blair also took the step of disfranchising hundreds of Adams County citizens who confessed, usually for a five-year period. Scores of impoverished farmers made it to Judge Blair's bench to tell their story. One woman confessed that she had sold the votes of her husband and son. Another Civil War veteran told Judge Blair about the incipient culture of corruption that ruled Adams County: "I took it because it was there to take," he said, adding, "I know it isn't right, but this has been going on for so long that we no longer looked upon it as a crime."

John A. McCarty, a Democratic Central Committee member from the county, put it best: "It has been going on for years. The very best and most honorable men in the county purchased votes. The buyers are made up of ministers, lawyers, businessmen, farmers, teachers, laborers, Sunday School superintendents, in fact all kinds of men." When two ministers pled guilty to accepting five dollars for their vote, Judge Blair decided to keep their names secret. News soon spread that evangelist Billy Sunday would even come to Adams County to admonish the local citizenry on the error of their ways. McCarty encapsulated a prevailing fact: that this culture was so powerful, no one really questioned the morality or legality of the vote-buying: "It's just a condition down there."

The religious overtones of the Adams County case had a certain irony. The long hordes of "sinners" waiting to confess their transgressions to Judge Blair, and the usual indictments of the "immoral" activity of the county, soon grew to be too much for the citizens of the county, many of whom deeply resented the notion of a self-righteous judge singling them out while many in other neighboring counties went unpunished. Rumors even circulated of attempts on Judge Blair's life, while others saw his actions as little more than political grandstanding. By the end of the hearings, Blair had disfranchised nearly 1,700 voters for five years for their role in the vote-buying, over one quarter of the entire electorate in Adams County.

The Adams County case became a national sensation, and even the *Literary Digest* published a poem in its wake:

Many people sold their vote
For to buy an overcoat
Or to buy a sack of flour

Thinking it a prosperous hour
Men of different age and size
For five years are disfranchised.

Despite the criticism that Blair had been too harsh on his rural constituents, former president Theodore Roosevelt applauded the judge's actions and noted that the case revealed that election fraud did not just occur "in cities and among our foreign-born population." In Adams County, in Roosevelt's estimation, "its people practically all belong to the old American stock." The ultimate point was not lost on TR, who wrote that without honest elections, "popular government is a farce."

The Adams County episode demonstrated, in ways not readily acknowledged, that it was just one of hundreds of counties throughout the country whose political and social culture, to its very core, was sullied by election fraud. For the people of those counties who paid close heed to the campaigns and voted their conscience, their votes were stacked against the ballots of bought and bribed voters.

"Worse Than Dynamite"

In the end, election fraud remained a local or state matter, and few doubted the outcome of any investigation or efforts at prosecution. That would change in 1915, when the U. S. Supreme Court ruled that local election officials were subject to federal indictments when they conspired to suppress votes. Writing for the court, Justice Oliver Wendell Holmes noted: "We regard it equally unquestionable that the right to have one's vote counted is as open to protection by Congress as the right to put a ballot in the box." Federal prosecutors were buoyed by the knowledge that they could start indicting local officials in races involving Congressional contests. That year, in Terre Haute, Indiana, federal prosecutors indicted 114 men for conspiracy to corrupt an election held there in 1914, including Mayor Donn M. Roberts, the sheriff, and a circuit judge.

Unlike the Adams County case, which remained a local affair, the Terre Haute case took on a national perspective when a number of

Southern Democrats, led by Kentucky's Senator Ollie James and Congressman A. O. Stanley, intervened to block the prosecutions. To these Democrats, the federal courts had no jurisdiction over local elections, and the actions of the Supreme Court constituted an assault on the rights of the sovereign states. Yet as Mayor Roberts wrote Stanley, much more was at stake with the court's decision:

> With the evident intentions of the Supreme Court of the U.S. to let the federal courts take jurisdiction of elections, the white man had just as well move out of the South and turn the offices over to the Negroes.

Before any trials began, eighty of the indicted men pled guilty. Other defendants, including Mayor Roberts, went on trial in March 1915. In attendance in the Indianapolis courtroom were a number of women who belonged to the Mississippi Valley Suffrage Conference, who obviously wanted a first-hand appraisal of how voting really worked by the very same men who denied them that right.

As the trial progressed, more details of how Terre Haute elections were conducted were carefully spelled out. The prosecution showed how the election machinery of Terre Haute was ruled by Mayor Roberts, the "Czar," who was also a Democratic candidate for governor. Roberts allegedly oversaw an election that was complete with false registrations, a sizeable "slush fund" to buy votes, and gangs of toughs to threaten voters at the polls. One city employee, who said he wrote out fictitious registration cards at the police chief's command, testified that when he ran out of cards, he "made men out of my imagination. I gave them a name, an age, and set out the place of birth." When another told Mayor Roberts on Election Day that he was unable to "put anything over" in a specific precinct because of Republican watchdogs, Roberts instructed him to "get something to put in their pockets and have them arrested for carrying concealed weapons."

The highlight of the trial came when Edward Holler, the city police chief, testified that Roberts had ordered him to make 2,500 false registration cards. The cards were then to be given to floaters on Election Day, who were paid $5 for their services. Yet one floater, Cortlandt Rector, testified he was paid $8 to vote ten times, and that he received his instructions from Mayor Roberts. Rector was outpaced by another floater who testified he voted twenty-two times on Election Day. Rep. Stanley's defense crumbled as more of his clients pleaded guilty. By early April, the federal jury found all remaining defendants, including Mayor Roberts, guilty. In his sentencing, Judge Anderson ruled that Roberts was the "arch conspirator" and sent him to Fort Leavenworth for six years. An appellate judge later ruled that Roberts's crime was "worse than dynamite; that it amounted to treason."

A local circuit judge and a sheriff received five-year sentences, and fifteen others were also sentenced to prison. The *New York Times* editorialized that Roberts and his cohorts had been convicted of crimes that "to people with a decently developed sense of civic and social responsibilities seem to be about the most serious that can be committed." The *Times* understood that Mayor Roberts was convicted of something that was intrinsic to the "game of politics," but felt that something new was in the air. "The misfortune of Mayor Roberts and his accomplices and henchmen was in not noticing that political fashions, like others, change once in a while, and that what is safe and even commendable one year may be dangerous and reprehensible the next."

"NEXT TIME, BE MORE CAREFUL"

If the *Times* felt that a new day had arrived in American elections, all they had to do was walk around the neighborhoods near their offices to be sorely disappointed. In November 1923, a Times reporter stood in a pouring rain at the corner of Houston Street and Bowery late on Election

Day, talking to a good "Bowery Democrat" who complained that he "had done a hard day's work—'voting in various places.'" After the polls closed, the two men walked to the 253rd Precinct of the 14th Ward, located at Public School 106. When they arrived, a kindly man inquired if they wished to vote. When the reporter said he could not because it was too late to do so, the man replied, "Never too late here."

As the Bowery vote was counted, stories were swapped of the infamous Barney Rourke, who was "responsible" for the delivering votes in another precinct. On one election night, Rourke was having dinner on Grand Street when his lieutenant walked in, reporting on the election results. "How's this, Barney," he said, "139 votes for our ticket and one for the opposition." While expecting a ringing endorsement from his boss, the young man only received scorn from Rourke. "What sort of business is this coming in with such a return?" Rourke said, adding "What were you thinking of when you let him vote?" Shocked, the young man was further badgered, "Were you asleep? Next time, be more careful."

As the onlookers exchanged more stories, the vote counters finished their work. In the 253rd precinct, there were 300 voters, of whom sixty were Republicans; except for a smattering of Socialists, the remainder were Democrats. The official results were:

ASSEMBLY:	Galgano, Democrat, 300 votes; Cohen, Republican, 0.
ALDERMAN:	Grauband, Democrat, 300 votes; Berzoni, Republican, 0.
MUNICIPAL COURT:	Schimmel, Democrat, 300 votes; Ellman, Republican, 0.

The reporter then described what happened next.

When the various formalities connected with the voting and the declaration of the official result were completed, the election officers separated and left for their respective homes in the downpour of rain. There were no angry collisions of embittered or extreme partisans; there were no recriminations over any unfair advantage taken by one side over the other. There were no threats of court proceedings, prosecutions, or disclosures. They separated, most of them going east. An honest count of the votes cast, it seemed to the writer, had gone west—decidedly!

The reporter reflected on what he had observed on New York's Bowery:

> In other election days election night on the Bowery was a gala occasion for many of those whom a sinister destiny or their own weakness had joined in the army of the down and out. The saloons were open, and especially on a wet and cheerless night there was a greeting in each for all newcomers. There was singing, cheers, and the occasional blowing of horns. It was not so last year, when what Swift described as a "rain of cats and dogs" added something to the cheerlessness of the great thoroughfare which continues to supply an abnormal number of those who vote early and often to the huge electorate of the great City of New York.

In so many ways, the culture of corruption that this lone observer discovered was repeated in cities and towns all across the country. The blatant vote-stealing revealed how little anyone cared about getting caught, and the casualness of the overall assault upon democracy belied how endemic these methods had become to election insiders.

THE SUFFRAGE ISSUE

By the 1920s, two Constitutional amendments had been ratified that allowed for the direct election of United States senators (1913) and gave women the right to vote (1920). The sudden swelling of the ranks of the electorate as well as the increase in the power of the individual voter certainly changed some of the ground rules for election fraud. While reformers could point to the amendments as sure signs of an expanding and more democratic electorate, the states themselves were often headed in the opposite direction, taking steps to disfranchise millions and make voting more difficult, except for the privileged. Literacy tests, poll taxes, lengthening residency requirements, and prohibiting non-citizens from voting were adopted. As Alexander Keyssar has written, "Stripping voters of the franchise was a politically delicate operation that generally had to be performed obliquely and without arousing the ire of large and concentrated groups of voters."

Women fighting for the right to vote saw some of the ways in which men had controlled elections for ages. Local politicians and city bosses were obviously not supportive of women's suffrage, in some part due to paternalism, but also because an enlarged electorate was much harder to manipulate and control. In the early 1900s, various states placed the question of women's suffrage as referenda for voters to consider. Either way, as the suffragist Carrie Chapman Catt understood, fraud was a major factor in some of the early defeats of women's suffrage. In Wisconsin and North Dakota, the ballots for the suffrage referenda were a different size and color than regular ballots, while in New York there were three separate ballots. All of these could be used by opponents to check and effectively control the matter of suffrage. Catt concluded that the suffrage movement was confronted by "an unscrupulous body [that] stood ready to engage the lowest elements by fraudulent processes to defeat suffrage." Catt's experience had taught her a vital lesson about American politics: "There was no protection against fraud on Election Day for a measure unsponsored by the dominant party, and that after fraud there was no redress."

In a Texas suffrage election in 1919, suffragists were wary of election fraud, and one male supporter of the suffragists who was steeped in how Texas elections proceeded warned supporters to pay close attention to how the votes were counted. "The counting is what counts and gets results," he admonished, adding, "Just count and then count some more and you will be sure to win." Yet the question failed in Texas by over 25,000 votes, some of it due to polls that never even opened in precincts that supported suffrage. Obviously, it is hard to start counting when the process never commences in the first place. The movement for women's suffrage was too well organized to quit, and with the support of even President Wilson, the ratification process took flight. When Tennessee approved the measure in 1920, the amendment was secured.

As women gained the right to vote, African-Americans, especially in the deep South, had seen their voting rights evaporate by 1920. White Democrats used a variety of methods—legal and illegal—to remove African-Americans from the voting rolls and to keep them away from the polls for good. Yet in the face of these overwhelming obstacles inherited from the Reconstruction era, Southern African-Americans fought courageously for the right to vote, and the reaction from whites was often brutal. In Florida, blacks registered to vote in the 1920 general election, hoping to transform the tradition of one-party rule and Jim Crow. On Election Day, what the historian Paul Ortiz has described as the "bloodiest presidential election in the history of twentieth-century America," the KKK declared open war on black voting; with the encouragement of state authorities, an estimated 30 to 60 black Floridians were killed that day, along with hundreds more wounded or chased away from the state.

CONGRESSIONAL REMEDIES

As demonstrated in Louisville, Adams County, and Terre Haute, courageous judges sometimes interceded to punish vote buyers or election thugs and reverse elections. Without judicial intervention, many elected officials assumed power with no check on the methods used to get them there. An exception was Congress, where both chambers reserved the right to withhold seating a member in cases where fraud had provided the mode of victory. When an election was contested, special committees would hear the evidence and make recommendations to the entire chamber, which could possibly unseat someone or declare a seat vacant. Between 1789 and 1901, 217 separate election contests had been waged in the House charging fraud, and in 94 instances, or 43 percent, the House voted to either award the seat to the contestant or declare the seat vacated. Partisan loyalties, of course, usually determined how a member interpreted a contested election. In the 1860s, Thaddeus Stevens, a Republican, was listening to a contest case when a colleague described both of the candidates as "damned scoundrels." Stevens agreed and wanted to know only one thing—"Which one is the Republican damned scoundrel?" Yet from 1908 to 1951, charges of election fraud swayed fewer House members, and only thirteen contestants were awarded their seats, while two elections were declared null and void.

Even when fraud was proven, the remedy could be hollow. In the Tenth Congressional District of Pennsylvania in 1918, the Democrat, Patrick McLane, was at first declared the winner, while, the Republican, John R. Farr, contested the election. Over nearly two years, a Congressional committee examined the case; they determined in February 1921 that "wholesale fraud" had indeed cheated Farr out of his seat, and, by a 161 to 121 vote on the House floor, McLane was unseated and Farr sworn in to serve out the remainder of his term—six days. For all intents and purposes, cheating had paid off for McLane's supporters, which only fueled the culture that tolerated such activity. The distant likelihood of the House refusing a seat based even on significant evidence of fraud belied the simple fact that this is what often happens when the players also act as referees.

Senate contests took a new turn with the passage of the Seventeenth Amendment. With direct elections, seats in the most powerful legislative chamber in the land were up for grabs, and the methods long used in electing governors and presidents were now employed to elect U.S. senators. In the 1920s alone, there were four election contests in the Senate. Not surprisingly, senators almost always voted along party lines in such disputes, and a candidate contesting a result who was not a member of the party in control of the Senate usually had no hope of even a hearing. Yet even if the majority party heard a claim for one of its own, the tradition-laden Senate was not disposed to overturn elections.

Less Than a One-in-Eight Chance

Yet in rare cases, even the Senate was forced to take action against the pervasiveness of fraud. One of the most famous Senate contests involved a primary election in Pennsylvania in May 1926. The winners of the party primaries were the former U.S. Secretary of Labor William B. Wilson, a Democrat, and the Republican, William S. Vare, the acknowledged political boss of Philadelphia. Vare won the general election in November, but Wilson contested the results, claiming the Vare campaign had won by employing legions of "floaters," stuffing ballots, and intimidating voters.

The question of whether to allow Vare his seat quickly arose. Governor Gifford Pinchot, in his letter to the Senate certifying Vare's election, wrote that Vare "appears to have been chosen," although his seat was "partly stolen" by frauds that had "tainted both the primary and the general election." In his public statements, Pinchot, a Republican, said: "When men in other states now think of Pennsylvania, they first think of one man—Vare—and one thing—corruption of the ballot box." Complicating the issue further was that after Pinchot sent the letter, his successor, John Fisher, was sworn in as governor and quickly sent a second letter that certified Vare without any qualifications. When Vare presented his credentials to Congress on

December 9, 1927, there were loud objections from some Democratic senators and he was not allowed to take his seat.

As the committee began investigating the Pennsylvania election, the details of the charges came to the fore. In several Philadelphia wards, Wilson did not receive even a single vote. The committee found over 21,500 poll-tax receipts that had been illegally issued, and in 395 voting divisions in Philadelphia the number of certified ballots exceeded the number of people registered to vote. Allegheny County Commissioner Charles McGovern told the committee that the election was nothing more than the "pure purchase of votes." A random check of just 150 divisions found 1,547 forged signatures on the registration books, and over 9,500 "illiterates" had no corresponding affidavits to prove their need for "assistance" from party workers when they voted. In all, the committee estimated at least 14,000 fraudulent registrations in Philadelphia; and 635 people were found to have signed their names at least twice as having voted. In a biting indictment of the election, the committee wrote: "The fraud pervading the actual count by the division officers is appalling," and concluded that a typical legal voter in Philadelphia had less than a one-in-eight chance of having his or her vote counted correctly.

The special committee submitted its findings to the full Senate on February 22, 1929. The committee stated that due to the overwhelming amount of fraud that marked the 1926 election, Vare was not entitled to his seat. The Senate delayed taking action against the senator, since Vare had fallen ill. Later that year, a weakened Vare took to the floor to defend his seat, but the best he could do was claim that the mountain of evidence against him was little more than clerical errors. Meanwhile, the Committee on Privileges and Elections reported to the Senate that Vare would have won even if the disputed votes were removed. This move effectively ended Wilson's claim to the seat. On December 6, 1929, over three years after voters had gone to the polls in Pennsylvania, the U.S. Senate—despite the committee's findings—voted 66 to 15 to deny Vare his seat, and then voted 58 to 22 to deny it as well to Wilson.

In other instances, the Senate could act in contested elections in ways that turned party politics upside down. In 1924 in Iowa, the Republican incumbent Smith W. Brookhart ran to retain his seat against the Democrat, Daniel F. Steck. Brookhart ran afoul of the GOP when he refused to endorse Calvin Coolidge, the popular Republican president. Some Iowa Republican organizations distributed sample ballots to voters indicating that they should vote the party line all the way with the exception of Brookhart, who, voters were advised, should be passed over in favor of Steck.

When Brookhart won by fewer than 800 votes, Steck contested the election. The hard feelings from the election had not subsided, and Brookhart soon learned that he would not have the full backing of his own party during the recount. At the heart of Steck's case were thousands of ballots that had been marked as invalid since they all displayed an arrow drawn all the way to Steck's name. These voters had apparently taken a Steck ad carried in a number of local newspapers too far. The committee noted that there were other problems with the ballots, including broken seals on the ballot boxes and discrepancies between the numbers of ballots and registrants in a number of precincts. All the same, the investigators determined that although the arrow constituted an extraneous mark and, in a purely technical sense, made the ballot illegal, the arrows clearly indicated the voters' intent. Consequently, the committee credited them to Steck. In the end, it found that Steck had won the election by 1,420 votes.

One committee member dissented. Unwilling to hand the seat to a Democrat, Senator Hubert D. Stephens claimed that the committee had counted over 1,300 straight Republican ballots that had individual marks beside each Republican with the exception of Brookhart. Stephens felt that voter intent was not clearly ascertained in these cases and contended that Brookhart should be seated. What made

Stephens's claims so unusual was that he was a Democrat. Although there were obvious partisan overtones to the dispute in which some angry Republicans exacted some revenge on Brookhart, and there were Democrats eager to capitalize on the situation to seat Steck, there were still some members who worked to find the real winner of the election based on some objective reasoning that they understood might be applied to their own reelections in the future.

In April 1926, the Senate vote on the Brookhart–Steck contest saw many members cross party lines for a variety of reasons. By a vote of 45–41, the Senate removed Brookhart from his seat and replaced him with Steck. Although the Republicans controlled the Senate, one of their own was replaced by a Democrat, but under circumstances that were unlikely to be duplicated. Brookhart's crime seemed to be that he was not a loyal Republican, and party stalwarts felt no inclination to come to his defense. Had he been a Coolidge supporter, the methods used to elect him would not have mattered.

"ACCEPT DEFEAT LIKE A MAN"

In the Solid South, the general election was never as important as the Democratic primary. In some of these pivotal races, even the U.S. Senate would be called to make some difficult political decisions. In a 1930 Democratic primary in Alabama, John Bankhead defeated the incumbent, Senator J. Thomas Heflin. Heflin contested the election before the Senate, claiming Bankhead's victory had been obtained by illegal registrations, fraudulent absentee ballots, miscounting of votes, and the illegal payment of poll taxes by the Democratic party. The Alabama legislature was indignant that Heflin would make such charges, claiming that he refused to "accept defeat like a man."

When the Senate committee on Privileges and Elections investigated the case, the Republicans on the committee felt that the fraud had been so massive that the Senate should declare that no election had taken place. The Democrats on the committee noted that Alabama law, like so many other states, declared that no election could be voided unless the number of votes proven to be fraudulent was enough to change the outcome of the race. Since Democrats claimed that Bankhead would still have won even if the illegal votes were discarded, they urged the committee to seat him. In April 1932, the Senate voted 64 to 18 to allow Bankhead to retain his seat. The Alabama election initiated an important precedent for how the Senate considered instances of election fraud in party primaries. The Senate committee wanted no part of investigating primary elections, and ruled that in future cases "The legality of the primary is not a proper matter for the consideration of the U.S. Senate."

While the first decades of the twentieth century saw a number of reforms aimed at expanding the electorate and curbing fraud, the Senate's move in the Southern primaries demonstrated some of the other changing political and cultural winds. By the 1930s, politicians and judges were ready to look the other way when confronted with evidence of election fraud rather than apply the remedies used in Terre Haute or Adams County. With fewer courts and fewer Congressional committees prepared to challenge election larceny, the general trend was to leave local elections to their own devices. With the onset of the Great Depression, a new era in American elections was about to commence.

CHAPTER SEVEN

The Real Foundations of the Gateway Arch

"I don't like to be a dictator."

F undamentally, elections are about who decides public policy and spends public money. This concept, however, is usually presented as little more than an abstract political understanding devoid of human details. Even seemingly insignificant elections can have profound social consequences that can eventually demolish neighborhoods, close businesses, and overturn lives. Elections have the singular power to carve in stone policies that cannot be reversed without gunfire.

Sometimes, elections allow skilled pols—with their own private and financial agendas—to use any means necessary to win an election while seemingly covering their larceny in the most democratic manner. After all, nothing is as powerful as the claim to a mandate rightfully earned from the people—even if the people did no such thing. In at least one case, election crimes have been buried underneath a soaring architectural masterpiece. To see how this can happen, we turn our attention to an obscure bond-issue referendum in depression-era St. Louis.

THE ST. LOUIS TRADITION

Even in the best of times, the desire to win can be consuming. But when times are bad, that desire is compounded. This was never more the case than during the Great Depression, as production levels, wages, and stock prices plummeted and unemployment, bank failures, and misery rose. With Franklin D. Roosevelt's victory in 1932, a more activist federal government took power and soon produced a sea change in the political and economic lives of all Americans.

Ever since the city of St. Louis had seceded from the county in the 1860s, Republicans had essentially controlled City Hall. Because of its riverfront location and the itinerant nature of some who lived in St. Louis, virtually every city election was met with charges of illegal voting and widespread fraud. Democrats claimed that one of the reasons Republicans had won in St. Louis, especially in the early 1900s, was due to the massive "colonizing" of illegal African-American voters, from across the river in East St. Louis, Illinois. Although the evidence suggests this was more a tool by white Democrats to intimidate and suppress legal black voters, the racist tone of the charges carried over to the summer of 1917, when white anger over hiring practices in East St. Louis resulted in a riot that killed 39 African-Americans and nine whites—one of the bloodiest race riots in American history. The riot "could not have occurred," the historian Elliott Rudwick has written, "if people had believed there was law instead of 'rotten' politics." Politics in St. Louis was a deadly serious business, and underneath the customary partisan acrimony were layers of racial and economic frustration that were ripe for political exploitation, especially on Election Day.

In a 1922 Republican primary, state party boss and former Congressman Fred Essen pulled out the stops to keep a Fusionist ticket sponsored by the Clean Election League from winning control of the city. Essen lost and was later indicted with seventy-three other men for election fraud. The jury was presented with evidence of massive tampering with ballots, of which many were literally found in cesspools behind the polling places. By the onset of the Great Depression, Democrats had gained control of City Hall, and were not above using some of Essen's methods to stay there.

DEVELOPING THE RIVERFRONT

For years, St. Louis officials had been trying to refurbish some downtown property near the river. Since 1889, a dream of city leaders had been a riverfront development project that envisioned various proposals to bring more people to downtown St. Louis and, consequently, raise property values and tax revenue. The overwhelming problem was in securing the funds necessary to build these projects, which in 1928 had been estimated at approximately $50 million. The city simply could not afford to issue a bond for the entire amount, since that would absorb all of the city's debt load and ensure that no other projects could be funded. So city leaders tried some inventive, if not illegal, ways to proceed. One suggested approach involved condemning land not used for the project and subsequently selling or leasing that property at increased rates because of the proposed development. Such a process involved amending the state constitution to permit what was termed "excess condemnation," but that failed. With the onset of the Depression, the ability to finance the project in any way seemed remote.

Yet by 1933, some city leaders, led by a local attorney, Luther Ely Smith, saw opportunities emerging with FDR's New Deal that seemed to make the possibility of a riverfront project more likely. Smith envisioned a commemoration to the Louisiana Purchase that would become a riverfront park. In 1934, a committee of city leaders went to Washington to ask for a Congressional resolution calling for a commission to plan such a park. While Congress obliged and Roosevelt supported the resolution, it clearly stated that the federal government was "not liable for any incidental expenses." City leaders assumed the project might be considered a Public Works Administration development, yet the president made clear to city leaders that "this is scarcely the type of project that falls under the PWA." Not to be deterred, city leaders went to Interior Secretary Harold Ickes, who was also interested in the plan but made no promises of federal funding. Yet with little more than a mild resolution in their hands, Smith and his supporters forged ahead and started planning what the riverfront project might entail.

In July 1934, W. C. Bernard, the city engineer, presented another plan for the riverfront. In Bernard's estimation, the problem with the riverfront "is strictly economic." With the Depression hurting the central part of the city, the riverfront was in even direr straits. His answer was a riverfront freeway that would bring more traffic to the city and would also include a "pedestrian park." Bernard hinted that the park would be highlighted possibly by a "monumental arch" that he even thought would be "described as the 'Gateway to the West.' "

Numerous blocks would have to be cleared, but Bernard saw this as another advantage, since some destitute families living in the area would be cleared away as well. Bernard's engineers had conducted a study and found 1,248 people living on the riverfront site, and most of them had no plumbing. "Unless corrected by a movement for the rehabilitation of these people, this condition will eventually produce one of the worst slums in America." To Bernard, the construction of the freeway "should be made the occasion for an enforced slum clearance program." Bernard's proposal, however, was accompanied by a whopping price tag that exceeded $20 million.

All of these plans lacked any realistic plan to secure the millions necessary to fund a riverfront park. But one possibility remained. Considering how the federal government provided massive sums for monuments to former presidents, city leaders took another tactic, asking the federal government to help the city create a monument to Thomas Jefferson. As the city leaders saw it, a memorial could be erected depicting Jefferson's Louisiana Purchase, and they hoped that the federal government might foot the bill. The stalled riverfront development project suddenly became the Jefferson National Expansion Memorial, and was quickly approved by Congress and President Roosevelt in June 1934. The funding mechanism would have the federal government match the city at a 3 to 1 ratio. Since the proponents of the project estimated a cost of $30 million, the city needed to raise $7.5 million. This would be the only chance for the developers in St. Louis to have their riverfront project and have it funded mostly by the federal government. It was an ambitious plan that involved clearing 37 blocks of riverfront properties to make way for a spacious memorial. To float the bonds, the city would need the approval of the voters, and a special election was called for September. Yet one significant obstacle remained: To win, the bond issue needed more than the mere approval of the voters—to pass, city statutes required a two-thirds majority.

THE DICTATOR

While Luther Ely Smith was the front man for the project, the political muscle was provided by Mayor Bernard Dickmann, the former president of the St. Louis Real Estate Exchange. In Dickmann's estimation, the project was a crucial ingredient in the city's resurgence. Cities all across the country were starting to receive New Deal funds to put people back to work, but none was requesting funds for a project on such a scale. Much was riding on whether Dickmann could deliver this election—the public works jobs that would come from the memorial's construction, and, most of all, the money that would flow to the developers and merchants of downtown St. Louis.

Accordingly, Dickmann was prepared to use all of his mayoral powers to secure victory at the polls. Here, the Depression aided him. With unprecedented unemployment levels, Dickmann's control of city jobs gave him more clout than usual, and the fear of possibly losing coveted jobs provided another weapon to deft practitioners of the political arts. Yet the city government was not the only place where job security was leveraged to coerce voters. An assistant vice president of the Columbia Terminal Company, a railroad company, wrote to one of Dickmann's aides, "You are familiar with the manner in which we attempt to acquaint our employees with any worthwhile issue in order to insure [*sic*] a large percentage actually getting to the polls." The executive promised City Hall that his workers would provide many votes for the bond issue. "While we have never attempted to use any coercion," he added, "almost 100% of those voting actually supported the issue in the manner in which we asked them to."

Despite the supposed civic-mindedness of the project, the odds of winning the necessary two-thirds majority seemed unlikely. Dickmann knew that Republicans and conservative Democrats were leery of incurring such a debt at a time of economic misery, and the project offered dubious benefits to the city. Dickmann countered by launching an aggressive public-relations campaign, and claimed that the bond issue would immediately bring jobs to the city and clear away blocks of unsightly and mostly derelict warehouses. The *Post-Dispatch* noted that the mayor was "also a real estate man" who had expressed confidence that the memorial project would "make property throughout the city worth more than at present."

Less than a month before the election, Mayor Dickmann raised the stakes. All 7,000 city employees were utilized as campaign workers for the bond issue. "Attitude of the employees toward the issue will be an evidence of their loyalty toward the administration," the mayor said in language that usually goes unspoken in most American elections but is tacitly acknowledged by those on the patronage payroll. With thousands

on relief rolls waiting desperately for a job, a job within the city administration was more coveted than ever, and Mayor Dickmann wanted to
make sure that he used this to his advantage in securing the necessary
votes. It also created some bitter feelings among his fellow Democrats
that would surface come Election Day.

Despite the supposed civic-minded appeal of the bond issue, Dickmann had some staunch opposition. One group, led by Marquard
Brown, organized the Taxpayers Defense Association, which claimed
the bond would not deliver the immediate jobs promised, that it would
remove property from the tax rolls that accounted for $200,000 in rev-
enue, and that the federal government had made no definite commit-
ment to starting the beautification project. The Taxpayers association
promised that in the end, the project would be little better than a "37-
block mudhole" or a "glorified parking lot." However, the Taxpayers
group could not match Dickmann's control of the city's workforce or
his public-relations skills in selling the bond to prospective voters. Just
days before the election, Dickmann began announcing early poll
results that indicated that the bond issue was enormously popular. In
the Eleventh and Twelfth wards, Dickmann claimed that a recent
straw vote gave the supporters of the bond issue a lead of 13,000 "yes"
votes to 2,100 "no" votes. Already at this early stage, Dickmann and his
associates were cooking the numbers in hopes of obtaining their two-
thirds majority.[*] If swelling straw-vote results—to put it mildly—were
not enough, large ads exhorting voters to "put 5,000 men to work"
were published in the local newspapers days before the election. The
ads further claimed that actual work on the memorial would start ten
days after the successful passage of the bond issue.

The most powerful group contesting the bond issue called themselves the Citizens' Non-Partisan Committee, led by Paul O. Peters.
This group felt that Dickmann's claim of providing jobs was overblown

---

[*] On Election Day, the "no" votes actually defeated the "yesses" in the Eleventh and
Twelfth wards by a combined margin of 6,938 to 5,937.

and would only saddle the city with more debt. The Non-Partisan committee informed city voters that bankers would be the only ones to ultimately benefit from the project: "The Shylocks of finance must get their pound of flesh before we can say 'It's paid for and it's ours.' " Peters also used another proven tactic designed to kill popular support by warning that "it would only benefit the colored people."

Dickmann also had some allies who were not on the city payroll. Bertha K. Passure wrote Luther Ely Smith that she was willing to "take charge" of various women's groups and "foreign born citizens" to get them to vote for the bond. Passure expressed some of the underlying concerns these groups had about the bond issue. "They must be convinced that a small tax increase must not stand in the way of such a splendid achievement." To make up for lost revenue that would occur when the proposed property was condemned, association advocates predicted that all St. Louis property owners would pay an additional three cents per $100 of assessed value the first ten years, and then a sliding rate that would reach 12 cents in ten years. Such increases, coming in the middle of the Depression, obviously worried small householders and landowners throughout the city. Councilman Otto Lietchen, for one, asked why his constituents should "have their taxes increased to benefit the downtown merchants and property owners?"

Several weeks before the election, Dickmann participated in a gridiron dinner that performed skits poking fun at some issues of the day. In a rather ironic twist, Dickmann played the role of the levee district that would be transformed if the bond issue passed and the reclamation begun. Dickmann joked that he was ready to "wreck home owners and cripple business" in the area once the project started, and added that he expected to spend his old age on the riverfront, "watching crates and dead animals float down the muddy Mississippi." Yet this was no joke to a number of St. Louis citizens, who worried about the city going further into debt and the consequent strain on the city's finances, nor was it humorous to those who lived and worked on the riverfront.

A pamphlet printed by Dickmann's supporters clearly stated that if the bond issue passed, St. Louis would "get U.S. funds; cut relief rolls; clear 37 blocks; put 5,000 men to work; build a memorial park; perpetuate our nation's history," and, sweetest of all, the memorial would be "maintained by the federal government." Yet there were other reasons provided by additional groups. The leaders of forty local trade unions were staunchly in favor, saying that jobs would come to the skilled laborers of St. Louis. Yet stuck in the middle were African-Americans, who wondered what benefits would come to them, Paul O. Peters's warnings aside. Several of the city's African-American leaders wrote to Smith and his associates: "Knowing that the city of St. Louis is dominated by union labor and knowing the attitude of union labor to Negro workmen," the leaders asked "What will be the status of the Negro workmen to the work in general?" Additionally, "If said bond issue is approved and the memorial completed, what will be the attitude toward Negro citizens as to their rights and privileges in the enjoying of said improvements?" Despite these concerns, the city's African-American newspaper, the *Argus,* endorsed the bond issue, saying, "It means bread, clothing, and other sustenances of life to those who have been without work for some time."

Worried that the bond-issue vote was in jeopardy, Dickmann's rhetoric grew more heated and threatening as the election approached. To those on the city payroll, Dickmann could not have been clearer. "We will know who is shirking because there is going to be a checkup" the day after the election, Dickmann claimed, adding, "and I don't mean maybe. No matter who may have recommended any city employee, if he is disloyal he will be got rid of." In a nakedly brutal sentence, Dickmann explained:

I don't like to be a dictator, but I don't want six or eight people to interfere and break down what we are trying to do to build up a progressive city.

Despite the mayor's efforts to the contrary, the appearance of a dictator running the bond election was not lost on wary opponents of the bond issue. Meanwhile, another canvass of the various precincts, overseen by the mayor's cronies, revealed that the bond was more popular than ever. In sixteen wards, the bond was favored by a whopping 67,678 to 19,984, easily more than the necessary two-thirds vote. Despite these glowing numbers, the precinct captains were not taking any chances. Captains in 669 precincts conducted door-to-door canvasses in late August, getting signed pledges from prospective voters in support of the bond issue. With these signatures in hand, the captains could reassure City Hall that the votes were there for passage of the bond issue.

DELIVERING THE VOTE

The Chamber of Commerce, which endorsed the bond issue, surveyed 290 businesses within the area that would be demolished, and found that thirty-four of those businesses' owners said that they would definitely go out of business if the bond passed. Dickmann's forces dismissed such claims as "ridiculous." After all, the memorial would only be a few blocks long. Since the riverfront around St. Louis was calculated at 25 miles long, "with ample and better locations at less expensive rentals," any displaced businesses located in their current "cramped and forsaken quarter" would have better opportunities to relocate. To the supporters of the bond issue, no one could possibly lose.

While the area was portrayed as a wasteland of destitute and abandoned buildings ravaged by time and the Depression, the Chamber of Commerce study revealed another story. Fully 55 percent of the area was occupied by "substantial businesses" that employed between 3,000 and 5,000 workers. The types of businesses in the area varied: printing companies, fur and wool traders, seed and feed distributors, and some wholesale grocers. The Chamber of Commerce then arrived at the heart of their study: that if the project commenced,

> There will be a definite tension placed on industrial real estate available outside the riverfront area if the proposal to erect a Memorial Plaza is fulfilled. Just how much tension, it is difficult to express precisely.

For the owners of this property outside the riverfront, the only "tension" would be in how far to raise the rents on the displaced businesses. The study noted that "The absorption of this large amount of space, together with the short period of time available for procuring new locations, will temporarily, and perhaps, permanently, increase real estate values in St. Louis."

A crucial moment occurred the day before the election, when the city elections supervisor, James Waechter, stated that he expected 110,000 to 115,000 people to vote in the special election. If so, then approximately 75,000 votes would be needed to approve the issue. Yet on Election Day, over 94,000 votes had been cast by 4 P.M. alone. When the polls closed, the "yes" votes won by an official margin of 123,299 to 50,713, the supporters of the bond issue receiving 70.9 percent of the vote, over four percentage points more than necessary. The number of votes in the election exceeded 174,000, a considerable leap from Waechter's estimate. With the bond issue approved, the Jefferson Memorial Expansion project seemingly had the democratic will of the people on its side, and with it, the bonds could now be floated to start the bulldozing.

The relative calm was suddenly disturbed late on Election Day, when shots rang out in City Hall. The violence stemmed from heated exchanges within the Democratic factions in City Hall, namely those supporting Mayor Dickmann and those who opposed his rule. The guns were drawn in the private office of the city's Democratic City Committee, and when it was over, four men had been wounded, including a Missouri state representative. Two of the wounded were Dickmann's men responsible for delivering the Twenty-fourth Ward but who had failed to do so with appropriate margins. The blood on the floor of City Hall testified to the intensity of the arguments behind the bond-issue election and the pressure some partisans felt to deliver the votes to the mayor.

Elsewhere, some of the precinct handlers had succeeded in securing thousands of votes, many more than were expected. One such precinct committeewoman was Mrs. Charles Carnali of the Twenty-third Ward. She proudly noted that the vote in favor of the bond issue in her ward was 3,419 to 426, an approval rate of nearly 89 percent. She humbly attributed the result to "the untiring work of all connected with it." The publicity chairman of the project, William D'Arcy, proclaimed: "In a few months you won't find a man or a woman who will claim that they fought it—that they even voted NO." After selling the city on the supposed historic value of the project and the imme-diate jobs that would flow to St. Louis, D'Arcy was more candid after the election was over. No longer did he stress imminent jobs or the monument to Jefferson: "We have made every retail corner in the downtown area more valuable," he boasted.

The Citizens' Non-Partisan Committee, for one, knew they had been robbed and refused to let the election rest. Committee leader Paul Peters had been trying to get the attention of anyone who cared, even sending a letter to President Franklin Roosevelt, asking that the results of the election be nullified due to extensive fraud. The Non-Partisan Committee printed a pamphlet outlining the enormity of the vote theft, adding that "Money flowed like water amongst those political workers, judges, and clerks who not only supported the bond issue, but were vile enough to deliberately stuff ballots or make false counts."

The committee began investigating registration lists in St. Louis, and soon received the considerable support of the St. Louis *Post-Dispatch*. It did not take long to discover the enormity of the false reg-istrants. At first, "hundreds" of names could not be found residing at the listed addresses, which were often abandoned buildings or vacant tenements. In other cases, unanimous votes in favor of the bond issue were found in some precincts, including Police Commissioner William Igoe's precinct, where the bond passed 505 to 0. Thirty-four precincts recorded over 97 percent of their votes in favor of the bond issue, and all nineteen wards that favored the resolution witnessed significant amounts of false registration and vote stealing. Within these wards, the vote favoring the bond issue was a combined 8,753 to 330, yet the *Post-Dispatch* easily found 543 voters who either signed affidavits that they had voted "no" or were willing to testify in court of their negative vote that had obviously not been recorded as such. As the investigation broadened, the scale and scope of the vote-stealing in St. Louis were exposed.

The stories were compelling. In one barbershop on Franklin Street, 392 names were placed on the registration rolls in a thirteen-hour period as residing there. In an abandoned building that had not been occupied for over a year, 137 people were registered to vote. At the Atlantic Hotel, 160 people were registered, yet the hotel owner claimed only six had ever resided there. When a couple was found to have registered in at least two separate residences, it was not lost on anyone that one of the residences belonged to Robert Hannegan, a former chairman of the City Democratic Committee.

In order for the massive duplicity to occur, election judges were shifted at the last minute to areas where they were not familiar with the local residents, making false registration easier to pull off. The judges were not exacting when it came to demanding identification and proper registration. Leonard Bernstein was an election judge who admitted that he knew none of the voters in the precinct where he was assigned, but did not seem particularly worried about the situation. "We just take down their names and let them sign the books," said Bernstein, claiming, "It is up to the clerks to check up to see if they are qualified voters." Bernstein disclosed that he received his placement

Even in the midst of a vote fraud investigation, State Sen. Michael Kinney (middle, facing opposite of camera), one of the bosses of St. Louis politics, openly distributes money to prospective voters outside the polls in a 1936 election. Kinney won his ward 3,652 votes to 2. Credit: *St. Louis Post-Dispatch*

orders from a state senator and St. Louis city boss, Michael Kinney, who had given him a job in the City License Collector's office. After being asked a series of embarrassing questions by a reporter for the *Post-Dispatch*, an obviously troubled Bernstein went off to consult with Senator Kinney. Election overseers like Bernstein understood that their job on Election Day was to look the other way in order to stay in good favor with people like Kinney. In all, these were the crucial dynamics in building a false registry list of thousands of voters.

To those on the ground in St. Louis, these tactics were nothing new. A former member of the St. Louis Board of Election Commissioners stated that ward heelers were well educated in padding registration lists. How?

Ward and precinct heelers collect persons from rooming houses and boarding houses and other persons willing to earn a few dollars.

> They give each of these people a name and an address. Some of the
> names are the persons' real names, some are fictitious. A copy of this
> list is retained by the ward heeler. He then arranges with a friend
> having either a flat, a residence or a rooming house, and, for a con-
> sideration to the friend retains a copy of the list with the names of
> persons supposed to be registered at the address.

At other times, a resourceful ward heeler would have his relatives
residing in neighboring counties or states come to St. Louis on registration day, swear that they were residents of the city, and register to
vote, providing the address of the ward heeler as their place of residence. If asked by an election inspector who lived at the residence, the
conspiring voter would simply present the list provided him by the
ward heeler. On Election Day, then, those who had registered under
the process could go to the polls, or repeaters hired for this purpose
could then vote as the individual registered illegally.

Over the next days, the *Post-Dispatch* revealed more of the latent
corruption in city elections. In some precincts, over thirty percent of
the registry rolls were fraudulent, and the total number of false registrants in the city ballooned. As one Republican poll watcher claimed,
"Irregularity seemed to be the rule. At the very start a man registered,
stepped outside, re-entered and registered again." The watcher's
friends cautioned him about challenging the ways St. Louis politics
ran by warning him not "to see too much." An even more revealing
glimpse inside the vote-stealing machine was unearthed by investigators. By law, each precinct was required to show the time at which the
ballot boxes were returned from each precinct. Using this "condition
card" record, then, allowed investigators to learn how long it took
precinct officers to make their official counts. When investigators
went to the Board of Election Commissioners a year following the
election requesting this record, they were informed that the record
could not be found. Not to be outdone, the *Post-Dispatch* carefully

pieced together a time sequence that the missing records would reveal. When the paper had sampled precincts at 9 A.M. on Election Day, they found that 21,000 ballots had been cast so far. That meant an average of 7,000 ballots per hour were cast in that period (the polls opened at 6 A.M.). At other intervals throughout the morning and early afternoon, the average remained between 7,500 and 17,300 per hour. Considering that over 173,000 votes were officially cast, the investigators were able to surmise that in the final three hours of the election, an average of over 26,600 votes were cast each hour. Fully one third of the entire vote was supposedly cast in the final three hours of the election. Considering how little time each voter would have had in order to accomplish this number, it was patently obvious that thousands of votes had been stuffed in the final hours; it was not surprising that records that could have revealed this were suddenly lost by the Elections Board.

Part of the problem was that the city Elections Board merely accepted the recommendations of the parties for precinct officers, rather than assigning qualified officials itself. Not surprisingly, the Elections Board was not pleased with the exposés of the *Post-Dispatch* and refused to inspect the city's registry rolls. Rather, board chairman Waechter said the board would only agree to investigate those cases of fraud exposed by the newspaper, and refused to expand the inquiry. After Governor Guy B. Park intervened and demanded that the board purge the rolls, the board relented and ordered the recheck to proceed.

By the end of July 1936, the numbers of false registrants were beginning to startle even the most cynical observer. In their investigation into the city's false registrants, the Elections Board found 46,301 registrants to be listed as "not found." This constituted nearly twelve percent of the electorate of St. Louis. Chairman Waechter, hoping to put the best public face on the findings, dismissed any suggestions of "wholesale" fraud and claimed 20,000 of these were probably due to deaths or people leaving the city. A Democratic member of the Elections Board went even further, claiming "Why, during the heat wave, they were dying at the rate of 400 a day"—which, since only an estimated 350 died the entire summer from the summer heat wave, was an astonishing medical calculation. In wards Four and Five, controlled by Mike Kinney, the number of false registrants reached over half of the entire registry list.

"Voted 'Em Like Soldiers"

The details of the St. Louis bond issue are insightful when trying to understand the larger culture that pervaded American politics at the time. Michael Krautchel ran a barbershop in the Sixth Ward, which was used as a polling place on Election Day. Krautchel later related that the Democratic machine "Voted 'em like soldiers" in his shop. Throughout the day, Krautchel observed poll officials examine a registration list and say "this man and that man would not be in to vote, that he was sick, or not at home, and a bunch of ballots for the bond issue would be marked, put in the box, and those voters names would be checked off as having voted." In all, Krautchel saw at least fifty votes stuffed in such a manner. The bond issue passed in the precinct housed in Krautchel's barbershop by 312 to 12.

Some election officials added to the growing chorus. Robert E. Puls, a Republican election official in the blatantly corrupt Fourth Ward, claimed that Democrats in his ward had made use "of the printed list of registered voters in the precinct":

One of the Democratic precinct officials goes through the printed list of voters and copies off certain names they intend to vote. Probably they will begin at the top of the list and copy off every third or fourth name. They draw a line through these names on the printed list, and assign a ballot number to each one. Sometime during the day they retire to the back room, taking a supply of blank ballots which the judges and clerks have initialed, and there they mark and number the ballots which are later deposited in the box.

If a genuine voter arrived whose name had been crossed out, there was a process available whereby no one would suspect anything was amiss. Puls described:

> A precinct official finds the name on his printed list, sees that it has been voted, but calls out to his fellow officials and adds the word "hold," which is a signal to them that this name has already been voted. He hands the applicant a ballot and when it is numbered the number is placed following the first unvoted name following that of the applicant. They always have plenty of names to take care of the genuine voter.

Puls noted that those registered did not need to actually vote, "because they know they don't have to come to the polls to vote. Everything is done beforehand." He then described how the counting of votes took place:

> They don't actually count the ballots. They dump the ballots on a table and sort the Democratic and Republican ballots in separate piles, so that they know how many ballots were in the box. Then they arbitrarily give each candidate a certain number of votes.

To Chairman Waechter and his men on the Elections Board, their dismissal of the excessive "not founds" were aggravated by an August 1936 primary, in which only 2,852 of the "not founds" showed up at the polls, leaving well over 40,000 fraudulent names from the previous registration lists. In Mike Kinney's bid for re-election to the state senate, he received 3,656 votes to his opponent's two in his home Fifth Ward.

When the details of the fraud were fully exposed, the outcry against the results of the bond issue election naturally intensified. The *Washington Post* concluded that considering the extent of the false registration, it was obvious that "The people of St. Louis really did not vote to spend $7.5 million." The *Post-Dispatch* declared that the election "must not be allowed to rest under this doubt" of fraud hanging in the air, and that "The city can not afford to have it said that the building of a great monument with the people's funds is being promoted by fraudulent methods." Yet back at City Hall, City Counselor Edgar Wyman argued that even if overwhelming evidence of fraud existed, there was no recourse to overturn the bond issue election because no statute existed on fraud that covered bond-issue races. Governor Park, meanwhile, fired the St. Louis Election Board, citing that it was "necessary for the betterment of the public service." Before doing so, Dickmann and Bob Hannegan tried to persuade the governor to keep the old board "for the good of the Democratic party." Park told reporters that Hannegan had made his plea "based on practical politics."

Due to the work of the *Post-Dispatch* and protests by various groups, a grand jury convened to investigate the bond-issue election. Whether the grand jury could actually examine the ballots used in the election, however, was a matter of some debate. State law held that all ballots in an election had to be destroyed within one year after the contest, unless an investigation was started within that year. Yet the grand jury surprised everyone and decided not to investigate at all because a number on the jury felt the riverfront project "would be a good thing" for the city and best left alone. Paul Peters's Citizens' Non-Partisan Committee, which had been the first to call attention to the fraud, was outraged, and rallied at the Municipal Auditorium in protest. Peters stated the obvious when he said: "An election in which city hall employees were coerced into going down the line by the city's chief executive could not be called a free and fair election." Yet the motives of the grand jury may have extended beyond community development. The grand jury foreman, Patrick Fitzgibbon, had a nephew who was an election judge in one of the most fraudulent wards in all of St. Louis. He also had three other relatives on the city payroll.

The project stalled in Washington as well, when Attorney General Homer Cummings ruled that the president could not issue an executive order permitting the start of work on the St. Louis project. Yet after Dickmann threatened to campaign against FDR in St. Louis, the administration changed course rather quickly, and Cummings was able to find language in the newly minted Historic Sites Act that authorized the president to issue an executive order to start work on the project. The administration issued a one-year appropriation of $9 million to clear the 37-block area. A disgusted Ickes confided in his diary that "since we are all committed up to our eyes on this project, I think we ought to go through with it under whatever guise."

Even after another grand jury indicted sixty-six people in the aftermath of the *Post-Dispatch* revelations, a city primary election in September 1936 saw even more widespread fraud and election corruption. An incredulous *Post-Dispatch* called the frauds in the newest election "amazing," and concluded there was "little relation between the count and the actual vote" in eleven St. Louis precincts. Six Democratic nominees for circuit judge, in fact, were credited with nearly twice as many votes as were actually cast. Throughout the ticket, candidates were either severely under- or over-counted. Poll officials were hardly bothered by the recent exposés and acted with impunity. "So brazen was the fraud," wrote the *Post-Dispatch*, "that in most instances no effort was made to reconcile the certified count with the number of ballots in the boxes." Instead, poll officials made a rough estimate of the overall count and divided the votes as they pleased. When a grand jury opened the boxes to actually count the votes, they found that countless precincts had simply made up their vote totals. In one race for circuit judge in the Eleventh Precinct of the Fifth Ward, one candidate was credited with having 170 votes. His six opponents received none. In actuality, the "leader" had only 12 votes, and his opponents split the other 158.

Despite the fact that the details of St. Louis elections had been exposed, the cheating only grew more open, and Dickmann himself paid no price at the ballot box for his own role in rigging the bond issue count. In 1937, when Dickmann ran for re-election, his Republican opponent tried to highlight the fraud involved in the 1935 bond-issue matter, saying the election had been "stolen." A thoroughly unimpressed Dickmann cruised to an easy re-election victory.

"A Miscarriage of Justice"

The supporters of the memorial encountered more resistance. Due to pending suits launched by the Citizens' Non-Partisan Committee, banking groups refused to bid on any of the bonds offered in April 1936. The next month, thirty-six property owners within the proposed site sued to stop Interior Secretary Ickes from releasing any federal funds to begin the project. Edmund Toland, the attorney for the property owners, claimed that the project was "a grand scheme to get rid of this property at the expense of the Government of the United States." Toland outlined the general zones of downtown businesses, and argued that promoters of the project "decided that if they could vacate" the riverfront district, "then the leaseholders would have to move." Toland summarized:

> That's the scheme. It's not intended to memorialize Thomas Jefferson or anyone else. It's a scheme to promote real estate value.

After a federal judge threw out the suit, the plaintiffs appealed, and by August the U.S. Court of Appeals had issued a temporary injunction against the federal government until it could hear the case in full. Property owners along the riverfront were delighted, and reported that business was "brisk," and that several new companies had even moved into the area. The business owners were also buoyed by the impending investigation into massive election fraud that also threatened the legality of the bond issue.

Responding to charges of fraud, Luther Ely Smith remarked that if "mere evidence of fraud" could stop the issuance of bonds, then all future bond issues would be postponed until after the required year had passed for the ballots to be destroyed. Paul Peters asked Smith where the memorial's supporters stood "when the mask has been torn aside and the fraud and corruption connected with the election made public?" What angered Peters so much was the enormity of the fraud that crossed a certain acceptable line. To Peters, it was "Fraud not of the occasional type, but fraud, so widespread and so common that it became almost general, has been established in each of the nineteen wards in which the bond carried." Furthermore, Peters was just beginning to see how even after the stories of fraud were revealed, most officials seemed to look the other way, none more so than those at the National Park Service, whose interest in building the project rendered it "entirely indifferent to the fraud." Smith replied that while "there may have been some irregularities" in the bond-issue election, he was sure that it "was freer from fraud than are most elections." Using a formula that allowed so many to dismiss rigged contests, Smith was confident that any "irregularities" in the bond-issue election "were certainly very far from being sufficient to affect the result."

Peters's attempt to overturn the election ended in March 1937, when the federal appeals court denied the property owners' appeal for an injunction. The court's opinion, written by Judge Josiah A. Van Orsdale, issued a thunderous declaration of the validity of the bond-issue election:

> We think that the action of the city of St. Louis in raising its portion of the money and paying it into the Treasury constituted an acceptance of the offer of the United States and resulted in a contract.

The court declared that the city of St. Louis, by passing the bond issue, had essentially entered into a binding contract with the federal government. The fact that the necessary margin was achieved by wholesale fraud was considered irrelevant. The election served as the city's signature, regardless of whether that signature was forged. The property owners tried one last appeal, this time to the U.S. Supreme Court, which refused to hear the case. Considering all that had transpired, the *Post-Dispatch* withdrew its endorsement of the project—something the paper did not loudly proclaim decades later when trumpeting the benefits of the Gateway Arch.

In May 1938, the Missouri Supreme Court halted any further examination of the widespread fraud in the bond-issue election. The court found that since the one-year limit had expired when the case was first heard, the ballots should have been destroyed. Even though the ballots were safely locked in a vault and ready for inspection by a grand jury, the court ruled that for all intents and purposes, those ballots did not exist and could not be used as evidence. The court admitted: "This may result in destroying evidence and covering up fraud." Yet Missouri law clearly stated the ballots were to be destroyed in order to preserve the secrecy of the ballot. "On the other hand frauds, coercion, and the sale of votes," the court reasoned, would be even more possible "if the secrecy of the ballot box were not strictly guarded." The *Post-Dispatch* called the decision a "miscarriage of justice" and "one of those instances where good law conflicts with justice, the interest of the community, and ordinary horse sense." Despite the overwhelming evidence that fraud had carried the bond-issue race, state and federal courts refused to intercede for a variety of reasons, and the election's results were carved in stone.

To those who had sued to stop the bonds, they really had no chance, considering what they were up against. Not only were the courts predisposed to dismissing what had happened, the power of those who stood to gain from the memorial project could not be denied. The most substantial group opposing the project were businesses like the Levison and Blythe Manufacturing Company, Hill Brothers Fur, and G. S. Robins Company, firms that leased property owned by real estate companies and stood to receive nothing from the federal government. They would either have to relocate, pay higher rents, or go out of business altogether.

"IT STINKS"

The frustration felt by those few who saw the fraud surrounding this "contract" did not go away. One member of Congress was not ready to spend the millions on a project that reeked of election fraud. Representative William Lambertson of Kansas proclaimed on the House floor that "The St. Louis proposal smells. It stinks." Lambertson discussed the revelations of fraud in the bond-issue election, and noted that throughout the rulings of the federal courts on the lawsuits challenging the project, "The matter of election frauds was given no consideration whatsoever." To Lambertson, the entire affair was essentially "a real estate proposition," by St. Louis real-estate promoters "to unload 37 blocks of business property in downtown St. Louis onto the Federal government."

As a member of the Interior subcommittee that oversaw funds for the National Park Service, Lambertson was indignant that the Park Service would acquiesce to being associated with such a project. "Think of the National Park Service leaving the lofty grandeur of the Yellowstone to dip into the cesspool of St. Louis." The very notion of using the pretext of a memorial to Jefferson struck Lambertson as odd. "There is no more sense in tearing these buildings down than there would be to advance on the city of Chicago, and demand the right to condemn half the downtown area as a memorial to the great historic fire created when Mrs. O'Leary's cow kicked over a lantern in 1871."

Lambertson's futile hope was that President Roosevelt would intervene and suspend the building of the memorial until the bond-issue
election was properly investigated. "Surely no one would want to proceed with the building of a $30 million memorial to that great Amer-
ican, Thomas Jefferson," Lamberston claimed, "whose principles of
honesty and democracy are beyond question, and have future generations point to it as a monument to fraud, corruption, graft, and waste."
Another congressman, Robert F. Rich, a Republican of Pennsylvania,
said the entire project was "Pendergastism, Dickmannism, and
machine politics at its worst." Rich pleaded with his colleagues not to
allow "the memory of the fraud and corruption behind the St. Louis
bond issue election to fade out with the memorial in the eternal
shadows." In time, Rich's fears would be realized.

Was Lambertson right? Was the project principally a real-estate
deal? Were the 37 blocks of condemned property as destitute as
advertised? In order to understand the origins of the bond-issue vote,
a central question is: Who would benefit most from the project, and
who would lose? To see the memorial project in its fullest context, it
is necessary to go back months before the bond-issue referendum. In
January 1935, backers of the memorial project met with Dickmann's
old board, the St. Louis Real Estate Exchange. The city's real estate
leaders heard an urgent appeal from the leader of the project to solicit
contributions in order to facilitate that Association's purpose of
building a riverfront memorial. During the discussion, one of the real
estate brokers mentioned, "I have been very much interested in some
disposition of the properties . . . for several years. I am speaking from
a selfish standpoint, as a real estate man." He continued,

> Of course, this is not supposed to be a real estate venture, so far as
> St. Louis is concerned, but it will enter into it more or less, because
> in taking the historical features in connection with it, it very well
> happens that that section is a section that has been on the minds of
> the property owners, real estate men, for a good many years.

Claude Ricketts, chairman of the Real Estate Exchange, was even more candid: he told those in attendance the project really had nothing to do with jobs or memorializing Thomas Jefferson. Those items served as essential political cover for the real point, to increase real-estate values downtown. "It has always been my idea that if we could make Fourth Street valuable," Ricketts claimed, "it is absolutely a certainty that Sixth and Seventh streets would continue to get the rent that they contracted to get for the next thirty-five years." Another member of the board spoke of seeing a memorial in Rome to Victor Emmanuel. When he noticed old buildings near the monument still standing, the broker saw it as a shame to the glorious monument next to them. Luckily, Mussolini's government cleared the area and, in the words of the St. Louis broker, "that wonderful monument stands there in all its glory. But it took a Mussolini to do it." Ricketts implored the members of the real-estate community to contribute all it could to help the memorial project, since it would ultimately benefit from the passage of the bond issue more than any other interest.

Perhaps what motivated the St. Louis Real Estate Exchange was something more than increased land values or the "tension" of accommodating more businesses in available space. Even more basic was a simple fact: Real estate companies held a sizeable amount of property in the 37-block area, and stood to make a considerable profit from the government's condemnation and purchase of land. Real estate companies owned eighty properties, nearly 28 percent of the total, and their combined assessed value was $1,479,950. Banks and investment firms owned an additional 29 properties valued at $360,540. All told, the city's real estate and financial sector owned 109 properties and 35 percent of the "blighted" area's assessed value. Three real estate firms were in the top five largest property owners in the area, and eleven financial and real estate companies were within the top twenty-one. Considering that the project's legal committee had been advised by "experienced real estate men" that the property in the proposed area would be condemned at a rate 25 percent in excess of the assessed value, it was simple math for the real estate companies of St. Louis to look upon a mostly industrial area as a new source of immediate income. In turn, its condemnation would immediately raise neighboring property values. The residents of the area, of course, would pay higher rents.

In the month before the bond-issue vote, the *Post-Dispatch* noted that hundreds of firms would be forced to move from the site if the referendum passed. "Real estate men are uncertain whether available buildings will absorb all the concerns in event of evacuation of the riverfront." What one anxious realty executive then said may have been more revealing than he intended. New structures would have to be built to accommodate the migrating businesses, he noted, but there was a problem: "Tenants east of Third Street have for many years been accustomed to low rents and possibly may not be willing or able to pay enough to create a large volume of new construction." Rather than empty warehouses or destitute buildings, it seems one of the major problems of the area, from the real-estate sector, was whether some of the businesses were capable of paying enough rent to suit their aspirations.

Four months after the election, the Real Estate Exchange produced another resolution backing the project—this time in prose that grounded their economic interests with the democratic consent of the people. "Whereas the city of St. Louis, by an overwhelming vote, authorized the issuance of bonds," the board wrote, by "wiping out this blighted area, it will undoubtedly produce renewed and extensive activity in the real estate market." The *Post-Dispatch* reminded its readers as late as the summer of 1939 that it now opposed the memorial project—not only because the results of the bond-issue election had been obtained by fraud, but also because "most of the funds would go for property," and not for the jobs that had been promised.

An indicator of the real condition of the "blighted" area was conveyed in 1939, when the final appraisal bill for the condemned property came to nearly $7 million, a whopping 65-percent increase over the 1938 assessed value. Interior Secretary Ickes, in fact, threatened to cancel the project because of the "excessive" nature of the bill. Ickes warned that the federal government would not support "a speculative real estate boom based on how much a landowner could get through selling a holding to the government."

Despite the claims of the city administration and the Chamber of Commerce, the reality of the riverfront was mixed. Homeless people were living in some abandoned buildings. Yet there were 196 businesses in the area that would have to relocate, along with their employees. To the forgotten people whose homes or businesses happened to be in the way of Dickmann's project, their lives were overturned in the name of urban renewal, all in order to make way for a presidential memorial. The relief that was promised to thousands of unemployed laborers also did not pan out. The property along the riverfront, which included several historic sites, was summarily razed and nothing was developed in its place for nearly three decades.* The only real outcome of the initial money spent on the project was the clearance of the 37-block area. Between 1939, when the area was cleared and nothing but a parking lot remained, and 1959, the memorial site obviously produced little income for the city. In fact, during these years the city lost an estimated $5.4 million in property taxes.

Who were some of these forgotten people who stood in the way of the memorial? One was A. W. Albrecht, who was not pleased with the city's offer for his property. Albrecht's business netted him $3,000 a year, a rather impressive sum for the middle of the Depression. The city assessed his property at $7,900, at which Albrecht wondered, "Will you please tell me where I can invest $7,900 to bring me an income of $3,000 per year?" Some of the angriest voices along the riverfront were fur and wool traders, along with a number of manufacturers, whose

---

* The riverfront area razed by the Jefferson National Expansion Memorial included the courthouse where the Dred Scott case was first heard, and several historic buildings noted for their distinctive architecture and once occupied by luminaries such as U. S. Grant.

dislocated businesses would never return anything approaching what they were then earning.

Mrs. Elsa Pappas rented a grocery store at Second and Valentine. She noted that she "supposed the memorial plan marked progress," but had no idea where she would go. "The government made no allowance for renters," she added. While the area noted that "real estate men have been thick in this district" as the appraisals were conducted, the same could not be said of the businesses that were being driven away. As one observer noted, the area was beginning to look like a ghost town, compared to the activity in 1935—the same time when supporters of the project said the area was virtually empty and "blighted."

"THE GREATEST MEMORIAL SINCE THE EIFFEL TOWER"

After World War II, Luther Ely Smith revived the plan for a memorial. An architectural competition ensued in 1947, and Eero Saarinen won the contract to design the memorial. Saarinen proposed an inverted catenary arch made of stainless steel that would rise over six hundred feet. Hopes for constructing the Arch, however, were dashed by the outbreak of the Korean War. Only by the 1960s did the federal government spend the necessary funds to begin construction. Nearly thirty years after the bond issue, the promised construction jobs finally came to St. Louis. When the keystone was completed in 1965, among those attending the grand opening was former mayor Bernard Dickmann, who boasted that the Arch was "the greatest memorial since the Eiffel Tower."

Interestingly, in the late 1960s, two more bond issues were presented to the voters of St. Louis concerning the arch. With both local and federal funds exhausted, the money to complete the park surrounding the arch was gone, and in 1966 a bond issue was put before the voters that would float $2 million in order to complete the entire project. Once again needing a two-thirds vote, the referendum failed to pass, getting only 59.5 percent of the vote. Yet just four months later, the same bond was approved in a special election, this time getting 69.5 percent of the vote. Heading the campaign to pass the second bond-issue election was none other than former mayor Dickmann, who told reporters afterward: "Never at any time did I think it wouldn't pass."

The story of the St. Louis election fraud investigation produced a sweeping purge in the city's registry rolls, and won the *Post-Dispatch* a Pulitzer Prize in 1937. Yet the remnants of the corruption remained unimpeded by either judicial intervention or journalistic outcries. The buildings were demolished and the businesses removed. Many of the accomplices in stealing the election rose to substantial posts on the national scene. Dickmann went on to serve as postmaster of St. Louis for fifteen years. Robert Hannegan became chairman of the Democratic National Committee, and fellow Missourian Harry Truman appointed him postmaster general for his efforts on behalf of the party. (In the bond-issue vote, Hannegan's precinct delivered 1,486 in support of the bonds to only 52 votes against. Later, 321 people swore they voted "no" in Hannegan's precinct.) Luther Ely Smith's dream of a riverfront development was eventually realized beyond their wildest hopes. The story of the thirty-year drive to build the memorial is a complex one, as some civic-minded citizens of St. Louis worked tirelessly to produce one of the most spectacular architectural and engineering triumphs of the twentieth century.

Yet that is not the entire story. Dickmann's public expressions of building a monument to the spirit of westward expansion was camouflage for less lofty motivations. His pronouncements about providing jobs were, at best, disingenuous, considering that the project actually contributed to the city's *un*employment, as dozens of businesses were shut down when property was condemned. Dickmann's maneuverings may be perceived as acts of inspired politics to exploit the opportunity afforded by the largess of the New Deal, but most contemporary citizens of St. Louis benefited little from the memorial. Those living in the downtown area paid higher rents for their homes and businesses. That was why they had opposed the bond issue in the first place. The only real, immediate winners were Dickmann's old protégés, the real-estate companies, which owned a good deal of the "blighted" area and made good returns on the federal money spent to buy their property.

Even if Dickmann had not intimidated city workers by acting as a "dictator," and had been motivated by nothing more than his civic-mindedness; even if it had been nothing but a well-intended jobs program bogged down by federal bureaucratic red tape, or a desire to beautify the riverfront with a dazzling architectural triumph; in the end, one thing remains. In 1935, the bond issue was actually rejected by the voters of St. Louis. The electoral victory for Dickmann and his supporters was obtained by intimidation and massive fraud. Once done, there was no looking back. Indeed, rather than overturn the election, the courts validated what had occurred and described it as an agreement to a contract. The Jefferson National Memorial was created in spite of the election, and it profoundly changed the lives of the people who lived and worked on the riverfront in ways that normal elections rarely approach. For those who exposed the fraud and were dismissed at virtually every corner, they learned a painful lesson—that an accurate election count sometimes is beside the point.

After the Gateway Arch was built, it became many things to many people. For the citizens of St. Louis, it symbolized their city as the Eiffel Tower had Paris or the Colosseum Rome. Some hailed it as a monument to Jefferson, or the Louisiana Purchase, or the hearty spirit that fueled the pioneers. In time, it was known simply as the Gateway to the West, and one of the most recognized structures in the world. For tourists visiting the Arch, the pamphlets read that the people of St. Louis had started everything back in 1935, when they approved the bond issue. In the end, the Arch stands as a monument to something more than what is usually carted out for tourists. The Arch vividly displays the power of a determined city hall and the clout of the city's real-estate interests to overcome staunch political opposition, and stands as a reminder of what a stolen election can sometimes produce.

CHAPTER EIGHT

"Consistency, Thou Art a Jewel"

"You have no idea how the people are intimidated, especially in depressed times."

Due to the lingering financial crisis produced by the Great Depression and the increasing power of those who could curry favor with the Roosevelt administration, the need to acquire and retain political power was magnified at every level. Consequently, some of the more seasoned practitioners of the art of delivering votes came to the fore. In their wake, the civic life of the nation was battered in ways not seen in such open displays since the Gilded Age.

PENDERGAST

After the exposés concerning the St. Louis election, one might conclude that that city was the nation's most corrupt in the 1930s. Yet one could make a strong case that St. Louis was not even the most corrupt city in Missouri. That distinction fell to Kansas City, run by Tom

Tom Pendergast of Kansas City. Credit: Missouri Valley Special Collections, Kansas City Public Library, Kansas City, Missouri

Pendergast, a man whose control of city politics generated considerable dividends. While St. Louis would one day boast of the Gateway Arch, the Pendergast machine would claim one of its own as occupant of the Oval Office.

Tom Pendergast inherited his position from his brother, "Alderman Jim" Pendergast, who had built his power base in the working-class districts of Kansas City's First Ward. When Jim died in 1911, Tom took over and expanded the ring and its patronage. With a barrel chest, a quick temper, and a penchant for gambling and cigars, the surviving Pendergast looked like what we think of today as the stereotypical big-city boss. Through favorable contracts, lobbying his powerful friends, and receiving bribes, Pendergast had grown rich at the public trough. His concrete company generated a small fortune from the contracts he secured to build the city's new airport and municipal auditorium. At the height of his power in the mid-1930s, Pendergast built a palatial home in Kansas City whose costs were estimated to exceed $125,000. Pendergast's source of power came specifically from the northern wards, which produced the gaudy vote margins to which many local and state politicians eventually owed their offices. When it came to winning elections for his candidates, Tom Pendergast understood that "The fundamental secret is to get the vote registered—and then get it out after it's registered. That's all there is to it."

STEALING SECOND BASE

Like all big-city bosses, Pendergast rewarded his friends with jobs, contracts, and access to power, and punished his enemies by cutting off these lines of patronage. One of his better-known friends was Harry Truman from nearby Independence. Truman was a failed haberdasher who, with the Pendergast machine's support, had won election as a county judge and, in 1934, a U.S. Senate seat.

Truman's victory in the 1934 Democratic primary was one that revealed why having Pendergast on one's side was essential on Election Day. Truman's major challenger, Congressman John Cochran of St. Louis, had strong support from Bernard Dickmann and the Democratic machine of the city. The election boiled down, in the historian Alonzo Hamby's words, "between the Kansas City and St. Louis politicians to see who could create the most votes." Neither city machine worried about a third contender, U.S. District Attorney and Pendergast foe Maurice Milligan. In St. Louis, Cochran beat Truman 121,048 to 4,614, while Milligan won just over 10,000 votes: In a three-way race, Cochran won 89.1% of the total St. Louis vote. In the Fourth Ward alone, Cochran won 5,568 to Truman's 8. In Kansas City, Pendergast returned the favor, and Truman won Jackson County by a total of 137,529 to Cochran's 1,525 and Milligan's 8,406— Truman winning 93.2% of the total vote. (In a previous race in 1932,

Cochran—then enjoying Pendergast's support—won Jackson County by 95,000 votes.) Elsewhere in the state, where the vote totals were tainted with a certain degree of honesty, Truman won 134,707 votes, Cochran 113,532, and Milligan 128,401, an indication of just how formidable Milligan would have been had honest elections been conducted in St. Louis and Kansas City. In all, Truman beat Cochran by over 40,000 votes. In the words of the historian Richard S. Kirkendall, Truman's victory erased "any doubt that Pendergast was the most powerful figure in Missouri politics."

For the rest of his political life, as he climbed from the Senate to the vice presidency and, finally, the White House, Truman was known derisively by his critics as "the gentleman from Pendergast." GOP national committeeman Barak T. Mattingly said Truman occupied the presidency due to "70,000 ghost votes" he had received in 1934 from Pendergast's machine. "Without those votes," Mattingly claimed, "Harry Truman's political career would have ended with the end of his term as Jackson County Judge."

The details of Pendergast's methods reveal the extent of the fraud to which his machine would resort. Even with over 50,000 phantom voters on the registry rolls, Pendergast used carloads of armed thugs to carry a 1934 municipal election against a Fusionist ticket of disgruntled Democrats and Republicans. The chairman of the county Republican committee wired Governor Guy Park describing the conditions in Kansas City as "intolerable," saying that more bloodshed would follow unless "this orgy of wholesale slugging and intimidation of voters is stopped." In a runoff race held later in the month, the situation only grew worse. One precinct captain was killed in a gun battle with thugs patrolling neighborhoods in a car.

In other areas of the city, ballot books were stolen and repeaters voted by the carload. A driver simply taking voters to the polls was assaulted, and one reporter was chased by gun-wielding men. The *Kansas City Star* decried the "reign of terror" that had seized the city's elections. A citizens' group supporting the fusion ticket went to police headquarters to demand protection for their voters, where they were met by the police chief's secretary who responded, "You're getting protection" and refused to do anything more. By the end of the day, approximately a dozen men had been beaten, one shot, and four killed, all of which was incidental to the city's acknowledged political kingpin. Pendergast remarked he was "tickled to death" over the election, as his candidate for mayor won by nearly 60,000 votes. A small Kansas newspaper commented that while the Pendergast machine won by killings and beatings, "we sent marines to Nicaragua to supervise elections."

The manner in which election judges were appointed in Kansas City was equally corrupt. Although judges of both major parties were to be on hand at the precinct as a check on one another, the Pendergast machine managed to evade bipartisan accounting for a less troubling system. Since ward committeemen were responsible for submitting the names of precinct officials, the machine surreptitiously placed over 250 "Republicans" on the lists who were all loyal Democrats. One African-American woman confessed to a reporter posing as a Democratic official that she would look out to protect party concerns, since "I've been a Democrat all my life." One member of the Pendergast machine responded: "We don't have to bother about voting them from vacant lots," he said, adding, in a not-so-delicate jab at his St. Louis counterparts, "we just see to it that the election officials are 'right.' " To one observer of the situation, the system of widespread fraud was well known in Kansas City and was a major contributor to the cynicism that so many voters had toward voting and politics. Vote-stealing was so much a part of the political culture of Kansas City that average voters had come to regard "the stealing of a vote akin to stealing second base in a baseball game."

In the general election in November 1936, no bloodshed occurred in Kansas City, but behind the apparent peace and calm was yet another electoral crime. In many precincts, all the candidates, from constable to President of the United States, received the exact same number of votes. To U.S. District Attorney Maurice Milligan, understandably sensitized to how fraud could be used to defeat candidates, this was too obvious. Milligan brought the case before a grand jury. The legal proceedings began by opening a sack of 95 ballots that had been altered from a straight Republican ticket to a straight Democratic one. The grand jury learned that when one WPA worker refused to go along with a machine plan to use names on a hotel registry in an attempt to falsely register fraudulent voters, he was told by a Pendergast man, "If you want to eat, help out here." One precinct worker, Chloe Albright, testified that after the polls had closed, she was confronted by a Democratic election official, Edson Walker, who told her, matter-of-factly, "You know we are not going to count those votes." When she refused to turn over the books, Walker threatened to take her "on a one-way ride." In time, Milligan convicted 259 people in the Jackson County area for election fraud. His work in uncovering the prevalence of fraud in city elections was not well received by Pendergast's Senator Truman, who after his presidency referred to Milligan as nothing more than a "dumb cluck."

In 1939, Pendergast went to prison for income tax evasion, a charge often used against powerful figures. Even after Pendergast was sent to prison, a new day for Kansas City elections did not arrive. In a 1946 Democratic primary, remnants of the Pendergast machine revealed that said machine was not quite finished. In races for county commissioner and attorney, the "leaders of the resurgent machine" sent word to support selected candidates for the respective offices. When the votes were counted, two Pendergast candidates won by 545 and 1,011 votes respectively, out of nearly 125,000 votes cast. Veterans of Kansas City politics recognized what had happened when the machine wards returned votes for the machine candidates of over 95 percent. The *Kansas City Star* sent reporters and hired students from a local law school to investigate, and eventually 5,000 people were interviewed.

Some patterns began to emerge. Approximately 45 percent of the election judges did not even serve in the primary; in some precincts the poll takers deliberately miscounted the votes, and in others there was no count taken at all: they were simply "announced" as Pendergast tickets (meaning that machine candidates received the number of votes equivalent to the number of ballots); and there was always the usual assortment of false registrations and voting the dead. Although Pendergast himself was gone, the remnants of his machine knew how to continue in the tradition of Kansas City politics.

OUTDUMMIED

Tom Pendergast and his machine still took a backseat to Louisiana in the hierarchy of corruption. After all, this was the state where Governor and U.S. Senator Huey P. Long ruled the state like no other individual had ruled in American history. The "Kingfish" may not have created the political culture of his state, but he and his cohorts took corruption of all kinds to new heights, and elections were where it all began.

Huey Long had grown accustomed to charges that he and his men dabbled in election fraud. His brother, and future governor, Earl, testified before a Senate committee that a day after one particular election, Huey was on the phone with a crony from the notorious Plaquemines Parish about a Congressional race between James O'Connor and "Bathtub Joe" Fernandez. Huey's discussion, according to Earl, concerned how the vote should be counted in the Parish. At first, O'Connor seemed to have won the race by 3,500 votes. But after Huey's phone call, when the Plaquemines count came in, Fernandez suddenly was the victor by 1,500 votes. The Long machine's hold over the St. Bernard Parish was on vivid display in a January 1932 gubernatorial primary, where Long's handpicked candidate, O. K. Allen, won 3,152 votes in the parish. His four opponents did not win a single vote there.

Long's support in the Plaquemines and St. Bernard parishes originated with a rival boss, Leander Perez. Few people in the United States
had the command of a local community as Perez did, and his hand-
picked candidates often received majorities of over 95 percent. When
Long ran for the U.S. Senate in 1930, he received 3,977 votes in St.
Bernard, even though there were only 2,454 registered voters. Alphabetical voting was common in the two parishes, and without Perez's
endorsement, rival candidates saw their chances for winning disappear.

Anti-Perez candidates, in fact, sometimes could not even get on the
ballot in Plaquemines and St. Bernard. When one candidate sought a
qualifying form, he was told at the courthouse that none remained.
Others who were able to complete the forms were later disqualified
because they had not paid the proper filing and postage fees. Twenty-
five anti-Perez candidates suffered this fate, while others tried to fight
their way onto the ballot by appealing to the state Supreme Court. If
successful at placing their names on the ballot, they simply lost by the
same outrageous margins as had so many before. Although rumors
swirled about virtually all of Long's own elections to various offices in
the state since the 1920s, it would be a constitutional amendment referendum in 1932 that would produce the most revealing reaction from
Long against inquiries into Louisiana elections.

As a freshman senator, Long had to answer charges before a U.S.
Senate special committee involving his own colleagues. In September
1932, Long's candidate, John Overton, ran against the incumbent
Democrat, Edwin Broussard, for the party's nomination. As in most of
the Southern states, the Democratic primary was the only election that
really mattered: the winner would either run unopposed in November
or against a hapless Republican who had no chance of winning. In this
case, Overton won handily, but Broussard contested the results and
requested that a Senate committee look into the Overton campaign.
Broussard's specific charges claimed that state employees were coerced
into supporting Overton, as well as other tricks used by the Long

forces to intimidate voters. In Leander Perez's St. Bernard Parish, for example, Overton won 3,080 votes to Broussard's 15. As the Senate committee began its work, there was no doubt in any astute observer's mind that the real subject of the committee was not John Overton, but the senior senator from Louisiana.

The strongest charges against Long and his forces concerned the skillful manipulation of the state election laws through the use of "dummy candidates." This was a familiar tactic in Louisiana. Dozens, sometimes hundreds, of candidates for local offices would be put on the ballot, most of them with no intention of ever serving if elected. The purpose of such a tactic was straightforward: Local election commissioners were chosen in Louisiana by lot, and every candidate for a local office could put forward one name for the pool. Long's forces paid the filing fees for thousands of such candidates in order to increase their chances of having favorable election commissioners chosen at random. In New Orleans, over a thousand such fake candidates were on the ballots, and each put forward a name to be chosen for election commissioner. All were Longites, while Broussard's side had only sixty. Such methods, of course, greatly increased the odds, ostensibly legal, of Long's supporters packing the election commission. Thus armed, the Longites could then control the election itself.

Huey vowed that he would never be "outdummied" by his opponents. Julius Long, another of Huey's brothers, testified that at least 50,000 votes were controlled by Long throughout Louisiana; when asked what effect Long's dummy candidates had on the election, Julius was candid:

> You would ordinarily think they would stampede, but the people of this state have been in such desperation for two or three years that they are absolutely afraid to go against the man who is going to win, whether he steals it or not. . . . They said "You cannot beat them. Don't you see what would happen? I will lose my job and starve to

death." You have no idea how the people are intimidated, especially
in depressed times.

The committee reported its findings without any recommendations.
Overton and Long took their seats, and both protested that the investigation was politically inspired.

THE PROPER PROTECTION

In November 1932, fifteen constitutional amendments were on the
Louisiana ballot, including two that were vehemently opposed by
Long's opponents—one that issued bonds to cover Board of Liqui-
dation expenses, and another that would enable the city of New
Orleans to purchase a ferry. Neither of the amendments seemed
especially significant at the time, but both were supported by Long
and both involved big money for the right insiders. All of the proposed amendments passed, but the self-appointed Honest Election
League looked a bit deeper into the returns, and found that in sixteen precincts in New Orleans, the votes to approve the amendments
important to Long were unanimous, and in twenty-eight others the
vote totals were all identical. Orleans Parish District Attorney
Eugene Stanley began presenting evidence to a grand jury that massive fraud had occurred.

As Stanley began his work, he soon encountered some of the means
by which Louisiana politics was protected from charges of stolen elections. The Louisiana Attorney General, Gaston Porterie, called Stanley
to ask him to drop the case, claiming that it would hurt the legitimacy
of the bond issues. When Stanley demurred, Porterie reminded him
that under state law, the attorney general could supplant a district
attorney in the prosecution of a case. On November 29, 1932, Porterie
did just that. He then met with the grand jury and soon announced

that no action would be taken in the vote fraud investigation. No one doubted who was really behind Porterie's actions.

The tension within the grand jury room increased. When the jury returned a "no-true" bill, effectively saying there was no case of fraud, the presiding judge, Frank T. Echezabal, refused to accept the verdict. The grand jury was ordered to go back and inspect the ballot boxes and conduct a "thorough" investigation. In June 1933, the jury once again returned a no-true bill, and another judge, Alexander O'Donnell, angrily refused to accept it. O'Donnell ordered an "open court inquiry" into the election, and appointed Stanley to conduct the investigation. By this time, the Kingfish himself had returned to Louisiana and seemed worried about the turn of events.

Soon, the Registrar of Voters was accused of scratching out the names of legal voters from the registry rolls, and the stakes in the episode were raised again. Huey felt that he had to stop it all. He conferred with Governor O. K. Allen on July 30; the next day, the governor declared martial law in New Orleans. His action allegedly came in response to the request by some of the grand jurors for protection. Yet for those who saw beyond this ruse, Allen's actions were nothing more than the Long forces using the state militia to intimidate the court system. One witness claimed he saw Allen sign the order in Long's hotel suite. What the usual amount of election fraud and political covering-up could not accomplish, the National Guard would. O'Donnell and Stanley proceeded without being bullied, and the remarkable sight of grand jurors opening up ballot boxes was conducted while national guardsmen placed machine guns on the registration desks. Realizing how this appeared, Allen suddenly reversed course (no doubt under orders from Long) and recalled the troops. To worried election officers, Long boasted that "no one need fear that any election commissioner will not have the proper protection to which he is entitled."

Meanwhile, a new grand jury was impaneled and their investigation proceeded. As the ballot boxes were opened and the votes carefully counted, wide discrepancies became apparent. In one precinct, the certified vote had given the amendments a vote of 177 for and 68 against. In the grand jury's recount, however, the actual vote was 59 votes for and 154 against. Throughout New Orleans, the vote for the amendments was reduced by over 18,000 votes. This was not enough to overturn the election, but it was suggestive of how creatively the city had done its counting. By September 1933, Stanley had brought indictments against 513 New Orleans election officials.

In December, three officials who were members of Long's circle were convicted of falsifying returns. With the pressure mounting, Long acted quickly, and had a special session of the legislature pass a bill saying that for election fraud to be proven, even ex post facto, prosecutors would have to show that the fraud had been done "willfully." Lacking the undisputed power to read minds, prosecutors dropped charges against the remaining 510 defendants, and Governor Allen pardoned the three convicted officials for good measure. Long's biographer T. Harry Williams summed it up: "Huey had kept his promise to protect the commissioners."

The New Orleans case and Long's handling of it have raised a number of questions among scholars of Louisiana politics and Huey Long. Why would Long and his machine worry so much about the obscure amendments, and the New Orleans investigation, when they were not especially crucial to Long's overall ambitions? The bonds had been issued and Long could explain the discrepancies as hasty counting done without "willful" intent. So why block the grand jury? Why declare martial law? Williams concluded that Long was in an "abnormal depression" at the time, and saw the ballot box episode as "another attempt to destroy him."

A better case can be made that Long also understood how his power ultimately rested on winning elections, and how even a seemingly insignificant race could possibly reveal the widespread methods of cheating that were so common and truly at the heart of Louisiana politics. Eighteen thousand stuffed ballots may not have been enough to change the vote on the amendments, but Long didn't need or welcome investigations by grand juries into the mechanics of how elections worked in New Orleans. While he may have been depressed, Long worked feverishly to have a special session make it much more difficult to indict election cheaters, and to protect the convicted commissioners.

By the end of 1934, all was back to "normal" in Louisiana; without the glare of the press and an investigating district attorney, Governor Allen could claim to FBI Director J. Edgar Hoover that the 1934 primary election was "the most peaceful election held in New Orleans in years." That "peace" would be disturbed the following year when Long was assassinated in the state capitol.

WOMEN AND THE HONEST ELECTION LEAGUE

Not all citizens of Louisiana were intimidated by Long or were willing to look the other way at his methods. The Honest Election League's women's division understood the root cause and went after the way election commissioners were appointed to their posts. The division hired attorneys to train hundreds of women in New Orleans in election law, and many of them became election commissioners. The women's division proved instrumental in helping purge thousands of illegal names from New Orleans voting rolls. In 1940, another group of New Orleans women (including the future congresswoman Corinne "Lindy" Boggs) checked poll books and conducted house-to-house canvasses to verify registration lists. The Long faction was not above using intimidation to harass these women, including using vicious dogs to frighten them away. Undaunted, the women went to the precincts and, armed with verifiable registration lists, challenged fraudulent voters.

Yet their actions made little headway against the powerful forces controlled by Governor Earl Long, Huey's brother, who beat his opponent by a two-to-one margin in the city, yet ultimately lost the governor's race in a run-off election marred by both campaigns sinking to ever-lower depths in race baiting. The atmosphere of Louisiana elections was not hospitable to women participating in any way, much less in the role of watchdog. The historian Pamela Tyler writes: "In places where swaggering policemen boldly flaunted their allegiance to one faction, where mayhem was not uncommon, where the simple act of placing a paper ballot into a wooden box could be accompanied by taunts, jeers, threats, or even fisticuffs, numbers of women certainly hesitated to cast votes."

EPIC

The Depression allowed some candidates far from the mainstream to become immediately competitive. In 1934, the novelist and socialist Upton Sinclair ran for the Democratic nomination for governor of California and shocked state and national observers by beating his nearest rival by a three-to-one margin. With less than three months before the general election, in which Sinclair would be pitted against the Republican, Frank Merriam, the fear that Sinclair's End Poverty in California program (EPIC) might begin a radical redistribution of land and wealth worried both parties in ways that dwarfed the anxiety Huey Long's politics produced in Louisiana.

One Republican organization, United for California, was prepared to ward off the Sinclair challenge. Former U.S. Attorney George Medalie provided some cagey suggestions to the group about how to challenge suspected illegal Sinclair voters, many of whom were transients. Medalie noted that while illegal registrants could be challenged in court before Election Day, courts usually sided with the voters. A more effective way, Medalie proposed, was for United of California to compose a list of alleged illegal registrants that would be filed with the prosecutor. The sealed list would be a source of great mystery, with no one knowing how many names were on the list. The important thing was that any Democrat's name could be on the list, and if a listed voter appeared at the polls attempting to vote, they could be arrested. Medalie stressed that legal voters who were uncertain whether they were on the list would be "scared away from the polls."

United for California filed suit against nearly 60,000 alleged illegal registrants, yet all voters who challenged the suit in court had their suffrage rights fully restored, giving weight to the argument that the list was nothing more than an effort to frighten away legitimate voters. On October 31, just days before the election, the California Supreme Court issued a writ prohibiting further purge efforts. The court ruled that the Republican suit was "a sham proceeding and a perversion of the court process. It can have no other effect than to intimidate and prevent eligible voters from going to the polls."

Perhaps part of the court's anger was fueled by a letter that a disgruntled member of Albert Parker's law firm released to the press. In the smuggled letter, Parker revealed that the true purpose of the Republican purge effort was simply: "to terrify many people from coming near the polls." On Election Day, Sinclair lost to Merriam by over 230,000 votes. Although in conceding defeat Sinclair claimed "the election has been stolen," the margin of his defeat minimized any claims of its actually being a stolen election. Yet had it not been for Parker's private confession, few would have suspected that the purge effort was part of an intimidation campaign instituted by the GOP. California would not have a socialist governor.

BLOODY HARLAN

As the Depression took an already corrupt election system to new heights, no area was more vulnerable to electoral corruption than the coalfields of Appalachia. Large coal corporations in eastern Kentucky and West Virginia ran their operations like small empires, and used their economic leverage to coerce local politicians to do their bidding. The control the companies wielded over their workers and their families was no abstract concept. Workers literally lived, shopped, and prayed in coal camps owned and operated by the companies. The power of these companies was everywhere, yet was never more on display than on Election Day.

In 1920, the Republican, Richard Ernst, edged out the Democrat, J. C. W. Beckham, by roughly eight thousand votes in a U.S. Senate race in Kentucky. Beckham was a former governor while Ernst was a corporation lawyer who was virtually unknown, yet Ernst won his seat due to some "late returns" from some eastern Kentucky counties. In Harlan County, Ernst racked up a margin of six thousand votes. The head of the state Republican party noted the irony of the situation— Democrats charging that fraud had made the difference for the GOP: "The Democratic organization of Kentucky, long the beneficiary of fraudulent election practices, now is confronted by an organization too efficient to be cheated." The practice of waiting until all other precincts had reported in order to know the number that was necessary to carry the day was a well-established art in Kentucky, where Republicans controlled the eastern part of the state and Democrats the western part. Republicans had always counted on Harlan County, and the town of Lynch, for special help when they needed votes.

Located in the eastern Kentucky coalfield, Harlan County was also home to the R. C. Tway Coal Company, which dominated virtually every local aspect of the economic and political world in which miners and their families lived, and knew which politicians would do their bidding in Frankfort or Washington. When the National Guard was called out to patrol the streets after a series of murders before the August 1933 primary, gunfire erupted at a precinct in the R. C. Tway Coal Camp. All told, an estimated five hundred rounds were fired in two hours, and machine guns and dynamite were even used in the "battle" in which three men were seriously wounded.

Three months later, in the general election, where the major issues on the ballot included an amendment to repeal prohibition, six men died in a shootout at the polls in the Harlan County coalfields. The election deaths, combined with the intense labor conflicts, gave the county its own national distinction as "Bloody Harlan." Countless other people were stabbed or beaten, yet the enormity of the violence was lost on the state's major paper, the Louisville *Courier-Journal*, which reported the killings on page four in a single column. This made clear to what extent violence and even murder had become an accepted part of election culture in the mountains.

In that same election in Harlan County, the race for jailer showed the ability of the Tway Company to deliver an election. The Democratic nominee, Clinton Ball, had beaten his Republican challenger by 8,212 to 8,003 votes. Standing out above all other precincts was the Tway precinct, where although the certified vote showed Ball winning by 626 votes to 63, an investigation revealed that no more than two hundred people had even voted in that precinct. The election officials in Tway had acted in the open, taking ballots out of the book, marking them, and placing them in the box, as well as compelling and intimidating employees of the coal company to vote for Ball. The officials knew two things for sure: Not rigging the vote would cost them their own livelihoods, and no one would dare question their tactics. A number of the false names voting in the election came directly from the coal company's payroll sheets.

The National Guard was called out yet again in November 1937 to restore order at the polls in Harlan County, and forty-one men, including the county sheriff and five of his deputies, were arrested on election law violations. In 1938, eight more men died in Election Day violence in Kentucky, four in Harlan County alone, where the race for jailer was a source of considerable fraud. More than a hundred sheriff's deputies controlled the polls, making certain that the "right" votes were cast and throwing out any "objectionable" ones. Chain voting and alphabetical voting was also widely used for the Democratic candidate, and whiskey was plentiful as liquid bribes. In the Black Mountain No. 10 Precinct, the ballot boxes were stolen the night before the election, causing nearly 500 people to be disfranchised the next day. Consequently, state courts threw out the results of the 1938 Harlan election.

"SOBER, SQUARE, AND HONEST"

Harlan County saw its most notorious election in 1942 in a race for the U.S. Senate between the incumbent, the Democrat A. B. "Happy" Chandler, and the Republican, Richard J. Colbert. On election eve, the local Harlan newspaper reminded its citizens that they owed it to the troops fighting in Europe to vote. "If you fail to vote, you are sabotaging the very thing they are giving their lives to preserve," said the *Harlan Daily Enterprise*, admonishing its readers to "appreciate this democracy by casting your ballot tomorrow." By all accounts, no one could criticize Harlan County for failing to cast their votes the next day. As a popular incumbent, Chandler had little trouble in disposing of Colbert in the statewide election, and won by a margin of 11,228 to 1,477 in Harlan County.

Yet Chandler's overwhelming vote margin in Harlan aroused suspicion. A skeptical local columnist wrote that "If there were 11,228 ballots cast in ballot boxes for [Chandler] then I am Hitler's first cousin." The editorial in the Harlan paper warned its readers not to worry that the votes might not be counted because, in words that could have been used to describe countless American counties by the 1940s, "nobody gives a damn about election frauds," but hoped the FBI might investigate the election nonetheless.

A few days after the election, a soldier from Harlan County wrote home about the coverage he had just read about the election: "Harlan County sends her boys to die for democracy and then makes a farce and mockery of democracy at home," wrote the soldier, adding, "Corrupt elections and democracy are opposed to each other." C. K. Whitehead, the local editor, agreed: "Our boys are ready to give all, and Harlan County gives her boys a carton of cigarettes each when they leave, for democracy, and then guts democracy by stuffing almost every ballot box in the county. Consistency, thou art a jewel."

The details of Chandler's popularity in Harlan County drew even more ire from angry Republicans. In the precinct located in the Harlan County courthouse, Chandler received 627 votes to Colbert's 17. In Verda, Chandler won 432 to 23, and in Pansy he won all but one of the precinct's 304 votes. In the Closplint precinct, Chandler won by a whopping margin of 425 to 2. In all, Chandler received 93 percent of his majority in Harlan from just 42 percent of the precincts. A cynical columnist for the Louisville *Courier-Journal* recalled that "the crooks" stealing votes in Harlan County "have grown bold, or old and fat and lazy, for these irregularities are obvious."

Dr. O. F. Hume, a Republican national committeeman, called for a Senate investigation of the election due to "ample evidence of wholesale fraud and corruption," but the Senate declined. Despite the Democratic majority's refusal, in 1943 a federal grand jury began investigating the charges of fraud in the Harlan County Senate race. Within weeks, prosecutors had indictments against nearly a hundred Harlan Countians. Indeed, careful inspections of the returns hinted that far from winning the county by a whopping margin, Chandler probably would have lost in a fair contest. In four selected precincts where Chandler had won by a combined vote of 740 to 70, the FBI calculated that Chandler had actually eked out a mere 195 to 186 lead.

Yet just as the indictments were handed down against the ninety-nine Harlan defendants, Federal District Judge H. Church Ford ruled that the indictments were invalid because no federal statute specifically outlawed ballot-box stuffing. According to Judge Ford, public protection against such "reprehensible election fraud" was covered by state law, and, therefore, no federal crime existed that applied to election fraud. Three months later, the U.S. Supreme Court reversed Ford's ruling, deciding by a 6 to 3 margin that ballot stuffing was indeed covered by the federal code. Writing for the majority, Justice Owen Roberts said that ballot-box stuffing violated section 19 of the Federal Criminal Code. "For election officers knowingly to prepare false ballots, place them in the box and return them, is certainly to prevent an honest count.

After the Supreme Court's ruling, the case proceeded against the ninety-nine defendants in Harlan County. Among the ninety-nine was the county sheriff, two members of the election commission, a probation officer, a son of a circuit judge, a state highway patrol investigator, a police judge, a former county magistrate, a former county jailer, a deputy court clerk, the superintendent of the Mary Helen Coal Corporation, and over fifty precinct officers. By the summer of 1945, sixty-five pleaded guilty or no contest, while six others went to trial and were found guilty. Twenty-one defendants had their cases dismissed, six had died in the interim, and one defendant's case was continued due to his military service. In all, Judge Ford handed down to over seventy Harlan Countians sentences that ranged from stiff fines to two-year prison sentences.

Throughout these trials, some of the defendants revealed the underlying dynamics of Harlan County politics. C. C. Ramey, a miner and a poll worker, testified that on the morning of the election, R. C. Collins, a mine manager for the Tway Coal Company, had told Ramey that "he wanted 300 votes for Chandler." Ramey added, "I understood it was that or my job." Judge Ford asked Ramey if that was the reason he stuffed the ballot boxes. "Yes, your honor," Ramey replied, "but my own motto is sober, square, and honest." An incredulous Ford wondered, "When did you begin to exercise that motto, before or after the election?"

Another poll official, Vess Cottrell, told the judge that Collins had approached him as well, and ordered a precise count that would come from Cottrell's precinct—250 votes for Chandler and 17 for Colbert. Another precinct officer told the court that officials from another coal company, the Harlan-Wallis Coal Corporation in Verda, instructed the precinct officers that Chandler needed a 2 to 1 majority. At 2:30 P.M. on Election Day, a "contact man" for the coal company came to the precinct, asked how the vote stood, and upon hearing a suitable margin said, "Close the box, boys, that's the limit." Following the testimony of Ramey and Cottrell, the prosecutor told reporters he was considering pursuing indictments against the coal company officials. Yet he never did. "The whole sordid business reflects the inadequacy of an election system which depends on the honesty and the loyalty of partisan representatives set to watch one another," the *Courier-Journal* editorialized.

One month after the close of the trial, another primary election was held in Harlan County, and early reports stated that voting was relatively light and that the general feeling among the county's citizens was rather "apathetic." Yet even in the shadow of the recent trial and its damning indictment of the county electoral system, nothing had changed. During the election, one man was arrested for running a chain ballot and another for voting under a false name. By September, five more were indicted for election fraud. In a move that displayed for everyone how little democracy existed in the coalfields, one precinct cancelled a 1947 primary election, the second consecutive time the constituents of the precinct were disfranchised. To those living in the coal camps, it was no surprise that the precinct was located in the R. C. Tway Coal Company.

PART THREE

The Path to
Popular Resignation

CHAPTER NINE

Uncomfortable Majorities

*"I don't think our poll managers would let a
dead man vote."*

S ince the 1890s, Southern Democrats had resorted to stealing
elections less frequently because the game was already decided
by the time the prospective white voter stepped into the booth. An
assortment of "legal" devices designed to disfranchise African-
Americans—poll taxes, literacy tests, white primaries—had all bccn
deployed to replace fraud and violence. Yet when white supremacy
was challenged in the South after 1945, Democrats were well armed
to defend it, especially on Election Day.

"GOD ALMIGHTY, SEARS ROEBUCK, AND GENE TALMADGE"

In 1942, Ellis Arnall, a progressive for his day, beat the incumbent, Eugene
Talmadge, to become the governor of Georgia. This was a surprising

Governor Eugene Talmadge of
Georgia campaigning in 1946.
Credit: Special Collections Dept.,
Georgia State University

development, since Talmadge was a quin-
tessential white supremacist, who had even
appointed a leading Klansman to head the
state highway patrol. Upon winning the
governorship, Arnall pushed through a
series of reforms, including lowering the
voting age to eighteen, abolishing the poll
tax, and revoking the charter for the Ku
Klux Klan. Yet Arnall was constitutionally
prohibited from running for re-election,
and as the 1946 election approached, Talmadge loomed as the leading candidate to
assume the office once again.

White Southerners like Talmadge were
especially on the defensive after the U.S.
Supreme Court struck down one of the hallowed instruments of white
supremacy. To avoid federal investigations of black disfranchisement in
general elections, Southern Democrats had used the primary election in
its place. Since the Solid South was firmly in the hands of one party—the
Democrats—and the Court considered the primary election to be a
matter of "private" discrimination, the primaries were places where white
Democrats could openly disfranchise African-American voters without
worry of federal intervention. However, in 1944, the Court finally abolished the white primary in *Smith v. Allwright*, noting that "the right to
vote in such a primary . . . is a right secured by the Constitution." With
this "legal" disfranchisement now outlawed, Democrats were left with
some old options. Senator Theodore Bilbo of Mississippi expressed it in
the most candid of terms: "The best way to stop niggers from voting is to
visit them the night before the election. I don't have to tell you any more
than that. Red blooded men know what I mean."

Gene Talmadge was ready-made for the campaign to intimidate
prospective black voters. He vowed that if elected back to the governor's

mansion, no black man in Georgia would vote thereafter. He portrayed himself as the defender of white rural Georgians: "The poor dirt farmer ain't got but three friends on this earth," Talmadge boasted, "God Almighty, Sears Roebuck, and Gene Talmadge." He was avidly supported by the Georgia Klan, which vowed to "punish" any African-American who dared vote.

Following the *Smith v. Allwright* decision in 1944 that outlawed the white primary, African-Americans in Atlanta await to register. Credit: Special Collections Dept., Georgia State University

In the July 1946 Democratic primary, Talmadge ran against James V. Carmichael, who was aided by the tens of thousands of new African-American voters registered after the *Allwright* decision. Remarkably, Carmichael beat Talmadge in the popular vote in Georgia, but Talmadge did not lose the election. In another clever device used by rural reactionaries to maintain power, the "county-unit" system was employed in Georgia elections, whereby counties earned "points" that were often nowhere near reflective of their population. Small, rural counties therefore had much greater weight than urban areas, and the influence of black votes in Atlanta, for instance, was minimized. Talmadge built his career on the system, knowing that all he needed for victory was to cultivate the sparsely populated rural counties while ignoring the urban areas. Thus, although more Democrats in Georgia voted for Carmichael, Talmadge won. Without Republican opposition, he was assured of going back to Atlanta as governor, and white supremacists throughout the state rejoiced.

Yet before Governor-elect Talmadge could assume office, he died of cancer. In most similar circumstances, the lieutenant governor would assume office, who in this case was the newly elected Melvin E. Thompson, an Arnall supporter. The reactionaries had to ward off a

Thompson governorship, and had one last ace in the hole—Gene's thirty-three-year-old son, Herman, who had received a handful of write-in votes. Talmadge supporters read the Georgia constitution carefully and saw that the lieutenant governor would, indeed, succeed the governor once the governor was sworn in. But what if the governor had not been sworn in? Then, an opening presented itself. The state legislature would be compelled to decide the new governor from "the two persons having the highest number of votes." Because the general election had produced no Republican opposition, a write-in candidate could conceivably become the next governor.

"These Are the Same Old Cracker Tactics"

In early 1947, the Georgia legislature convened to decide the matter. With so much on the line and with only a handful of votes in the offing, the politicos in the Georgia statehouse began plying all of the old tricks of the trade in support of the young Talmadge. When the official vote was recorded, Gene Talmadge had 143,279 votes, James Carmichael managed 669, a tombstone salesman named Talmadge Bowers had 637 write-in votes, and Herman Talmadge had received 617. Legally, the legislature would have to decide between Carmichael and Bowers. But word quickly spread among Talmadge supporters to scratch out Gene's name and write in Herman's on some selected write-in ballots.

In a display that would be repeated many times in major Southern elections over the next few years, the Georgia election took an unexpected turn when another ballot box was suddenly "found," months after the election. This one came from Telfair County, Talmadge's home turf. Fifty-eight new votes were found for Herman, pushing his total now to 675, making him the new leader among write-in candidates. As Robert Sherrill wrote, "There was no finesse, no effort even to save Georgia's face by delicate cheating." Rumors of bribes circulated in the statehouse, but the outcome was never really in doubt. By day's end, the Democrats in the legislature selected "Hummon" as the state's next governor, although he had received a grand total of just 617 votes from the Georgia electorate, a microscopic .004 share of the vote.

The race for governor was far from over, however. An incensed Governor Arnall called Herman Talmadge "a pretender" and refused to acknowledge him as the legitimate chief executive. Throughout the night, as tensions flared, Talmadge forces changed the locks and prevented Arnall from entering his office the next morning. Arnall eventually changed his mind and relinquished his office, but felt confident the courts would throw out the legislature's actions and install Lt. Governor-elect Thompson as the new governor. In the meantime, Herman Talmadge was sworn in. As if the charade his partisans had just undertaken were not enough, Talmadge had the state legislature repeal all laws regarding primary elections. Then, the real story of Talmadge's "election" was revealed.

The source for the revelation was the *Atlanta Journal* (whose motto was that it "covers Dixie like the dew"), which began investigating the voting methods used in Telfair County. In the critical precinct of Helena, where the mysterious extra votes were found to make Herman governor, names of dead and nonexistent people were discovered to have been voted in the November election. In many offices, the figure (1) was placed before certified vote totals to automatically add one hundred votes to the totals. In the Temperance precinct, for example, Gene Talmadge was credited with 127 votes, although only 27 were ballots were cast. Thirty-four names were found to have voted in alphabetical order, and a total of six hundred more votes were certified from the county than actually voted. The manner in which these voters were distributed was odd. After the first fifty-five names, which corresponded to Gene Talmadge's total, the next thirty-four were in alphabetical order. When the *Journal* sent their reporter George Goodwin to Telfair County to interview some of the thirty-four people who had voted in alphabetical order, what he discovered was not surprising. Most of the people could not be located, and many of those who were found stated they had not voted that November. Olin Dennis, in fact, told Goodwin she had never voted in her entire life, and her husband, who was listed as having voted before her, had been dead for seven years.

Governor Talmadge reacted with considerable anger. He issued a blistering statement that accused the *Journal* of "yellow journalism," and said that the paper's publishers were "mad because they couldn't keep the white primary destroyed. They are mad because they could not destroy the county unit system." And, Talmadge insisted, the paper was "mad because they cannot control Georgia politics." Members of the legislature who opposed Talmadge did not see things in the same light. Representative Myer Goldberg said "the claim of Herman Talmadge to the governorship was conceived in conscienceless fraud." Representative William S. Morris was familiar with the outlines of the voting mechanics in Telfair, because "These are the same old Cracker tactics that were employed so successfully for so many years in Augusta."

It was clear why one of Talmadge's priorities as the new governor was to repeal all laws regarding Georgia's primary elections. "Even under the protection of the law trickery like this is used," said one mayor, who asked, "How much more will it be used without safeguards against fraud?" Some outraged citizens voiced their concerns. H. H. Sapp wrote that politicians like Talmadge managed to "keep our state in poverty and its citizenry in turmoil over frivolous issues." Sapp pleaded: "Give us a chance to get a clean slate where an honest election, based on the sanity of the people to choose an honest governor may be held."

In the State Senate, Sen. E. F. Griffith of Eatonton, a leader of the anti-Talmadge forces, noted that "Most people in Georgia just waste their time in going to the polls at all, because the election officers count their votes the way they want to count them anyway." Talmadge's cronies, however, were not impressed by the stories coming out of Telfair County. Sen. Iris Blitch of Homerville attacked the *Journal* as "that piece of yellow journalism" that everyone knew "was northern-owned and has as a policy of the division of this state. They deserve really no reply." Others were less irate. Sen. L. T. Mitchell of Clayton had heard enough about the election and the alleged irregularities, and urged his colleagues to "get down to business and do something."

Two weeks later, the state Supreme Court did just that. It declared M. E. Thompson was the rightful governor, not Herman Talmadge. The 5–2 decision did not mention anything about the Telfair County fraud, and ruled along more technical lines that the legislature "had no jurisdiction to elect the Honorable Herman Talmadge or any other person as governor." The court ruled that Lt. Gov. Thompson was the only one legally able to ascend to the governorship, and a special gubernatorial election would have to be held the following year. Talmadge accepted the Court's order as humbly as he could, clearing out his desk within minutes and simply smiling when asked if he planned to run for governor in 1948.

The following year, Talmadge beat Thompson by 40,000 votes out of over 600,000 cast, calling his return to the governorship a "restoration." Talmadge stated his politics clearly for all Georgia voters: "My platform has one plank . . . my unalterable opposition to all forms of 'civil rights' programs." Not surprisingly, Talmadge was keenly interested in matters pertaining to elections, and openly vowed that he would use voting-list purges and literacy tests to keep African-Americans from voting in Georgia.

The forces that had tried to stuff the younger Talmadge down the throats of Georgia's voters and legislature finally had their man in office without having to resort to the trickery used in 1947. But memories of how their methods had been revealed in Telfair County were vivid. As in so many other Southern counties, whites in Telfair County did not react to these exposés kindly. A bomb went off at the home of one of the *Journal*'s reporters. One minister who dared to tell his congregation they should not "put the name of Talmadge before God" was fired and quickly left the county.

"WE DIDN'T STEAL AS MANY COUNTIES AS YOU THINK"

Fraudulent elections followed Talmadge. In 1950, he was challenged for the governorship by former Governor Thompson. On primary day in late June, Thompson was ahead of Talmadge by 6,000 votes approaching midnight and held a slight lead in the county units. Suddenly, the returns stopped coming in for several hours. Then, some counties that had reported that Thompson had won reversed course and now proclaimed Talmadge the winner. In Chatham County, Thompson led by nearly four hundred votes in the first reports, only to lose to Talmadge by over 6,000. The biggest turnaround came in Fulton County, where the first returns had Thompson with a commanding 16,000-vote lead. In the final returns, Talmadge won by 8,000 votes, a margin that seemed very dubious late on Election Night.

Talmadge's campaign, using white supremacy as their battle charge and justification for cooking the numbers, had been down this road before. They knew the popular vote was meaningless: In the county-unit count, Talmadge won by a veritable landslide, 305–115. Roy Harris, one of Talmadge's henchmen, later revealed to Thompson, "M. E., we didn't steal as many counties as you think." How many counties were actually stolen? Harris replied "Only about thirty-five." Whether the voters of Georgia installed him as governor, Talmadge had already shown, really did not matter. To Talmadge and his forces, the only thing that counted was winning, and beating back "northern-inspired" challenges bent on promoting civil rights.

In 1955, following the *Brown v. Board of Education* decision outlawing segregated public schools, Talmadge penned his political views in a pamphlet, *You and Segregation.* Talmadge railed at the black "bloc vote" that threatened to undermine Southern politics. The South needed more candidates, Talmadge urged, who "forcefully [believe] in Constitutional government, States' Rights and the preservation of our traditional separation of the races." More than ever, Talmadge warned, Southerners needed to be "United at the ballot." In 1956, Talmadge rode a united white vote to the U.S. Senate, where he served until 1981. For over thirty years, "Hummon" was a major power in Georgia politics, taking great pride in the support given him by the people back home, whether they happened to have elected him or not.

THE DUKE OF DUVAL

Just as Harry Truman would never have been a national figure without the Pendergast machine, Lyndon Johnson would never have emerged as a leader of the Democratic party and a presidential aspirant without the support of a number of powerful Texans who knew how to deliver the vote. In 1948, they were ready to put their knowledge to work in perhaps the most infamous case of election fraud in twentieth-century America.

South Texas, especially the counties along the Rio Grande, had long been the scene of some of the nation's most fraudulent elections. *Patrones* who controlled the area exercised daunting political and economic power over their workers, many of them Mexicans who had crossed the border. On Election Day, thousands of voters were imported from across the river to mark their ballots as instructed, and then were promptly returned. In Jim Wells and Duval counties, bosses ruled in ways that would have humbled Tom Pendergast. None was more powerful than the legendary "Duke of Duval," George Parr, who had inherited his role from his father, Archie. To be elected to anything in the region, and in some cases statewide, George Parr's support was essential. Without it, the truckloads of votes he could furnish would never materialize. Parr, in turn, made a fortune by manipulating county contracts, and owned, among other things, a 57,000-acre ranch which he paid for by "borrowing" a half million dollars from the Duval County government. The rest of Texas was no shrine of virtue on Election Day, but south Texas was the most notorious area for made-to-order majorities.

Parr's aide and feared enforcer, Luis Salas, later related how the Parr machine ruled: "Parr was the Godfather. He had life or death control. We could tell any election judge, 'Give us 80 percent of the vote and the other guy 20 percent.' We had it made in every election. I carried a gun all the time. Oh, I tell you we had real power." One of the election counters was Salas himself, who commonly fabricated any totals he liked without any regard to the actual vote. Salas, who had once ridden with Pancho Villa, had a direct system of producing the required majorities in his precincts. "If they were not for our party, I make them for our party." If Duval and Jim Wells countries returned enormous margins of victory for Parr's favorite candidate, no one dared say a word, not even in Austin. An indignant politician knew that Parr might be needed to provide a suitable return someday in another close race.

The 1948 election had a precursor in an earlier Senate primary election held in 1941, when Congressman Lyndon Johnson apparently beat W. Lee "Pappy" O'Daniel by several thousand votes. Johnson had obtained the support of the south Texas bosses such as Parr, who sent in the number of votes the Johnson camp had told them were necessary for victory. But Johnson broke a cardinal rule: Wait until your opponent reports all his votes before reporting yours. An overconfident Johnson wanted the numbers in early, in order to build his lead. After all of Johnson's votes were recorded and he seemingly had the election won, O'Daniel's forces reported some late returns that put their man over the top. A number of Johnson's aides, as well as the chairman of the Texas Democratic party, encouraged Johnson to contest the race. Yet Johnson refused, telling one supporter that he did not wish to have the details of the campaign and the election opened for Senate investigators—"I hope they don't investigate *me*," he said. For Johnson, it was a bitter lesson. If the opportunity to run for the Senate ever presented itself again, Johnson would not make the same mistake.

In 1948, that opportunity came, but it made the battle against Pappy O'Daniel look easy. Johnson's opponent in the primary was the former governor, Coke Stevenson. Stevenson had assumed the governorship in 1941 when Pappy O'Daniel won the Senate seat after his primary victory over Johnson. When Stevenson ran for the governorship in his own right in 1942, he won nearly 69 percent of the Democratic primary vote, the largest margin ever for a primary race. He broke that record two years later, when he received 85 percent of the primary vote. Part of his enormous margins of victory came from his support in south Texas and among the *patrones*. Stevenson had served as an honorary pallbearer at Archie Parr's funeral, and George Parr had supported Stevenson in four past races, giving him nearly 97 percent of the vote. But in 1948, Parr felt betrayed when Coke refused to appoint a Parr crony as district attorney in Laredo County. From then on, Johnson had Parr's backing. Stevenson's deeply conservative politics—he was fiscally frugal with the people's money, was a staunch isolationist, and had described the 1944 *Allwright* case outlawing the white primary as a "monstrous threat to our peace and security"—and frontier image were enormously popular. He was known throughout the state as "Mr. Texas." As the election approached, Gene Autry even considered producing a movie based on Stevenson's life. Defeating Stevenson in a Senate primary would take a miracle, or so it seemed.

On primary day in July 1948, the results were not surprising: Stevenson beat Johnson by 71,000 votes and won 168 counties to Johnson's 72, although in six south Texas counties—Duval, Starr, LaSalle, Brooks, Jim Hogg, and Zapata—Johnson won 98 percent of the vote. George Parr had dutifully delivered his share of the vote to the Johnson campaign, but it was not enough to overtake the popular Stevenson. Yet the election was not yet over. According to Texas law, a party nominee needed to win a majority of the vote, and since a third candidate, George Peddy, had received twenty percent of the vote to go along with Stevenson's 40 and Johnson's 34 percent, Johnson faced Stevenson in a runoff election to be held in late August. The votes for Peddy had come from very conservative eastern Texas counties, and since Johnson had finished third in the counties that Peddy had won, those Peddy votes were sure to go to Stevenson in the runoff. All Stevenson needed to do, in fact, was just pick up half of those Peddy votes to win.

"AS CLEAN AN ELECTION AS EVER HAS BEEN HELD"

That Democratic runoff proved to be one of the most contentious in historical memory, even by south Texas standards. A poll taken just one week before the runoff had Johnson closing Stevenson's lead somewhat, although the former governor still commanded a considerable 54 to 46 percent majority among likely voters.

On Election Day, Johnson's campaign poured massive sums of money into highly ethnic areas such as the west side of San Antonio, where votes could be bought by the truckload. In south Texas, Johnson's campaign was more vigilant than ever, especially in Jim Wells County, where Luis Salas was counting the votes. When Jim Holmgreen, a poll watcher, demanded to look at some of the ballots he was sure Salas was taking from Stevenson and putting into Johnson's column, Salas had Holmgreen put in the city jail.

Soon after the polls closed, some of the outlines of the election came into focus. Although just a few weeks before, Stevenson had beaten Johnson 2–1 in San Antonio, this time the money that poured into San Antonio from the Johnson campaign had bought thousands of votes, enough to give Johnson a 500-vote lead. Other counties began producing overwhelming majorities for Johnson, to the tune of 5–1. In the six counties that Parr controlled in south Texas, Johnson won 93 percent of the vote. Yet even with these figures, Stevenson still held a lead of 854 votes out of almost a million cast as the next morning dawned.

It would not be enough for Johnson's campaign to "find" a few more votes and overtake Stevenson like O'Daniel had overtaken Johnson in 1941. Stevenson's veteran aides were likely to hold out any last-minute returns or changes until they saw all that the Johnson forces had up their sleeves. As Johnson aide Walter Jenkins remembered it, "We didn't rush the people in the counties where we had strong votes. We rather hoped that they would hold back, so if there was any sort of fraud," the Stevenson camp would have as little time to react as possible.

After some Houston precincts reported suspicious changes that produced additional Johnson votes, Parr announced to the Election Board that one precinct in Duval County had not yet sent in its final returns. Originally, Johnson's lead in Duval had been in excess of 99 percent ("about the same percentage but not the same purity as Ivory soap," said one disgusted local), but Parr could improve even upon that. On an amended return, Parr reported an additional 427 votes, all but two of them for Johnson, which put his margin in Duval County at 4,622 to 40.

By Sunday afternoon, Stevenson's lead had shrunk to just eight votes, and by nightfall, Johnson suddenly held a 693-vote lead thanks to various "revisions." Stevenson decried the "bloc voting" in south Texas yet expressed confidence of victory. Not even Duval County's "peculiar position in Texas politics" could prevent it, Stevenson insisted. With approximately 10,000 ballots still to be counted, both camps were scurrying to find more votes. To John Connally, a Johnson aide, "It's tighter than a tick but I think it's going to be all right." Yet as the days passed, it looked as though Stevenson had prevailed. Six days after the election—an eternity in political time—the unofficial "complete" returns gave Stevenson a lead of a mere 113 votes.

Then Parr had one final trick at his disposal. When the Democratic executive committee met in Jim Wells County to certify its vote, every precinct came in as reported on election night, except for one. In Precinct Number 13, Luis Salas's precinct, where he had manufactured a vote for Johnson of 765 to 60, the tally was now different. When one of the committee members read the totals for Salas's precinct, the new total was 965 to 60. In the interim, obviously, one of Parr's men had simply taken a pen and closed the top loop of the "7" to create a "9." With the stroke of a pen, Lyndon Johnson was in the lead, by 87 votes. By about one hundredth of one percent, Lyndon Johnson was ready to claim victory. "I can assure my fellow Texans," Johnson said in his victory statement, "that I have won by a comfortable majority." Amid a swirl of allegations, Johnson was indignant: "Lyndon Johnson did not buy anybody's vote." George Parr was even more adamant, saying that the election in Duval "was as clean an election as ever has been held."

Stevenson and his supporters knew better. "I was beaten by a stuffed ballot box and I can prove it," Stevenson claimed. E. H. Shomette, the editor of the *Freer Enterprise,* a Duval County newspaper, dismissed any charges that improper voting had occurred there. While Shomette was certain that no more than forty people would have voted for Stevenson in Duval County, there was a disturbing qualification to his boasts: "At least they wouldn't admit it after the election came out like it did." Did democracy reign in Duval? Shomette understood that "It isn't democracy to have political machines and bloc voting, but I guess the majority of the people in Duval County are getting the kind of government they want." Such was the descriptive terminology used to rationalize the prevailing culture of corruption.

BALLOT BOX 13

Stevenson took his case to court, and his attorneys focused on Ballot Box 13. If the Stevenson camp could get the state democratic executive committee to throw out the 200 manufactured votes from Precinct 13, Stevenson would be back on top. Although Stevenson was not allowed to examine the voting lists, one official who did so informed Stevenson that the last 203 names on the voting list were written in alphabetical order and in the same ink.

A quick investigation of some of the 203 names did not surprise anyone—they had never voted in the primary, yet they all contained Luis Salas's signature. Johnson's camp was noticeably worried and decided to take the offensive. Johnson's attorneys went to a state judge and informed him that the Stevenson campaign was unlawfully trying to have the vote "thrown out on grounds of fraud." The judge ordered an injunction until a hearing could be held on September 13.

While the legal battle was being waged, so was the political one within the state Democratic party, where Johnson was anxious to have the party certify his returns so that he would be the party's nominee for the U.S. Senate in November. As the party executive committee met, a judge in Alice ruled against Stevenson and continued the injunction until a contest could be properly filed. Meanwhile, no changes could be made to the Box 13 returns, and Johnson's 87-vote lead held. The executive committee heard Stevenson's attorney claim that "The issue is whether Jim Wells County is to elect a United States Senator." In no unmistaken terms, Lyndon Johnson "was trying to get the office with votes of people who never appeared at the polls." When a committee member asked a Stevenson aide if he had any more information from Duval County, the aide responded: "I have never been able to penetrate the iron curtain around that county." Johnson's attorneys contended that any evidence obtained in Jim Wells was from "Latin Americans under duress." By the narrowest possible margin, the committee voted in support of Johnson, 29 to 28.

By that one vote, Johnson now had the backing of the subcommittee, whose motions were almost always accepted by the party stalwarts. A minority report was offered, claiming that Johnson had won with "palpable fraud and irregularities," but it could not carry the day. The convention accepted the committee report and made Johnson its standard-bearer in the November election. Yet the legal battle was not yet over: Stevenson's attorney went to Federal Judge T. Whitfield Davidson, asking him to sign a temporary restraining order prohibiting Johnson's name from being placed on the November ballot until a hearing could be held. The fraudulent votes in Jim Wells County had deprived Stevenson of his civil rights, his attorneys claimed, and Davidson signed the order. On September 21, Davidson suggested the bizarre option that the best way to settle the election dispute would be to have both Johnson's and Stevenson's name on the November ballot, which was quickly rejected by Johnson's attorneys. With that, Davidson continued the restraining order against placing Johnson's name on the ballot until hearings could be held in Duval, Zapata, and Jim Wells counties.

To ward off an unfavorable ruling by Davidson, Johnson's legal team, now composed of such heavyweights as Abe Fortas and Thurman Arnold, appealed to Federal Fifth Circuit Judge Joseph C. Hutcheson, arguing that Davidson had no jurisdiction in such a case. On September 24, Hutcheson denied Johnson's motion, ruling that since the Fifth Circuit was in recess, the appeal would have to wait until October 14, which was dangerously late in the game for Johnson if that proved a defeat. By law, county election boards needed to post the official ballot in public places, and have the ballots printed by October 24—just two weeks before the election. Johnson's legal advisers decided to take their appeal to Supreme Court Justice Hugo Black, the justice responsible for the Fifth Circuit.

On September 29, Black agreed with Fortas that a federal judge had no power to issue an injunction in a state election. With that, Judge Davidson then dismissed Stevenson's claim, and ordered Lyndon Johnson's name as the Democratic candidate on the November ballot. Stevenson's attorneys quickly appealed to the U.S. Supreme Court, which in early October denied the motion. A few weeks later, Johnson beat the Republican nominee, Jack Porter, by 350,000 votes. In Duval County, Johnson beat Porter 1,829 to 58 votes, the usual 95-plus percent. Despite the margin of his general election victory, Johnson would be forever haunted by the 87-vote margin that earned him the nickname "Landslide Lyndon."

Stevenson contested the primary election results to the Senate. In his statement, Stevenson underscored how Johnson and his forces had simply gone too far in the usual game of vote manipulation. The violation of the electoral code was simple: "This is the first time that the manipulators of the voting in those counties (Duval, Jim Wells, Zapata, and Starr) were not content with all-out bloc voting, but reopened the boxes in secret long after the election had closed and stuffed them with a directed number of ballots." Yet with the Democrats in control of the Senate, Stevenson's ploy had no chance. Johnson issued a public statement that must have embarrassed even his most partisan supporters who knew of the dynamics of the primary vote: Stevenson was trying "to overrule the will of the people," and the fraud charges were "flimsy."

Stevenson also asked the Justice Department and the FBI to investigate the election, but this proved as ineffective as court challenges had been, showing how personal relationships could color political activities. Johnson was friendly with the two most powerful figures who would decide whether to pursue the investigation. J. Edgar Hoover had been Johnson's neighbor in Washington, and Attorney General Tom C. Clark was also a close friend. When the Supreme Court refused to hear the case, Clark dashed off a letter to Johnson saying: "Congratulations, Senator, Perhaps that makes it 'finis.' " Not surprisingly, the Justice Department's investigation concluded that nothing illegal had occurred in the run-off election and essentially whitewashed the entire episode.

An interesting footnote to the 1948 election came two decades later, when Lyndon Johnson was in the White House. The Texas journalist Ronnie Dugger interviewed Johnson and inquired about the details of the 1948 election. Dugger later recalled that Johnson then went to a dresser used by his wife and retrieved a photograph of five men surrounding a ballot box marked "13." The men were a combination of law-enforcement officials with guns and political figures with suits, including George Parr's cousin. With a grin, Johnson proudly showed the photograph to his astonished guest. Dugger wrote that the president "held it forward to me with a kind of pride." When asked about the picture, Johnson said not a word and quietly returned it to its hiding place. Johnson well knew Dugger was not a hagiographer, but his need to show Dugger the photograph that memorialized the stolen election speaks volumes of the culture that countenanced election fraud. Later, Luis Salas confirmed to Dugger that the photograph was taken on the day of the run-off election *before* the polls had even closed.

The infamous "Ballot Box 13" used in the 1948 Texas primary race that won "Landslide Lyndon" his Senate seat. Credit: LBJ Library, Photo by unknown

"YES, IT'S TRUE"

The Texas election of 1948 produced a belated but definite verification from a future president, while another race that year generated an even more candid appraisal from a Southern Democrat—one with a considerable political lineage. Russell Long, Huey's son, defeated

Robert Kennon by less than 11,000 votes in a Louisiana Senate election in which the lead seesawed between the two candidates in the days following the election. Some odd majorities accumulated in remote areas, and in ways that mirrowed Duval County, Texas. In St. Bernard Parish, Long beat Kennon 3,039 to 121, and he received nearly 85 percent of the vote in Plaquemines Parish. In Plaquemines, Long's support by Parish boss Leander Perez was crucial. With a considerable volume of stolen and manufactured votes evidently coming in from these two rural parishes, some doubt was cast on Long's electoral legitimacy. Long and his supporters brushed aside such claims, casually noting that the number of votes in Plaquemines and St. Bernard was not enough to overcome his overall margin of victory throughout the remainder of the state.

Yet Russell Long soon fell out of favor with Perez, and the two became bitter enemies. Enough so that Senator Long, in a heated moment at a state party caucus at the 1952 Democratic National Convention, admitted some of the seamier ways one could be elected in Louisiana. He told an astonished audience:

> Yes, it's true that [Perez] gave me stolen votes ... I accepted all Perez did, the stolen votes and the ruse to confuse the voters by the marking of the ballot. I'm sorry that I did. I was wrong and I regret it.

The following day, after headlines appeared saying Long had admitted to accepting stolen votes, the senator quickly backtracked once he realized the political implications of his words, saying that the votes were not needed, and insisted he had not received a single stolen vote. In yet another revealing sentence, Long claimed, "I am sure I would have beaten [Kennon] anyway." The very fact that there was some doubt, even in Long's own mind, of his election in the party primary cast some shadows over his initial claim to the seat. Yet similar to Johnson, Long pressed ahead, won more elections, and became one of the most powerful members of the U.S. Senate before his retirement in 1986.

"THE GOOD, THE TRUE, AND THE BEAUTIFUL"

While Johnson and Russell were conventional Southern Democrats, an election in central Kentucky in 1948 displayed what could happen to a young Democrat who was not so mainstream. Edward F. Prichard, Jr., had been a New Deal *Wunderkind* during the Second World War, serving in a variety of posts in the Roosevelt and Truman administrations, all before he reached thirty. Prichard was an ardent defender of civil rights who helped craft the party's 1948 minority plank that prompted Strom Thurmond to bolt for the Dixiecrats. When Prichard returned to his home of Bourbon County, Kentucky, a Senate seat and, possibly, the White House seemed in store for him one day.

On the morning of the general election in November 1948, as officials opened the vaults in the county courthouse in Bourbon County to prepare them for delivery to the polls, the sheriff heard a distinct rustle within one of the boxes. Using his penknife, he extracted a marked ballot for the U.S. Senate race. In all, 254 marked ballots were found in the boxes before the polls had opened, all but one marked for a Bourbon county native, Virgil Chapman. FBI agents came to Bourbon County, and in the first week of their work sent various memos and teletypes to J. Edgar Hoover. At first, Hoover was uninterested in the Bourbon County case, and claimed that no investigation would be undertaken unless he was directed to do so by the assistant attorney general. This was the typical Hoover response to allegations involving election fraud. Yet when Prichard's name was mentioned as a possible suspect, Hoover suddenly reversed course and wrote in the margins of the teletypes "Press Vigorously and Thoroughly." By the spring of 1949, the case had been built against Prichard and his law partner, and the trial took place that summer. Because Prichard had confessed how he had obtained the ballots to a local judge who then testified against him, the jury quickly returned a guilty verdict and Prichard was sentenced to prison.

Prichard's case displayed how the role of Hoover and the FBI was crucial. While the FBI was ready to look the other way in cases involving the likes of Harry Truman's Pendergast machine and the election of Lyndon Johnson in Texas, Ed Prichard was a target of Hoover's from the moment he came to Washington. In 1941, Hoover had noted that the young Prichard's advocacy of anti-lynching legislation and elimination of the poll tax were very similar to the platform of the American Communist Party. Prichard's case demonstrated how a Democrat without the proper racial politics was a marked man. The lesson was clear: when election fraud cases came before the FBI, conservative Democrats could expect a friendly Justice Department and FBI to look the other way, while civil-rights advocates such as Prichard would receive a far different treatment. When the right people cooked the numbers or intimidated voters, J. Edgar Hoover considered that a harmless part of the game. When the wrong people stuffed ballots, it was an unconscionable crime that threatened the moral foundations of the Republic.

In his later years, Prichard admitted fully to his participation in stuffing the ballots. Yet he also acknowledged that election fraud "was not a thing in our county in which only thugs and other totally disreputable people indulged. It was done by the most respectable people who were leaders in the church." Prichard voiced the essential paradox of a democratic progressive trapped within a corrupt political culture:

I was raised in a county where monkeying with elections was second nature; my father did it, my great-grandfather did it. I was raised to believe it was second nature. There I was on the one hand with all those great moral and intellectual principles, believing I ought to stand for the good, the true, and the beautiful; and on the other hand thinking it's perfectly all right to stuff a ballot box.

Prichard concluded: "That's an absolute dichotomy, but that's the kind of dichotomy I got into."

"ONE PERSON, ONE VOTE"

By the early 1960s, a series of pivotal Supreme Court decisions had refashioned the structure of American elections, especially in the South. The power base of so many reactionaries in Dixie rested on the disproportionate power of rural legislative districts over more heavily populated urban areas. In Georgia, the county-unit system mimicked one of the problems of the Electoral College. While Fulton County contained 14 percent of the state's population, in the county-unit system it had only 1.46 percent of the vote. In Echols County, with a population in 1960 of just 1,876, one county-unit vote there represented 938 residents, while one unit vote in Fulton represented 92,721 residents. The votes of urban dwellers, consequently, were significantly diluted.

In 1962, the U.S. Supreme Court ruled in *Baker v. Carr* that such constructions violated the equal-protection clause of the Fourteenth Amendment. The following year, Georgia politics were the focus of another apportionment case that introduced a new standard in national voting rights. In *Gray v. Sanders,* the Court finally struck down the county-unit system. After considering the undemocratic nature of the Georgia system, Justice William O. Douglas, speaking for the majority, wrote: "The conception of political equality from the Declaration of Independence, to Lincoln's Gettysburg Address, to the Fifteenth, Seventeenth, and Nineteenth Amendments can mean only one thing—one person, one vote." A subsequent case, *Reynolds v. Sims,* also invalidated an Alabama districting system that allowed 25 percent of the state's population to determine a majority of the legislative seats. In that case, Chief Justice Earl Warren recognized the latent unfairness of the old system and wrote that "legislators represent people, not trees or acres. Legislators are elected by voters, not farms or cities or economic interests." Yet while the legal bastion of the old system may have been destroyed, older, more illegal methods were still at the disposal of county officials.

"YOU HAVEN'T LEARNED ANYTHING ABOUT VOTING MY WAY"

The same year that the *Baker* decision was announced, a young former naval officer from Plains, Georgia, named Jimmy Carter, whose only political experience to that point was serving on his local school board, ran for the state Senate. Carter was among a new generation of white Southerners who aimed to topple Jim Crow. Opposing Carter in the Democratic primary was Homer Moore, a businessman from Richland with deep political ties within his district.

Early on Election Day, Carter received word that the voting procedures were a sham in Quitman County, a small county of just 2,400 people bordering Alabama that was run by Joe Hurst, a cigar-smoking, fedora-wearing stereotype of a Southern country political boss. Hurst was himself a state representative and no fan of Carter's politics. Carter sent an aide, John Pope, to Quitman to see if the stories were true of Hurst rigging the election before arriving on his own later in the morning.

When Pope entered the courthouse in the county seat of Georgetown, he quickly understood that everything he had heard was probably an understatement. First, Hurst had moved the polling booth out of the courthouse and into the office of the county ordinary, a local probate judge who oversaw the election. Then, Hurst and his protégés lingered over every voter who came to the polls, exhorting them to vote for Moore. When one couple quickly placed their ballots into the box, hoping Hurst had not seen them, he simply reached inside the box and found the ballots, telling the couple, "You haven't learned anything about voting my way." He tore up the ballots and reached for two new ones and marked them for Moore. "That's the way you're supposed to vote," proclaimed Hurst, knowing full well he was being watched by a Carter man. "I have been running my county my way for twenty years," Hurst explained, and made a chilling threat: "I have put three men in that river out back for doing less than you are doing here today."

Due to the 224-vote margin Hurst's precinct in Georgetown gave Moore, Carter narrowly lost the election by 139 votes. Yet after seeing what had occurred in Quitman, where even the local newspaper reporters were friends with Hurst and refused Carter's indignant protests by casually responding, "Mr. Carter, everybody knows it's not right but this is the way they always run elections over here," Carter decided to contest the election. "I could still see the grin on Joe Hurst's face, and the image burned me up," Carter remembered, adding, "I had been betrayed by a political system in which I had had confidence, and I was mad as hell!"

Despite the looming odds against him, Carter went ahead with what he described as his "obsession." Carter's relative innocence about how Southern elections worked was subsumed by the injustice he felt in being cheated. Yet Carter was not alone; he was aided by the *Atlanta Journal*'s John Pennington, who wrote a series of articles that described how institutionalized election fraud had become standard practice in Quitman County. There were the usual accounts of alphabetical voting and false registrations, and after being confronted with evidence that a man who had died the previous summer was listed as having voted, Hurst himself claimed in one of the most remarkable responses in American political history, "I don't think our poll managers would let a dead person vote."

A man housed in the Atlanta penitentiary was also listed as having voted, as well as several large families who were out of town on Election Day. In all, while 333 votes were supposedly cast in Quitman, 420 were somehow recorded, and without this discrepancy, Carter would have won his seat in the state house. Carter's first legal recourse was to take his case before the Quitman County Democratic party executive committee, which was headed by none other than Hurst. Although no one in Carter's camp believed Hurst's committee would find in

Carter's favor, at least Carter could have his case placed in the record as prescribed by the Georgia Democratic party, which would then allow him to appeal. Yet the crafty Hurst outflanked Carter when on October 29 his committee refused to even hear Carter's complaint, which was the common outcome of so many challenges to local rural bosses on charges of election fraud.

Yet Carter refused to quit, and his legal team continued to interview dozens of Quitman residents to build their case. Later, Carter remembered being struck by how "so many were willing to endanger their financial and maybe their physical well-being to bring free elections to their county." Armed with a host of affidavits, Carter decided to take his case before a Democratic recount committee. That committee included a representative from Carter's team and one from Moore's team, and was headed by Judge Carl Crow of the Albany Judicial Circuit. For all intents and purposes, since any decision by the committee would be split by the Carter and Moore representatives, it came down to Judge Crow to decide the outcome of the election contest.

On November 1, just days before the general election, the ballot box from Georgetown was opened in Judge Crow's court. Carter's attorneys asked the judge to have the clerk simply turn the ballot box over, which revealed that the flaps on the box were folded together and not sealed. Much to the shock of observers, when the contents of the box were finally made public, the ballot stubs were missing, which would make any attempt to determine the disparity between those listed as having voted and the total number of certified votes impossible. Various elections officials testified that they simply could not remember how many people had voted in the election just days before.

Then a voter named Tom Gary testified that he was one of the last people to vote before the polls had closed. He remembered his ballot stub as 330, and he thought only three more voted after him. Remarkably, when an election official told Gary she thought over 400 people had voted, he asked about why he was just the 330th voter and among the very last. Gary was told that the absentee votes would make up the difference, which stood in contrast to the fact that no absentee votes had been deposited.

After listening to a long litany of charges against Hurst and his men, Judge Crow made his ruling on November 2. He noted the disparity between 431 ballots in the box and the testimony that only 333 had voted. He also described the testimony concerning the details of the Georgetown vote and the real lack of anything approaching a secret ballot. Then he came to his dramatic conclusion:

> The ballot box showing to have been stuffed and it being impossible to separate the illegal from the legal votes, if any, a majority of the committee finds that the Georgetown precinct vote should not be counted.

By throwing out the entire Georgetown election, Carter suddenly led Moore by 75 votes. Judge Crow's decision was one that few judges have dared to make in American history. By judging the Georgetown election to have been fraudulent, he not only threw out the corrupt votes, but in the process had also thrown out some that were legally cast. In virtually all similar cases, cries of disfranchising legal voters were usually more than enough to stop a judge from taking such a stand. The no-nonsense, conservative Crow had also proclaimed that "Under existing election laws, any election can be stolen." A defiant Joe Hurst and the Quitman County Democratic executive committee sought to hold the judge's finding in abeyance just long enough to legally keep Carter off the ballot, but the state party chairman, J. B. Fuqua, said Carter's name would be printed in time for the upcoming general election, which he won. In a few short years, Carter would be governor of Georgia.

In remembering the case, Jimmy Carter gave virtually singular credit to one man for saving his political career—John Pennington of the *Atlanta Journal*. While the rest of Georgia's major dailies ignored the Quitman County case, Pennington's articles kept the issue burning in the minds of Georgia's citizens and helped shape the legal and political maneuvering that followed. Like so many that preceded Carter's, most major cases of overturning a stolen election involve an energized reporter or newspaper revealing the details to an outraged citizenry and forcing some remedial action to occur. Without Pennington's articles, it would have been much easier for the Georgia Democratic party to dismiss Carter's recount effort. Along with a courageous Judge Carl Crow, Pennington helped restore some democratic integrity to Georgia elections.

The significance of the Quitman episode extended far beyond the fact that it established a future president's career: It also displayed how Southern politics after *Baker* was changing in some dramatic ways. Local rural bosses like George Parr and Joe Hurst would soon be replaced by large, well-financed, and centralized campaigns geared toward reaching voters in the urban areas. Television ads would instantly reach larger audiences than Hurst could bully in a lifetime.

Yet amidst the stunning developments, one constant remained in Southern politics—race. After all, in the same year Jimmy Carter won his election to the Georgia state Senate, George Wallace won the governor's race in Alabama on a segregationist plank that echoed Gene and Herman Talmadge's earlier appeals to white supremacy. In order to rid Congress and the statehouses of demagogues like Talmadge or Wallace, voter registration drives became a critical element of the civil-rights movement. "Give us the ballot," said Martin Luther King, Jr., "and we will fill our legislative halls with men of good will." The ensuing struggle between these competing visions of Southern elections was one that would ultimately redefine American politics.

CHAPTER TEN

"Elections Are Like Cement"

*"Candidates don't win elections. Precinct
captains win elections."*

O ver the course of American history, election fraud has naturally
evolved in response to changing political and social conditions.
By the 1960s, Election Day violence and killings, for the most part,
were no longer a routine component of political life. Ballot boxes were
not taken by thugs and dumped into rivers. Thankfully, mass importa-
tions of illegal voters were relics of a different era. Yet even more effective methods of controlling the ballot box had emerged, often in ways
hidden from our historical memory.

An example is the 1960 presidential election. In short, our collective wisdom tells us that John F. Kennedy beat Richard Nixon by a
slim margin in the popular vote; that part of Kennedy's electoral victory was grounded in some "irregularities" in Richard Daley's Chicago,
but these were probably offset by GOP chicanery in other parts of Illinois; and even in the face of serious problems with the results, Richard
Nixon valiantly conceded the race. In the end, it was simply a very

close race. The 1960 election and its aftermath can serve, therefore, as a laboratory for understanding how modern fraud works at the precinct level. It is also a telling reminder that what we remember about a critical contest often has little to do with what really occurred.

LEGALIZED BRIBERY

In order to win the 1960 Democratic nomination, Kennedy beat Senator Hubert Humphrey of Minnesota in a crucial primary in West Virginia. The details of how West Virginia was won are often overlooked in the making of Camelot. Winning the support of county bosses who provided the "slate" to their constituents was the key to winning in West Virginia. In effect, these slates instructed voters who the bosses endorsed for various offices, and those candidates who did not make it on the slate could count on certain defeat at the polls. In order to get on the slate, candidates knew that far more than oratory or debating skills were required. They had to outbid their opponents. As Robert Dallek has described, this was little more than "legalized bribery" that proved an expensive game in which Humphrey could not compete.

In Logan County, West Virginia, the local Democratic leader was Raymond Chafin, who also happened to work for one of the county's largest coal companies. Chafin initially endorsed Humphrey, whose campaign gave Chafin a total of $2,500 for various election "expenses." However, the way in which Chafin—and Logan County—ultimately became Kennedy supporters is instructive. Chafin admitted that James McCahey, a Chicago coal buyer and Kennedy supporter, came to Logan County to convince him that his initial support of Humphrey was misplaced. McCahey implored Chafin to support the Massachusetts senator and name him to a favorable slate. In return, McCahey allegedly gave Chafin $35,000 in cash. In Chafin's words, this money was for one purpose: "We bought votes with it. Regardless of what you want to believe, that's the way real politics works." The official results were enough to kill Humphrey's chances, as Kennedy won 55 percent of the vote in Logan. Later that year, twenty-nine people in Logan County were indicted for vote-buying charges in the primary. Before Lyndon Johnson was an active competitor for the nomination himself, or the vice presidential nominee, he alleged that Kennedy had stolen the West Virginia election.

Johnson was not the only senator (and future presidential candidate) to hold this view. Barry Goldwater, an Arizona Republican, authorized a secret investigation of the West Virginia election by a former FBI agent. That summer, when Goldwater read the agent's report, he remarked he was "utterly flabbergasted." The agent secured sixteen signed affidavits, each testifying to how Kennedy's forces bought the election. One stated he had not lived in West Virginia for over a decade but had run a county precinct and counted votes for Kennedy "regardless of what the ballots said." Others reported the extent of vote buying and of the Kennedy campaign buying "the organization strength" of numerous county leaders. Goldwater, acting on Nixon's orders, gave the report to Attorney General William Rogers, "fully expecting immediate action." Instead, Rogers did not publicize the report or follow it up, and throughout the campaign, an anxious Goldwater assumed "the whole, seamy, sordid mess" would keep Kennedy from winning the White House. Yet after examining the investigation, Rogers concluded that not enough evidence could be found to warrant prosecuting the case. Afterwards, Goldwater regretted having taken the report to Rogers rather than the press.

"IT WAS GOING TO BE ALL RIGHT"

As Election Day approached, the race between Kennedy and Nixon was too close to predict. With so much on the line, and considering that a handful of votes in a few selected precincts in certain states could make the difference in the Electoral College, the Republican general counsel Meade Alcorn warned the party faithful to "protect this election against election fraud." Alcorn was obviously worried that the Democrats might resort to "illegal votes in order to swing the election in closely balanced states."

It was no coincidence that Richard Daley's Chicago would figure so prominently in the 1960 election. As the electoral map played out, Illinois was crucial to Democratic chances for winning the White House. In 1956, Illinois had gone for Eisenhower, and with challengers for his own job as mayor emerging within the Republican party, Daley understood how crucial the 1960 race was for his own political career. Just as Daley had relied on countless precinct captains to deliver their precincts, the Kennedy campaign counted on Daley to deliver enough votes in Cook County to counteract votes Nixon was sure to receive in the southern part of the state. The precinct captains were the crucial cog in the Daley machine, since they served as the mayor's representative to the constituents of the precinct. Favors were always forthcoming from the captains, who expected the favor in return on Election Day from loyal constituents. When a store owner failed to vote in the 1960 primary, his precinct captain took notice and warned: "That guy is going to wish he had voted. The building inspector is going to visit him on Monday, and I can hear him crying now."

Chicago Republicans were also well aware of these dynamics and were noticeably worried as the election approached. Aiding them were the Republican newspapers of Chicago, notably Richard McCormick's *Tribune* and the *Daily News* and *Sun-Times,* controlled by Marshall Field IV, a descendant of the Chicago department store magnate. The *Daily News* began running stories in October describing how thousands of illegal names were on the poll lists, and showed how the Board of Election Commissioners was little more than an extension of Daley's machine, considering that 176 of 180 positions on the Board were held by Daley Democrats. In late October, David Brill, representing an organization called the Committee for Honest Elections, met with Daley to discuss the impending election and ways to prevent fraud at the polls. Daley dismissed the warnings, accused Brill of playing politics, and refused Brill's request to allow inspectors from the Honest Elections Committee to observe the election. To Daley, thinly disguised Republicans like Brill were doing little more than trying to intimidate Democratic voters: "You are in there to stop people from voting Democratic," Daley told Brill.

The presidential race was not the only one that concerned Daley. Perhaps even more important to the mayor was the contest for state's attorney. Benjamin Adamowski, a Republican, had won election as state's attorney in 1956 and, if he won re-election, seemed poised to challenge Daley for mayor in 1963. Additionally, from his post as state's attorney, Adamowski could take on Daley's machine and possibly expose its seamier sides in patronage matters and in the awarding of city contracts. For Daley, it became essential that Adamowski lose the state's attorney's race, as much as it was critical that Kennedy win the presidency. Indeed, to some within Daley's inner circle, it seemed likely that Daley was more interested in seeing Adamowski defeated than seeing Kennedy win. To secure the coveted post, Daley selected a former federal prosecutor, Daniel P. Ward, to challenge Adamowski. What most political observers understood was that while Ward may have been the nominal challenger whose name appeared on the ballot, Adamowski's real opponent was Richard Daley.

As the polls closed on Election Day, 1960, and votes were tabulated in the presidential race, it was obvious that this was a historically close election. Indeed, the popular vote in the presidential race was a nearly a statistical dead heat, with Kennedy winning 34,227,096 votes to Nixon's 34,108,546, a difference of just over 118,000 votes out of over 68 million cast, or .2 percent (Kennedy's popular vote margin should be seen in contrast to Al Gore's popular vote margin in 2000, which

exceeded a half million votes). In the Electoral College, however, the
vote was apparently not as close. Kennedy won 303 electoral votes to
Nixon's 219—a veritable landslide by 2000 standards.

Yet the ways Southern Democrats engineered their electoral votes
meant the Electoral College count was not firm. In Alabama, five
"unpledged electors" were committed to Kennedy but the remaining
six were free to bolt to the segregationist Harry Byrd of Virginia. In
Mississippi, eight unpledged electors also threatened to vote for Byrd
(with the addition of another bolting elector from Oklahoma, Byrd
actually won 15 electoral votes). In the unlikely event that recounts
would give additional states to Nixon, those unpledged Southern electors could prove troublesome for Kennedy.

Late on election night, GOP suspicions were raised when the
Democrats refused to release returns from over two hundred Chicago
precincts until they learned of returns from other parts of the state, one
of the oldest election tricks in the book. Theodore White wrote that
late on election night, Bobby Kennedy was on the phone often with
Daley, who told the candidate's brother not to worry—"Daley knew
which of *his* precincts were out and which of *theirs* were out, and it was
going to be all right." In Daley's own ward, Kennedy had won by
14,000 votes. Considering Kennedy had won the state by less than
9,000 votes, even uncovering a small amount of vote padding could
have significant consequences on the election and the perceived legitimacy of a Kennedy presidency.

In the days and weeks after the 1960 election, the GOP attacked
Democratic returns from two states that, if their collective fifty-one
electoral votes were placed in Nixon's column rather than Kennedy's,
would give the Vice President the Electoral College victory—Lyndon
Johnson's Texas, which Kennedy had won by over 46,000 votes, and
Richard Daley's Illinois.

Nixon and the GOP privately agonized over whether to concede
defeat and allow the vote returns to be certified, or to challenge the

election on the grounds of widespread fraud. Additionally, with the Electoral College set to convene in mid-December, the constitutional clock was ticking, and little time could be wasted if a recount were to proceed. If unsuccessful, Nixon and his party might appear sore losers who purposefully humiliated the country at the very height of the Cold War. Nixon also worried that a recount might diminish the presidency and American prestige abroad. On the other hand, if the recount were somehow successful, would the nation accept a President Nixon—who had received a minority of the popular vote—assuming office under such conditions? How would the nation and the world react to exposing the unseemly side of American elections? For Richard Nixon, an intense political brawler who relished a good fight, the thought that Kennedy and his father's millions had possibly stolen the race would haunt him for the rest of his life.

Heading the Republican effort at overthrowing the results of the 1960 race was the Republican national committee chair Thruston Morton, a senator from Kentucky. Morton walked a fine line between challenging the results and making his party appear as one that would not accept defeat. Days after the election, Morton stated carefully he was not "making charges of fraud," but pointed out that some counties in Texas cast more votes for a bond issue than for president. All along, Morton promised that a recount would be conducted in Chicago. He also called upon eleven states (Delaware, Illinois, Michigan, Minnesota, Missouri, Nevada, New Mexico, New Jersey, Pennsylvania, South Carolina, and Texas) to consider recounts, although at this early stage he admitted he did not think any such challenge could give the election to Nixon.

Meanwhile, Nixon put some distance between himself and Morton, declaring he was not in favor of seeking any recounts. Nixon was also careful enough not to use the word "concede," although future commentators would assume that he had. By the next week, the GOP centered their inquiry in eight states, headed, of course, by Illinois and

Texas. While Kennedy was busy selecting his cabinet, Morton and his supporters were forming a national recount and fair elections committee, and even by early December Morton claimed there was "an outside chance" of Nixon being proclaimed the winner.

Throughout November and early December 1960, a firestorm erupted in Chicago over the looming recount and the rumors that swirled about Democratic chicanery at the polls. Daley, of course, put up as many roadblocks to the recount as he could. Early on, the election board began the official recount by examining only one precinct a day, meaning that the entire recount would take years. When an official ballot application list from a suspect precinct suddenly disappeared from City Hall in late November, GOP officials were quick to declare it evidence of a "widening vote scandal" in Chicago. In that precinct, the Fiftieth in the Second Ward, Kennedy beat Nixon 74–3, yet only twenty-two people were registered to vote. Alcorn called for a wider investigation to see how the list was removed in order to bring those responsible to justice, and to "determine just which candidate did carry Illinois."

"BE HELD FOR NAUGHT"

Meanwhile, the charges increased in Texas. The Texas state Republican Party contested Kennedy's victory in the Lone Star State, claiming that "in many boxes" the votes for president exceeded the number registered, along with a host of problematic ballots. Most unusual was the use of a "Negative Ballot" in a number of Texas counties. Forty years later, the entire country would learn of the notorious "butterfly ballot," but it was preceded in many ways by the more imaginative Texas ballot. Since 1957, all Texas counties using paper ballots were required to use a uniform ballot, in which columns for the major party candidates, as well as the Constitution and Prohibition parties, were printed horizontally. The instructions read:

Vote for the candidate of your choice in each race by scratching or
marking out all the other names in that race. You may vote for all
the candidates of a party by running a line through every other party
column.

Prior to the election, the Texas Secretary of State announced that
county election boards could determine the position of the parties on
the ballot. A Democratic board, for example, would have wanted the
Democratic column placed first on the ballot so that partisans would
see it first and properly mark through the other remaining names on
the ballot. Also, the Prohibition party only ran a presidential ticket and
not candidates for other offices, making it hard to notice on the entire
ballot. Because of the manner of voting that contradicted what so
many expected when they went into the voting booth, inspectors
found countless ballots that did not have marks that removed all of the
candidates leaving one, and many that had not marked out the Prohibition ticket.

Democratic county judges were quick to count those "spoiled" ballots for the Democrats, while denying the same to Republicans.
Republicans were particularly upset with vote patterns in southern
Texas, an area where some counties had "spoiled"-ballot rates
approaching thirty percent. Additionally, thousands of discarded Texas
ballots had not been rechecked, which was required by Texas law. To
the GOP, even weeks after the election, the stories emanating from so
many parts of the Lone Star State confirmed what they instinctively
knew—Richard Nixon had been cheated out of the presidency. But
knowledgeable Republicans expressed real doubt about overturning
the results in Texas because of the electioneering skills of Kennedy's
running mate, "Landslide Lyndon." One GOP official lamented: "You
can't outcount Lyndon Johnson."

By late November, the state Republican party had presented violations of election law in two Texas counties, while the head of the state

Democratic party dismissed fraud charges and called Republicans "poor losers." The FBI, meanwhile, investigated whether the names of deceased people were on the voting lists as having voted in the presidential election in Dallas, San Antonio, and Houston. The state attorney general, Will Wilson, selected thirty-four precincts in Wichita County to determine if "constructive" fraud had occurred. If that were determined, then Wilson could have the ballot boxes from those precincts brought to Austin and opened to see if fraud had occurred in the counting of the votes. If he concluded that fraud had occurred, then a statewide recount could be called. Yet Wilson's limited investigation, merely inquiring into the results of one county was not enough for the GOP, which accused Wilson of attempting to "sweep it under a rug and forget about it." A district judge, J. Harris Gardner, denied the GOP a chance to examine the discarded ballots in Wichita County. A Republican attorney Hardy Hollers implored the judge to open the boxes, in order to better understand why approximately 150,000 ballots were not counted. It did not matter whom those voters preferred for president, Hollers claimed, "what does matter is that all these people were denied the right to vote." In ways that would be echoed by their opponents forty years later, the Texas GOP decided to press their case in federal court, arguing essentially that thousands of Texans had been disfranchised by "inconsistent actions of election judges in throwing out improperly marked ballots," and requesting that the election—in what would have been an unprecedented development—"be held for naught."

On November 24, the *Houston Chronicle* revealed that thousands of ballots had been thrown out by election judges without being rechecked. Texas law stated that a special ballot box designated "Number Four" should be the depository of all mutilated, defaced, or unused ballots. After the polls closed, Box Number Four was to be locked, returned to the county clerk, and then opened to see how many ballots had been discarded. In a number of counties, county clerks were apparently not even aware of the law and the existence of Box Number Four. In Fort Bend County, 9,083 votes were cast in the presidential race, and Kennedy won the county, 4,339 to Nixon's 3,301. Therefore, 1,443 votes, nearly sixteen percent of the county's entire vote, were not counted and should have been placed in Box Number Four. The county clerk, Ella Stubblefield, said she did not know that she needed to maintain such a box, and claimed she had "no way of knowing" why the 1,443 votes were not counted. In Wharton County, clerk Delfin Marek said he had no intentions of opening his Number Four Box, which contained over 5,000 uncounted ballots.

In challenging the election in court, the Texas GOP charged that the election should be considered to be of "no legal force." In addition to the 100,000 or so invalidated ballots, the attorneys for the state Republican party claimed that in Duval County, election officials wore pistols and "coerced Spanish speaking voters." In the 23rd Precinct in Angelina County, 86 people voted for president, yet the official returns showed Kennedy beating Nixon in the precinct by 147 votes to 24, and similar patterns were noted in other counties. One particular election violation was noted by Republican officials that would be later echoed by Democratic attorneys in Florida in 2000: "Thousands of improperly marked ballots were thrown out by election officials. But other election judges corrected improperly marked ballots and counted them."

"A SAD DAY IN AMERICAN POLITICS"

By December 1, Morton claimed there was still a chance Nixon could have the election reversed due to the prevalence of "shocking irregularities and fraud." In Morton's words, what he had seen on Election Day was a "national disgrace." And to make it abundantly clear, Morton did not mince words when it came to Illinois—"I have no doubt whatever that, based on the evidence, Illinois belongs in Nixon's column." While Nixon preferred to remain invisible in the Chicago recount, the same could not be said for Ben Adamowski, who lost his race by 25,000 votes and was vocal in his charges that Democrats had stolen the election. If any one was in doubt, Adamowski was blunt about the significance of what had just happened: "I don't suppose I would mind if it was just a matter of stealing the courthouse," said Adamowski, "but when the manipulations and machinations of a political machine are used as a vehicle to take over the White House, it is a sad day in American politics."

With the nation's attention now turned to election methods in the windy city, Richard Daley came out fighting. "The Republican actions are cheap charges for publicity," said the mayor. He even accused the GOP of using "Hitler-like" methods in the post-election dispute. Daley suggested that the press investigate voter returns from down-state Illinois, where the results were "as fantastic as some of those precincts they are pointing at in Chicago." When grilled by reporters, Daley admitted he never said there was no fraud in the recent election, only that it had never been proven. Adamowski responded that Daley had "rigged" the election and was little more than a "ward comedian." President-elect Kennedy dismissed the Republican claims, while Henry Jackson, chairman of the Democratic National Committee, stated that the GOP charges were "dilatory proceedings" aimed at delaying certification of votes from enough states to deny Kennedy an Electoral College majority and thus throwing the election into the House of Representatives. The Chicago recount effort, under a severe time limit with the approaching meeting of the Electoral College, worked over the first weekend of December in order to speed things along. After checking 69 of 863 Cook County precincts, Nixon had picked up 147 votes. Republicans reacted angrily to those numbers, claiming Democrats were illegally counting "spoiled" ballots, hiding incriminating voter lists, and delaying the overall process.

To bring more national attention to the events in Chicago, Morton flew there on December 2 and vowed to pursue every legal means to "preserve the sanctity of the ballot" and get firsthand knowledge of the Democratic theft. When asked about possible court action, Morton said the GOP was inclined to take the issue to court, especially "to find the absentee ballots which are still drifting around somewhere." Countering charges that his actions were simply to delay the inevitable or to cast doubt on Kennedy's legitimacy, Morton claimed that all those working on the GOP's behalf in recounting the votes were "rendering a great service" to their country. An outraged Daley said Morton should investigate the voting methods in his home state of Kentucky rather than "investigating his own propaganda." Daley further charged that the entire episode was a "GOP conspiracy to deny the presidency to the man elected by the people." Although Nixon claimed he wanted nothing to do with the recount effort, Morton himself stated that he was directed to go to Chicago in early December to oversee the recount efforts, all "at Mr. Nixon's request."

A thoroughly bored Mayor Richard Daley (middle) listens to a Republican effort to throw out the 1960 presidential results in Chicago in December. Credit: © Bettmann/Corbis

HAWAII

While most eyes were on Chicago, Hawaii provided another twist in the 1960 election saga. The first returns in Hawaii had Kennedy in the lead, but upon a recount, Nixon took over by just 141 votes out of nearly 185,000 votes cast. On November 18, Hawaii officially certified Nixon as the winner of Hawaii's three electoral votes. Democrats filed suit, claiming that Republican poll officials had counted illegal votes for Nixon. A circuit judge ordered seven more contested precincts to be recounted, and by mid-December, Kennedy actually pulled back into the lead by a mere twenty-one votes. With such a close margin and the seesawing of the two candidates, the same judge next ordered more recounts in additional counties.

When the Electoral College officially convened on December 19, Hawaii abstained. Ten days later, after a contentious recount, a judge declared Kennedy the winner by 115 votes. Republicans countered by claiming that a form of chain balloting had helped give Kennedy his victory and moved that the results be nullified. As President-elect Kennedy planned his cabinet, Congress quietly honored Hawaii's three electoral votes for Kennedy, giving serious credence to the fact that even after a vote is "certified," and even after the Electoral College itself meets, there may still be attempts to gauge a state's electoral count accurately, and, if necessary, changed.

SET IN CONCRETE

Lawyers for the Texas GOP continued in their quest to prevent the Texas Electoral College count from being certified, citing that a full recount was necessary to determine the rightful winner. In addition to the problems they had already highlighted, the GOP claimed further problems with the election. In Fannin County (home county of Speaker of the House Sam Rayburn), 6,138 votes were cast, yet only 4,895 poll tax receipts were recorded. Republicans were also wary of how votes were thrown out, which seemed to be based on party alliances. In Eagle Lake, where Nixon beat Kennedy by 475 to 357 votes, 234 improperly marked ballots were discarded. In areas that were more likely to produce GOP votes, the votes were thrown out in a much higher proportion than in heavily Democratic counties.

In some contiguous precincts, large discrepancies existed in discarding "spoiled" ballots. In Fort Bend County, Precinct One, which

had delivered a one-hundred-vote margin for Nixon, had 182 discarded votes. In Precinct Two, which went 68 to 1 for Kennedy, no
votes were discarded at all. The Texas Democratic party hired a
Houston attorney, Leon Jaworski (a decade later, Jaworski would pose
even greater problems for President Richard Nixon as Watergate prosecutor), who said the entire case was without merit and, besides, with
the meeting of the Electoral College looming, it would be physically
impossible to conduct a complete recount. Texas Attorney General
Wilson expressed the common opinion that little could be done to
correct the vote—"I have found that elections are like cement. When
they are set, they harden, and that's it."

By December 7, Thruston Morton told a Republican audience that
chances of overturning the election were "remote," but that not all was
in vain. The process of cleansing American elections was a necessary
and noble one, and that "the people will know about it regardless of
how much criticism is heaped upon my head." While the party chair
was presenting the public posture of only proceeding with the recounts
for the civic good, at the state level in Illinois and Texas, party workers
had not yet given up hope that Richard Nixon might still be inaugurated in January.

On Sunday, December 4, 1960, the *Chicago Tribune* declared
Kennedy's election to be the result of theft: "Most of the people of
Cook County are convinced . . . that the recent election of Nov. 8 was
characterized by such gross and palpable fraud as to justify the conclusion that at least two Republican candidates were deprived of victory." The paper made it clear that Richard Nixon was one of those
candidates. The *Tribune* was less confident that justice would prevail
and give the electoral votes of Illinois to Nixon. The system in place,
controlled at the precinct and city level by Daley, "places a premium on
fraud and protects it once consummated."

Despite the pessimism of Morton and papers like the *Tribune*,
hope grew on December 7 that Nixon could still win Illinois. After
recounting the ballots in four hundred Cook County precincts, less

than half of the total, Nixon had picked up 2,978 votes. The chairman of the Republican recount committee was confident that when the remainder of the precincts was counted, combined with a recheck of some voting-machine errors in other parts of the state, Nixon would win Illinois. Democrats countered that by their totals, Nixon had picked up only 481 votes. On December 9, the partisan recount figures grew—Democrats claimed Nixon had gained 943 votes, while Republicans said that the real figure was nearly 4,500 votes and added that even the Democrats' own figures indicated the existence of fraud in the November election. As Adam Cohen and Elizabeth Taylor write, "if the Republican count was correct, this canvass of less than one-third of the Cook County precincts, looking at only one kind of voting irregularity, had erased more than half of Kennedy's margin of victory."

"Substantial Non-Complementary Miscounts"

Just as it would forty years later, the recount issue came to an abrupt end on December 12. Notwithstanding gains for Nixon, judges in both Texas and Illinois stopped the GOP recount dead in its tracks and brought the election to a close. In Chicago, Circuit Judge Thomas Kluczynski—a Daley loyalist—dismissed two Republican lawsuits that challenged the Kennedy victory on grounds of alleged irregularities. In Texas, U.S. District Judge Ben C. Connally dismissed the Republican petition to recount 1.25 million paper ballots, ruling that the Federal courts did not have jurisdiction in state contests, and added that the Republicans had not adequately proven that anyone's rights had been violated when the Texas ballots were thrown out. Republican attorneys termed Judge Connally's ruling "impetuous" and "shocking." Two hours after Connally's ruling, the Texas State Board of Canvassers met in Austin to quickly certify Kennedy's twenty-four electoral votes.

Yet the fight was not quite over in Chicago. Nixon's supporters encouraged Adamowski to press ahead. As one member of the Nixon Recount Committee stated, the Adamowski recount effort "gives us a means of proving the fraud and irregularities perpetrated against the Vice President." The recount covered 906 precincts that used paper ballots, but soon bogged down over partisan haggling on how to count the ballots. When it ended in March 1961, Adamowski had only cut Ward's lead by 8,875 votes, with nearly 2,000 votes set aside for the judge to determine later. While these numbers were not enough to overtake Ward's lead, it was stunning evidence of how many votes had been underreported on election night for Daley's archrival from just those areas using paper ballots.

While the Adamowski recount occurred, an investigation was launched that would keep the 1960 election controversy in Chicago burning a while longer. On December 16, 1960, Morris J. Wexler, a Democrat and a Special State's Attorney of Cook County, was ordered by Criminal Court Chief Justice Richard B. Austin—an unsuccessful Democratic candidate for governor in 1956—to investigate and prosecute cases of election fraud in the November 1960 general election. Over the next four months, Wexler and his staff interviewed "thousands of persons" involved in the election and examined over 1,300 precinct returns. In April 1961, Wexler issued his report. Throughout, Wexler found "substantial non-complementary miscount of the ballots"—a more legal term for stealing votes—in various wards, such as the Ninth Precinct of the Third Ward, where Nixon was credited with only four votes, whereas a recount showed he actually received forty-four. An overall pattern was distinct in the precincts Wexler investigated; the miscount in the Ward–Adamowski race actually dwarfed that of the presidential contest. Daley's machine had been much more concerned with the state's attorney race and the possible threat Adamowski posed to the mayor than the presidency.

Wexler brought contempt charges against 667 election officials involved in the 1960 Chicago election. Elated Republicans felt that this vindicated their charges of a stolen election, although Wexler would not go so far as to assert that Nixon and Adamowski had actually won. Daley's machine trumped Wexler's moves by placing the case in the hands of a Democratic judge from East St. Louis. His bench rulings essentially eviscerated Wexler's charges, and in the end he dismissed all charges against the defendants. With that, any further inquiries into the working dynamics of the election were stifled.

THE COLD LIGHT OF THE NEXT DAWN

While Nixon kept mum on the issue of fraud in public, privately he harbored a deep bitterness over the way the election played out. At a Christmas party that year, he told guests, "We won, but they stole it from us." Morton never allowed the party faithful to forget what had happened in 1960. Six days after Kennedy's inauguration, Morton spoke before party regulars in Chicago. For Morton, there were unmistakable lessons learned: "We all have discovered the utter futility of attempting to correct voting irregularities after the fact." In words that could be used about thousands of races from all eras, Morton related the essence of political campaigns and elections:

> Exciting speeches at roaring rallies are important, of course. But in the cold light of the next dawn, the only realities are the number of ballots in the box, how they were cast, and how they are counted and certified.

In the aftermath of the 1960 election, both candidates tried to place as much distance between themselves and the election controversy as possible. Kennedy used humor to deflect questions surrounding the legitimacy of his presidency, once joking that his wealthy father was prepared to buy his son a victory but would be damned if he would pay for a landslide. There were also suggestions that before the election, Joe Kennedy had obtained the support of the Chicago mafia, led by Sam Giancana, and the votes the mob could deliver, in return for a promise to back off from investigating organized crime.

Nixon felt the sting keenly, although in public he tried to remove himself from the contentions of a stolen election. In writing his memoirs *Six Crises*, Nixon instructed his staff on how to handle the coverage of fraud in retelling his story of the election. "What I want is six or eight pages indicating how the fraud story developed and using some specific examples. In Texas—In Chicago, of flagrant fraud as well as any other states where good examples might be pointed out." Nixon concluded in his notes, "What we need here are examples and quotes from other people rather than charges being made by me on this issue." As the memory of the election faded, the collective notion that Nixon and the Republicans fought for recounts, and even to overturn the election itself well into December, faded as well. In Nixon's mind, however, the image of the Kennedys stealing an election preoccupied him, and was a factor in his obsession that Democrats would undertake the same methods in his reelection campaign in 1972. Nixon's "dirty tricks" unit—a perfect description of the culture of corruption at work in modern politics—stole confidential documents from Democratic candidates and distributed anonymous letters suggesting that leading candidates had committed adultery. The notorious "enemies list," as well as the Watergate break-in and cover-up, were certain legacies of the 1960 election, in which Nixon felt Illinois and Texas had been stolen from him by unscrupulous Democrats.

Was Nixon right? Did he rightfully win Illinois? No exact determination can, of course, be made. In the most exacting appraisal of the 1960 election, undertaken by the historian Edmund Kallina, Nixon picked up anywhere from 4,674 to 7,968 votes in the Chicago area, neither of which would have been enough to overtake Kennedy's official lead of 8,858. In Kallina's words, "The fact is no one can say with

certainty who 'really' carried Illinois in 1960, especially considering
stories of GOP irregularities in other parts of the state." On the other
hand, Kallina finds that the calculations give a clear indication of the
state's attorney' race, where he estimates Adamowski picked up over
30,000 votes, enough to overtake Ward. Kallina concludes that
Adamowski was "cheated out of the election." The usual dismissal of
the entire affair would be to counter that Republicans had probably
stolen enough votes in downstate Illinois that the margin Kennedy
won by was fairly accurate—all of which gives a certain legitimacy to
his presidency. Yet the details of the Chicago and Texas elections certainly reduce Kennedy's popular-vote margin in the national race.

As usual, calls for the elimination of the Electoral College were
uttered immediately following the 1960 election, but they quickly
faded. Senator Karl Mundt, a Republican of South Dakota, called for
a reform of the Electoral College, whereby the "winner take all" system
would be scrapped in favor of a plan in which the winner of the state's
vote would receive the two "at large" votes. The remainder of the state's
electoral vote would be determined by who won the individual congressional districts. Under Mundt's proposal, interestingly, Nixon
would have beaten Kennedy in the Electoral College, 282–269.
Mundt's plan, and other calls for a more proportional accounting of
the Electoral votes, fell by the wayside, as they have after every other
contested presidential election.

Uncovering the Daley Machine

As Tip O'Neill once said, all politics is local; even more, all elections are
local. When examining elections from a national or state perspective,
we tend to lose sight of the fact that how elections work at the precinct
level is the most critical element in the outcome. In order to see how the
Daley machine worked, our focus should not be on the national party,

or, for that matter, on deliberations within City Hall. Rather, the real source of Daley's power—and this was true for other power brokers across the country—was the precinct captains. Suspicions of the magnitude of fraud that occurred in Chicago remained under the visible political layer for another decade until a rather nondescript primary election in March 1972 blew the lid off Daley's apparatus.

In order to verify the extent of fraud in a typical Chicago election, the staff of the Chicago *Tribune* hatched a plan whereby several of its reporters went through the legal steps to qualify as precinct officials. Undergirding their approach was the certainty that unless a way could be found to get inside the Daley machine on Election Day, the knowledge of the working mechanics of Chicago politics would never rise above the level of informed rumors. Along with the help of a local reform organization called the Better Government Association, the *Tribune* was successful in placing twenty reporters throughout the city in official posts as precinct officials, all in areas known especially for wholesale fraud. Neither voters, local politicians, nor other precinct workers were aware that the new precinct officials were also reporters. From this vantage point, with an insider's view at the local precinct level, the scale of the fraud and the ways in which it was done in Chicago were fully exposed as never before.

It did not take long for the planted workers to see some troubling practices. Besides observing countless cases of workers illegally helping voters or even distributing partisan campaign literature, vote-buying and chain balloting were done out in the open. When one voter was offered a ballot by a precinct official, the voter casually replied, "I already have one." In the Twenty-fourth Ward, called by one local politician the "vote fraud capital of the world," two Better Government Association workers who identified themselves to local precinct officials were threatened with death.

But the *Tribune* reporters did more than merely report some of these disturbing episodes: They went deeper to explain the dynamics of how elections really functioned in Chicago in the early 1970s. To Philip Caputo, the precinct captain was the crucial figure in stealing votes. The captain, in Caputo's words, "stakes his crown on a set of numbers written on a tally sheet," as well as his "livelihood, and that fact explains why vote fraud is an ugly reality in Chicago's electoral process."

In urban political lore, no one is as revered and as significant to the success of a political machine as the precinct captain. Captains were the eyes and ears of the machine, and throughout the year provided the necessary goods and services to the constituents in order to display how much they needed to support the party in power at City Hall. If someone lost a job, they would usually call the precinct captain, who would find a suitable city job or a referral to someone who was hiring; if someone was short on funds, the captain could be counted on to provide a loan; if a sick child needed medical care, the captain would see to it that the child was seen by a good doctor, and the captain usually took care of the bill. Through these countless daily acts of compassion and service, the captains were the crucial cogs of the machine, the link between City Hall and the people at the grass roots. Consequently, on Election Day, precinct captains rarely needed to resort to strong-arm tactics. Rather, by virtue of having provided so many benefits that flowed from City Hall to his constituents, all a good precinct captain needed to do was to make certain that those who received those benefits remembered as much on Election Day.

Caputo explained that long before any election was held, the ward captain was called upon to provide to his ward committeeman the exact number of votes the favored candidate in a specific race could expect to receive. The committeeman, in turn, passed that prediction on to Mayor Daley, who would fully expect those predicted votes to be delivered on Election Day. After the election, the mayor called the committeemen together to evaluate the "performance" of each captain. In the words of one committeeman, if Daley saw a precinct captain not living up to his promises of votes, the words from the mayor would be swift: "Get rid of him." If this occurred, the captain would lose his city job and any patronage that went with it. Consequently, ward captains had everything at stake in virtually every election, and would do anything to protect their own jobs. As one committeeman explained, "Candidates don't win elections. Precinct captains win elections."

The pressure on precinct captains to deliver the predicted numbers never eased, regardless of the election or even the margin of victory. If, say, a captain won his precinct by a vote of 300 to 50, he was expected to return that same margin in every successive election, regardless of how Daley's candidates were doing citywide. A Daley opponent stated it bluntly: "Daley's man might be winning by a million votes, but if that precinct captain doesn't turn in his quota, he loses his job." The major ways in which captains could ensure that their numbers were always right involved stuffing the boxes before the election or "leveling" the count after the polls closed.

According to the *Tribune* report, one such precinct captain was Sam "Smitty" Smith, who controlled the Fifty-ninth Precinct of the Fourth Ward. Smith's workers spent a good part of the morning giving illegal help to voters in the booth, and sometimes giving the right voters more than one ballot. But it was not enough for Smith, who was under considerable pressure to deliver his precinct in a way that would satisfy the Daley machine. At midday, Smith had the votes counted (illegally) and determined that the Daley man had only 98 votes, way behind what had been predicted. "This may be our last time here," Smith declared, claiming that City Hall "pushed us too hard, too fast." The desperation was echoed by another captain, who grew anxious that he could not deliver his quota of 185 votes, which he unsuspectingly told a reporter was usually obtained by hustling "drunks off the streets, elderly women, and illiterates," usually from a nearby vacant lot. Things worked more smoothly in the Twenty-fourth Ward's Fortieth Precinct, run by Eddie Simmons, who personally distributed campaign literature at the polls and often went in the booths with voters to "help" them cast their vote. Closing the polls early, Simmons counted the votes, whereby one Daley man was astonished that a maverick challenger was actually credited with receiving 14 votes out of 280. "He shouldn't have gotten any."

No one was more open about how to get the necessary quota than Illinois C. Daggett. She might not have been the "official" captain of the Fifteenth Precinct of the Twenty-seventh Ward, but she ruled the polls, in the words of the *Tribune,* "with an iron hand." Daggett was a loyal Democrat who worked in the federally funded Model Cities program in Chicago, and spent most of Election Day instructing poll officials on how to do their work. Her very presence at the polls violated the Hatch Act, but such technicalities did not impede Daggett, who understood that her job was on the line unless enough Democratic votes were delivered to Daley's machine. When she allowed one couple to vote without signing the proper papers, Daggett said, "We make our own rules here." Daggett's work was successful. Democrats beat Republicans by 125 to 3 in her precinct.

Over the succeeding days and weeks, more stories came from the BGA–*Tribune* study, including one about a Democratic precinct captain in a polling place inside the Chicago Housing Authority senior citizens building who offered free meals to senior citizens voting for his favored candidates. In other areas, precinct captains threatened challengers with visits from local gangs. One of the precinct captains was a longtime veteran of Chicago politics who learned from a former alderman, Paddy Bauler, that "Chicago ain't ready for reform yet." To some Chicagoans, such as the Rev. Jesse Jackson, the reports verified what he had long suspected: "We have known for a long time the inequities of the electoral system in Chicago." U.S. Attorney General Richard Kleindienst ordered the FBI to investigate the vote-fraud stories coming from Chicago.

Crucial to the work of the precinct captains was making sure that the "right" people were appointed as election judges, including their Republican opponents. In City Hall, Democratic party bosses effectively controlled the GOP appointments, and essentially placed loyal Democrats in the posts of GOP election judges, ensuring that no real challenge to elections could occur. An astonishing 82 percent of Republican election judges admitted that they had been recruited and appointed by Democratic ward bosses. Of these, nearly 60 percent admitted that they were really Democrats. By now, attention was turned to Mayor Daley, who could only respond with a meaningless platitude: "No one is in favor of vote fraud."

Meanwhile, ordinary Chicagoans, perhaps for the first time in their lives, saw an opportunity to speak out about the ways Chicago elections were conducted. They knew firsthand how the culture of corruption kept free elections from occurring in the Windy City. In a stunning example of the enormity of the ubiquitous fraud, over 20,000 people signed a White House petition asking for federal marshals to patrol the city's polling places in the 1972 general election. Most of these signatures were from African-Americans, who had seen enough vote buying and intimidation. "Vote fraud is a way of life on the West Side," said Wesley Spragens, a spokesman for Power, an organization of twenty-one community groups working to reform the city's elections. James W. Compton, president of the Chicago Urban League, underscored a larger reality within the African-American community. "One of the most often noted reasons for apathy we find among unregistered voters," Compton said, "is that votes are so often miscounted or uncounted."

In September 1972, a federal grand jury returned indictments against forty Chicagoans, and more were on the way. At the state capitol, a special Illinois House subcommittee began hearings into Chicago elections. Stories of vote-buying, intimidation, phony judges, and ballot stuffing were rampant. By working to penetrate the Daley machine's Election Day army, the *Tribune*'s reporters were able to put a concrete reality to what so many had suspected had been there all along. To those who asserted that Daley's machine did not need to resort to fraud in order to win and that therefore fraud could not be happening, the stories destroyed their dismissals. It also vividly displayed the impediments that scores of challengers like Adamowski faced in confronting Daley's machine.

By the mid-1970s, Daley no longer had the clout in Chicago to reward Democrats at every level with certain victory, and a new presidential candidate felt the consequences. In 1976, Jimmy Carter was in a tight race with the incumbent, Gerald Ford, and desperately needed Illinois in his column. Although on election night Daley exhibited his usual bravado and promised Carter that one thousand precincts would be withheld until the results from downstate were in, things had changed in the preceding sixteen years. With increased state and federal oversight of Chicago elections, including the announcement of thirteen indictments for vote fraud on the very day preceding the election, Daley's machine could not deliver the necessary margins, and in what the *Tribune* termed "one of the cleanest" election days in years, Ford won Illinois by over 100,000 votes.

CHAPTER ELEVEN

Thieves Who Steal Democracy

*"Sales is all about understanding people and
their needs."*

T he passing of the Daley machine seemed to mark yet another
moment of progress in the nation's electoral history. Having
apparently put to rest the last of the big-city bosses and their
machines, the nation's collective electoral energies could be harnessed
toward other problems that plagued Election Day—namely, in
stanching the increasing number of non-participating voters. Despite
the various safeguards, elections in some parts of the country continued to be stolen on a routine basis. For election officials, protecting
the polls while encouraging greater turnout became increasingly complex and, at times, contradictory. Few understood that some of the
rising discouragement and demoralization stemmed directly from a
weary electorate long accustomed to the workings of "practical politics" when they went to the polls.

THE FREEDOM BALLOT

Southern demagogues such as Herman Talmadge of Georgia, Strom Thurmond of South Carolina, and James Eastland of Mississippi, had built their careers on preserving white supremacy, knowing full well they never had to worry about black opposition at the polls. Even by 1960, some imposing barriers stood in the way of African-Americans achieving the rights supposedly given them by the Fifteenth Amendment. Literacy tests and poll taxes still disfranchised millions. To those who could pay the poll tax, the bills would not be sent, or the receipts conveniently lost by Election Day. Mississippi had instituted a more difficult literacy test called an "understanding test," which white poll officials used with great latitude to disfranchise the most literate of black voters, while yet another grandfather clause allowed exemptions for white voters. Federal attempts to pass civil-rights bills were thwarted in the U.S. Senate, where Southern Democrats used their seniority to block hearings at the committee level, or filibuster any bill that managed to make it to the floor.

In 1957, Senate Majority Leader Lyndon Johnson helped pass the first Civil Rights Act since Reconstruction, although it was hardly a triumph of racial justice. The heart of the bill was the supposed protection of black voting rights, yet its reliance on jury trials to prosecute violators removed any teeth the bill might have contained. A Civil Rights Commission was nevertheless created and a Civil Rights section was elevated to a division of the Justice Department. By 1962, only 5.3 percent of Mississippi's majority black population was registered to vote, and only 13.4 percent of Alabama's African-American citizenry was on the voting rolls. As the other side of the coin to the previous "formula" that meant that those who were registered illegally could vote legally, those unregistered by whatever means could *not* vote legally.

In 1963, Robert Moses and other civil-rights organizers in Mississippi staged a mock election to demonstrate that the low level of black turnouts had nothing to do with "apathy." "The freedom ballot will

show that if Negroes had a right to vote without fear of physical or economic reprisal, they would do so," Moses said. In that unofficial vote,
80,000 black Mississippians voted, roughly four times the number
"legally" registered. The following year, the Mississippi Freedom
Democratic Party (MFDP) tried to have itself recognized as the true
representative of Mississippi Democrats at the Democratic National
Convention, but the national party, fearing it would lose Southern conservatives, refused to seat the MFDP delegates. In the midst of this
episode, yet another landmark moment in the democratization of the
franchise occurred in 1964, when the Twenty-Fourth Amendment was
ratified, finally prohibiting the poll tax in federal elections.

When President Lyndon Johnson signed the 1965 Voting Rights
Act into law, the right of all citizens to vote without fear of violence or
intimidation was finally protected by the federal government. The act
authorized the attorney general to send federal agents into counties to
observe election practices, suspend literacy tests, and challenge the
constitutionality of poll taxes in state and local elections. The historian
Alexander Keyssar has written that the act "bore a strong resemblance
to the never-passed Lodge Force bill of the 1890s." In those counties
where less than fifty percent of the citizens had voted in 1964, a five-
year moratorium was placed on a series of "tests" that disfranchised
voters, and those counties and the affected states could not enact new
election laws without the approval of the civil rights division of the
Justice Department. While barriers to voting still existed, the Voting
Rights Act put the federal government behind a black claimant's right
to vote, and the registration rolls swelled. The percentage of blacks in
Alabama registered to vote by 1968 had climbed to 57 percent, and in
Mississippi that figure reached nearly 60 percent. A dawn of a new
democratic day had seemingly arrived in the United States, as millions
of previously disfranchised Americans gained their right to vote.

In other ways, however, changes in American politics have made
vote cheating easier. Since the 1960s, the American electorate has been

segmented into easily identifiable groups that claim clear political agendas and preferences. While parties rail against "special interests," voters are often identified as belonging to some specific subset to which parties market themselves: the NRA, Baptists, the VFW, Rotarians, AARP, teachers' unions, labor, and countless other organizations or ethnic and religious groups have their own particular interests, often producing strong turnouts for a specific party. Parties employ sophisticated polling techniques to measure how to reach these groups in ways that, the historian Lizabeth Cohen writes, segment voters into compartmentalized "political markets." By fragmenting the electorate into groups with predictable voting behaviors, the parties have an easier job identifying those who will likely vote for and against them, which make vote-buying and vote-suppression much easier tasks.

PROTECTIVE ZONES

Considering the long history of violence and intimidation at polling places, the twentieth century saw considerable efforts to protect voters from employers, police, or bribers when they went to the polls. Every state except Vermont erected protective circles around the polling places that would prohibit soliciting votes or even displays of campaign material. Implicit in the creation of these zones was the historical knowledge of how elections could be manipulated and stolen at the last minute by bribery or intimidation at the polls. Challenges along First Amendment lines were taken against these laws, and the U.S. Supreme Court heard such a challenge in a 1991 case from Tennessee.

In an effort to "prevent voter intimidation and election fraud," the Tennessee legislature had enacted a one-hundred-foot barrier in 1972. A political campaign worker filed suit, charging that the "campaign free zone" limited her ability to communicate with voters in violation of her First Amendment rights. The Tennessee Supreme Court agreed, and the state appealed to the U.S. Supreme Court. In 1992, in a 5–3 decision, the high court overturned the Tennessee decision and ruled that such zones did not violate the First Amendment. Justice Harry Blackmun wrote that "Tennessee's compelling interests in preventing voter intimidation and election fraud" outweighed any apparent encroachments upon the First Amendment. "In sum," Justice Blackmun wrote, "an examination of the history of election regulation in this country reveals a persistent battle against two evils: voter intimidation and election fraud." Blackmun concluded:

> A long history, a substantial consensus, and simple common sense show that some restricted zone around polling places is necessary to protect the right to cast a ballot in an election free from the taint of intimidation and fraud.

With the constitutionality of the zones upheld, the states were allowed to keep their respective prohibitions around the polls, many of which were similar to Tennessee's one-hundred-foot line. Some states erected very modest barriers, such as Pennsylvania and New Hampshire, which maintained ten-foot zones. Vermont was the only state to prohibit electioneering only inside the polls themselves. Kentucky and Wisconsin, on the other hand, enacted five-hundred-foot zones, which, at least in Kentucky's case, displayed the legislature's recognition of the long history of fraud and violence at the polling place. "Under the guise of legitimate [campaigning]," said one Kentucky court clerk, "hides the vote buyer and the vote intimidator." Louisiana enacted a "campaign-free zone" of six hundred feet. The nation's largest electioneering-free zone belonged to Hawaii, which prohibited any such activity within one thousand feet of the polls. Opponents of the zones, usually citing First Amendment protections, continued to challenge the more restrictive zones, and in 2004 were successful in getting a three-judge panel from the U.S. Sixth Circuit to throw out Kentucky's line of five hundred feet.

PLAQUEMINES—"THIS IS THE FIRST TIME WE'VE HAD AN OPEN ELECTION"

In studying the history of election fraud, a familiar pattern often emerges: Areas where corruption has become a way of life keep producing tainted elections. In 1974, a Congressional election in Louisiana was so laden with fraud that an appellate court voided the results completely and ordered a new election. Two years later, in a Democratic primary for Congress, Rick Tonry beat F. Edward Hebert by just 184 votes. Hebert actually led in every parish with the exception of St. Bernard and Plaquemines. In St. Bernard alone, Tonry garnered over seven thousand more votes than Hebert. Months after the election, twenty poll commissioners in St. Bernard pled guilty to casting 432 fraudulent votes for Tonry. Tonry came under fire for allegedly casting fraudulent votes himself and personally offering one poll commissioner $100 to pad his vote totals. Tonry denied the allegations, and said, "If I ever wanted to steal an election, I wouldn't be stupid enough to walk into the same precinct and vote several times for myself." Amid charges of campaign finance violations, Tonry resigned in May 1977, but vowed to win back his seat. The following month, a House committee found "substantial voting irregularities" in the two parishes, and heard testimonials from locals who commented on how "casual" the vote-stealing seemed. Election commissioners "simply entered voting booths, 'rang up votes,' then falsely listed names of voters as having cast their ballots."

The House committee also found other disturbing trends in the Tonry election, but in ways that implicated his opponent. The absentee balloting in Plaquemines drew the notice of the Congressional committee, since Hebert was supported by remnants of the infamous Leander Perez political machine. At the time of the Tonry investigation, the president of the Plaquemines Parish Administrative Advisory Panel was Chalin Perez, Leander's son, and the county district attorney was none other than Leander Perez, Jr. In Plaquemines

Parish, the parish that had seen colonizers in the nineteenth century, the absentee ballot count drew considerable attention. There had been 657 absentee ballots cast in the parish, and 653 of these were for Hebert. Since Tonry had resigned his seat, the committee said any further investigation of the absentee ballots would be "moot," but added that "the irregularities cited in the absentee voting in Plaquemines Parish appears to be part of a long-standing tradition, ignored, if not endorsed, by parish officials." After losing another primary race, Tonry pled guilty to campaign finance violations and went to prison.

For several generations, no one in Plaquemines stood a viable chance of winning any election without the support of the Perez family. Yet there is more to the case than a simple family-run machine stuffing a few votes. As the Plaquemines case demonstrated, stealing elections often means stealing money. Not only are the people of a given area denied the basic democratic right of a fair election, it also allows those who control the votes to obtain the economic benefits that controlling elections provides.

Few regions of the country are as rural, remote, and utterly wealthy in oil and sulfur deposits as Plaquemines. Since a good deal of these resources resided under public lands, for many years Leander Perez skillfully manipulated those public leases for his personal benefit. Leander obtained the lease to these lands at bargain-basement prices, and leased the land to oil companies for a staggering profit. By the 1970s, Leander's private fortune was estimated at over $100 million. After Leander's death, his sons became the heirs to his political and financial kingdom. A 1982 documentary of the Perez family, "The Ends of the Earth," highlighted how one impoverished African-American district in Plaquemines could not even persuade the parish to bring in water lines until the early 1980s, when an awkward Chalin Perez presided over ceremonies that finally brought running water to the area. This kind of grinding poverty existed in Plaquemines for decades. In no uncertain terms, the Perez affluence came at a high price for those on the bottom of the political ladder in Plaquemines.

After years of fighting the Perez family and the closed milieu of Plaquemines elections, a federal court redistricted the Plaquemines School Board due to evidence of racial discrimination. Taking advantage of a bitter disagreement between the Perez brothers, a jubilant parishioner commented on how the school board race in 1980 was the first time elections were not controlled by the Perez family in fifty years: "This is the first time we've had an open election. It's exciting." Not surprisingly, the Perez-supported candidates lost, signaling a wider reality that might have occurred in countless other contests had some measure of democracy existed in Plaquemines. Chalin Perez himself lost his position as president of the parish commission council in 1983, the same year evidence was uncovered of his father's complicity in taking control of the parish's oil leases. The parish sued the Perez family for $80 million, claiming that an equivalent sum had been illegally taken from public property in oil royalties that rightfully belonged to the parish. In 1988, the suit was settled for just $12 million, a small remedy for years of one family enjoying the bounties that stealing countless elections had brought them.

"TO GET 50 PERCENT OF THE VOTE, YOU'VE GOT TO BUY IT"

A similar pattern played out in the coal-rich Appalachian mountains, where election fraud was practiced in the 1980s in ways that had remained essentially the same for generations. Coal companies still exercised considerable leverage in election contests, and local races could still produce sporadic violence. In these remote and often impoverished communities, long-held customs that surrounded Election Day were difficult to change. Liquor and cash were displayed in large quantities when the polls were opened, and while repeaters and floaters may

have been rare, a new way of importing votes was seen in the wide use
of "vote-hauling." While cast as a way to get voters to the polls, it was
often little more than an efficient vote-buying operation that provided
"walking-around money" to those willing to sell their votes.

A compelling look at elections in the mountains was on display in
Leslie County, Kentucky, where County Judge-Executive C. Allen
Muncy ran for re-election in 1981 despite having earlier been convicted of vote fraud conspiracy. A federal jury had concluded that
Muncy had defeated a party rival in a previous race by obtaining hundreds of absentee ballots, marking them for himself, and having his
"friends" sign the ballot. During a campaign appearance at the courthouse, Muncy did not exactly deny having participated in the absentee
ballot scheme. Instead, he implied that his opponent was currently
doing the same thing: "I don't guess he had anything to do with
absentee ballots," Muncy claimed. "He just got ten in his newspaper
mailbox, but for some reason nobody never asks about that."

In the heavily contested Democratic primary in May 1987—an
election that would essentially decide who would become Kentucky's
next governor—a businessman, Wallace Wilkinson, defeated a
number of competitors, including former governor John Y. Brown, Jr.
The election had all the major ingredients of modern campaigns: big
money, highly paid advisers, and endless television ads. Yet in some
parts of eastern Kentucky, vote-selling remained a way of life. The
respective gubernatorial campaigns understood this, and worked
through local intermediaries to corner the market in votes.

In Magoffin County, a liquor store owner named Don Bailey
worked to deliver his county to Brown by openly paying people five to
ten dollars per vote. How did he know he was getting what he paid
for? As voters went into the polling place in Lakeville, one of Bailey's
associates watched carefully behind a window as the voters left the
polls, making certain no one else entered the voting booth. When he
nodded toward a specific voter, Bailey would meet the voter and thrust

the requisite bill in his hand. When he saw a reporter witnessing the episode, Bailey said he was just paying campaign workers. Afterward, Bailey admitted to paying people to vote for Brown, which he said was necessary for anyone to compete for the vote in Magoffin County, especially against the vote buyers for Wilkinson.

Inside the county courthouse, election officers were seen escorting voters into the booth and looking over their shoulders as the votes were recorded. Most of these voters were not asked to sign affidavits saying why they needed assistance. In the hallway outside the polling place, an exasperated Brown supporter was talking to a couple preparing to enter the polls. "Now, who do you want me to vote for again?" they asked. "John Y. Brown," they were told. A few minutes later, they returned, where the Brown worker handed them something that a reporter wrote "appears to be money," and the couple left quickly. In a rural precinct, L. C. Arnett was openly buying votes but was encountering some problems. Arnett was worried that after being paid for his vote, the unscrupulous vote seller might try to find a higher price and vote differently. Arnett sent eighteen such people home without voting because he feared they would not do as instructed. Arnett bemoaned the introduction of the free market to vote-buying: "It used to be when you bought a vote, it was yours."

When the polls closed in Magoffin County, Wilkinson won the county with 1,695 votes, while Brown finished a distant third (in the state count, Wilkinson won by over 57,000 votes). Insiders understood that besides having a considerable amount of cash to buy votes, a crucial ingredient in Wilkinson's victory rested in his alignment with the county Democratic chairman and the county Republican school superintendent, who together controlled the appointment of election officers—who, of course, counted the votes. A commonwealth's attorney in Magoffin went a step farther, claiming that Wilkinson's forces "basically stole the election."

For poor families in eastern Kentucky, elections were opportunities for extra income. For all involved, the issue became one of timing. An inexperienced seller might take the first offer in the morning during a close election, while more crafty sellers would wait the entire day as the price increased. Yet that simple equation did not always work. In tight races, the best money might come early before either side had an idea of how many votes they would need. If vote buyers felt that they had padded the totals enough in an easy race, they would not pay as much in the afternoon. Experienced vote buyers and vote sellers played a certain cat-and-mouse game throughout the day: buyers trying to get the most votes while keeping the price down, while vote sellers wanted to wait until the market peaked to get the best price.

In the 1987 Kentucky race, that price could reach as much as $200. One Harlan County politico noted: "To get 50 percent of the vote, you've got to buy it, or else you wouldn't get 10 percent." In Perry County, one vote buyer estimated that nearly half of the county's vote in the May primary had been purchased. The rationale for the culture of corruption on display here was straightforward, according to the buyer: "People got no respect for politicians, think they're all thieves." One seller admitted: "They're up there stealing my money. I gotta work for mine. I want some of it back." There had been sporadic attempts to prosecute some for vote-buying, but local juries were usually inclined to exonerate people for vote-selling so prosecutors rarely even bothered pursuing such cases. One small-town editor who published a list of vote sellers, complete with the type of whiskey they preferred, received an unwelcome reminder of what happened when the local press publicized the details of vote-buying—a shotgun blast at the newspaper's offices in the middle of the night.

Vote-buying, of course, is a two-way street and involves the raising of enormous amounts of money. In a memo sent to Gov. Brown in 1982, a cabinet official warned that election fraud in Kentucky was commonplace, and new laws were needed to make these crimes punishable by prison sentences. The memo stated that not only vote-buying, but absentee-ballot fraud, tampering with voting machines, and the old practices of illegal registration and voting the dead were still common. No action was taken, and by 1987 Brown could not even recall ever having received the memo.

The call for cleaner elections in Kentucky was loud, and a 1987 commission proposed changes in the ways Kentuckians voted, concluding that "by allowing corruption to erode the foundation of our political freedom, we have neglected to ensure that the promise of one person, one vote is fulfilled." The commission's recommendations included establishing a toll-free hotline in the state attorney general's office to report alleged fraud at the polls and a one-thousand-foot "campaign-free zone" to protect voters from intimidation at the polls (later reduced to five hundred feet by the legislature). Other recommendations concerned the abuse of absentee ballots and the presence of campaign workers and others supposedly helping disabled voters. Yet no laws could touch the practice of vote-hauling, which was defended as sometimes the only viable way to bring shut-ins, the disabled, and those without transportation to the polls.

To some Appalachian officials, election fraud was more widespread than anyone imagined. "People not involved in vote fraud don't comprehend the magnitude," said Pike County Judge-Executive Paul Patton in 1987. Patton knew that behind the democratic façade of vote hauling was a more pragmatic function: "I think the bulk of the money used to influence votes, is used under the guise of hiring people to haul voters." Most of the money used for hauling, of course, went to direct payments to the voters themselves, while the driver kept a certain percentage for himself. If the operative did not have a car, then his or her support could be purchased through the ruse of hiring "campaign workers." With this device, the cash payment could be made up front and the seller could dispense the money to his friends or family. In a 1985 race, Patton stated he spent $27,000 to hire 144 "contract laborers" to help with his campaign. "That's the way that it's done,"

Patton admitted. "There are lots of people that expect to be hired to work on behalf of the candidate in elections. If they or somebody in their family is not hired," Patton said, "they're not going to support that candidate." Patton was as experienced in winning elections as anyone in the state. Indeed, in 1995, he was elected governor of Kentucky.

Despite the best efforts of reformers, vote buying remained a common component of Appalachian elections. In a 1998 primary election, twenty people were indicted in eastern Kentucky for vote-buying. In Pike County, ten indictments were handed down, including one against a former state senator. Because those who bought the votes often ran the county, only a few courageous souls could be found to testify, and that was usually not enough to secure a conviction. A glimpse into the difficulty of obtaining convictions for such a crime came in September 2003, when one woman prepared to testify in federal court that she had taken a $50 bribe for her vote. "I needed the money, so I took it," she related. Before she came to court, however, she was visited by a local owner of an auto parts store, who warned her not to testify. According to the witness, the man told her that "The police—like, state police and county police—would be after me, after my family." If there were any doubts in her mind, he added: "You know who governs the county, don't you?"

That same year, students from Alice Lloyd College in Knott County were convicted of selling their votes for thirty dollars. One of the vote buyers taught at a local elementary school. After a federal prosecutor claimed that this case would warn vote buyers and sellers that their days were over, a local judge was not impressed. He understood that the culture of corruption was in the very political air one breathed and would not be eradicated with the mere successful prosecution of some college students. The judge noted that, after all, those being sent to prison were "guilty of engaging in activity that, historically, George Washington engaged in."

ABSENTEE BALLOTS AND BULLETS

Another more modern and effective device for fraud, especially in rural counties, is absentee-ballot fraud. In a 2001 report written by the Kentucky secretary of state, the magnitude of the problem was candidly expressed: "Absentee vote fraud in Kentucky is as serious a threat to legitimate elections as outdated punch cards are in Florida." Absentee ballots are easy to obtain—voters can simply go to the county clerk and obtain an absentee ballot if they state they cannot be in the county on Election Day. Buyers prefer absentee ballots because they can mark the ballots themselves after payment, making certain that the bought voter voted correctly.

In a May 2002 primary race in Clay County, Kentucky, one option for those who might be away on Election Day was to come to the county clerk's office two weeks before the election and obtain an absentee ballot. In Jefferson County, the largest in Kentucky with over 240,000 voters, only 248 voters had requested an early absentee ballot. In Clay County, however, with less than 16,000 total voters, 269 had applied for such a ballot within the first hour. "Chaos" seemed to be the rule until Sheriff Edward Jordan shut down the polls. In response to queries about the extent of vote-buying, Jordan shrugged: "How come there was that many people there all at once? That's all I can say." The election in Clay only grew more bizarre, as four people linked to the Republican primary race for county clerk, including two candidates, were involved in shootings before Election Day. When the election was finally over, the extent of the role of absentee votes was evident. All told, 853 absentee ballots were cast in Clay, over five percent of the eligible electorate of the county, well above the state average of 1.16 percent. One candidate for sheriff stated he could prove that votes were being bought, "if I wanted to get killed."

Murder was not out of the question. With two candidates for sheriff murdered and other local races scenes of gunfire, the *New York*

Times noted that the 2002 election season in the eastern Kentucky mountains was "one of the bloodiest in more than fifty years." The Kentucky attorney general's office received over two hundred complaints and reports concerning vote-buying in the May 2002 primary election alone. Making matters worse was the changing nature of "treating voters," where a new commodity replaced liquor used in purchasing votes: the drug OxyContin, a powerful addictive prescription painkiller.

"A SUCCESSFUL FLEA MARKET"

Absentee fraud and vote-buying are still practiced in the open. In Dodge County, in south-central Georgia, a primary was held in July 1996 for an assortment of local offices. In a race for county commissioner, Don McCranie beat Doyce Mullis by 31 votes. Mullis contested the results, and a county superior court voided the election due to extensive fraud. In a new election, McCranie won again, but the residue of the first contest lingered.

A subsequent investigation revealed that both McCranie and Mullis were engaged in buying the ballots of absentee voters. Meanwhile, one person testified he was given $4,000 in $20 bills, for the sole purpose of paying vote haulers to buy votes. There were other ways to get votes, and economic intimidation was always available. McCranie's employees in the road department were required to work in his campaign or lose their jobs. Bank records revealed that McCranie alone obtained $15,000 in $20 bills throughout the campaign, which was used to buy votes. As one unrepentant vote buyer stated, "Vote-buying is a way of life in Dodge County."

One of the most remarkable aspects of the Dodge County election was what occurred in the courthouse itself on Election Day. McCranie and Mullis set up tables at opposite ends of a hall in the courthouse, where they were openly bidding for votes. One disgusted magistrate who witnessed the episode referred to it as a "successful flea market." The cash payments, in which the going rate was $20 per vote, were usually distributed in a bathroom or handed out by the hauler on the ride home. Ironically, both candidates—McCranie *and* Mullis—were convicted of a conspiracy to buy votes and were sent to prison.

PHANTOM VOTERS

Some old tactics occasionally resurfaced in some familiar areas. In the fall of 1990, the *St. Louis Post-Dispatch* reported on a variety of disturbing patterns in East St. Louis, Illinois. In a casual conversation with the director of the city's election board, a *Dispatch* reporter had learned that East St. Louis had more registered voters than it had residents. In ways that had not changed significantly since the 1930s, the city's registry rolls were filled with false registrants, many of them long dead. In seventeen elections since 1981, at least twenty-seven deceased residents had somehow voted. In just a sample of five precincts, 113 people were registered as living in vacant lots or abandoned buildings. In another instance, 55 people were registered on Bond Avenue from burned-out buildings and vacant lots.

The precincts in question were Democratic strongholds that often supplied the margin necessary to defeat Republican candidates. In a special Congressional election in 1988, Jerry Costello, a Democrat, defeated Robert Gaffner, a Republican, by 1,973 votes. Without the problematical precincts, Gaffner would have won by over two thousand votes. Yet in an area in which some dead people had cast votes, Costello beat Gaffner in East St. Louis by 4,724 to 608 votes. "Phantom voters," it seems, had not only helped pass the bond issue that built the Gateway Arch across the river, but had been voting in congressional and other elections since.

THE PARADOX OF MODERN CIVIC LIFE

The twentieth century presented a strange twist that greatly troubled civic-minded people. The franchise had been extended to citizens older than eighteen with but a few exceptions, yet voter turnout rarely reached over half the eligible electorate in a presidential contest, and appallingly low percentages in state and local races was common. To some, there was a single reason that accounted for the low turnouts: The registration process was too cumbersome.

In the late 1970s, President Jimmy Carter had supported federal legislation that would have allowed voters to register on Election Day, yet the bill encountered stiff Republican opposition. Democrats argued that easing registration restrictions would bring more people into the democratic process, while Republicans countered that it would encourage election fraud. Behind the debate were more partisan reasons—Democrats thought lower-income or minority groups would necessarily be inclined to vote for them, and Republicans were not about to let themselves be hurt at the polls. In the late 1980s, a drive to make registration much easier took shape in Congress with the Motor-Voter Bill. Under its provisions, people could register as they applied for a new driver's license. When the bill reached George Bush's desk in 1992, he vetoed it, saying the proposed reform was little more than "an open invitation to fraud and corruption." The following year, Bill Clinton signed a similar bill into law that mandated that states allow people to register at their motor vehicles bureaus, as well as by mail, or where social service agencies were located.

On its face, the law seemed to produce the desired results. By 1995, over nine million people had registered through motor-voter, yet voter turnouts in 1996 and 2000 were not appreciably better than before. Despite the straightforward process, half the eligible electorate still stayed home, even for presidential contests. The reasons for the lack of interest in voting seemed to extend far beyond the registration process.

Others turned to the act of voting itself, of which certain parts seemed anachronistic by the 1990s. Voting in all elections was usually a one-day affair, almost always conducted during the work week. The general election still occurred on the first Tuesday after the first Monday in November, and required voters to go to local schools, libraries, or other public facilities and often wait in line to cast one's vote by paper ballot or by machine. While some citizens received a day off for Election Day, many still had to find time in the early morning hours before going to work, on their lunch breaks, or on their way home.

Considering the difficulties, some states began experimenting with other ways of casting a vote. Tennessee and Texas adopted early voting programs, whereby voters could cast their ballots weeks before Election Day, and nine more states followed suit. But despite all these innovations that seemingly made voting more convenient, voter turnout did not increase dramatically. In Texas, voter turnout has actually lagged behind national averages since early voting began in 1988.

Because elections were local affairs, a variety of voting techniques existed throughout the country, from outdated mechanical devices to touch-screen computers, to the old reliable paper ballots. No state had gone as far as Oregon, where, beginning in 1996, all elections were conducted by mail. Candidates in Oregon can obtain lists of those who have not returned their ballots days before the election. These voters are besieged by campaign staff, and the opportunities for vote buying multiply. A study of the 2000 Oregon election showed that five percent of voters acknowledged that others had marked their ballots and 2.4 percent admitted someone else had actually signed them. Since Oregon has no central statewide database to check for duplicate voting, one analysis concluded that "the potential for massive overvotes, including widespread fraud, exists."

Other states have experimented with Internet voting. In March 2000, the Democratic primary in Arizona became the nation's first trial in a binding election where the votes were cast on the Internet. All such initiatives—similar to other reforms adopted decades earlier—increase the possibility and likelihood of fraud and call into question the evident disregard of the secret ballot. A California task force that examined the feasibility of Internet voting concluded: "It is technologically possible to utilize the Internet to develop an additional method of voting that would be at least as secure from vote-tampering as the current absentee ballot process," which, considering the extent of fraud in absentee ballots, should not calm many worries. By 2000, election officials throughout the nation were still struggling with the age-old dilemma of making elections more accessible to a wider populace without opening up new opportunities for cheating.

"DEMOCRACY IS DISPENSABLE IN MIAMI"

Before the events of 2000 in Florida turned American perceptions about elections on their head, a Miami mayor's race three years earlier foreshadowed some of the problems of and possible remedies for the rising epidemic of absentee-ballot fraud. Two bitter rivals, Joe Carollo and former Mayor Xavier Suarez, competed for the job of leading the city. Carollo was a self-described Ronald Reagan conservative who blasted Suarez as a Harvard-trained liberal. Suarez countered by claiming Carollo was a "false prophet" who, like Fidel Castro, seemed promising at the beginning but who would prove little more than a merciless tyrant. With three other minor candidates in the field, the race was on to win a majority of the vote, in hopes of warding off a possible runoff election which, by law, would come the following week.

On Election Day, November 4, 1997, Carollo beat Suarez, 21,854 to 20,602, but Carollo fell just short of the required majority, winning 49.6 percent of the vote. Some strange anomalies quickly arose with the returns. While Carollo beat Suarez 51 percent to 45 percent in Election Day balloting, Suarez won 61 percent of the absentee vote compared to just 35 percent for Carollo. Considering that 4,739 votes, fully 11 percent of the Miami vote, was cast by absentee ballot, Carollo was denied his outright victory by Suarez's margin in absentee votes. While it was considered abnormally high for as much as five percent of the Miami vote to come from absentees, one district saw as many as twenty percent cast their votes in this manner. As both candidates readied themselves for the following week's runoff, serious questions were raised about how those absentee ballots would be distributed and counted.

Before the week was up, those concerns produced some troubling discoveries. When investigators uncovered an absentee ballot cast by one Manuel Yip, a quick search of Social Security records revealed that Yip had died four years earlier. Yet Yip's absentee ballot was considered legal since it bore the signature of a witness, 92-year-old Alberto Russi, who claimed his signature was forged. "I am not a magician. I am an honest man," he said. Yet suspicion grew around Russi, whose signature appeared on 75 other absentee ballots, and ten were listed as having voted from his home.

Russi's signature was not forged. In fact, he was among many "vote brokers" in the Miami area who helped collect absentee ballots for candidates. As David Leahy, the Miami-Dade Elections Supervisor, noted, beginning in the 1980s, "Campaigns began to use absentee ballots as a tool." While using people to collect absentee ballots was not illegal, it was rife with fraud. Once an absentee ballot was sent in the mail, Leahy admitted, "we lose control of it. That's where the vote broker comes in. They can buy it, take it, or talk a vote out of someone who doesn't know what to do with it." In an attempt to accommodate Florida's elderly population, the state legislature had written some of the most lax absentee-ballot regulations in the nation, regulations that allowed great latitude to unscrupulous brokers. Brokers could call the elections office and order ballots, so long as they could provide names, addresses, and Social Security numbers of those supposedly needing a ballot. When the ballots arrived, all the broker needed to do was mark the ballot, sign it as a witness, and send it back.

One of the absentee votes Russi collected was from Maria Danger, who did not even live in Miami but visited her fiancé, who rented a room at Russi's house. "I thought he was gathering signatures to show support for his candidate," Danger claimed, "I didn't realize it was for a vote. I'd never known you could vote like that." Russi told reporters that "Maybe her boyfriend punched the ballot," but when reminded that he had signed as a witness, he quickly changed his story. "Well, then she must have voted. I do things legally." Russi then boasted about his role as a local boss in the Little Havana community and his ability to gather absentee votes. "Sales is all about understanding people and their needs," Russi said, and added that "Politics is a similar art form." As the November 12 runoff began, Russi went to the county election headquarters with more completed absentee ballots. As he stepped off the elevator to the 19th floor, he was promptly arrested for election fraud. When state agents went to Russi's home, they discovered more than a hundred absentee ballots and fifty blank applications for more absentee ballots. All Russi could say was "Oh, my God."

In the runoff, Suarez made up considerable ground and defeated Carollo by nearly three thousand votes. Despite the attention given to absentee-balloting fraud the previous week, election workers, according to the *Miami Herald,* were "buried under a small mountain of absentee ballots" for the runoff contest. The number of absentee votes actually increased to 4,982, with Suarez winning the vast majority of them. But Carollo was not finished; he took his case to court, asking a judge to overturn the results of the previous week's election. Carollo's lawyers based their case on a 1984 Florida Supreme Court ruling that stated courts could invalidate an election's results if fraud could be proven to have permeated the balloting. A county grand jury also began investigating the role of absentee ballots in the mayoral race. One of Carollo's lawyers, Kendall Coffey, said that brokers "can work retirement homes, nursing homes, swoop through and potentially take advantage of the elderly and the infirm. That shouldn't be the way it happens." (With the experience provided by the 1997 mayoral election, many local politicians and lawyers, such as Coffey, would be intimately involved in the Bush–Gore contest three years later.)

In February 1998, a grand jury found that absentee-ballot brokers were essentially "thieves who steal democracy," and concluded that fraud had "tainted" the election results. "Based upon the information we have gathered and the testimony we have heard, we find that absentee ballot fraud clearly played an important part in the recent city of Miami elections." While the grand jury was not authorized to overturn the election, it recommended that absentee ballots should be mailed on a random timetable in order that brokers would not know when to check mailboxes. Miami-Dade County had already implemented one reform that required two witnesses to sign an absentee ballot.

Carollo's civil suit against the Suarez campaign went before Circuit Judge Thomas S. Wilson, Jr., on February 9. Suarez's attorneys were noticeably worried, calling Carollo a "sore loser" and warning about a possible judicial "coup." Before Judge Wilson, Suarez's attorneys dismissed the role of brokers like Russi, saying their role was not "enough to throw out an election in a major American city," and redefined the whole episode as "the final political battle between the Hispanics in Miami and the *Miami Herald*," whose exposés had certainly not benefited Mayor Suarez. As Liz Balmaseda, a *Herald* columnist, wrote, the trial told the citizens of Miami: "With each bad ballot that is discovered, that democracy is dispensable right here in Miami, that the will of the voting majority is not as important as the appearance of the will of the voting majority. Who cares what people want as long as you have their votes, one way or another?"

Twenty-four subpoenaed witnesses pled the Fifth Amendment to charges they were involved in the absentee fraud. Handwriting experts testified that the signatures on at least 225 absentee ballots were questionable, and sixteen witnesses testified to the harassment they endured from vote brokers. The choice for Judge Wilson was a difficult one: invalidate the fraudulent absentee ballots and award the office to Carollo, or stay out of the political mess that would necessarily ensue and refuse to investigate the returns? Either way, legal voters would claim they had been cheated.

On March 4, Judge Wilson issued a ruling that the *Herald* described as one "that shook Miami's power structure and thrust its government to the brink of chaos." Wilson agreed with Carollo that rampant fraud characterized the absentee voting and invalidated the election. To settle the issue as to who should be mayor, Judge Wilson essentially split the difference and ordered a new election in two months.

"A cornerstone of American democracy is that each citizen's vote has equal value," wrote Judge Wilson. "In the November 4, 1997, election, the value of every honest vote was greatly diminished or devalued by this fraud." Wilson was reluctant to throw out all of the absentee ballots and declare Carollo the winner since that would disfranchise some honest absentee voters, and so he settled for a new election. "It's a great day for democracy," said Carollo, while a disappointed Suarez readied himself for yet another election.

But that election was not to be. A three-judge panel from the state Third District Court of Appeals agreed with Judge Wilson that the election had been rife with fraud, but they went one step further. The judges threw out all of the absentee ballots and ruled that Carollo had been fairly elected and should assume his office as mayor of Miami; no new election was necessary. In a ruling that would have great significance far beyond the mayor's race in Miami, the court found that absentee voting was not a constitutionally protected right but a privilege. "The sanctity of free and honest elections is the cornerstone of a true democracy," the court wrote, which placed greater value on those who "exercised their constitutionally guaranteed right to vote in the polling places of Miami" rather than those who voted by absentee ballot. "Invalidating all absentee ballots," wrote the court, was not "an unjustified disenfranchisement of those voters who cast legal [absentee] ballots." To simply call for another election, the court reasoned, would implicitly reward election fraud. "Were we to approve a new election as the proper remedy following extensive absentee voting fraud, we would be sending out the message that the worst that could happen in the face of voter fraud would be another election."

To some of those who had cast legal absentee ballots, their reactions were mixed. "You mean I'm sick and I'm blind and my vote is not counted?" said 77-year-old William Ward. Gladys Harden, a 68-year-old-retiree, said "I feel pretty bad my vote got thrown out. What about everyone who can't get to the polls?" Predictably, the bulk of the reactions fell along partisan lines. A suit brought by some of the legal absentee voters met with no success, but a U.S. District Court in Florida noted: "The absentee voting scheme as it now exists in Florida lends itself to fraud, manipulation, and deceit."

Absentee balloting was growing increasingly popular as the 2000 presidential election approached. In the name of producing higher turnouts, the criteria for voting absentee grew more lax, as "convenience" replaced strict adherence to residency on Election Day. In California, roughly five percent of voters had requested absentee ballots in the 1970s. As the state actively encouraged voters to routinely use absentee ballots, their usage exploded. In 1992, over 17 percent of the ballots in California were cast absentee, and by 2000, that figure would reach nearly 25 percent. In Washington state, over half of the ballots cast in the 2000 election were absentee. A study conducted by Caltech and MIT concluded: "The convenience that on-demand absentees produce is bought at a significant cost to the real and perceived integrity of the voting process." Unfortunately, that integrity was not a high priority as the 2000 election approached.

CHAPTER TWELVE

A Hidden Time Bomb

*"It was our first battle, but nobody noticed it.
And it could have ended the whole case."*

T he 2000 presidential election quickly faded into the national memory as primarily an electoral aberration—one where quirky ballots, imperfect machines, and honest "misunderstandings" raised some issues about vote verification, but little else. Though camouflaged by the most modern of methods, the debacle in Florida exposed how the culture of corruption had evolved into its modern form, and demonstrated once again that the engaged intent to cheat and mislead is a highly accomplished craft within American politics. While its modern practitioners may be more sophisticated than their nineteenth-century counterparts, their underlying contempt for democracy is every bit as dangerous.

SUSPICIOUS ACTIVITY

There were ominous signs of possible voting problems in the early primary season. Although most Americans assumed that issues of ballot access and disfranchisement were just historical relics, the primaries provided a small taste of what was to come in the general election. After Senator John McCain of Arizona won a stunning victory in the New Hampshire Republican primary, South Carolina proved a crucial state on the road to the nomination. If McCain won in this traditionally conservative state, he could overtake George W. Bush among the party's right wing. If Bush won, he would seize the political high ground and claim "front-runner" status—a key ingredient in raising even more funds for the fall campaign against Al Gore, the likely Democratic nominee.

On primary day in the Palmetto State, 21 of 135 polling places were suddenly closed or "consolidated" in Greenville County even though the party was under court orders to open as many polls as possible. The orders resulted from a recent lawsuit claiming that South Carolina had a history of excluding minority voters. With the party's nomination possibly hanging in the balance, the sites in Greenville were nonetheless closed or changed at the very last minute, causing considerable confusion among a number of voters. McCain's aides were quick to charge that the location of the closed or moved polls was no accident. The senator himself said, "I thought the court had already dictated that all polling sites should be open," and he, along with his fellow candidate Alan Keyes, demanded a "full investigation."

Considering that McCain was depending on independents and minorities in the primary, his campaign understood that these problems with the polls did not bode well for his chances of defeating Bush. A GOP attorney dismissed McCain's criticisms, claiming that only two of the twenty-one polling sites were in predominantly African-American areas (where McCain was expecting a heavy turnout), and added, in language that belied the reality of conducting elections in South Carolina, "compared to state elections, this is as smooth as silk." Yet of those polls closed in Greenville, nine of the twenty-one had higher percentages of black voters than the county as a whole, and six of the precincts had been carried by the Democrats in the 1998 governor's race—suggesting that the centrist McCain would have found support in these precincts.

Bush beat McCain in South Carolina by eleven points, and the suspicions about the poll closings faded as the Texas governor moved steadily closer to the nomination. Yet McCain's campaign considered the poll problems to be "very suspicious," and his national field director called the episode "a last-minute switcheroo." An underlying current in South Carolina was the fact that Bush held the loyalty of the state's party apparatus, while McCain was regarded as an outsider. In areas where McCain might have picked up votes, such as the Greenville precincts, no major effort was launched by the leadership of the state party to find the necessary workers to conduct the election. Because of the relative size of Bush's victory in South Carolina, nothing more was mentioned about opening an investigation of the voting problems in Greenville, and it was quickly brushed aside as a story by the national media.

DEAD MAN RUNNING

In Missouri, a hotly contested senatorial race presented the unique situation of the incumbent, the Republican John Ashcroft, running against a dead man. After a plane crash killed Mel Carnahan in October 2000, his name remained on the ballot, according to Missouri law. Carnahan's widow, Jean, agreed to assume the seat if he were to be elected posthumously. That would not be the last bizarre ingredient to the election in Missouri.

In St. Louis, local Democrats were pleased with the early turnout on Election Day, especially in areas of high African-American population. Under the rubric of wishing to accommodate all those who wished to exercise their suffrage rights, Democrats went to St. Louis City Circuit Court at 3:20 P.M., asking for an extension beyond the lawful closing time of 7:00 P.M. At 6:30 P.M., the court agreed and issued an order keeping the polls open until 10:00 P.M. Outraged Republicans immediately sought an injunction to stop the order and close the polls at the legally established time, which was fast approaching. Already, cries of a possible stolen election were being heard, but not from Democrats.

By 7:45 P.M., the Missouri Court of Appeals stepped in to block the Circuit Court's order to keep the polls open late. In the days to come, Republican suspicions turned to outright anger when they learned of the conditions preceding the lawsuit. On the morning of November 7, the state Democratic party filed suit on behalf of a plaintiff named Robert D. Odom, claiming that he had been denied his right to vote and asking for an extension so that other voters would not be turned away. The lawsuit's avowed purpose crumbled when it was discovered Odom had died in 1999. Backpedaling as fast as they could, Missouri Democrats admitted that they had made a mistake in their haste to file the suit, and the actual plaintiff's name was Robert M. Odom (a campaign aide to a Democratic Missouri congressman). Yet that story did not hold water either, considering that a quick glance at poll records revealed that Robert M. Odom had voted early in the day without any trouble.

The language used in the St. Louis suit was strikingly similar—in some places verbatim—to that of a suit filed in Kansas City that same day asking for more time. Clearly, the suits were not attempts to address Election Day problems, but were preconceived plans designed to keep the polls open well beyond the legally prescribed time. Under the guise of prohibiting long lines that would keep lawful voters from voting, Missouri Democrats used the courts to buy them more time to round up potential voters. The simmering problems in Missouri quickly faded from view considering the events in Florida, and because Carnahan beat Ashcroft by nearly 50,000 votes and George W. Bush carried the state by almost 80,000 votes. Yet Missouri was not the only Midwest state to witness questionable tactics by Democratic workers.

In Wisconsin, Republicans claimed that Democrats were offering cigarettes to homeless people in exchange for voting for Gore.

"From the Comfort of Your Home"

As Gore and Bush wrapped up the party nominations, the campaigns had begun adding up their "safe" electoral votes as they planned their strategy for the fall campaign. With Gore putting California, New York, and most of the northeast into his column, and with Bush placing the deep South and the plains states into his column, the election seemed too close for comfort on either side. One thing was certain: Both candidates desperately needed Florida's twenty-five electoral votes. And in this regard, George W. Bush was essentially playing on home turf.

Bush's brother, Jeb, had been elected governor of Florida in 1998, and a number of the state's highest ranking officials were Republicans loyal to the Bush brothers. While having a brother as the chief executive in Florida had obvious advantages, little did anyone guess that having the Florida secretary of state within the Bush camp might be even more significant. The job was held by a former state senator, Katherine Harris, who had campaigned for Bush in the New Hampshire primary. In her role as the official certifier of elections, her office would normally have played only a pro forma role in the election, unless it was contested.

The GOP held another distinct advantage in Florida: Bush's campaign had aggressively sought absentee ballots in ways that far eclipsed the Democratic effort. The Florida GOP spent $500,000 in a mass-mailing campaign that contained a letter from Jeb Bush. Under an old state seal, Bush told the party faithful they could easily vote "from the comfort of your home" by simply requesting an absentee ballot. The letter was instrumental in persuading over 700,000 Floridians to use absentee ballots in the presidential contest, an increase of nearly 50 percent from the 1996 election. Yet encouraging voters to cast absentee ballots for convenience ignored some elements of Florida law, which stated that only those voters who could not be at the polls on Election Day could use absentee ballots. Bush's letter bypassed that critical legal aspect. Democrats, not fully understanding the power of the absentee effort, spent their time concentrating on Election Day votes. By the time the polls opened, Bush already had a 125,000-vote lead in domestic absentee votes in Florida.

In the weeks and then the days leading up to the election, seasoned observers of Florida politics had no idea of the perfect storm brewing over their heads. On the Monday before the election, one Florida newspaper displayed a photo of a voting machine and casually editorialized, "These days, voters walk up to a semi-private cubicle, grab a felt-tip pen, and silently change history. Then a computer tallies the totals and tells the tale." A prescient editorialist, however, warned: "Hopefully there will not be a repeat of the 1876 tardiness in counting the Dade vote," he claimed, adding "what's past is prologue." Another reported that the problems with voting in the Miami area had been ironed out, although David Leahy, Elections Supervisor, acknowledged that one problem possibly remained with paper ballots. If a voter did not clearly punch through the hole indicated, it might prove a problem in the event of a recount. The *Miami Herald* wrote: "Election officials even have a term for this—'hanging shad.'" In just hours, the world came to know a somewhat different term—"chad"— all too well.

Despite the pundits' claims of expected low turnouts, the early signs of turnout, especially among Democrats, were much higher than expected on Election Day. Senior citizens, African-Americans, and union members came out in droves for Al Gore and his running mate, Sen. Joseph Lieberman, the first Jewish vice presidential candidate on a major party ticket. Young suburbanites, rural gun owners, and middle-class Protestants flocked to the polls for Bush, anxious to rid the White House of Bill Clinton and his vice president. The crush of voters produced long lines in many areas, but in Palm Beach County, Florida, an indication of things to come appeared early on. A number of Jewish voters were worried they had "accidentally" voted not for Al Gore, or for George W. Bush for that matter. Because of the confusing design of the ballot, they were afraid they might have cast a vote for Pat Buchanan, an ultra-conservative candidate who had once questioned the extent of the Holocaust. It made no sense that Buchanan would get many, if any, votes in the heavily Jewish precincts around Delray Beach. These were certain Gore votes, and in an election that promised to be close, if those votes were not ending up in the Democratic column, this spelled potential problems for the vice president. Yet in Palm Beach County, Buchanan won nearly 3,400 votes, or one for every 70 votes for Gore.

Statewide, Buchanan received one vote for every 167 Gore votes. One of those votes probably came from Kurt Weiss, whose parents were killed by the Nazis and who worried that he had inadvertently voted for Buchanan. "I hope I didn't. I pray I didn't," Weiss said, adding, "we wouldn't vote for that man for anything. Even Alzheimer's victims wouldn't vote for Pat Buchanan." Buchanan's sister and campaign manager, Bay Buchanan, acknowledged that her brother's totals in Palm Beach County were likely inflated. "As a good citizen," Buchanan admitted, "this vote is much larger than one would expect from us." Buchanan's candid appraisals of honest vote counting proved one of the last to emerge from any campaign in 2000. In contrast, Bush aide Karl Rove dismissed reports that thousands of Gore voters might have mistakenly voted for Buchanan, saying that Buchanan's showing in Palm Beach County was due to the "extraordinary effort" of the Buchanan team to register supporters in the area.

By mid-afternoon, the phone had not stopped ringing in the office of Palm Beach County Supervisor of Elections Theresa LePore, who in any other election would have been just another obscure election official overseeing the mundane chores of designing ballots and super-vising the election process. After hordes of voters complained of the confusing "butterfly ballot," Pore's design of the presidential ballot in her county came under immediate fire, mostly from angry Democrats.

LePore's explanation for the confusing design was simple. She said she had hoped to accommodate the large number of candidates (ten party tickets were on the 2000 ballot) for president on a single page, as well as to accommodate a predominantly elderly population who wanted larger type. LePore came up with what seemed a suitable com-promise: a ballot that listed all of the candidates on both sides of a folded-out page. The names of the candidates were on both the left and right hand sides, and the punch holes were located in the middle. The names were tiered, in order to match them up with a correspon-ding hole. Hence the term "butterfly," as it looked like a winged ver-sion of a single-page ballot.

Perhaps the luckiest thing for the Texas governor was that his brother had been elected governor of Florida in 1998. That gave him some obvious political advantages in a contested race, and another edge that played itself out in Palm Beach County. Under Florida law, in listing the candidates for president, the party of the sitting governor was automatically listed first, giving Bush the top slot and, obviously, no problem matching his name up with the top punch hole. The problem came below, where the Gore/Lieberman ticket came second on the left side of the ballot, but the corresponding second punch hole actually belonged to the Buchanan/Foster ticket, which was on the top of the right-hand side of the ballot. While an arrow directed the voter wishing to vote for Gore/Lieberman to punch the hole labeled "5," confused voters came out of the booths afraid they had mistakenly cast their votes for Buchanan, who received more votes in Palm Beach County than in any other Florida county.

As more voters in Palm Beach County considered the state of things, they grew increasingly worried about their vote. Siggy Flicker, a 33-year-old who had been born in Jerusalem and whose father worked at an Israeli memorial, said she had sleepness nights worrying that she might have unintentionally voted for Buchanan. "Yasser Arafat would get more votes here," Flicker claimed. But the anguish of voters like Flicker was quickly dismissed. Some understood that the secret ballot could not be corrected for errors after the vote was cast and had little sympathy, claiming that elderly voters in south Florida had no problems playing bingo. Lester Zimmerman, a retired electronics engineer, took offense at claims that he was too stupid to understand a crowded ballot: "I hold a patent on an artificial kidney," Zimmerman claimed, and when he went to vote, he "saw Bush was 1 and Gore was 2, and pressed the second box."

Palm Beach was not the only county to experience extensive problems with its ballot design. In Duval County, located in northeastern Florida, it took two pages to list the presidential tickets on the ballot, and sample ballots were placed in the *Times-Union* the Sunday preceding the election that informed voters they must "vote all pages." At the polls on Tuesday, voters were told something different. The votomatic machines instructed voters to only "vote appropriate pages." Florida law required that "sample ballots shall be in the form of the official ballot as it will appear at that polling place on Election Day." Duval voters like Helen Garland came to vote for Al Gore, but later realized her vote had been rejected. After voting for Gore on page one, Garland wondered, "Why are there people back here?" She then made a move on page two that invalidated her vote: "I was confused, so I just punched out a name. I thought I had to vote for somebody." In Duval, nearly 27,000 ballots were rejected because of such double votes, and more than 11,000 votes were cast in predominantly African-American areas where Gore was expected to build considerable leads over Bush.

In other areas of the state, more stories surfaced of voter disenfranchisement. First-time Creole-speaking voters were not allowed assistance in voting and many were subsequently turned away; one precinct had partisans who presented themselves as Democratic supporters distributing punch cards with the likeness of Al Gore and Joe Lieberman on them, yet the punch numbers listed were those of George W. Bush and Richard Cheney. In other areas, last-minute complications arose in some unlikely ways. When railroad workers began cutting up track near a polling place in Suwannee County, election officials created an alternative precinct so those cut off from their usual precinct could still vote. The director of the state Division of Elections noted: "These supervisors can be pretty enterprising."

At 7:49 P.M. Eastern Standard Time, although the polls had not closed along the western panhandle of the state, the major networks announced that Gore had won Florida. To observers within both campaigns, as they watched the electoral map take shape, they knew this was the big prize, the crucial state that, with Gore's almost-certain victories along the west coast, would give him the necessary votes to surpass the constitutionally required 270 electoral votes.

Yet the Bush camp was conceding nothing after the initial shock of the Florida news. The candidate himself cautioned against discounting Florida, as did his top aides. As the evening wore on, the election played out with Bush taking the South and the Midwest, while Gore's victories came in the heavily populated Northeast and the industrial North. Although the polls remained open in a number of states, if the votes held up, it seemed certain that upon the closing of the California polls, Al Gore would win the presidency.

At around 9:00 P.M., the networks suddenly announced that new results had changed their estimates and Florida was now "too close to call." As the number crunchers added it up in the respective campaigns and in the networks, the election was coming down to who could claim victory in the Sunshine State. After winning California, Gore's electoral total stood at 267, Bush's at 246. If Gore had won his home state of Tennessee, or even the usually safe Democratic state of West

Virginia, the problems in Florida would have been little more than an afterthought. With a growing victory in the popular vote that ultimately reached over a half million, and with enough to win in the Electoral College, President Gore would have claimed his mandate despite any lingering doubts about the Florida vote. After all, Gore's popular-vote margin was five times that of John F. Kennedy's in 1960.

Yet because of the Electoral College and its winner-take-all system, Bush could still become president if he could win Florida. By 10:00 P.M., that seemed likely, as Bush's lead in Florida was now approaching 100,000 votes. As midnight neared, that lead shrank to just over 50,000 votes, and by 2:00 A.M., the networks finally called Florida for Bush. Yet even that proved premature, as a glaring mistake in the counting of votes in Volusia County reduced Bush's lead to just 6,000. With over six million votes cast in the state, this was well below the threshold that required a mandatory recount. While on his way to concede, Gore realized that the election was still up in the air and promptly withdrew the concession in a phone call to Bush. As bleary-eyed Americans awoke the next morning, they were greeted with the news that the election had not been decided.

Count Till You Win

Over the next thirty-six days, an election drama played itself out, one that drew parallels to a scene in the 1948 film *Key Largo* where Johnny Rocco, played by Edward G. Robinson, lectures a deputy on how he controls Florida politics: "Get my boys to bring the voters out. And then count the votes over and over again till they added up right and he was elected." As the recount grew in intensity, defining exactly how to count an official vote became a national pasttime—would "hanging chads," or a partially perforated paper punch hole, be counted as a legal vote, or even a protruding, or "pregnant," dimple provide adequate voter intent? The competing political camps understood one essential truth: The ensuing contest was not about finding a fair, objective way to determine who had won Florida; rather, it became a game of "count till you win." With so much on the line, the players inside the parties— and well beyond the view of the networks' cameras—manipulated the election to their own benefit. What became apparent only afterward was that even though the 2000 election had not seen bands of thugs roaming neighborhoods or gangs of "repeaters," the election nonetheless displayed how the culture of corruption operated behind the scenes in modern American politics.

A central rule about recounts is that a candidate needs to immediately claim frontrunner status. Frontrunners can stake a claim to the office, while those who trail and contest the results can quickly be burdened with the mantle of "sore loser" and therefore the obligation of having to prove why the perceived frontrunner should be denied the office. In terms of public relations, frontrunners have all the political and legal advantages. Throughout the 2000 recount in Florida, the Bush camp quickly seized the role of frontrunner, while Gore accepted the role of the one behind in the count. On November 8, Secretary Harris claimed that Bush's official lead stood at 1,784 votes, while acknowledging that fourteen counties had not produced their recounted totals. The Associated Press, however, in looking at 66 of 67 counties, showed Bush's lead to be a scant 229 votes. While this was a paltry .00381 percentage lead, in the hardball world of election recounts, this "lead" was still formidable. Bush could portray himself as the "winner" who needed to plan his cabinet, while Gore was to blame for the embarrassing election imbroglio. In fact, just three days after the election, the *Orlando Sentinel* editorialized that threats of a pending lawsuit by the Gore camp were "reckless, nation-rending foolishness," and that "reducing a national election to a lawsuit would be calamitous."

Immediately after the election, as Harris's office released the returns showing Bush having a lead of varying amounts, the Gore camp had a crucial decision to make: Should it ask for a statewide recount, including "overvotes" (ballots where more than the legally prescribed marks were given for the same candidate) and "undervotes" (ballots with no preference stated for president)? Or should it ask for recounts in only selected counties? In the end, the Gore campaign asked the courts to recount only the "undervotes" in three selected counties where, of course, they expected to pick up the necessary votes to overcome Bush's slim lead.

Yet Bush's official "lead" was not all that it appeared. In stark terms, the official certified results clarify the issue.

	ELECTION DAY	LATE FEDERAL OVERSEAS ABSENTEES	TOTAL
BUSH	2,911,215	1,575	2,912,790
GORE	2,911,417	836	2,912,253

Despite Bush's 125,000-vote head start with the domestic absentee ballots, the national obsession with butterfly ballots and hanging chads, and the ways Harris included dubious Republican votes while excluding Democratic ones, the fact remains that Al Gore still won 202 more votes on Election Day in Florida. Bush's ultimate margin of victory came from late overseas absentee votes, which were counted from November 17 to 26.

There were problems with these ballots on several fronts. Over 340 had late postmarks; 183 had U.S. postmarks (they were supposed to be from overseas sources), while others had no postmark at all. Ninety-six lacked even the required signature. A fierce debate raged over whether the problematic ballots should be counted. Despite the media's obsession with hanging chads and the undervote controversy, some within the campaigns knew where the real game was being played. Bush's lead attorney in Florida later acknowledged that the overseas absentee ballot issue was "a hidden time bomb. It was our first battle, but nobody noticed it. And it could have ended the whole case."

These ballots were critical because they were the only new votes that could be found and counted afresh after Election Day. Considering that Bush actually trailed Gore in Election Day votes, the GOP needed to shore up their total with additional votes

The ballots that made the difference. An elections supervisor from Leon County, Florida holds up a late overseas absentee ballot in the 2000 Florida recount. Credit: © Reuters/Corbis

that had an essential component: they could not be questioned or closely examined. The Republican campaign understood the importance of these ballots early on, and had spent eight times as much as the Democrats in advertising for the overseas vote. The GOP had also mailed unsolicited ballot requests to thousands of military personnel overseas who had previously voted Republican. Some of these absentee voters may not have even lived in Florida. Considering that Florida had no income tax and the residency laws were relatively lax, it was well known that an untold number of military personnel listed Florida as their place of residence. One elections supervisor noted "we have people who registered here 20 years ago and haven't been back, but they're allowed to vote."

On November 18, headlines in Florida stated "Bush Leading in Overseas Ballot Counts." According to the official count, Bush had a comfortable margin in the overseas count of 1,057 to Gore's 597. Yet as Gore picked up votes in the recount, the Bush camp knew two things needed to occur. First, by placing restrictions on when the recounts from some selected counties could be submitted, Harris needed to discount as many Gore votes as possible while making sure to include questionable Bush votes. Second, more Bush votes needed to be found, and the only place they could be located were on late overseas ballots.

By insisting that questionable overseas ballots be included in the mix, the GOP portrayed their efforts in patriotic terms that put Democrats on the defensive. Bush's aide Karen Hughes was indignant: "No one who aspires to be commander-in-chief should seek to unfairly deny the votes of the men and women he would seek to lead." Bob Poe, the chair of the state Democratic party, criticized GOP standards: "They use the law when it suits their purposes, and ignore the law when it suits their purposes." When the *Miami Herald* ran a story that noted that 39 convicted felons had voted in Broward and Miami-Dade counties, and their crimes ranged from murder and rape to passing bad checks, Republican leaders seized on it. Montana's Governor Marc Racicot claimed, "There's something terribly, terribly wrong with what's going on in Florida," adding, "How can felons be allowed to vote when the men and women in our armed forces cannot?" Retired Gulf War General Norman Schwarzkopf spoke gloomily about the fact that brave men and women were "denied the right to vote," because of a mere "technicality."

To counter GOP charges, Gore's running mate, Sen. Joseph Lieberman, appeared on NBC's *Meet the Press*. The first question dealt with whether the Gore camp favored invalidating the votes of military personnel because of alleged "technicalities." Lieberman was in headlong retreat, saying emphatically he would not tolerate invalidating any of these ballots, and he went even further, claiming he would give "the benefit of the doubt" to those ballots, and urged Florida election officials "to go back and take another look" at the rejected absentee ballots. The "benefit of the doubt" standard was precisely what his Republican counterparts wanted to hear. One Democratic congressman from Florida understood what was under way: "We're getting kicked around for saying illegal votes are illegal votes," and he added that "the Republicans got a lot of illegal votes counted on Friday that never would have been let in before, and now we're the ones retreating? Incredible."

Hyper-Technical Reliances

On November 21, a crucial moment occurred when the Florida Supreme Court handed down a unanimous decision extending the recount, a decision derided by the GOP as judicial usurpation. A furious James Baker said that two weeks after the election the Florida Supreme Court had suddenly changed the rules, and "invented a new system for counting the election results." Democrats were ecstatic with the ruling, feeling assured this would give them adequate time to make up the few hundred votes that would give them victory.

Yet this ruling planted the seeds by which Bush would claim victory. The Florida high court wrote that "the will of the people, not a hyper-technical reliance upon statutory provisions," should be the overriding principal in recounting. While Baker and the GOP cursed this decision and ask the U.S. Supreme Court or, possibly, the Florida legislature, to overrule it, GOP lawyers also saw an opening in the court's language that allowed them to look again at hundreds of rejected late overseas ballots. Once again, while most were focused on the court's decision to extend the recounting of pregnant chads, Republican attorneys knew it allowed them to revisit more questionable overseas absentee ballots.

Simply put, GOP leaders understood the vital importance of overseas absentee ballots far better than their Democratic rivals. During the recount, some House Republicans had even solicited the Pentagon for phone numbers and E-mail addresses of servicemen and -women. "The information was used to put sailors in contact with Florida Republicans who were organizing a public relations campaign to persuade counties to reconsider rejected ballots," the *New York Times* said, and that it was "part of a broad effort by the Bush campaign to turn public opinion against Al Gore." Rep. Steve Buyer of Indiana defended the E-mails as entirely appropriate and claimed they were sent because "he was furious that Gore campaign lawyers had urged county canvassing boards to reject absentee ballots without postmarks." The Bush campaign team, incidentally, wanted Democratic absentee ballots rejected for this very reason. The difference was that since any questions concerning the overseas absentee ballots would be met with charges of disfranchising military personnel, Republicans had political cover.

While the media was focused on hanging chads, Bush lawyers used the Florida Supreme Court ruling to aggressively pursue more rejected overseas absentee ballots. Postmarks were especially fertile ground for considering a ballot rejection on account of "hyper-technical" reasons, and Republicans worked in the county canvassing boards to count previously excluded absentee ballots, while at the same time arguing in court against the same standard for the statewide recount. Jason Unger, a GOP attorney, demanded that an absentee ballot from a registered Democrat in Leon County, which was postmarked November 8 and sent from Maryland, be rejected "based on the postmark alone." Yet another Republican lawyer in Escambia County, which was heavily Republican, argued that a ballot sent from a registered Republican, postmarked November 10 and sent from Missouri, be accepted. "Just because it has a U.S. postmark does not mean that it was mailed from the United States," he argued. The Leon County ballot was rejected, while the Escambia ballot was accepted. In another instance, GOP attorneys opposed a civilian absentee ballot because it had no postmark. That ballot was sent from a registered Democrat and was ultimately rejected because of GOP objections that "the envelope was mailed but does not bear an APO, FPO [military postmarks] or foreign postmark." Similarly, when a military ballot from a registered Republican, lacking the same kind of postmark, came before a GOP lawyer in Bay County, he argued, "I don't think the postmark matters. I don't think you should disenfranchise members of the armed forces." That ballot was accepted.

Andres Viglucci of the *Miami Herald* commented on the developments: "The GOP's legal and political push to force 14 Florida counties to reconsider disqualified overseas absentee ballots paid off over the Thanksgiving weekend with a net gain of 115 votes for George W. Bush," wrote Viglucci, who noted that these votes were "potentially enough to save the day." Viglucci added that eleven counties, "under pressure from Republicans," went back and reinstated scores of absentee votes in a way that was hypocritical to the charges the GOP had been firing at Gore—in essence, the canvassing boards changed "the rules in the middle of the game." Those rules, which the GOP was eager to ignore, Viglucci reminded his readers, "are designed to prevent fraud."

Since the votes within the absentee ballots were, of course, secret, no one could say for certain how they were distributed and, accordingly, how the results of the Florida election would have necessarily been changed. Out of over 2,400 late overseas absentee ballots, 680 contained flaws or errors that violated state election or administrative rules. The *New York Times* carefully examined these flawed ballots and the ways they were counted. The paper found a glaring difference in the manner in which problematic ballots were accepted or rejected by county election officials:

	LATE OVERSEAS ABSENTEE BALLOTS		
	ACCEPTED	REJECTED	% ACCEPTED
Counties Won by Bush	530	523	50.3%
Counties Won by Gore	150	666	18.4%

In Republican counties, problematic overseas ballots were nearly three times as likely to be counted as those in Democratic ones. Although equal protection claims would later be central to the 2000 election, the way the overseas ballots were counted was hardly equitable or democratic. These late overseas absentee ballots, combined with the intense partisan counting of Election Day votes, made the crucial difference that would give Bush the White House.

"UNTIL VOTERS GET TO SPEAK AGAIN"

Political commentators weighed in on the election recount, revealing their lack of appreciation of how American politics worked. Just as in so many other past elections, their comments were almost outdated the moment they were spoken or written. Besides the strong partisan claims that the opponent was trying to steal the election, there was strong sentiment that the Electoral College should be quickly abolished by a Constitutional amendment. Others made more bland pronouncements about the effects of the election controversy. Some wondered whether it really mattered who was declared the eventual winner, since so many aspersions would be cast on the legitimacy of the claim as to make the office suddenly unattractive. Some were especially Machiavellian, claiming that it might be good in the long term for a party to allow their opponent to claim the office and then win big in the Congressional elections in 2002 and the next presidential election in 2004.

The most unusual scenario was offered by Robert Steinback, a *Miami Herald* columnist, who suggested that since Bush was ahead in the recount and would likely be president, he should acknowledge the unique circumstances surrounding the election and "establish a 'caretaker' government, in which some executive power is shared between Republicans and Democrats, until voters get to speak again in 2004." Steinback even saw the new president inventing new ways to make policy decisions:

> Bush could establish an advisory "policy cabinet," made up of Republicans and Democrats, with the power to make decisions—by

consensus only—on nominations and certain domestic policy matters. It would be responsible for such things as issuing executive
orders, selecting ambassadors and nominating candidates for the
federal courts—including the Supreme Court—which Bush would
be bound to respect.

Steinback concluded that perhaps the people would "speak again" in
2004; but had their voices been adequately heard in 2000? Democracy,
when put on hold for four years, is no democracy at all.

"WIDESPREAD VOTER DISFRANCHISEMENT"

Amid the recount arguments, the fact that 175,000 Floridians had
their votes invalidated—a figure greater than the population of either
Ft. Lauderdale or Tallahassee—never seemed to attract the appropriate concern or outrage. To statisticians, this was merely three percent of the total vote, which fell within so-called "acceptable" levels.
Perhaps these people voted more than once for the same office on a
ballot, or misread the directions, or purposely did not vote for a specific office. These figures belied a national figure that soon shocked
concerned citizens. One study found that throughout the country,
somewhere between 4 and 6 million votes were not counted in 2000
because of confusing ballots, faulty equipment, and other problems.
Illinois, South Carolina, and Georgia, in fact, had rates of spoiled or
uncounted ballots that exceeded Florida's.

Upon closer inspection, the issue of spoiled ballots smacked of
another form of disfranchisement, which may not have been as blatant
as earlier forms, yet was just as effective. The crucial factor was race.
While approximately eleven percent of the Florida electorate was
African-American, a whopping 54 percent of the spoiled ballots were
from predominantly African-American precincts. The chances of

having one's vote "spoiled," therefore, increased tenfold in Florida if one were African-American. In Gadsden County, the only Florida county with a predominantly black population, 1 in 8 votes were not counted, whereas in Leon County, a predominantly white county, the same spoilage rate was less than 1 in 500. Counties with significant African-American populations did not have the same kind of access to machines that could detect erroneous votes and give the voter two more tries. Counties with this updated technology (predominantly affluent, mostly white counties) had a far lower spoilage rate (.83%) than those with optical-scan equipment (5.68%) or punch cards (3.93%), which were more frequently used in African-American precincts.

African-American voters in Florida faced daunting challenges that went far beyond spoilage. Thousands did not even know what happened to their franchise until they went to vote. Some black voters were denied the right to vote because they had been placed on a no-vote list following a purge of felons, deceased voters, or mentally incompetent voters following the 1998 election. Nearly 58,000 African-Americans found themselves unable to vote because of the purge. Yet this purge system was fraught with errors, and an estimated 14 percent of the names on the list were erroneous. The company that the Republican Secretary of State Sandra Mortham had hired to assemble the list, DataBase Technologies (which had become Choice-Point by 2000), did not extensively check their lists that were compiled from matching birthdates, gender, and other characteristics, to a list of more than ten million felons. Naturally, errors appeared from such a casual match, and DBT suggested that further checks be used by the state, such as financial records and address histories to confirm the veracity of the list. Katherine Harris's office dismissed the suggestion, placing a note in the files that read "DO NOT NEED."

What was even more astonishing, at least three hundred "felons" on the Florida list were convicted of crimes dated in the future (one as late as 2007!). While some counties responded to Harris's pre-election directive to remove the names from the voter rolls, some did not. In Madison County, Supervisor of Elections Linda Howell discovered her own name in the felon list. Others were denied the vote for mistakes in the registration system. About fifty students at Bethune-Cookman College in Daytona Beach complained that they could not vote because their names were not officially on the Volusia County voter rolls, even though these students had participated in a voter-registration drive at their college six weeks before the election and had received their registration cards in the mail. In the aggregate, a study by the U.S. Commission on Civil Rights found that the "despite the closeness of the election, it was widespread voter disenfranchisement, not the dead-heat contest, that was the extraordinary feature in the Florida election."

Like so many other examinations of the election, the Commission's report, issued the following summer, was grounded in partisanship. The majority report was signed by Democrats, while a stinging dissent was written by Republicans on the commission. Those in the minority, led by Abigail Thernstrom, took issue with the methods and conclusions of the majority. Their criticisms were not entirely off base. Commenting on the "numerous" people who testified before the commission as to how they had been disfranchised, the dissenters noted that only 26 witnesses had been called, who resided in just eight of Florida's 67 counties. Additionally, the dissenters correctly pointed out that although one can gauge what was a predominantly African-American precinct or county, one could not distinguish whether the votes that were thrown out were those of an African-American or a Hispanic. The "testimony of witnesses fails to support the claim of systematic disenfranchisement," the dissent claimed, which said that for obvious partisan reasons, the majority failed to distinguish between "bureaucratic problems" and "actual discrimination." The core problem behind all of the "irregularities" in Florida, according to the dissent, was simple—voter error.

Indeed, many of the witnesses cited by the commission did not reveal any systematic efforts to disfranchise them. Although rumors were rampant of Florida State Highway Patrol troopers intimidating black voters by setting up roadblocks in African-American neighborhoods, only one was documented and it proved to be a vehicle checkpoint located "within a few miles" of a polling place in a largely African-American neighborhood. Specifically, the checkpoint was in southern Leon County, and was located over a mile from the First Baptist Church precinct in Woodville, where one third of the voters were African-American. The checkpoint operated from 10:00 to 11:30 A.M., and the assistant attorney general verified that the stop "was not done in accordance with normal procedures." Thirteen drivers were cited for driving violations, and eight of them were white. No proof was offered of anyone denied the right to vote by the checkpoint or even of anyone feeling sufficiently intimidated to avoid voting.

Yet the essential point of the majority on the commission could not be dismissed. The details of the Florida election revealed a system that did not provide the same access or quality of machines, or of the chance of having one's vote counted correctly, to all races and locations. Simply applying "voter error" to the events in Florida ignores the fact that over 175,000 citizens who went to the polls had their choices invalidated. Some made egregious errors in their ballots that made them impossible to record as votes; others were the victims of incompetent or inexperienced election officials; others encountered bureaucratic snafus or inexplicable inconveniences. The obvious inequity revealed by the election was disturbing, and whether one was mistakenly on a purge list or had to use outdated machines with confusing ballots, the fact remained that the chances of low-income African-Americans having their votes invalidated were significantly higher than for affluent whites.

The politics of race was injected into the Florida election for an obvious reason. African-Americans are one of the few demographic groups who vote overwhelmingly one way. While one can make a reasonable stab at someone's political ties based on gender or education or religion, nothing was as certain in Florida politics in 2000 as the partisan leanings of African-Americans, 93 percent of whom voted for Gore. The disfranchisement of African-American voters in Florida did not occur necessarily because of their race, but because of their politics. And the dynamics that resulted in removing those citizens from the rolls or in discounting their votes did not happen entirely by accident. It was part of a not-so-subtle effort to diminish and suppress a considerable voting bloc.

"COUNT EVERY VOTE"

While the disfranchisement issue might be readily dismissed as "voter error," as the minority report of the Civil Rights Commission said, there were other charges that merit a closer examination. In Seminole County, Bush led Gore in absentee votes by 10,006 to 5,209, yet the applications for absentee ballots that had been mailed to voters had a problem. The company hired by the GOP to print the application forms omitted asking for voter identification numbers, as required by state law. When the applications began pouring into the county office, they could not be processed unless the numbers could be obtained. Florida law specifically stated that only the applicant, members of the immediate family, or a guardian could supply the information on the application. Yet Supervisor of Election Sandra Goard allowed local GOP members to manually add the numbers to the applications. She later admitted that one Republican official, Michael Leach, joined another man in using laptop computers to search a database in order to quickly add the missing numbers to roughly 2,146 applications. No such courtesy was extended to the local Democratic party. Hundreds of absentee applications—mostly from Democrats and Independents—stacked up without being corrected. Even the former state Republican chair expressed worry over the legality of the move, and stated, "It is absolutely an issue of controversy as to whether public documents can be altered on an after-the-fact basis." Following the election, Democratic attorneys sued to have the entire Seminole County absentee vote thrown out. A similar suit was launched in Martin County, where Republican officials were allowed to fix about 500 tainted application forms. The Martin County elections supervisor allowed GOP officials to take these applications home, while hundreds of Democratic applications sat idle. The GOP claimed that only applications, not ballots, were altered, and considering Gore's mantra to "count every vote," it was a powerful argument against throwing out the votes in Seminole County.

On the other hand, this was a matter that Republicans could not quickly dismiss, either legally or on the public-relations front. These were not ballots designed by a Democrat, as had been the case in Palm Beach County. Nor were these ballots sent to military personnel overseas. Those ballots were confusing, but so were the butterfly ballots, and no party official could correct any potential "voter error" there. Rather, these were applications printed by the Republican Party, and were treated in anything but equitable fashion by the GOP-led elections supervisor.

The lower court and the Florida State Supreme Court refused to throw out the absentee votes in Seminole and Martin counties, in the process validating the partisan treatment of the applications. The court managed to find that there was no evidence of "fraud or other intentional misconduct" that justified rejecting all of the ballots, although it did conclude that the handling of the applications was "troubling." The quick action by some enterprising election supervisors had been indispensable in helping to save hundreds of GOP votes.

A strange twist in the recount happened in heavily Republican Nassau County in the northeastern corner of the state. On election night, Bush carried Nassau 2 to 1. In the recount, in a state where

4,000 additional votes were counted and 56 counties reported more votes after Election Day, Nassau actually lost 51 votes for Bush. As in the other counties throughout Florida, the election board dutifully certified the second count. Yet late Friday, November 24, on the eve of Harris's official state certification, the Nassau canvassers reversed themselves and certified the original count. Harris quickly accepted the first count, restoring fifty-one precious votes to the GOP column.

"SEMI-SPONTANEOUS COMBUSTION"

Despite the events in Seminole and Martin counties, and the overseas absentee ballots, a handful of votes could still make all the difference. With the manual recounts going on in Palm Beach County, another tactic was utilized by partisans that worked to diminish the democratic nature of the election or even the recount itself. Hordes of interested partisans, led by the Rev. Jesse Jackson and conservative Congressmen, flocked to Florida to see the tumultuous events themselves. But many were not there by accident.

In West Palm Beach, a fourteen-year-old boy named Chris Miller was riding a skateboard, and happened to ride by the Palm Beach County Governmental Center, where an angry crowd of GOP stalwarts was congregating. The crowd was led by a West Palm radio host, Dick Farrel, who was among many conservative radio personalities in southern Florida encouraging the faithful to stop the recount. For Miller, his mistake was in stopping near the crowd and mentioning to someone he liked Al Gore, because "He's pro-choice and he's against school on Saturday." An outraged Farrel screamed, "You don't vote!" and the crowd clustered around the boy. Photographers caught the image of a glaring Farrel jabbing his finger at the boy's chest. Despite the pathetic demonstration, bullying tactics like Farrel's were becoming more commonplace. Indeed, Farrel was seen by his followers as a crusading hero. Nowhere was there an objective attempt to ascertain the people's will. Rather, in some areas it had become a contest of who could yell the loudest. Observers and media at first dismissed these antics as the acts of a few rabid partisans whose behavior would not affect the outcome of the election, but events soon shifted.

In Miami-Dade County, the canvassing board's recount took place in public view, as wearied canvassers inspected each ballot by hand, peering through perforations to determine how the vote should be recorded. On November 22, an angry crowd appeared in the halls just outside where the recount was under way. A well-planned Republican effort to bring as many angry marchers as possible to the courthouse had been going on for days. Hundreds of calls had been made on GOP telephone banks to implore interested members of the party to go to the Stephen P. Clark Government Center to protest the recount. People also had been egged on by talk radio hosts, particularly those who appealed to staunchly Republican Cuban-Americans. New York Congressman John Sweeney led a group of Republicans to the Center to, in Sweeney's words, "shut it down."

As hundreds of pro-Bush marchers chanted outside the closed doors, the canvassers began the process of counting over a half million ballots. Supervisor David Leahy suggested, above Republican objections, to limiting the recount to just 10,000 "undervotes," and to moving the proceedings to another floor where the counting machines and his own office were located. Leahy considered the new location a more appropriate locale for counting the ballots, where representatives from both parties could observe and monitor the recount. Yet there were no windows for outsiders to observe the proceedings, and when GOP-led protestors realized they would not be able to see the recount themselves, they grew violent. The chairman of the county Democratic party had to be escorted away by police for his own safety after he was chased down by protesters who thought he was stealing a ballot (he was seen taking only a sample ballot). Protesters demanded access to the room where the recount was to occur, and when they were refused, the *New York Times* reported, "several people were trampled, punched, or kicked." Sheriff's deputies had to be brought in to restore calm; the canvassers inside could hear the commotion and the angry shouts.

Suddenly, the canvassers became cowed, and voted unanimously to call off the recount entirely. Leahy admitted the angry protest outside the doors of his office was "one factor" that "weighed heavily" in the decision. The crowd's intimidating tactics had worked beyond their wildest hopes, and Republicans cheered the board's decision while Democrats cried foul. *Wall Street Journal* columnist Paul Gigot wrote approvingly of the "semi-spontaneous combustion" in Miami-Dade County that produced a "bourgeois riot." After first denying any involvement, local GOP leaders then took the stance of quiet pride in having worked up party activists to stop the recount. Democratic party leaders described the actions of the crowd as smacking of "fascism." The recount stopped as Gore had picked up 157 votes. A commentary on the episode came from a cartoon in the *Orlando Sentinel,* which showed several bearded men in military uniforms watching a small television set next to some chickens. In this clear representation of a banana republic, the soldiers laughed heartily at the news that stated: ". . . and now more on the democratic elections in America."

537 Votes

On November 26, Secretary Harris certified George W. Bush the winner in her state by a margin of 537 votes. Harris refused Palm Beach's requests to extend the recount and, in the process, rejected over four hundred votes in Palm Beach, Miami-Dade, and Nassau counties that Gore had seemingly picked up in the process. While most eyes were on pregnant or hanging chads and butterfly ballots, the late overseas absentee ballots had quietly provided Bush with his ultimate margin of victory. Democrats

vowed to extend the count and to fight the certification in the courts, but
as the convening of the Electoral College approached, the chances of
Gore winning Florida were fading fast. Considering what had transpired
since Election Day, one thing remained: Bush's 537-vote margin was
essentially a fictional number that had no grounding in reality, except that
it would make him the 43rd president of the United States.

BUSH V. GORE

A final aspect of the 2000 election was the matter of the judiciary,
which had long been seen as the final arbiter in many election cases. Yet
the U.S. Supreme Court had been diligent in avoiding intrusion upon
the sovereignty of the states in cases of contested elections. In fact,
when considering how best to solve disputed presidential elections following the 1876 debacle, Congress refused to allow the Supreme Court
to settle future disputes. Senator John Sherman of Ohio was one of the
most vocal critics of giving the court such power, calling the matter of
determining who could settle a disputed presidential election "a question that is more dangerous to the future of this country than probably
any other." To Sherman and other members of Congress, elections were
political issues that should never involve the courts.

When the U.S. Supreme Court interceded in 2000, there was no
mistaking the fact that an extremely partisan court was taking on the
most highly charged political case in memory. In this realm, Gore was
a considerable underdog. The high court's makeup was decidedly
Republican: Only two justices had been appointed by a Democrat
(Stephen Breyer and Ruth Bader Ginsburg). Chief Justice William
Rehnquist and Justices Antonin Scalia and Clarence Thomas were
conservative Republicans. Scalia, in fact, had two sons working in the
Republican recount effort, and his own inclinations were revealed in
his decision to grant *certiorari* in the first place:

The counting of votes that are of questionable legality does, in my view, threaten irreparable harm to petitioner [Bush] and to the country, by casting a cloud upon what he claims to be the legality of his election.

No mention was made of the potential harm that might come to Gore and his claims from the "legality of his election." Scalia's comments betrayed his partisan perception of the case from the outset.

Although appointed by Reagan, Justice Sandra Day O'Connor was seen as a "moderate" by court observers. Yet her "moderation" in this case was outweighed by her own partisan proclivities. While watching the election results with friends, she exclaimed "This is terrible" when news of Gore's victory in Florida was announced early on. When a reporter asked the justice if she denied making these comments, a spokesman at the Supreme Court had no comment. What went unstated throughout the days leading up to the Supreme Court's final decision was that Bush had four votes solidly in his pocket from conservative Republicans appointed by administrations which his father either led or in which he was vice president. All he needed was one more vote to end the game once and for all.

On separate occasions in early December, the court heard the case that was simply known as *Bush v. Gore*. In the first instance, the court blocked a Florida high court ruling in early December that extended the recount, and sent the case back to Florida for further consideration. During oral arguments, Scalia voiced an unspoken assumption that had become all too clear since election night. In a discussion about the rights of Florida citizens to vote for president, Scalia reminded Democratic lawyers, "In fact, there is no right of suffrage under Article II."

The high court interceded again on December 12, 2000, when it brought the election of 2000 to a close. In a 5–4 decision (along with Rehnquist, Scalia, Thomas, and O'Connor, Justice Anthony Kennedy, a Reagan appointee, joined the majority), the court ruled that no further recounting would be permitted and, thus, Harris's certified results should stand. In a *per curiam* opinion, the majority did some judicial calisthenics that seemingly contradicted a good deal of their own judicial philosophy. Having spent their careers restricting the Fourteenth Amendment's "equal protection" clause, the majority used an expansive view of this very same clause to justify halting the recount. When the Florida Supreme Court had used the standard of "clear intent" to determine the validity of a challenged ballot, the high court ruled this was unconstitutional, since that standard was subject to varying interpretations and was not, thus, equal protection. The court's language was clear: A state may not, by "arbitrary and disparate treatment, value one person's vote over that of another."

A wave of reaction, almost exclusively on partisan grounds, met the ruling in *Bush v. Gore*. Democrats assailed the five members of the majority for cynically using the equal protection clause to validate their political leanings and award the election to Bush. In the process, claimed the detractors, the court had hurt its own reputation as an entity above the clamor of partisan politics. Considering the disparate ways Republicans had suppressed or counted votes, using the equal protection clause to validate the decision smacked of rank hypocrisy. Yet to Republicans, the court's majority had courageously stopped an out-of-control process and validated the rightful victory of George W. Bush.

To answer all future inquiries considering the application of the equal protection clause and elections, the court made a most remarkable statement, one that had the weight of an imperial *decree* rather than a precedent-setting *decision*. The majority members of the court wrote:

> Our consideration is limited to the present circumstances, for the problem of equal protection in election processes generally presents many complexities.

For future reference, then, the complex issues concerning counting votes, in the court's reasoning, could not be scrutinized along the lines of *Bush v. Gore*. It was simply a decision that affected the 2000 election and would go no further. Although in his dissent John Paul Stevens wondered if we would ever know the actual winner, Harris's 537-vote majority for Bush was carved in stone.

"OUR VOTES ARE NOT SACROSANCT"

On January 20, 2001, at the time prescribed by the Constitution, George W. Bush was sworn in as the 43rd president of the United States. Along the parade route, thousands of angry protesters demonstrated against the new president. Donald Johnson, a D.C. bus driver, remarked, "the people of America were robbed of their choice." A consulting engineer from New York came to Washington to protest "the disenfranchisement of black voters." But the scattered protests were relatively quiet. No arrests were made and newspapers generally avoided the whole subject of questioning the election.

In the spring of 2001, one of many recounts of the disputed Florida votes was published. The one commissioned by the *Miami Herald* and *USA Today* found that had the recount been allowed to proceed under the standards set by the Gore campaign, Bush would actually have widened his lead to 1,665 votes. The story was reprinted across the country and reiterated what many had suspected in the immediate wake of the election: the election results were maddeningly close, but nonetheless, Bush would win most scenarios by varying margins. What was lost, however, was a rather simple notion buried well within the story: had the recount proceeded "from scratch," and had the most inclusive standards been used, Gore would have won by 393 votes. The exercise taught *Herald* reporter Tom Fiedler that "our votes are not sacrosanct."

A year after the election, the *New York Times* reported that when the "over" and "under" votes in Florida were carefully counted, Bush would still have won. Yet had a recount of all 175,000 rejected ballots been undertaken, Gore would have won, "no matter what standard was chosen to judge voter intent," with margins ranging from 60 to 115 votes. The White House seized on the confusion generated by the report and released a statement that displayed how nonplussed the administration was by the assertion that perhaps the nation's chief executive should not be in office: "The American people moved on a long time ago. . . . The election was settled last year."

Yet attempts to ascertain the "real" winner missed the point. By focusing solely on how various recount scenarios could have played out, the 2000 election has been relegated in our memory to little more than a one-time electoral nightmare that could never occur again. The historical evidence, however, tells us differently. If the circumstances of the 2000 election had changed only slightly, and the Electoral College hinged on a razor-thin margin of votes elsewhere, and if we look closely at how votes were cast and counted in any one of a number of counties or parishes throughout the nation, what occurred in Florida does not seem so nightmarish after all.

In the end, the vote in 2000 was another timely reminder that elections are not necessarily about getting the most votes, but about winning. From the outset, the Bush campaign understood the working realities of elections far better than did Gore's. Bush's supporters in Florida were more aggressive in purging likely Democratic votes from the rolls, claiming frontrunner status, counting problematic overseas absentee votes, and using local and state officials to discount Gore votes in the recount. As our history informs us, this was not a new development. Rather, the events in the Sunshine State validated once again Boss Tweed's stark pronouncement: "The ballots didn't make the outcome, the counters did."

CONCLUSION

"Something Very Personal"

"You know why we never paid attention to this until now? Because we don't want to know that our democracy isn't really so sacred."

F ollowing the events in Florida, any lingering doubts about the integrity of American elections were eased by the reassurances that 2000 was just a glitch in the nation's electoral system and that corrective steps would soon follow. Conjecture about new voting procedures was plentiful, and so was the speculation about how outraged voters in Florida and throughout the nation would respond in upcoming contests.

Then came September 11. In the aftermath of the terrorist attacks in New York and Washington, D.C., reminders that the 2000 election was a national embarrassment were obliterated by the focus on the war on terror. So little did the anticipated outrage play in the next election cycle that the GOP reversed the usual mid-term party losses by regaining control of the U.S. Senate, and Jeb Bush was easily reelected governor of Florida. Katherine Harris won a seat in the U.S. House of Representatives, and Al Gore later declined to run for president in 2004.

For added measure, Congress passed the Help America to Vote Act (HAVA) in 2002, which provided nearly $4 billion to the states to replace outdated voting equipment, initiate voter-education projects, and train poll workers. Although by the time the next presidential race came around only half of that money had actually been spent, at least the federal government had reacted to the crisis in Florida with major legislation in order to restore public confidence.

If 2000 did anything, it showed that a disputed election could change the course of American history in dramatic ways. Hardly had Bush entered the White House than it became clear that the ideological differences between the president and Al Gore were far wider than many had assumed. The election of George W. Bush, in retrospect, and his later enunciation of a doctrine of pre-emptive military action without multilateral support, may mark one of the greatest turning points in American domestic and foreign policy in a century. No one needed more to be reminded how elections can transform everything than 140,000 American soldiers deployed to Iraq.

But the election of 2000 did much more. By closely examining the election methods in just a few Florida counties, Americans were given an unwelcome civics lesson in the ways political power is sometimes acquired. "You know why we never paid attention to this until now?" asked the co-director of the Indiana Elections Division during the 2000 recount. "Because we don't want to know that our democracy isn't really so sacred."

While many Americans might have quickly forgotten the means by which the president had come into office, other nations kept somewhat longer memories. Similar to the ways Jim Crow was used against the United States by its Cold War adversaries decades ago when discussing abuses of human rights, American pronouncements on fair elections abroad were casually rebuffed as little more than hypocritical posturing, considering what had happened in 2000. In March 2004, Russian's president Vladimir Putin easily won reelection by winning over seventy percent of the vote. Amid charges of vote-buying, ballotbox–stuffing, and distributing ballots to patients in psychiatric hospitals, Putin had little trouble tossing aside American concerns. "Four years ago, we were watching in amazement how the electoral system in the United States was faltering," Putin responded acidly. "So I hope that by criticizing us, they will draw certain conclusions for themselves and will perfect their own democratic procedures, too."

2004

As the 2004 contest between Senator John Kerry and President Bush approached, worries of another tight race and the legitimacy of the election system itself increased. The slightest hint of possible equipment malfunctions drew immediate indignation, and pundits warned of an avalanche of lawsuits that threatened to forestall the selection of the president. Yet nothing of such dramatic proportions occurred on Election Night as had happened four years earlier, and Bush won reelection with a small but clear popular vote majority, yet with the slimmest Electoral College margin for an incumbent since Woodrow Wilson. When Senator Kerry conceded the contest the next day, most Americans felt a sense of relief that the troubles associated with 2000 would not be revisited.

Yet the 2004 race was not trouble free. The new Florida this time was Ohio, whose twenty electoral votes held the presidency in the balance. At first, Kerry trailed Bush by 136,000 votes, but approximately 155,000 provisional votes remained.* These occurred where a voter appeared at a precinct and his or her name was not on the registry rolls. Under the new rules implemented in the wake of 2000, the vote would be cast, sealed, and (where legally registered) counted later.

* Bush's certified margin of victory in Ohio was 118,457 votes.

Coupled with early exit polling that indicated a probable Kerry victory in Ohio, some Internet bloggers circulated stories of definite election theft in the Buckeye State. To account for the discrepancy in the exit polls, one pundit even suggested that there might have been fraud in the exit polling process.

Reasonable explanations might be found for Kerry losing surprisingly badly in Ohio counties with significant Democratic majorities, but the possibility of untraceable electronic fraud was suspected all the more after the ugly disputes of 2000. Indeed, the doubts remained for months thereafter, along with an undercurrent of unease and a cottage industry of conjectures about how Kerry had been cheated. Christopher Hitchens, no fan of the Kerry campaign, later noted the strange anomalies in Ohio and how they all seemed tilted toward the Bush campaign. "Whichever way you shake it," Hitchens writes, "there is something about the Ohio election that refuses to add up." Another observer warned that because of 2000, a new era had dawned where "ballot booths with electronic voting machines become the new Grassy Knoll for conspiracy theorists." Some of the skeptics included academic specialists and computer scientists, which demonstrated how the 2000 recount had made many Americans increasingly suspicious about the reliability of our election systems.

"HAVE A NICE DAY"

In the context of election fraud, the most striking contest in 2004 did not involve the presidency. In the governor's race in Washington State, Democrat Christine Gregoire apparently lost to Republican Dino Rossi by just 261 votes. During a mandatory recount, state GOP officials were furious when a local judge ordered officials to give the names of provisional voters to the Democratic Party. When the voters were called, Democratic workers asked them for whom they had voted. If the answer was Rossi, one party worker stated candidly, "we just tell them to have a nice day." If the answer was Gregoire, then the party helped supply written oaths to the voters testifying they had voted Democratic. The results of the recount shrank Rossi's official lead to just 42 votes. Then, Democrats "found" more than 150 "misplaced" ballots in a plastic tray at a King County polling site. Understandably, Washington Republicans compared the belated discovery of uncounted Gregoire ballots to the remarkable additions to Lyndon Johnson's senatorial vote in 1948. In late December, another recount gave Gregoire a ten-vote lead. After adding more lost votes from King County, her official margin of victory stood at 129 votes.

Six months after the election, a trial began in Washington Superior Court in which the GOP argued that Gov. Gregoire should be removed from office and a new election ordered. To the GOP, this was not a case of some accidental irregularities or technical malfunctions. In his opening statement, Republican attorney Dale Foreman was clear: "This is a case of election fraud." Superior Court Judge John Bridges was not persuaded by this line of argument and ultimately ruled for Gregoire. Bridges's response indicated how by 2005 the judiciary and the larger culture recoiled from using the political "F" word. Whereas a court in the early 1900s had used the word "slavery" to describe the condition of voters living in a society without free and fair elections, no court today would go quite that far. Rather, courts and reformers alike take comfort in the assumption that modern election problems can usually be reduced to correcting unintentional errors.

NEW MACHINES

Distrust of election results is, of course, a dangerous thing in a democracy, but the worst may be yet to come. One element of the danger is the increasing privatization of American elections. Counties and states are relying more on private companies that specialize in election equipment, and these companies sometimes have questionable agendas and security precautions. A popular solution to the outdated machines in Florida was the widespread use of the newest equipment to register votes, the touch-screen machine. By 2004, one of the largest manufacturers of touch-screen voting machines was Diebold, Inc., whose CEO, Walden O'Dell, was a member of the elite "Rangers and Pioneers," a group of wealthy businessmen committed to raising $100,000 each for President George W. Bush's reelection campaign. In a 2003 fundraising letter, O'Dell boasted, "I am committed to helping Ohio deliver its electoral vote to the president." New Jersey Senator Jon Corzine said, "Not only does Mr. O'Dell want the contract to provide every voting machine in the nation for the next election, he wants to 'deliver' the election to Mr. Bush." A Diebold vice president, Thomas Swidarski, dismissed charges that programmers could steal votes, and in a phrase eerily reminiscent of Boss Tweed, stated: "Programmers do not set up the elections, election officials do."

Another danger, however, came in the very technology that seemed intended as a means of preventing the paper-ballot fiascos of 2000. Diebold's product, the touch-screen machine, had a perilous potential, even if all partisan suspicions were somehow laid to rest. Computer specialists who examined the Diebold equipment concluded that it lacked adequate security precautions. David Dill, a Stanford computer scientist, claimed that the problem extended to all manufacturers of touch-screen systems. "If I was a programmer at one of these companies and I wanted to steal an election, it would be very easy." Programmers could simply insert software that would "be impossible for people to detect, and it would change the votes from one party to another. And you could do it so it's not going to show up statistically as an anomaly."

Dill and many of the nation's leading computer scientists and engineers began devising election systems that could better ensure accuracy and minimize opportunities for fraud. They came up with a straightforward solution to verifying the accuracy of a vote. The touch-screen machines could print a paper receipt that the voter would check to ensure that his or her vote had been recorded correctly, and then be deposited in a ballot box. In a recount, the paper receipts would serve as the ultimate source for verifying the true count. At first glance, the paper receipts seemed to solve one of the major problems arising from 2000. With a receipt, voters would no longer have to worry whether they had voted for, say, Al Gore rather than Pat Buchanan.

This reform, however, represents the triumph of hope over history. The creation of a paper trail actually could bring back many of the methods used in the nineteenth century when paper ballots were first common. Then, too, voters were supposed to leave the polls, having deposited the one proof of how they had voted; as we have seen, how-ever, there were ample ways around it. The history of American elections clearly shows that whenever technology raised new safeguards against fraud, the manipulators, bribers, and intimidators found ways to adjust. Paper receipts, even now, could not withstand the ingenuity of computer programming. Hackers would have little difficulty pro-gramming a machine to record a vote for X every so often, when it was actually cast for Y; and it would take little more trouble to add in a corollary, that a printed receipt for Y be issued along with it. With apparent proof in hand of how he or she had voted, the voter would be all the less likely to suspect something was amiss. It is poor consola-tion to be cheated but in the freshest, most up-to-date way, and poor comfort to imagine that touch-screen machines will deter corruption where the other methods of reform have failed to do so.

"The Long and Ugly Tradition"

The debate over paper receipts demonstrates how reformers may have misread some of the most crucial lessons from the 2000 election. By focusing exclusively on verification and equipment, they overlook how modern elections really work. New machines and paper receipts cannot solve some of the more fundamental barriers to free elections— one of which is to keep some people from voting at all. Minorities across the country are finding themselves increasingly on the defensive in registering and going to the polls, since many are easily identifiable for their party affiliation.

In a purge before a Louisiana Senate race in 1986, an internal Republican memo stated that the purpose was not in curtailing fraud, but to help "keep the black vote down." In 1990, Sen. Jesse Helms of North Carolina used a not-so-subtle technique to accomplish this purpose that bypassed purging. Helms's campaign distributed 125,000 letters to predominantly African-American districts, warning potential voters that any misleading statement concerning residency could result in a prison sentence of five years. Purging was used against Native Americans in South Dakota in 2004, where poll officials jeered at "Indian" names and created roadblocks to registering, while Republican poll watchers in Arkansas took photographs of African-Americans as they went to the polls. In Texas, a Republican district attorney threatened students at a predominantly African-American college if they attempted to vote using their campus addresses, which state law allowed them to do.

Just weeks before the 2004 presidential election, Florida state police officers interrogated elderly black voters in Orlando as part of an investigation into some absentee abuses. Many of these voters were members of the Orlando League of Voters, which mobilized the city's African-Americans to go to the polls. The officers remarked that their efforts were not part of an intimidation campaign against people registering certain Democratic votes, but were "just the people we selected out of a random sample to interview." Bob Herbert of the *New York Times* later discovered that the investigation was conducted in August, even though the Florida Department of Law Enforcement had found three months earlier that "there was no basis to support the allegations of election fraud." Yet armed troopers visited the homes of black voters nonetheless. Their presence happened to fit the Florida Republican party's goal, best expressed by one anonymous party member, who said, "It's no secret that the name of the game for Republicans is to restrain that turnout as much as possible." Herbert concluded: "The long and ugly tradition of suppressing the black vote is alive and thriving in the Sunshine State."

Another form of intimidation occurred in the 2004 Michigan presidential primary. Michigan Democrats were allowed to use the Internet in the February caucus, in addition to voting by mail at 576 caucus sites. Union leaders brought laptops to work sites in order to provide their members a convenient way to cast their ballot, all in ways that preceded the arrival of the secret ballot. One union head offered a lukewarm defense of the process, dismissing suggestions that voters were coerced: "No one bothers to check to see how people vote." The executive chairman of the state Democratic party admitted there was not even a "pretense to secrecy" with Internet voting, and made the unhelpful claim that online voting was as secure as absentee balloting.

In terms of effectiveness, absentee ballots remain the easiest way of buying votes in advance, or swinging them after the results are in, whichever way works. This is due, in part, to the widespread use of absentee ballots, even in all of their honest uses. On its face, this seems perfectly legitimate; each side wants to get out all of the vote, if it can. But absentee voting also allows party operatives to avoid prohibitions against electioneering near the polling place, as well as essentially bypassing secrecy. According to one party official, absentee balloting presents an opportunity for swinging votes. "You can't stand over their shoulder and move their hand for them," he said, "but you can certainly suggest to them that this is the candidate that deserves their vote."

Supporters of absentee voting point to decreasing levels of voter participation as a primary reason to retain them. Yet the evidence does not bear this out. Although absentee balloting has doubled since 1980, overall voter turnouts have not significantly increased. Oregon's mail-in vote, for example, increased turnout by just 3.5 percent in 2000, barely above the national average increase of 2.1 percent. While having a negligible affect on turnouts, these initiatives have, however, made a vote buyer's job considerably easier.

A series of municipal elections in Dallas from 2001 to 2003 displayed how absentee fraud can have profound consequences. In a race for city council, vote "brokers" in south Dallas exploited a Texas law that required the names of all people requesting an absentee ballot to be printed in the newspaper, along with the day that the ballots were mailed out. In numerous instances, the brokers, or "contractors," literally waited at the mailboxes for the ballots to arrive, especially at nursing homes. The law even allowed brokers to then take the marked ballot from the mailbox and deliver it. The brokers usually received from the campaigns that hired them five to twenty-five dollars for each returned absentee ballot.

Many of the areas in which the Dallas absentee fraud occurred were in poor and predominantly African-American neighborhoods, where the margin for victory in tight races was often produced. Not only did the absentee ballots make the difference in the city council race, but also in a referendum on a $2 billion Trinity River Project that passed by just 1,600 votes. In ways that St. Louis voters in the 1930s would have understood, the river project would have a profound impact on the landscape and the citizens of Dallas, and whether the election had been honest would not matter once the project was under way.

Add together the latest technology and balloting procedures, and the mixture is a potent one, all the more so because many of those who brewed it often have no idea of its toxicity. In 2004, the Pentagon tried to implement an Internet absentee voting system for the upcoming general election. In January, a panel of computer experts determined that this system was "inherently insecure and should be abandoned." It combined the two most vulnerable areas in modern fraud—absentee ballots and the Internet—in a system that could produce, in the experts' opinion, a "catastrophic" result. Secure Internet voting, the panel concluded, is an "essentially impossible task." Of the seven states that were ready to use the new system in 2004, one was Florida.

In early February 2004, the Pentagon reversed itself and canceled plans to use the Internet for overseas absentee balloting. The disappointed president of the company developing the project tried to reassure critics that Internet voting was "viable, valuable, and secure enough to use for filing absentee ballots." Her claims that sending absentee ballots through the Internet "is just as secure and reliable as sending them by mail" provided a certain commentary on how little some election designers know about the intricacies of delivering votes.

RECLAIMING DEMOCRACY

What, then, can be done? What does this history tell us? Is it possible to create a system of American elections as good as its people? Or is this little more than the baseless fabric of a naïve dream? Realistically, the culture of corruption is too endemic to be eradicated quickly. Yet at the very least, there are some changes that might not prove popular but could curb the cheating and make voting abuses more difficult.

For a start, states should consider making absentee balloting the rare exception to the rule. Absentee voting began long ago as a way to allow soldiers to exercise their franchise when stationed far from home. Those conditions, of course, merit continuation of voting away from the precinct. Yet in too many instances, the integrity of the ballot is traded for casual convenience for millions of voters who are at home on Election Day. The moment the ballot leaves the precinct, secrecy and integrity are compromised. If voters cannot be near home on Election Day, they could vote in a secure machine beforehand rather than submitting it by mail.

Yet new proposals are making obtaining and manipulating absentee ballots easier than ever. In May 2004, Jeb Bush signed into law a bill that allowed Florida voters to cast absentee ballots without even a witness signature. If this safeguard had been removed in 1997, the evidence to overturn the Miami mayor's race would not have existed. The new law stated: "Requiring a witness signature placed an undue burden on law-abiding voters, resulting in legitimate ballots being rejected on a technicality." The *Orlando Sentinel* casually noted that "Florida will essentially vote by mail," since all a voter needed to do was request an absentee ballot, sign it, and return it without ever leaving home. Leon County's Supervisor of Elections, Ion Sancho, who had previously tried to reject some absentee votes if the same witness signed more than six ballots, worried that the lax requirements raised "the spectre of fraudulent activity." Florida was not alone in relaxing rules for absentee ballots. In nineteen "swing states" in the 2004 election, only six required witness signatures. In many of these states, party operatives can even help voters complete their ballots and collect them for mailing. As a West Virginia fraud investigator noted, "Everybody was worried about the chads in the 2000 election when in fact by loosening up the restrictions on absentee voting they have opened up more chances for fraud."

Mail-in votes and the Internet may help end long lines of people waiting to vote, yet they cannot guarantee that the votes will be accurately counted, and they provide an easy target for vote buyers. Internet voting discriminates against poorer and less educated people with limited access to a computer, no doubt raising equal-protection claims. The modern proliferation of identity theft, especially with online purchases, should also give us pause as voters are distanced ever further from their local polls. This is not necessarily a desperate outlook; it is simply a reminder that countering the culture of corruption means looking ahead and not just backward.

For over two hundred years, reformers have noted how eliminating the Electoral College would make selecting the nation's chief executive more democratic. But there is another argument in favor of abolishing it. It would diminish many of the opportunities for fraud at the presidential level. At the very least, state legislatures could decide to award electoral votes in proportion to the popular vote. Although the standard argument against this holds that states would lose clout in presidential contests, eliminating the winner-take-all design would certainly help discount the temptation to steal or suppress a handful of votes in some selected areas. With the Electoral College, the election essentially boils down to fifty separate state elections, and the opportunities for mischief are significantly increased in a tight race, as evidenced in 1844, 1876, 1884, 1888, 1960, and 2000.

Yet it would be unrealistic to conclude that with the elimination of the anachronistic Electoral College, fraud would not be practiced in future presidential races or might not even provide the margin of victory in especially close contests. However, for partisans hoping to steal votes, the complexities of doing so in a national election involving over one hundred million votes would be multiplied no end with the elimination of the Electoral College. In 2000, Bush supporters would have had to find a half million more votes to win, rather than a mere few hundred in Florida. In 2004, Kerry supporters would have had an even more daunting task, considering Bush's popular vote lead of well over three million.

Vote "brokering" or "hauling" is another time-tested means of vote buying, although it is usually presented as an effective way to get people to the polls who have no means of transportation. Without such intermediaries, as the defense goes, the disabled, the shut-ins, and the poor would effectively be disfranchised. Without a proper recognition of the role these agents play in modern election fraud, no honest discussion of regulating their activities can occur. Additionally, virtually all discussions of campaign-finance reform ignore how part of the funds raised in modern elections is spent to pay brokers to bribe voters, and to purchase absentee ballots.

Low voter turnout and election corruption of the ballot are not mutually exclusive. In fact, the steady persistence of election fraud helps explain some of the declining participation levels among American voters. If the game is perceived to be rigged, many will opt not to play. Additionally, if one is going to play where the field is not seen to be level, the temptation to cheat is increased. In recent elections in rural West Virginia, observers pondered why voter-participation rates in some counties were in the low twenties. The standard answer from cynical voters was, "Why bother, the election has already been decided anyway." Some choose to sell their vote as a way to actually get something from a state or local government to which they have no connection anymore, while some choose to stay away from the polls entirely. If the only situation in which voters accept the legitimacy of election results occurs when their side wins, the longevity of the culture of corruption is ensured.

More than ever, the civic life of the nation needs people going to public polling places to cast their votes, rather than through the Internet or by mail. The voting machines and procedures used in East Harlem should be the same as those in West Palm Beach. Voters should be able to go to the polls protected by expanded electioneering-free zones. Courts must be willing to throw out illegal votes. Finally, voters must understand that civil rights safeguards involve the counting, not just the casting, of a free ballot.

Even with some or all of the above changes, history provides us with another sobering assessment: No matter how many reforms are implemented, no matter how trustworthy the new voting devices appear, partisans will find new ways to manipulate and cheat. Considering the rare penalties, the payoffs are simply too high for partisans to ignore the opportunities to pad their leads or minimize their opponents' advantages, and the future promises more of the same. As the issues of abortion, stem-cell research, privacy rights, and public displays of religion produce even more bitter political divisions, so does the justification to win at all costs on Election Day.

"SOMETHING VERY PERSONAL"

American voters have long assumed that our elections are the gold standard for the rest of the world to emulate. But sometimes budding democracies have something to teach us about our collective desire to "move forward" once an election is over. If the evidence indicates that the vote totals may not reflect the will of the electorate, the recent example from Ukraine shows what is democratically possible from an electorate that refused to "go on." Just days after Bush's victory in 2004, the Ukrainian presidential contest was marked by widespread intimidation of government workers and election officials, ballot stuffing, absentee fraud, "fantastically high" turnouts, repeat voting, and even the attempted assassination by poisoning of the opposition candidate, who it seemed had lost the race to the candidate endorsed by Vladimir Putin.

However, the theft did not succeed. While many of the methods deployed in the Ukrainian election had long histories in the United States, the European reaction was stunning to American observers. Crowds in the streets protested the enormity of the fraud and the threat to democratic forms. The Ukrainian Supreme Court declared the election results invalid and called for a new election. When the opposition candidate won the revote, the "Orange Revolution" became a reality. "This was a case in which something very personal was being stolen from us—the right to vote," one participant in the uprising explained.

It is an irony that contemporary American voters, to use the old cliché, believe "it can't happen here." The example from Ukraine is a reminder of what can occur when an engaged electorate and judiciary refuse to accept a tainted election. There was and is no means for voiding an American presidential election and calling a new one; or, for that matter, elections for governor or the local school board. But perhaps there ought to be; despite what some may say, new elections would damage the credibility of the election process far less than a result that nearly half the electorate considers illegitimate, leaving them prepared to win other election contests by any means possible.

Not all crises in a democracy show themselves in an angry crowd or in an explosion of outraged violence. Some of them can be lingering, pervasive, a constant, corrosive force, gradually destructive of the values in which faith in the consent of the governed is based. The degradation of the polling place ranks among these, even when its manifestations are less sensational than Bleeding Kansas, the stolen election of 1876, "Ballot Box 13," or the hanging chads of 2000. After two centuries of persistent electoral corruption, Americans have become resigned to a different reality, one where they do not even recognize that "something very personal" has been taken from them.

To reclaim the ballot box, we must start with the humblest of beginnings, the awareness that there really is a problem, and confront the uncomfortable truth that election fraud has been a common component of our nation's electoral history, and, in the aggregate, undermines the only check that the people have over their leaders. This fundamental threat to our democratic birthright must no longer be dismissed by partisan finger-pointing or trivialized by technological updates. The stakes are too high.

Endnotes

INTRODUCTION

p. xv   Before the polls even opened . . . *North American Review* (December 1887): 679–82.

p. xviii   a crime that usually pays . . . : A recent appraisal of modern American society makes a similar argument. In David Callahan's *The Cheating Culture*, the ways doctors, attorneys, athletes, CEOs, and various other groups cheat are detailed. Callahan notes that societal and professional temptations to cheat have grown markedly stronger since the 1960s. The culture of corruption that I suggest is an important component of American politics has many similarities with the culture Callahan analyzes. Yet unlike many of Callahan's subjects, who commit fraud or steal fully knowing what they do is morally indefensible or an affront to professional ethics, the politicos in this book have no such qualms. Rather, they see their actions as contributing to the public good and, therefore, fully justified.

p. xix   "Man's capacity . . ." Reinhold Niebuhr, *The Children of Light and the Children of Darkness*, xi.

CHAPTER ONE

p. 3   Colonial elections in . . . James H. Kettner, *The Development of American Citizenship*, 144; Gordon Wood, *The Creation of the American Republic*, 166–70; Chilton Williamson, *American Suffrage*, 5–8, 100; Richard P. McCormick, *The History of Voting in New Jersey*, 22–23, 37–47; Harry C. Silcox, *Philadelphia Politics From the Bottom Up*, 18–19.

p. 3   In 1742, . . . : Norman S. Cohen, "The Philadelphia Election Riot of 1742," *Pennsylvania Magazine of History and Biography* (July 1968): 310–13; William T. Parsons, "The Bloody Election of 1742," *Pennsylvania History* 36 (July 1969): 290; Steven Rosswurm, *Arms, Country, and Class*, 92–93.

p. 4   While paper ballots . . . : Gary B. Nash, *The Urban Crucible*, 16–18, 89, 235–38. Nash notes that in Boston, the most important offices, such as clerk or treasurer, were not elected posts but "were regularly filled from a small pool of acknowledged leaders to whom the lesser people ordinarily deferred (17)." One exception to the issue of secret ballots was South Carolina, which employed paper ballots as early as 1670, although in 1745 Governor James Glen supported *viva voce* because "any person who attends the balloting box, may with a very little sleight of hand, give the election to whom he pleases." See Albert McKinley, *The Suffrage Franchise*, 141, 156–57; Charles S. Sydnor, *Gentleman Freeholders*, 14–15, 19–26, 67–69; and G. B. Warren, *Boston: 1689–1776*, 31–32.

    Montesquieu, among others, was worried about the ability of those without land who, through the device of the secret ballot, could conspire to destroy property rights. He supported *viva voce* because "the lower class ought to be directed by those of higher rank, and restrained within bounds by the gravity of eminent personages." Quoted in Williamson, *American Suffrage*, 11–12, 40–41. On the other hand, Tom Paine thought it was wrong to "disfranchise any class of men," because the vote was "the primary right by which other rights are protected." Quoted in Eric Foner, *Tom Paine and Revolutionary America*, 144.

p. 5   In running . . . : Rupert Hughes, *George Washington*, 366–68; Worthington Chauncey Ford, ed., *The Writings of George Washington*, vol. II, 52–53; Robert J. Dinkin, *Voting in Provincial America*, 102–06, 115–16; Dumas Malone, *Jefferson and His Time*, vol. I, 129–30. See also Arthur M. Schlesinger, *The Birth of a Nation*, 14.

    Treating was not confined to colonial America. It had a direct link to election practices in Great Britain. Treating had become an elaborate ritual in England, complete with sumptuous dinners and picnics in areas such as Beverley, Hull, and Kent. A student of this period in Hanoverian England states that treating was used to reward loyal voters, or, in a considerable understatement, in also "arousing their anticipation." If a party refused to treat voters, they paid the price at the polls. In some areas, election breakfasts often directly preceded party nomination elections. See Frank O'Gorman, "Campaign Rituals and Ceremonies: The Social Meaning of Elections in England, 1780–1860," *Past and Present* 135 (May 1992): 85–86.

p. 6   In general, . . . : Williamson, *American Suffrage*, 50–51. Connecticut Governor Oliver Wolcott wrote in 1821 a summary of voting practices in New York in the previous century. Then, "few men of decent character have failed at some time to acquire the qualification when desired." Even some paupers, Wolcott wrote, had at times been permitted to vote. Quoted in Williamson, *American Suffrage*, 49. The practice of "fagot" voting was not new to the colonies. In England, Parliament attempted in 1711 to curb the practice of splitting up estates to qualify someone to vote. See McKinley, *The Suffrage Franchise*, 8–9.

Alexander Keyssar has authoritatively demonstrated that enfranchisement varied according to locale. "As the Revolution approached," Keyssar writes, "the rate of property ownership was falling, and the proportion of adult white males who were eligible to vote was probably less than sixty percent." Keyssar, *The Right to Vote*, 7; Robert E. Brown, *Middle-Class Democracy and the Revolution in Massachusetts*, 40–48; Jamin B. Raskin, "Legal Aliens, Local Citizens: The Historical, Constitutional, and Theoretical Meanings of Alien Suffrage," *University of Pennsylvania Law Review* 141 (April 1993): 1399–1401.

p. 7   The practice became . . . : Williamson, *American Suffrage*, 53–55; Dinkin, *Voting in Provincial America*, 117; McKinley, *The Suffrage Franchise*, 458–59, 465.

p. 7   Sheriffs were among . . . : McCormick, *The History of Voting in New Jersey*, 46–60. The 1725 law required New Jersey sheriffs to post news of an election at least twenty days prior to an election, and prohibited moving the location of the polls. The sheriffs also appointed clerks representing each candidate to administer oaths to voters. These clerks then registered the name and address of each voter. A sheriff found violating this statute could face a fine up to 300 pounds.

p. 8   In New York . . . : Nash, *The Urban Crucible*, 87–98, 143–46.

p. 8   With the outbreak . . . : Williamson, *American Suffrage*, 77–78; Nash, *The Urban Crucible*, 54–56.

p. 9   In some states . . . : James Schouler, "Evolution of the American Voter," *American Historical* Review 2 (July 1897): 666; John Chalmers Vinson, "Electioneering in North Carolina, 1800–1835," *North Carolina Historical Review* (April 1952): 171–88.

p. 9   Perhaps no elections . . . : Samuel Eliot Morison, "Struggle Over the Adoption of the Constitution of Massachusetts, 1780," *Massachusetts Historical Society Proceedings* L (May 1917): 353–412; Gary B. Nash, *The Unknown American Revolution*, notes that "The people of the Commonwealth of Massachusetts would now live under a constitution they had rejected (303–04)"; for Adams's role in writing the constitution, see David McCullough, *John Adams*, 220–25. While guaranteeing that "all elections ought to be free," the Massachusetts constitution also noted that "with grateful hearts," the people of Massachusetts thanked "the great Legislator of the Universe," who allowed the people to form the compact "without fraud, violence, or surprise."

p. 10   As the framers . . . : Keyssar, *The Right to Vote*, 21–25. Abigail Thernstrom notes that although there is no explicit right to vote in the federal constitution, that right is "certainly implicit" in the guarantee that every state shall have a republican form of government, and members of the House would be selected by "the People of the several States." Determining exactly who "the People" were who could vote was left to the states. "Right to Vote," in Kermit L. Hall, ed., *The Oxford Companion to the Supreme Court*, 899.

p. 10   "The election . . . : W. B. Allen, ed., *George Washington: A Collection*, 448.

p. 11   An example . . . : Williamson, *American Suffrage*, 168–84; Robert A. Dahl, *Who Governs*, 16. Connecticut repealed the Stand Up Law in 1817, but only after a concerted Federalist effort to keep the law. Raskin, "Legal Aliens, Local Citizens," 1400.

p. 11   In the infamous . . . : Leonard L. Richards, *The Slave Power*, 40–43; Garry Wills,
            "Negro President", 1–13, 50–61. A recent analysis of the 1800 election in the
            context of the 2000 election is Joyce Appleby, "Presidents, Congress, and
            Courts: Partisan Passions in Motion," *Journal of American History* 88 (Sep-
            tember 2001): 407–14; William W. Freehling, *The Road to Disunion*, 559;
            Joanne B. Freeman, *Affairs of Honor*, 199–261.

p. 12   While the structure . . . : Keyssar, *The Right to Vote*, 29, 330–32.

p. 13 .   While the debate . . . : Robert V. Remini, *Henry Clay: Statesman for the Union*,
            234–50; Freehling, *The Road to Disunion*, 267.

p. 13   Besides expanding . . . : Leonard D. White, *The Jacksonians*, 342–43. In the 1824
            presidential election, six of the twenty-four states still selected their electors in
            the state legislatures. Jackson's supporters in New York within the Tammany
            Society elected a slate of pro-Jackson candidates in an 1827 primary by
            employing repeaters as well as intimidators brandishing hickory sticks to ward
            off voters loyal to John Quincy Adams. See Gustavus Myers, *The History of
            Tammany*, 73–74; Jerome Mushkat, *Tammany: The Evolution of a Political
            Machine*, 84, 107.

p. 14   Kentucky had a chronic problem . . . : "The Importance of a Register Law to the
            Purity of the Elective Franchise" (Louisville, Ky.: N. H. White, 1840).

p. 14   One loyal Whig . . . : William Smith King to Thurlow Weed, November 27, 1858,
            Thurlow Weed papers, University of Rochester; *Detroit Free Press*, April 8, 1860.
            Early attempts to challenge the constitutionality of registry laws proved unsuc-
            cessful. See *Capen v. Foster* 12 Pickering 485 for an 1832 case in Massachusetts.

p. 15   In the 1857 . . . : Iowa Constitutional Convention Proceedings (1857), 863–64;
            Maryland Constitutional Convention (1851), 41; Anthony Gronowicz, *Race
            and Class Politics in New York City Before the Civil War*, 111–12; Joel H. Silbey,
            The Partisan Imperative, 141–43; Eric Foner, *Free Soil, Free Labor, Free Men*,
            230; Williamson, *American Suffrage*, 275–76.

p. 15   In the Maryland . . . : James W. Harry, *Maryland Constitution of 1851*, 38, 73.

p. 15   The essential arguments . . . : Kenneth J. Winkle, *The Politics of Community*,
            76–83.

p. 17   In Massachusetts . . . : New Bedford *Mercury*, quoted in the Massachusetts
            Constitutional Convention, vol. I (1853): 582–83; Jerrold G. Rusk, "The Effect
            of the Australian Ballot Reform on Split Ticket Voting: 1876–1908," *American
            Political Science Review* 64 (December 1970): 1221; J. Allen Smith, *The Growth
            and Decadence of Constitutional Government*, 36, 48–55, who noted "To enfran-
            chise the wage earning population without at the same time ensuring a secret
            ballot was to give, in large measure, the form without the substance of political
            power." To Smith, "conservatives appreciated the advantage of *viva voce*." (36);
            Richard Franklin Bensel, *The American Ballot Box*, 55–57; Reeve Huston, *Land
            and Freedom*, 30; Schouler, "Evolution of the American Voter," 670.

p. 17   In a constitutional convention . . . : Proceedings of the Kentucky Constitutional
            Convention (1849–50), 201, 226.

p. 17   In Massachusetts . . . : *Hartford Courant*, November 22, 1853; Williamson, *American Suffrage*, 274.

p. 18   In New York . . . : Mushkat, *Tammany*, 186. Mushkat also writes of the considerable help Marcy received in 1851 from Tammany Hall, when ballot boxes were stolen and violence at the polls was exercised to wrest control of key county offices from the Whigs. Myers, *The History of Tammany Hall*, 118–19.

p. 18   The source . . . : Edwin G. Burrows and Mike Wallace, *Gotham: A History of New York City to 1898*, 823–25; Kenneth D. Ackerman, *Boss Tweed*, 37–59; Myers, *The History of Tammany Hall*, 120, 135; Leo Hershkowitz, *Tweed's New York: Another Look*, 8–9, 18; Alexander B. Callow, Jr., *The Tweed Ring*, 110–12. See also *New York Evening Post*, October 10, 1856.

p. 19   Tammany employed . . . : *New York Evening Post*, October 10, 1851 and October 28, 1854; Larry J. Sabato and Glenn R. Simpson, *Dirty Little Secrets*, 276; Peter Livingston quoted in Williamson, *American Suffrage*, 56; John I. Davenport, *The Election Frauds of New York City and Their Prevention*, 93–94.

p. 22   One St. Louis . . . : Kate Kelly, *Election Day: An American Holiday, An American History*, 86.

p. 22   In New Orleans . . . : New Orleans *Commercial Bulletin*, October 30 and November 1, 1852; New Orleans *Bee*, November 1, 1852; New Orleans *Louisiana Courier*, November 11, 1853; Mark Wahlgren Summers, *The Plundering Generation*, 57.

p. 23   The practice . . . : Roy P. Basler, ed., *The Collected Works of Abraham Lincoln*, I, 212–13. Other major newspapers that kept close tabs on election procedures are the *New York Evening Post*, *New York Herald*, *Detroit Free Press*, Indianapolis *Daily Sentinel*, Philadelphia *Daily News*, Providence *Journal*, *Daily Chicago Times*, New York *Morning Express*, Chicago *Times & Herald*, Cincinnati *Daily Commercial*, and the Newark *Advertiser*.

p. 23   In New Orleans . . . : *New Orleans Bee*, October 16, 1855; "Address of Charles Gayarre, to the People of the State, on the Late Frauds Perpetrated at the Election Held on the 7th of November, 1853, in the City of New Orleans," in Edward Clifton Wharton Family Papers, Folder 10, Special Collections, Hill Memorial Library, Louisiana State University Library.

p. 25   How widespread . . . : William E. Gienapp, "Politics Seem to Enter Into Everything: Political Culture In the North, 1840–1860," in William E. Gienapp, et. al., *Essays on American Antebellum Politics*, 23–29.

        Cushing, *Massachusetts Election Cases*, 583; *People v. Cook* 8 New York 67; *People v. Cicott* 16 Mich. 295; *People v. Tuthill* 51 N.Y. 550; in Frederick C. Brightley, *A Collection of Leading Cases on the Law of Elections*. Determining whether one's knowledge in breaking existing election law constitutes fraud was examined by a number of state courts. In Massachusetts in 1835, a court decided that a defendant is not criminally liable for illegally voting unless he knew he was not a qualified voter and was also attempting to vote as an illegal act. Courts in other states, however, ruled that ignorance of the law was not an excuse. In

Tennessee, a defendant could be tried for vote fraud even if he was not aware that he was breaking state statutes; yet, in order for conviction, "it must appear that the voter know of a state of facts which would, in point of law, disqualify him." In California, the law stated "where an unlawful act is proved to have been done," the law assumes "it to have been intended, and the proof of justification or excuse lies with the defendant." *Mc Guire v. State of Tennessee* 7 Humph. 54; *People v. Harris* 29 Cal. 678.

Several methods of fraud, including intimidation, illegal registration, and paying one not to vote, would not be found in simply examining vote returns. Looking solely at whether returns were inflated over an arbitrary five percent mark misses the culture of fraud that did, indeed, permeate antebellum elections. See also the exchange by Walter Dean Burnham, Philip E. Converse, and Jerrold G. Rusk in the *American Political Science Review* 68 (September 1974): 1002–57; Burnham, "Those High Nineteenth-Century American Voting Turnouts: Fact or Fiction?," *Journal of Interdisciplinary History* (Spring 1986): 613–41. In "New Perspectives on Election Fraud in the Gilded Age," Peter H. Argersinger notes that "the subject of election fraud thus not only represents a challenge to the methodology of the new political history in terms of raising the problem of data validity, but also raises questions of deeper significance concerning the portrayal of political culture and the party system." *Political Science Quarterly* 100 (Winter 1985–86): 672–73.

p. 25   In 1844, . . . : Thomas F. Redard, "The Election of 1844 in Louisiana: A New Look at the Ethno-Cultural Approach," *Louisiana History* 22 (Fall 1981): 419–33; John M. Sacher, *A Perfect War of Politics*, 124–25, 237; Michael F. Holt, *The Rise and Fall of the American Whig Party*, 198, 203; Mushkat, *Tammany*, 219; Charles Sellers, "Election of 1844," in Arthur M. Schlesinger, Jr. and Fred L. Israel, eds., *History of American Presidential Elections*, vol. I, 791–95; Sellers, *James K. Polk: Continentalist*, discusses allegations of Whig impropriety in Pennsylvania and New York (155); Henry Clay to P. R. Fendall, October 28, 1848, Miscellaneous Letters, Henry Clay papers, Filson Club, Louisville. In looking ahead to the 1848 election, Clay warned that Whig candidate Zachary Taylor "may be cheated out of Pennsylvania as I was in 1844." Remini, *Henry Clay*, 663–65.

In the 1848 presidential race, a curious anomaly arose in Virginia. Although the Free Soil candidate, former president Martin Van Buren, received more than ten percent of the vote nationwide, in Virginia he tallied only nine votes. When Free Soilers charged fraud in the election, one unrepentant official replied: "Yes, fraud. And we're still looking for the son of a bitch who voted nine times." Jimmie Rex McClellan, "Two Party Monopoly to Third Party Participation in American Politics" (Ph.D. diss., Union for Experimenting Colleges and Universities, 1984), 75.

p. 26   In an 1855 . . . : *New York Evening Post*, November 2, 1855; *Providence Journal*, April 14, 1854.

p. 27   In Louisville . . . : American Party of Kentucky, "Proceedings of the Grand Council of Kentucky" (August 20, 1856), 5; Thomas P. Baldwin, "George D. Prentice, the Louisville *Anzieger*, and the 1855 Bloody Monday Riots," *Filson Club History Quarterly* (October 1993): 482–95; Charles E. Deusner, "The Know Nothing Riots in Louisville," *Register of the Kentucky Historical Society* (April 1963): 122–47; Holt, *The Rise and Fall of the American Whig Party*, 935–36.

p. 28   The City Council . . . : *Louisville Weekly Democrat*, August 8, 1855; George H. Yater, *Two Hundred Years at the Falls of the Ohio*, 66–70; Baldwin, "George D. Prentice, the Louisville *Anzieger*, and the 1855 Bloody Monday Riots," 485–88.

p. 28   By midday . . . : *Louisville Daily Courier*, August 8, 1855; Yater, *Two Hundred Years at the Falls of the* Ohio, 69–70; Lowell H. Harrison and James C. Klotter, *A New History of Kentucky*, 123; Baldwin, "George D. Prentice, the Louisville *Anzieger*, and the 1855 Bloody Monday Riots," 494; Stephen E. Maizlish, "The Meaning of Nativism and the Crisis of the Union: The Know-Nothing Movement in the Antebellum North," in Gienapp, et al., *Essays on American Antebellum Politics*, 190–91; Summers, *The Plundering Generation*, 65–67; New York *Evening Post*, August 15, 1855. The *Chicago Daily Tribune* concluded that a March 1856 mayoral election had been stolen by Irish and Catholic "foreigners" pouring into the city to stuff ballot boxes for "the Black Democratic ticket." See *Daily Tribune*, March 5 and 8, 1856.

p. 29   In New Orleans . . . : Leon Cyprian Soule, *The Know Nothing Party in New Orleans*, 46–80.

CHAPTER TWO

p. 31   "I may here be . . . : Alexis de Tocqueville, *Democracy in America*, vol. II, 110.

p. 34   "The people of every . . .": Douglas quoted in David Herbert Donald, *Lincoln*, 232.

p. 34   In the village of Douglas . . . : "Special Committee Appointed to Investigate the Troubles in the Territory of Kansas," U.S. House of Representatives, 34th Congress, 1st Session (Serial 869), no. 200, 3–5, testimony, 2, 882 (hereinafter referred to as the Howard Committee).

p. 34   Although Whitfield . . . : Howard Committee, 5–9; Chester H. Rowell, *A Historical and Legal Digest of all the Contested Election Cases in the House of Representatives of the United States from the First to the Fifty-Sixth Congress, 1789–1901*, 56th Congress, 2d Session, Doc. 510, 1901, 145–47. See also R. H. Williams, *With the Border Ruffians*, 82.

p. 34   The outcry . . . : Howard Committee, 9–35, 132–33, 168, 174–75, 357, 389–91, 990–91, 1012–13, 1060–61; David M. Potter, *The Impending Crisis*, 201–02; *Chicago Daily Tribune*, January 5 and 28, 1856.

    The Kansas requirement for residency was very lean compared to other territorial examples. In 1789, the first Congress reenacted the Northwest Ordinance of 1787 to allow freehold aliens who had been residents for two years the right to vote. See Raskin, "Legal Aliens, Local Citizens: 1402–03.

p. 37   In May 1856 . . . : Kenneth Stampp, *America in 1857*, 145–46; Richard O. Boyer, *The Legend of John Brown*, 457, 494–503.

p. 37   "crime against Kansas": David Herbert Donald, *Charles Summer*, 278–82.

p. 37   The new pro-slavery . . . : *New York Times*, October 24 and 27, 1857, February 4, 1858; Stampp, *America in 1857*, 144–81; James A. Rawley, *Race and Politics*, 214; Jeffrey D. Schultz, *Presidential Scandals*, 98–100.

In June of 1856, Senator Robert Toombs of Georgia introduced a bill which would have rejected both the "border ruffian" government and the free state government in Kansas. Toombs wanted a new federal census ordered in Kansas supervised by officials appointed by President Pierce. After determining the proper voters in Kansas, a new election would then be ordered for November 1856 for a new constitutional convention. While Democrats supported the bill, Republican congressmen defeated its passage.

p. 38   Its essential ideology . . . : Foner, *Free Soil, Free Labor, Free Men*, 43–48, 59–61.

p. 38   In his inaugural address . . . : Richards, *The Slave Power*, 201.

p. 39   In the Oxford precinct . . . : *Chicago Daily Tribune*, January 5, 6, 10, 16, and 20, 1858; *New York Times*, October 24 and 27, 1857, January 26, 1858; McCaslin to William Bigler, December 25, 1857, William Bigler Papers, Historical Society of Pennsylvania; Potter, *The Impending Crisis*, 204; Stampp, *America in 1857*, 65, 155, 262–64.

p. 40   "In 14 or 15 . . .": McCaslin to William Bigler, December 25, 1857, Bigler Papers.

p. 41   The Lecompton constitution . . . : Stampp, *America in 1857*, 291–93, 328–29; Rawley, *Race and Politics*, 202–52; Richards, *The Slave Power*, 202–11; Richard H. Sewell, *Ballots for Freedom*, 343–45.

p. 43   In 1855 . . . : Madison *Daily State Journal*, August 31, November 3, 5, and 7, December 14 and 27, 1855, January 5, 25, and 28, February 26, March 21, 22, and 25, 1856; *Chicago Daily Tribune*, January 10, 14, 21, and 23, March 2, 27, and 28, 1856; Charles R. Tuttle, *An Illustrated History of the State of Wisconsin*, 306–09, 316–21; Robert C. Nesbitt, *Wisconsin: A History*, 232–33.

p. 44   "What is popular government . . . ": Madison *Daily State Journal*, March 25, 1856.

p. 45   In San Francisco . . . : *New York Evening Post*, August 20, 1856; Philip J. Ethington, *The Public City*,, 75–76, 118–20. For discussion of *viva voce* elections in another West Coast setting, see Paul Bourke and Donald DeBats, *Washington County*, 8–12, 174–81; and Kelly, *Election Day*, 92–94. See also Mary P. Ryan, *Civic Wars*, 148–49.

The 1856 election in New York City also witnessed Know-Nothing violence, but the party could not compete with the election skills of Mayor Fernando Wood, whose forces used brickbats, axes, and pistols to intimidate any opposition, also breaking into several ballot boxes. Not surprisingly, Wood easily won reelection. Samuel Augustus Pleasants, *Fernando Wood of New York,* 62–65. See also Edward K. Spann, *The New Metropolis,* 382–83.

p. 46   To defeat a slate . . . : *Washington Daily Union,* June 2 and 3, 1857; Washington *Daily National Intelligencer,* June 1, 2 and 3, 4, 1857; Baltimore *Sun,* June 2 and 3, 1857; *Richmond Dispatch,* June 2 and 3, 1857; New *York Daily Times,* November 6, 1856, June 2, 3, 1857; *New York Times,* November 6, 1856; Benjamin Tuska, *Know-Nothingism in Baltimore,* Bensel, *The American Ballot Box,* 48–49, 170–72; Sister Mary St. Patrick McConville, "Political Nativism in the State of Maryland, 1830–1860" (Ph.D. dissertation, Catholic University of America, 1928), 115–20; Sewell, *Ballots for Freedom,* 265–77. For Know-Nothingism in Cincinnati, see Zane L. Miller, *Boss Cox's Cincinnati,* 65–66.

p. 48   "It cannot have escaped" . . . : Baltimore *Sun,* June 3, 1857. The Washington *Daily National Intelligencer* even found the railroad companies which had transported the "plug uglies" from Baltimore to Washington to be partly liable: "Is not the Railroad Company responsible for any injury done to property in this way?" the paper asked. June 4, 1857.

p. 50   In the Twelfth Ward . . . : Donald, *Lincoln,* 255–56; Myers, *The History of Tammany Hall,* 195–96.

CHAPTER THREE

p. 51   "In the worst days . . .": Henry Adams, *Democracy: An American Novel,* 72–73.

p. 52   In 1862, . . . : Myers, *The History of Tammany Hall,* 203–04.

p. 53   Democrats . . . : James M. McPherson, *Battle Cry of Freedom,* 505–06, who notes that the election of 1864 saw "some irregularities," but dismisses their overall impact because the partisan cheating "tended to cancel each other out." In a statement that one can interpret in a variety of ways, McPherson concludes "the voting of soldiers in 1864 was about as fair and honest as 19th-century elections generally were" (805 n. 69).

p. 53   "It would be worse . . .": Seymour quoted in William M. Burcher, "A History of Soldier Voting in the State of New York," *New York History* 25 (October 1944): 462. Seymour vetoed a bill authorizing soldier voting in the field. After the legislature failed to override the veto, New York lawmakers hastily passed an enabling constitutional amendment that bypassed the governor. In 1872, a state constitutional revision assembly extended the suffrage to members serving in the state militia.

p. 53   Some states allowed . . . : Josiah Henry Benton, *Voting in the Field,* 306–09; Oscar Osburn Winther, "The Soldier Vote in the Election of 1864," *New York History* 25 (October 1944): 440–47; Joseph Allen Frank, *With Ballot and Bayonet,* 94–95.

p. 55   Rep. Lazarus Powell . . . : "Speech of Honorable L. W. Powell of Kentucky," March 3–4, 1864 (Washington, D.C.: Constitutional Union Office, 1864), 8–9.

p. 55   With so much . . . : McPherson, *Battle Cry of Freedom*, 690–94; Benton, *Voting in the Field*, 4–16; Frank, *With Ballot and Bayonet*, 95; Davenport, *The Election Frauds of New York*, Keyssar, *The Right to Vote*, 104–05. For a Missouri election where the local militia controlled the polls, see *Bruce v. Loan (1862)*, in George W. McCrary, *A Treatise on the American Law of Election*, 346.

Jean H. Baker, *Affairs of Party*, 314–16; Benton, *Voting in the Field*, 158–64. Benton concludes that New York Governor Horatio Seymour had "commissioned a lot of irresponsible, unscrupulous men as inspectors, to get the vote of New York soldiers for McClellan, and when they could not get the votes for McClellan they forged them (167–68)." See Stewart Mitchell, *Horatio Seymour of New York*, 376–81.

p. 56   Republicans, wary . . . : Myers, *The History of Tammany Hall*, 206; Davenport, *The Election Frauds of New York*, 60–64; *New York Times*, November 9, 1864; Glenn C. Altschuler and Stuart M. Blumin, *Rude Republic*, 176–77. For the 1863 draft riots, see Iver Bernstein, *The New York City Draft Riots*. Thomas Nast drew a *Harper's Weekly* cartoon that depicted "copperheads" copying the names of war dead in order to falsely register them; it appeared the weekend before the election. Lincoln remarked that "Thomas Nast has been our best recruiting sergeant." Kenneth Ackerman, *Boss Tweed*, 35–36.

p. 57   While Indiana . . . : Altschuler and Blumin, *Rude Republic*, 174–75; Winther, "The Soldier Vote in the Election of 1864," 452–53. After the Civil War, fifteen states had repealed acts allowing soldiers to vote by the end of the 1800s. Only Michigan, Kansas, Maine, Nevada, and Rhode Island kept those statutes on the books. As the role of the military grew in American life in the 1900s, the argument over allowing soldiers serving their country to vote by absentee method increased. For the statewide movement to repeal soldier voting, see Benton, *Voting in the Field*, 314–15.

p. 58   In 1867, . . . : Foner, *Reconstruction*, 314, 342, 442; Joseph G. Dawson III, *Army Generals and Reconstruction*, 75–77; Joe Gray Taylor, *Louisiana Reconstructed*, 150–53.

p. 58   The Ku Klux Klan . . . : Allen W. Trelease, *White Terror*, 34–35, 113–85. The historian Steven Hahn describes an ironic form of electoral intimidation after the Civil War: African-Americans intimidating other freedmen who dared vote Democratic. One Mississippi African-American justified the attacks on black Democrats: "We don't believe they have a right to acquiesce with a party who refuse to recognize their right to participate in public affairs." Hahn, *A Nation Under Our Feet*, 226. Paul Ortiz found the same dynamics used by African-American women in Florida. Ortiz, *Emancipation Betrayed*, 23.

p. 58   In Camilla, Georgia . . . : "Condition of Affairs in Georgia," 67–72; Hahn, *A Nation Under Our Feet*, 288–92.

p. 60   Former slaves in Mississippi . . . : U.S. House of Representatives, 40th Congress, 3rd Session (1868), Miscellaneous Document no. 53, 5–30, 149–50, 219; Trelease, *White Terror*, 88–89, 274–78.

p. 60   In St. Landry Parish . . . : U.S. House Reports, "Condition of the South,"
        763–65; Trelease, *White Terror,* 127–36. Trelease concludes that due primarily to
        Klan intimidation, Louisiana and Georgia were carried by the Democrats in
        1868 (185).

p. 61   When a joint committee . . . : Supplemental Report of the Joint Committee of
        the General Assembly of Louisiana, "Conduct of the Late Elections and the
        Condition of Peace and Good Order," v–xxvi; Gilles Vandal, "The Policy of
        Violence in Caddo Parish, 1865–1884," *Louisiana History* 32 (Spring 1991):
        164–78; Dawson, *Army Generals and Reconstruction,* 86–92; Taylor, *Louisiana
        Reconstructed,* 172. Dawson writes that with General Lovell Rousseau in com-
        mand of federal troops in Louisiana, there was a much more relaxed atmosphere
        in which to steal the election than with General Buchanan just a few months
        before. Dawson says Rousseau's actions bordered on "the point of negligence
        and had allowed the Democrats almost a free hand in several parishes" (92).

p. 62   Georgia provided . . . : U.S. House of Representatives, 40th Congress, 3rd Ses-
        sion (1869), "Condition of Affairs in Georgia," Miscellaneous Document no.
        52, 39–64.

p. 62   In New York . . . : Davenport, *The Election Frauds of New York,* 139–40, 168–72;
        Charles H. Coleman, *The Election of 1868,* 365–67; Hershkowitz, *Tweed's New
        York,* 325–26; Stewart Mitchell, *Horatio Seymour,* 474–80.

p. 65   In Arkansas . . . : "Election Fraud in Arkansas," 42nd Congress, 2nd session,
        Report no. 5; "Boles vs. Edwards," 42nd Congress, 2nd session, Report no. 10;
        Steven F. Lawson, *Black Ballots,* 4; Keyssar, *The Right to Vote,* 106. U.S. House
        Reports, "Condition of the South," 43rd Congress, 2nd Session, no. 261,
        352–61. For other examples of election fraud in Louisiana in the elections pre-
        ceding 1876, see *New York Times,* November 14, 17, 19, and 29, 1874, January
        1, 2, 7, 8, 9, 10, and 13, February 24, 1875. For examples in other areas of the
        country, see Philadelphia *Inquirer,* October 12, 1870; *New York Herald,*
        November 2, 1872; Howard Frank Gillette, "Corrupt and Contented: Philadel-
        phia's Political Machine, 1865–1877" (Ph.D. dissertation, Yale University,
        1970), 74–76; *New York Times,* December 20, 1869; Steven Jeffrey Fram, "Puri-
        fying the Ballot?: The Politics of Electoral Procedure in New York State,
        1821–71" (M.A. thesis, Cornell University, 1983), 101, 106–09; Cincinnati
        Enquirer, January 19, 1869; Milwaukee *News,* February 28, 1874; *Chicago Tri-
        bune,* March 11, 1875; *Detroit Free Press,* October 22, 1870.

p. 67   Not surprisingly . . . : Foner, *Reconstruction,* 565–68; James E. Campbell, *The
        American Campaign,* 171–75; Mark Wahlgren Summers, *The Era of Good Steal-
        ings,* 288–90; Alexander C. Flick, *Samuel Jones Tilden,* 320; *New York Times,*
        October 6, 7, 8, 10, 20, 24, 25, 26, and 27, 1876. New York City election super-
        visor John Davenport was prepared to address the possibility of wholesale fraud
        in the city's election by methodically verifying registry lists. On election eve, lists
        of fraudulent voters were published in the *Times.* See *New York Times,* October
        29 and November 6, 1876.

p. 67   In Mississippi . . . : U.S. Senate Miscellaneous Documents, 44th Congress, 2nd
         Session, "Testimony as to the Denial of the Elective Franchise in Mississippi at
         the Election of 1875 and 1876," Misc. Document no. 45, 316–18; Aberdeen
         Examiner, July 26 and September 28, 1876 and "Testimony as to the Denial of
         the Elective Franchise in Mississippi," 320–24. A federal grand jury concluded
         in somewhat purple prose that in the Mississippi election, "fraud, intimidation
         and violence" had been practiced to a degree "without a parallel in the annals of
         history." Hahn, *A Nation Under Our Feet*, 302. *New York Times*, October 9, 1876,
         January 1, 1877. The January 1 edition of the *Times* mistakenly lists the
         Alabama vote totals as coming from Mississippi.

p. 68   In Florida . . . : Jerrel H. Shofner, "Fraud and Intimidation in the Florida Elec-
         tion of 1876," *Florida Historical Quarterly* (April 1964): 323–24; Roy Morris, Jr.,
         Fraud of the Century, 147.

p. 69   In East Feliciana . . . : Dawson, *Army Generals and Reconstruction*, 232–34; Leon
         Burr Richardson, *William E. Chandler: Republican*, 184–87; Paul Leland
         Haworth, *The Hayes–Tilden Disputed Presidential Election of 1876*, 118; *New
         York Times*, November 7, 1876; for South Carolina, see *New York Times*, October
         18, 1876. Although troops were stationed in Louisiana ostensibly to protect the
         polls, the small number of troops in the state betrays the fact that they could not
         do their job effectively. In 1866, there were 9,772 troops stationed in Louisiana;
         by November 1876, there were just 800. See Dawson, *Army Generals and Recon-
         struction*, appendix III.
             In "The Negro, the Republican Party, and the Election of 1876 in
         Louisiana," *Louisiana History* (Spring 1966): 101, T. B. Tunnell, Jr., argued that
         the apparent loss of the black vote in Louisiana was not due to Democratic vio-
         lence but rather to dissatisfaction "with Republican rule." Years later, Tunnell
         recanted this view entirely. See *Crucible of Reconstruction*, 212.

p. 70   One resident explained . . . : *New York Times*, December 16, 1876.

p. 70   The election margin . . . : U.S. Senate Report, "Florida Election, 1876," 44th
         Congress, 2nd Session, Report no. 611, 12–13, part II, 12–15. This report is
         helpful in observing the partisan nature of the 1876 recount, as Democratic and
         Republican senators and their counsel differed on every contention of fraud.
         New York Times, November 14, 1876.

p. 71   When a train . . . : Lloyd Robinson, *The Stolen Election*, 148; C. Vann Wood-
         ward, *Reunion and Reaction*, 111–13; Allan Nevins, *Abram S. Hewitt: With Some
         Account of Peter Cooper*, 319–23; Haworth, *The Hayes–Tilden Disputed Presiden-
         tial Election*, 55; Jerrell H. Shofner, "Florida in the Balance: The Electoral
         Count of 1876," *Florida Historical Quarterly* (October 1968): 123–24. In *Samuel
         Jones Tilden*, Flick argues that Tilden won Louisiana, although "intimidations of
         the Democrats undoubtedly affected the voting, but not sufficiently to deter-
         mine the result" (343). In a formula that would be repeated by countless other
         scholars in analyzing the significance of fraud and intimidation, Flick con-
         cluded: "Republican frauds in registration offset Democratic intimidations"

(343). This zero-sum approach, it should be noted, is often offered without any corresponding evidentiary material.

p. 73   Both parties . . . : See Claude G. Bowers, *The Tragic Era*, 522–40, who termed the election the "Crowning Crime" of the era.

p. 73   In a Key West precinct . . . : U.S. Senate Report no. 611, "Florida Election, 1876," 5–7.

p. 74   Although on . . . : *New Orleans Republican*, November 14, 15 and 17, 1876; John Sherman to D. F. Boyd, December 7, 1876, in David French Boyd Papers, Box 4, Special Collections, Hill Memorial Library, Louisiana State University; "Testimony Taken by the Select Committee on Alleged Frauds in the Presidential Election of 1876," 45th Congress, 3rd Session, Misc. Doc. 31; Keith Ian Polakoff, *The Politics of Inertia*, 210–14; Taylor, *Louisiana Reconstructed*, 490–93.

By contrast, the New Orleans *Daily Picayune* found nothing corrupt in the 1876 election, reporting that the voting was conducted "with uninterrupted tranquility." If anything, the paper later claimed, it was the Democrats who were defrauded. Many African-Americans wanted to vote Democratic, the paper claimed, but were threatened by Republicans. Since the election, the paper found that with Tilden supposedly in the lead, the freedmen "have manifested the utmost enthusiasm over the results." The *Daily Picayune* gave Louisiana to Tilden by a margin of over 9,000 votes. See November 8, 9, 13, 14, and 15, 1876. See also Baton Rouge *Daily Advocate*, November 8, 1876; *New York Times*, February 14, 1877.

p. 75   In any event . . . : A meeting of selected Republicans and Democrats at the Wormley Hotel in Washington has sometimes been perceived as the location where a "secret" deal, or the "Compromise of 1877," was formalized whereby Democrats would support Hayes in return for the essential end of Reconstruction. See Woodward, *Reunion and Reaction*, who writes that something else was at stake in the spring of 1877: "This was the question of whether the country could regain the ability to settle Presidential elections without the resort to force (13)."

p. 76   Hewitt declined . . . : "Secret History of the Disputed Election, 1876–77," in Allan Nevins, ed., *Selected Writings of Abram S. Hewitt*, 168–85; *New York Times*, December 7, 1876 and March 2, 1877; Woodward, *Reunion and Reaction*, 153–54; Foner, *Reconstruction*, 578–81; Summers, *The Gilded Age*, 35–36; Polakoff, *The Politics of Inertia*, 232–314; Robinson, *The Stolen Election*, 115–27.

Also in dispute during the election of 1876 were the electoral votes of Oregon. Hayes had won Oregon's three electoral votes by a 500-vote margin, yet one of Oregon's electors was also a postmaster and was, therefore, constitutionally prohibited from participating in the Electoral College since he held a federal office. Oregon's Democratic governor refused the elector's certificate and appointed a Democrat to fill his place, who would then cast the 185th vote for Tilden. The Electoral Commission denied the Governor's action, saying that the popular will of Oregonians was clearly for Hayes and placed all of Oregon's electoral votes in Hayes's column. Outraged Democrats responded by wondering why the Commission did not give such prominence to the voters' wishes in Louisiana and Florida. See *New York Times,* December 8, 9, and 10, 1876.

p. 77   "No facts" . . . "is horrible": Morris, *Fraud of the Century,* 227–28. Another argument was offered by Paul Leland Haworth, who wrote "no one familiar with the evidence and with the attitude of the southern Democrats toward Negro suffrage will for a moment doubt that there was sufficient intimidation to change the whole result." In the final analysis, Haworth concluded, "*in equity* the electoral votes of the state of Florida belonged to Hayes." *The Hayes–Tilden Disputed Presidential Election,* 76.

p. 77   "violated the sanctity". . . Quoted in Ortiz, *Emancipation Betrayed,* 216–17.

p. 77   Earlier writers . . . : Woodward, *Reunion and Reaction,* 19; Foner, *Reconstruction,* 576 n 22; U.S. Senate Report 611, 12–13. Most recently, Roy Morris dismisses cries of Democratic suppression of the African-American vote and finds that what happened to Tilden was nothing less than a "virtual coup d'état." Morris's claims regarding the onslaught against the ability of former slaves to vote rests on quick references to other secondary works and ignores the social and political reality of the post-War South and the culture that saw African-American suffrage as a right that would take over a century to acquire outright. Morris, *Fraud of the Century,* 256. For the election results in South Carolina, see Ronald F. King, "Counting the Votes: South Carolina's Stolen Election of 1876," *Journal of Interdisciplinary History* 33 (Autumn 2001): 169–91.

p. 77   One Congressional committee . . . : *New York Times,* May 24, 1878. One remnant of the 1876 election was a bill passed in 1887 and signed into law by Grover Cleveland. It called for the counting of the electoral votes to be done in the states within six days of the Electoral College meeting. The six-day "window" was a relatively innocuous phrase that came to be of great significance in the 2000 recount. See Haworth, *The Hayes–Tilden Disputed Presidential Election,* 305–06.

p. 79   Potter and the Democrats . . . : *New York Times,* May 17, 18, 23, and 28, 1878; Haworth, *The Hayes–Tilden Disputed Presidential Election,* 307–08.

p. 80   "privilege and duty" . . . : *Nation,* May 2, 1878; *New York Times,* May 11, 14, 15, 16, and 28, June 6 and 9, 1878. The *Times,* a Republican paper, dismissed the McLin "confessions" since he had waited until after failing to secure a government post. "At first blush it seems a little singular," the *Times* felt, that McLin and his cohorts "waited so long before they cleansed their bosoms of the perilous stuff which must have weighed upon their hearts" (May 19, 1878.) In 1940, Leon Burr Richardson defended the Republican efforts in the South because of Democratic "intimidation or fraud," which he understood was "a matter of course in the South." Regarding McLin, Richardson dismissed him as a "somewhat unstable and shifty character." See Richardson, *William E. Chandler,* 186–89.

p. 81   "Here, then" . . . : "Investigation of Alleged Electoral Frauds in the Late Presidential Election," 45th Congress, 3rd Session, Report no. 140, 2, 67; Haworth,

The Hayes–Tilden Disputed Presidential Election, 311–28. The Potter Committee listed the individuals from the contested states who had received appointments from the Hayes administration. From Florida, there were eighteen people; in Louisiana, there were over sixty.

CHAPTER FOUR

p. 83   The *New York Times* . . . August 20, 1896.

p. 84   "believe it is" . . . : Glenn Feldman, *The Disfranchisement Myth*, 22.

p. 84   In 1880, . . . : Stephen Kantrowitz, *Ben Tillman and the Reconstruction of White Supremacy*, 75–76, 224–28; Francis Butler Simkins, *Pitchfork Ben Tillman*, 61; Chester H. Rowell, *A Historical and Legal Digest*, 381–84.

p. 86   Big Tim Sullivan . . . : *New York Times*, September 27, 1964.

p. 86   In 1884, . . . : Rowell, *A Historical and Legal Digest*, 399–400, 406–08.

p. 86   In Florida . . . : Rowell, *A Historical and Legal Digest*, 468–70; Ortiz, *Emancipation Betrayed*, 37–39; Kenneth C. Barnes, "Who Killed John M. Clayton?: Political Violence in Conway County, Arkansas, in the 1880s," *Arkansas Historical Quarterly* 52 (Winter 1993): 371–404.

p. 88   "These titans . . . cheated consumers": Callahan, *The Cheating Culture*, 15–16.

p. 88   An illustrative example . . . : Stephen Cresswell, *Multi-Party Politics in Mississippi*, 29–32, 50–51; Paul Lewinson, *Race, Class, and Party*, 76–78.

p. 89   Chicago ward heelers . . . : Paul Avrich, *The Haymarket Tragedy*, 48–49; Donald L. Miller, *City of the Century*, 468–82; Bruce C. Nelson, *Beyond the Martyrs*, 159, 177–200.

p. 91   "Men of the" . . . : *Nation*, November 18, 1880.

p. 92   In the South . . . : Mark Wahlgren Summers, *Rum, Romanism, & Rebellion*, 289–301; Kantrowitz, *Ben Tillman*, 95–96, 102–04; Gilles Vandal, "Politics and Violence in Bourbon Louisiana: The Loreauville Riot of 1884 as a Case Study," *Louisiana History* 30 (Winter 1989): 23–42.

    By 1880, the diminishment of the Southern black vote was already evident. A combination of what the historian Steven Hahn labels "paramilitary terrorism" with Democratic gerrymandering, poll taxes, and election fraud produced declining numbers of black voters. In Georgia and Mississippi, less than half the state's eligible African-Americans showed up at the polls, and the rest of the South was not far behind. To Hahn, these were no mere "precursors or preludes to the era of Jim Crow." Rather, these impediments to democracy were part of the "advent of Jim Crow itself" and of the "construction of state-sponsored and sanctioned social and racial hierarchies in search of formulas and constituencies of support." Hahn, *A Nation Under Our Feet*, 367.

p. 92   A bill . . . : Keyssar, *The Right to Vote*, 108; John A. Garrity, *Henry Cabot Lodge*, 118.

p. 93   "Well, now". . . . : Summers, *Party Games*, 255; Ortiz, *Emancipation Betrayed*, 57.

p. 93   The bill stalled . . . : Keyssar, *The Right to Vote*, 110–11. By 1913, in fact, Southern Democrats in the Senate chaired *all* of the eight major committees in the Senate. In the House, Southerners chaired eight of the nine major committees the same

year. All of these members benefited from the failure of the Lodge bill, which
allowed them to amass the seniority that would bring them to the chairmanships
twenty years later.

p. 93   In 1876 . . . : *U.S. v. Reese* 92 U.S. 214 (1876); *Ex Parte Yarbrough, et al.* 110 U.S.
651 (1884); *James v. Bowman* 190 U.S. 127 (1903). In *Williams v. Mississippi* 170
U.S. 213 (1898), the Court unanimously upheld the constitutionality of the literacy tests and poll-tax qualifications established by the Mississippi constitution
of 1890. Those requirements, the Court reasoned, "do not on their face dis-
criminate between the races, and it has not been shown that their actual administration was evil; only that evil was possible under them." For some of the ways
Southern Democrats stole elections from Greenbackers and other independent
candidates in the 1880s, see Michael R. Hyman, *The Anti-Redeemers*, 192–94.
Jim Bissett examines how fraud was stillfully used against Midwestern Socialists in *Agrarian Socialism in America*, 112–37.

p. 94   The 1888 election . . . : James L. Baumgardner, "The 1888 Presidential Election: How Corrupt?," *Presidential Studies Quarterly* 14 (Summer 1984): 417–22;
James Henry Jacobs, "The West Virginia Gubernatorial Election Contest,
1888–1890," *West Virginia History* 7 (April 1946): 159–220. The 1888 race also
saw a major dispute in West Virginia in the governor's race, where months of
manipulation finally cheated the GOP candidate out of the election. Democrats
claimed, for example, that returns from Lewiston should be thrown out because
the election commissioners there had not been properly sworn to their duties.

p. 95   Yet the most explosive . . . : *Nation*, November 22, 1888; Richard Jensen, *The
Winning of the Midwest*, 26–30; Baumgardner, "The 1888 Presidential Election," 421; Robert F. Wesser, "Election of 1888," in Arthur M. Schlesinger, Jr.,
ed., *History of American Presidential Elections*, 1615–1700.

p. 96   "practically of no avail" . . . : *National Economist*, April 27, 1889; Keyssar, *The
Right to Vote*, 151–59; Joseph P. Harris, *Registration of Voters*, 72–77.

p. 97   "If the act of" . . . : *Nation*, November 22, and December 13 and 20, 1888; L.
E. Fredman, *The Australian Ballot*, 31–39, 46; Peter H. Argersinger, "To Dis-
franchise the People: The Iowa Ballot Law and Election of 1897," *Mid-
America* 63 (January 1981): 18; Herbert J. Bass, "The Politics of Ballot Reform
in New York State, 1888–1890," *New York History* (July 1961): 253–72; John
F. Reynolds, *Testing Democracy*, 49–61; Sarah M. Henry, "Progressivism and
Democracy: Electoral Reform in the United States, 1888–1919" (Ph.D. dis-
sertation, Columbia University, 1995), 43–45; Alan Ware, "Anti-Partyism and
Party Control of Political Reform in the United States: The Case of the Aus-
tralian Ballot," *British Journal of Political Science*. 30 (Jan. 2000): 1–29. *Nation*,
January 4, 1894.

p. 98   But the evidence . . . J. Morgan Kousser, *The Shaping of Southern Politics*,
110–11; In *Colorblind Injustice* Kousser notes the secret ballot was deployed
mainly "with the intent and effect of disfranchising illiterates, who were very
disproportionately African-Americans or immigrants (34)." Reynolds, *Testing*

Democracy, ch. 3; see also Mark Schultz, *The Rural Face of White Supremacy,* 186–87.

p. 99   In Vermont . . . : Summers, *Party Games,* 242–45.

p. 99   If the secret ballot . . . : For information on the Myers machine, see the Web site of the Federal Elections Commission at www.fec.gov/pages/lever.html. Because voting machines contained so many movable parts, they were highly susceptible to mechanical breakdowns. The Belgian inventor was Albert Snoeck, whose machine differed from Myers's in that two doors were used. The voter entered one to vote, and another to exit. Once the exit door shut, the vote was recorded and the gears were reset for the next voter. *New York Times,* August 20, 1896.

p. 100   There is no better example . . . Gregg Cantrell, *Kenneth and John B. Rayner,* 220–21; Lawrence Goodwyn, *Democratic Promise,* 110–53, 515–55; Gene Clanton, *Populism,* 100; Woodward, *Tom Watson,* 241–42, 257–58; Woodward, *Origins of the New South,* 235; *National Economist,* April 27, 1889, October 29, 1892. Based on the results of the 1892 election, the national organ of the People's Party, the *National Economist,* predicted "It is highly probable that [the People's Party] will supplant the Democratic Party in 1896." November 19, 1892. Thomas E. Watson, *The People's Party Campaign Book,* 123.

p. 100   "It is the religious duty" . . . : William Ivy Hair, *Bourbonism and Agrarian Protest,* 260.

p. 100   In 1894 . . . : William Warren Rogers, *The One-Gallused Rebellion,* 283–89; Feldman, *The Disfranchisement Myth,* 21–22. In an 1892 campaign, Kolb was denied permission to speak in several counties, causing him to swear out warrants against those who had denied him a venue. *National Economist,* November 5, 1892. In his superb study of Mobile, Michael W. Fitzgerald notes that "If the stakes were high enough, the Democrats manipulated voting returns, but this was a last resort rather than the preferred option." Fitzgerald, *Urban Emancipation,* 249.

p. 101   A local judge . . . : Rogers, *The One-Gallused Rebellion,* 290–92.

p. 101   On Election Day, . . . : Cantrell, *Kenneth and John B. Rayner,* 239–40.

p. 102   In fact . . . : Woodward, *Origins of the New South,* 321–27.

p. 102   In the Alabama . . . : Feldman, *The Disfranchisement Myth,* 49, 122.

p. 102   "It is true" . . . : Woodward, *Origins of the New South,* 321, 326, 342; Kousser, *The Shaping of Southern Politics,* 224, 236–46, 251–61; Kousser, *Colorblind Injustice,* 15–16. In Texas, the aftermath of the populist revolt reveals that the disfranchisement among black voters occurred in rapid fashion. In 1896, 85 percent of black Texans had voted in that year's presidential race. Just six years later, that figure had plummeted to 23 percent. See Cantrell, *Kenneth and John B. Rayner,* 248.

p. 104   "started by whites" . . . : *Nation,* February 25, 1897; Woodward, *Origins of the New South,* 326.

p. 105   In 1894 . . . : Glenda E. Gilmore, "Murder, Memory, and the Flight of the Incubus," in David S. Cecelski and Timothy B. Tyson, *Democracy Betrayed,* 76.

p. 105   North Carolina Democrats . . . : Raymond Gavins, "Fear, Hope, and Struggle:

Recasting Black North Carolina in the Age of Jim Crow," in Cecelski and Tyson, *Democracy Betrayed,* 189.

p. 105   Led by Waddell . . . : R. D. W. Connor and Clarence Poe, *The Life and Speeches of Charles Brantley Aycock,* 239; Timothy B. Tyson, *Blood Done Sign My Name,* 273–74; Joel Williamson, *The Crucible of Race,* 195–96.

p. 106   In 1899, . . . : James C. Klotter, *William Goebel,* 33–35, 46–49; Louisville *Courier-Journal,* November 6, 7, 8, 1899; Louisville *Evening Post,* August 17 and November 7, 1899; Cincinnati *Enquirer,* November 6 and 8, 1899; Woodward, *Origins of the New South,* 377–79; *Kentucky Irish-American,* November 11, 1899.

p. 107   Election Day itself . . . : Cincinnati *Enquirer,* November 9, 1899; Louisville *Evening Post,* November 11, 1899; Klotter, *William Goebel,* 86–91; William D. Forester, *Flatland Election Thieves and Mountain Bushwackers,* 9–32. The *Kentucky Irish-American* explained how papers such as the pro-Democratic *Courier-Journal* responded to close elections: "The Courier-Journal received full returns just as the other newspapers did, and has withheld them from the public. This fact is well known in newspaperdom, if not by the public" (November 7, 1899).

p. 107   In early December 1899 . . . : *Outlook,* December 16, 1899; Louisville *Courier-Journal,* November 18 and December 8 and 12, 1899; Klotter, *William Goebel,* 91–93.

p. 108   By the end of January . . . : Louisville *Courier-Journal,* January 5, 17 and 21, 1900; Louisville *Evening Post,* November 17, 1899; Klotter, *William Goebel,* 92–99.

p. 108   On the morning of . . . : Louisville *Courier-Journal,* January 31 and February 1, 1900; Klotter, *William Goebel,* 100–04. Although he was not in Frankfort at the time of the shooting, Caleb Powers was indicted as an accessory to the assassination. He was tried three times, as packed juries convicted him with often perjured testimony. Each time, the Court of Appeals threw out the decision, and a fourth trial ended in deadlock. In 1908, Republican Governor Augustus Willson pardoned Powers, who later served in Congress. The question as to who fired the shot that killed Goebel remains unsolved. See Klotter, *William Goebel,* 114–25.

p. 108   Both sides . . . : Louisville *Courier-Journal,* February 2, 3, 4, and 15, 1900; *Outlook,* February 10, 1900; Klotter, *William Goebel,* 105–14; Woodward, *Origins of the New South,* 377–79. "Put a shirt" . . . : *New York Times,* February 9, 1900, originally printed in the *Lexington Leader,* n.d.

CHAPTER FIVE

p. 113   "No people . . ." Louisville *Evening Post,* May 22, 1907.

p. 114   After Reconstruction . . . : *Twelfth Census of the United States, 1900, Population, part I,* lxix; George C. Wright, *Life Behind a Veil,* 68–72; James T. Wills, "Louisville Politics, 1891–1897" (M.A. thesis, University of Louisville, 1966), 2–4. See also Tracy A. Campbell, "Machine Politics, Police Corruption, and the Persistence of Vote Fraud: The Case of the Louisville,

Kentucky Election of 1905," *Journal of Policy History* 15 (Summer 2003): 269–300.

p. 114   Throughout the 1880s . . . : Louisville *Courier-Journal*, December 1, 6 and 7, 1887; Charlene M. Cornell, "Louisville in Transition: 1870–1890" (M.A. thesis, University of Louisville, 1970), 93–100, 124–32. During the electoral crisis following the 1876 presidential election, Henry Watterson's *Courier-Journal*, in the estimation of C. Vann Woodward, was the "strongest Southern exponent" of violent resistance to ward off a Republican victory. Woodward, *Reunion and Reaction*, 110–11.

p. 115   After reading . . . : Louisville *Courier-Journal*, January 14 and 23, February 19 and December 5 and 6, 1888, and January 24, 1892; *Nation*, December 13 and 20, 1888, August 10, 1889, April 30, October 22, 1891, and January 14 and February 4, 1892; Cornell, "Louisville in Transition," 134; Fredman, *The Australian Ballot*, 31–32; Frances Fox Piven and Richard A. Cloward, *Why Americans Still Don't Vote*. Writing in 1887, William M. Ivins claimed that a secret ballot "would remove every one of the foundation stones that lie at the base of our present organized political machinery." Ivins, *Machine Politics and Money in Elections in New York City*, 90–91, 119; Keyssar, *The Right to Vote*, 142–43. In 1902, a European observer, Moisei Ostrogorski, noted the Australian system "has, in fact, put an end to the open intimidation and to the coercion which were practiced on the electors; the elections are now, with few exceptions, conducted in an orderly manner." Quoted in Arnaldo Testi, "The Tribulations of an Old Democracy," *Journal of American History* 88 (September 2001): 422. In 1888, Massachusetts became the first state to adopt the Australian ballot, and by 1891 thirty other states had followed suit.

p. 115   John Whallen . . . : Undated newspaper clipping, J. H. Haager Scrapbook, Louisville Police Records, Filson Club Library; undated clipping from Hugh McCullough Scrapbook, Louisville Police Records, Filson Club Library. For Whallen's rise to power, see Karen R. Gray and Sarah R. Yates, "Boss John Whallen: The Early Louisville Years (1876–1883)," *Journal of Kentucky Studies* (1984): 171–86; Karen R. Gray and Sarah R. Yates, "John Henry Whallen," in John Kleber, ed., *The Encyclopedia of Louisville*, 935; Cincinnati *Enquirer*, December 4, 1913; *Kentucky Elk*, n.d., Filson Club Clippings File; Wills, "Louisville Politics," 29–31. See also Wright, *Life Behind a Veil*, 71–75; Wright, "The Billy Club and the Ballot: Police Intimidation of Blacks in Louisville, Kentucky, 1880–1930," *Southern Studies* 23 (1984): 23. In the harsh winter of 1912, the Whallen brothers distributed over $10,000 in cash to needy Louisvillians. Louisville *Times*, February 7, 1912.

p. 116   Louisville native . . . : Arthur Krock, *Myself When Young*, 212–13.

p. 116   In 1892 . . . : *The Critic*, October 9, 1892; *Louisville Post*, October 12 and 15, 1892; Louisville *Courier-Journal*, October 4, 6, 11 and 14, 1892. The figure of 13,108 eligible Democratic voters was based on the number who had voted for the Democratic nominee in the previous gubernatorial election. Gary M. Cox and J. Morgan Kousser have noted the difficulty of locating vote fraud in contemporary sources. It is, after all, an illegal activity and ripe for exploitation by partisan sources. Even legislative hearings and court records, they contend, "were inherently biased, since the lawyers for each side were more interested in making a case for their clients than in dispassionately uncovering facts." In their study, Cox and Kousser examined forty-eight local newspapers in New York. In so doing, they admitted to casting "a wide and lengthy research net, and to counteract the bias of individual papers and reporters" by balancing their respective ideological and geographical persuasions. "Turnout and Rural Corruption," 651–53. In this study of Louisville, numerous newspaper accounts of various political persuasions, in addition to court and police records, have been utilized in a similar effort to balance all possible partisan loyalties in order to understand the scale and scope of the local corruption.

In "The Effect of the Secret Ballot on Voter Turnout Rates," Jac C. Heckelman asserts that within a "rational voter framework," the secret ballot eliminated a market for buying votes, and therefore voters "were rational to stay away from the polls" (107). As the example of Louisville affords, the secret ballot eliminated no such market. In "Revisiting the Relationship Between Secret Ballots and Turnout," Heckelman concludes that "income, rather than race or literacy, was the crucial determinant for voting in secret ballot elections" (211), in that with a decreased ability to bribe voters, those of lesser means were less likely to vote. The case study of Louisville calls into question the entire evidentiary base of such studies, which rely on voter turnout and not on the social reality surrounding the polls on Election Day.

p. 117   Whallen reappeared . . . : The *Courier-Journal* concluded "the voters of Louisville spoke in thunder tones against the continuance in office of the worst administration with which this city has ever been cursed." Louisville *Courier-Journal*, November 3, 1897; Wright, "The Billy Club and the Ballot," 26–27; Wills, "Louisville Politics," 117–118.

p. 118   Without the strong arm . . . : Zane Miller, *Boss Cox's Cincinnati*, 93–96, 165–67; William D. Miller, *Memphis During the Progressive Era*, 100–01, 141–45, 169–70; Robert M. Fogelson, *Big-City Police* (Cambridge: Harvard University Press, 1977), 2–5, 33–34, 67–68; Cyril D. Robinson, "The Mayor and the Police—the Political Role of the Police in Society," in George L. Mosse, ed., *Police Forces in History*, 281–82, 295–97; for a wider discussion of the techniques of police corruption, particularly the role of ward and precinct leaders in protection rackets, see V. O. Key, Jr., "Police Graft," *American Journal of Sociology* 40 (March 1935): 624–36. While not specifically discussing the role of the police, Peter McCaffery writes that boss rule in Philadelphia was dependent on its control over the process of city elections, "through a variety of extralegal and illegal practices." McCaffery, *When Bosses Ruled Philadelphia*, 136–40; for an extended discussion of the methods of controlling votes as well as the use of police and

firefighters on election day, see David Harold Kurtzman, "Methods of Controlling Votes in Philadelphia" (Ph.D. dissertation, University of Pennsylvania, 1935).

p. 118   By 1900 . . . : Wright, *Life Behind a Veil*, 186, 190; Ernest Collins, "The Political Behavior of the Negroes in Cincinnati, Ohio and Louisville, Kentucky"
(Ph.D. dissertation, University of Kentucky, 1950), 50. Within the 1891 Kentucky Constitutional debates, there was extended discussion of the secret ballot
and worries of election fraud, but no public proclamations of the intentions to
disfranchise African-Americans, such as occurred in numerous other southern
conventions. In fact, the framers were anxious not to disfranchise illiterate voters
and took steps to ensure their suffrage rights. The absence of such "legal" disfranchisement schemes in Kentucky made the Democratic machine in
Louisville especially willing to disfranchise African-Americans and well-to-do
Republicans by illegal means on Election Day.

p. 118   Pat Grimes . . . : Undated clippings, Haager Scrapbook, Filson Club; *Louisville
Times*, n.d.

p. 118   Yet when it became . . . : Louisville *Courier-Journal*, November 10 and 11, 1899;
Yater, *Two Hundred Years at the Falls of the Ohio*, 147. Future Kentucky Governor
Augustus Willson was one of the members of the League who did not support
violence, but called attention to the Declaration of Independence and the right
of the people to "alter, reform, or abolish" any form of government. Willson
added "I do not believe in violence, but I would say to Goebel and his followers,
'you have gone far enough!' "
   The evidence of Whallen's complicity in Goebel's murder was very thin. A
few weeks before the assassination, he allegedly attempted to bribe a Kentucky
state senator to oppose Goebel's contest. Whallen replied that he had merely
given the senator $5,000 "to act according to what he represented to be the true
dictates of his conscience." Also, a significant aspect of Goebel's election contest
concerned the election proceedings in Louisville, where Whallen was mentioned specifically as an "agent" of the L & N Railroad. Klotter, *William Goebel*,
46–48, 93–95; see also Urey Woodson, *The First New Dealer*, 208–12.

p. 119   An election in 1903 . . . : Speech of Marshall Bullitt before the Kentucky Court
of Appeals, 1905 Election Speeches, Bullitt Family Papers, Oxmoor collection,
Filson Club. Louisville *Evening-Post*, October 10 and November 3 and 4, 1903.
After the 1903 election, Thomas W. Bullitt and Judge W. O. Harris issued a
report finding "there was a preconceived plan to subvert the will of the electors
and to prevent a fair election."

p. 119   With the 1903 election . . . : Robert W. Bingham to undisclosed person, August
10, 1905, box 30, Robert W. Bingham Papers, Filson Club Library, Louisville;
Louisville *Herald*, July 14 and 18, 1905; Louisville *Evening-Post*, May 23, 1907.
In *Political Corruption in America*, George C. S. Benson concludes that "most
election frauds occur in areas of one-party dominance" (169). For an extended

analysis of various political insurgencies that sought to upset the existing two-party system, as well as the efforts by the major parties to end them, see Peter H. Argersinger, " 'A Place on the Ballot': Fusion Politics and Antifusion Laws," *American Historical Review* 85 (April 1980): 287–306. For an example of the success of fusionists in nearby Cincinnati, see Zane Miller, *Boss Cox's Cincinnati*, 165–67.

p. 120   When challenges were made . . . : *Scholl v. Bell*, no. 41519, and *Peter v. Wilson*, no. 41524, Jefferson Circuit Court, volume I, 16–17, 46, vol. III, 91–93, Special Collections, University of Kentucky (hereinafter referred to as *Scholl v. Bell*). This case formed the core of Helm Bruce's appeal to the Kentucky Court of Appeals and, as such, comprises thousands of pages of detailed sworn testimony concerning the 1905 election. It is a rare piece of social history that contains hundreds of Louisville citizens stating in their own words how an election was systematically stolen. Louisville *Evening-Post*, October 3, 4 and 5, 1905; Thomas D. Clark, *Helm Bruce, Public Defender*, 32–34; Wright, "The Billy Club and the Ballot," 27–28. Upon reading that the Louisville *Evening-Post* had accused him of hiring repeaters from St. Louis, John Whallen promptly charged the paper with slander and sued for $25,000 in damages.

p. 121   Roman Leachman . . . : Louisville *Evening-Post*, October 20, 1905; Kentucky *Irish-American*, October 14, 1905; J. F. Bullitt to Thomas W. Bullitt, October 18, 1905, file 308, Bullitt Papers; Yater, *Two Hundred Years at the Falls of the Ohio*, 147–48. McAuliffe was dismissed from the Louisville police force in April 1906 for "conduct unbecoming an officer." Louisville Police Force Book, 24, Louisville Police Records.

p. 121   In the Tenth Ward . . . : *Scholl v. Bell*, vol. V, 31–35.

p. 121   Charles Schuff . . . : *Scholl v. Bell*, vol. I, 231–44; vol. II, 292–93. For an extended analysis of turn-of-the-century methods of disfranchising African-Americans and thereby diminishing Republican totals in Southern states, see Kousser, *The Shaping of Southern Politics*. Cox and Kousser, "Turnout and Rural Corruption," 655, discuss the process of paying people not to vote as a form of vote-buying.

p. 122   Of 356 election officers . . . : *Scholl v. Bell*, vol. I, 634.

p. 122   Bank records . . . : *Scholl v. Bell*, vol. I, 230–31. The Fusionist fund was considerably smaller, totaling $23,078.09, which included $3,100.00 for registration-day costs, and $6,120.70 for election-day expenses. *Scholl v. Bell*, vol. IX, 1–3. As a comparison, James Bryce wrote in the early 1900s that "as much as $50,000" was being spent on a congressional race in New York. James Bryce, *The American Commonwealth*, vol. II, 148. Nearly fifty years later, V. O. Key found that a suitable candidacy for U.S. Senate in South Carolina had to spend $50,000. *Southern Politics*, 465.

p. 123   Fred R. Bishop . . . : *Scholl v. Bell*, vol. II, 190, 197–99.

p. 123   The manner in which . . . : *Scholl v. Bell*, vol. I, 202–03; Louisville *Evening-Post*, November 6, 1905; Clark, *Helm Bruce, Public Defender*, 36–38.

p. 123 "whatever they say". . ."laying around": *Scholl v. Bell*, vol. I, 204–09. For other examples of election fraud in Kentucky, see Malcolm E. Jewell and Everett W. Cunningham, *Kentucky Politics*, 16–18, 30–37, 53–71, 225–33, and Sabato and Simpson, *Dirty Little Secrets*, 298–300.

p. 124 After acquiring . . . : *Scholl v. Bell*, vol. I, 446–59; vol. V, 196–97; Louisville *Evening-Post*, October 2, 1905; City of Louisville, Board of Aldermen, *Annual Report for 1905*, 413–14; Speech of Marshall Bullitt before Kentucky Court of Appeals, Bullitt Papers; "Louisville Election Contest Cases: Report of James P. Helm, Chairman of the Committee of One Hundred," pamphlet, Filson Club; *Scholl v. Bell*, vol. II, 586–87.

p. 124 On election eve . . . : Clark, *Helm Bruce, Public Defender*, 35–36; "Fusionist Movement," *The Encyclopedia of Louisville*, 325.

p. 125 When the polls opened . . . : *Scholl v. Bell*, vol. VI, 1–5, 125–29, 289–93, 381–87, 555–63, 700–02, 823–29; vol. II, 299–304, 366, 682–84; vol. V, 272–73; Louisville *Evening-Post*, November 7, 1905.

p. 125 In the Sixth Ward . . . : *Scholl v. Bell*, vol. III, 179–86.

p. 125 In the Tenth Ward . . . : *Scholl v. Bell*, vol. V, 102–20.

p. 126 B. M. Rivers . . . : *Scholl v. Bell*, vol. II, 723–25.

p. 126 In the Twelfth Ward . . . : *Scholl v. Bell*, vol. VII, 368–72.

p. 126 Throughout the day . . . : *Scholl v. Bell*, vol. IX, 250–56.

p. 127 While Fusionists . . . : Louisville *Evening-Post*, November 7 and 11, 1905; Louisville *Courier-Journal*, November 8 and 9, 1905.

p. 127 Calling themselves . . . : Louisville *Evening-Post*, November 11, 1905. Ironically, a constitutional amendment was also on the November 1905 ballot that would have banned the Australian ballot, but it was defeated.

p. 128 Leading the Fusionist campaign . . . : Helm Bruce, "What Kind of City Do You Want?" September 26, 1917, pamphlet at the Filson Club Library. William Marshall Bullitt was appointed U.S. Solicitor General by President Taft in 1912.

p. 128 At the beginning . . . : *Scholl v. Bell*, vol. XI, 1–5, 125–29, 289–93, 381–87, 700–02; vol. XIII, 1–42, 128–29; vol. V, 423–24.

p. 128 "frauds perpetrated" . . . : Louisville *Evening-Post*, November 13, 1905.

p. 129 In March 1907 . . . : Louisville Election Contest Case, "Opinion of Chancellors Miller and Kirby, April 16, 1907," Filson Club; "Twelve Plain Facts About Col. Whallen and Judge Miller—Their Relations for Twenty Years," Bingham Miscellaneous Files, Bullitt Papers. *Outlook*, June 15, 1907, 306–07. In 1910, as head of the Democratic Committee, Whallen chose Miller to replace Judge Henry S. Barker on the Kentucky Court of Appeals. Barker had decided against the Democrats in the 1905 contest case; Louisville *Evening-Post*, March 23, 1907; Clark, *Helm Bruce, Public Defender*, 44–49.

p. 129 "We have the best election laws" . . . : Louisville *Courier-Journal*, January 13, 1906.

p. 130 "When the Apostle Paul" . . . : Speech of Marshall Bullitt, n.d., Bullitt Papers.

p. 130   Bullitt presented . . . : Louisville *Evening-Post*, April 18, 1907.

p. 131   On May 22, 1907 . . . : Louisville *Evening-Post*, May 22, 1907; Louisville *Courier-Journal*, May 23, 1907; Louisville *Herald*, May 23, 1907; *Outlook*, June 15, 1907, 306–07; Clark, *Helm Bruce, Public Defender*, 49–51, 84–85; *Scholl v. Bell*, vol. XIII, 23–50. Judge Lassing noted that had the disfranchised voters all voted for the defeated candidates in the various municipal races, "they would have been elected by majorities ranging from 3,425 to 5,332"(50).

In February 1907, the Court of Appeals invalidated an election in rural Princeton, Kentucky on grounds of vote fraud. Louisville *Evening-Post*, February 22 and 23, 1907. Writing for the majority, Judge Henry S. Barker wrote that the court understood it "ought not, for light and trivial causes, undo the work" of the voters, but if sufficient evidence warranted such drastic action, there was a fundamental principle at stake: "Whenever elections are not free and equal, the democratic principle is dead, and the republican form of government will exist in name only." *Orr et al. v. Kevil et al.*, 100 S.W. 314.

p. 131   Governor J. C. W. Beckham . . . : Robert W. Bingham to Bon Robinson, August 22, 1907, Bingham Papers; Louisville *Evening-Post*, June 27, 1907; William E. Ellis, *Robert Worth Bingham and the Southern Mystique*, 31–48.

p. 133   The day before . . . : Bingham to Eames MacVeagh, August 8, 1910, box 34, Bingham Papers; Louisville *Courier-Journal*, November 1, 3 and 4, 1909; Louisville *Evening-Post*, November 1, 2, 3 and 5, 1909; Louisville *Herald*, November 15, 1909; Kentucky *Irish-American*, October 30, 1909; Ellis, *Robert Worth Bingham and the Southern Mystique*, 42–48; Yater, *Two Hundred Years at the Falls of the Ohio*, 149–52; Wright, *Life Behind a Veil*, 190–92. When Bingham ran for a seat on the state court of appeals in 1910, Whallenites forcibly kept African-Americans from registering. Bingham lost the race by 1,600 votes. "It is true," Bingham wrote Governor Augustus E. Willson, "that we should have won, but for the most general and flagrant intimidation and bribery, and a victory won by such methods is always very dearly bought." Bingham to Willson, November 22, 1910, box 34, Bingham Papers. Bingham later bought the *Courier-Journal* and was appointed Ambassador to the Court of St. James by Franklin D. Roosevelt.

p. 134   By 1908 . . . : Louisville Police Department Records, Force Book, 1904–21, Filson Club; Robert I. Cusick, Jr., "The History of the Louisville Division of Police From the Founding of the City to 1955" (M.A. thesis, University of Louisville, 1964), 48–51. One officer involved in the vote corruption, Lt. James W. Kinnarney, resigned in July 1907 and later became chief of the special police of Churchill Downs, home of the Kentucky Derby. In 1930, Kinnarney was an honorary pallbearer at James Whallen's funeral. Louisville *Herald-Post*, March 16, 1930; Krock, *Myself When Young*, 138.

p. 134   In 1923 and 1925 . . . : Louisville *Courier-Journal*, November 7, 15, 19, and 22, 1923, January 29 and 30, 1924, June 13, 1925, November 1, 4, and 19, December 11, 1925, January 28 and 29, February 4 and 26, 1926, and June 18,

1927; David R. Castleman, "Louisville Election Frauds in Court and Out," *National Municipal Review,* December 1927, 761–69; *New York Times,* June 16, 1927; *New York Evening World,* June 16, 1927.

CHAPTER SIX

p. 136   In 1905, . . . : Lincoln Steffens, *The Shame of the Cities,* 198, 203; Steffens, "Rhode Island: A State for Sale," *McClure's Magazine,* February 1905. Some of E. L. Godkin's critiques of Gilded Age American politics can be found in *Problems of Modern Democracy,* and *The Triumph of Reform: A History of the Great Political Revolution, Nov. 6, 1894* (New York: Souvenir, 1895). See also John D. Buenker, "The Politics of Resistance: The Rural-Based Yankee Republican Machines of Connecticut and Rhode Island," *New England Quarterly* (June 1974), 212–37.

p. 137   New Jersey, for example . . . : Kelly, *Election Day,* 174–75; McCormick, *The History of Voting in New Jersey,* 200–06; Keyssar, *The Right to Vote,* 150–51.

p. 138   Hearst's father . . . : David Nasaw, *The Chief,* 67–142, 160–67, 180–83, 194–99; W. A. Swanberg, *Citizen Hearst,* 204–223.

p. 139   Although the role of money . . . : *New York Times,* November 7, 1905.

p. 140   One city newspaper . . . : *New York Times,* November 8, 1905; Nasaw, *The Chief,* 198–99; Mrs. Fremont Older, *William Randolph Hearst, American,* 281–85. The 1905 election coincided with the publication of *Plunkitt of Tammany Hall,* a candid appraisal of some of the inner workings of the machine. In G. W. Plunkitt's view, votes needed to be seen as "marketable goods," and the more one could deliver to the machine, the more valuable he became. Plunkitt's candor backfired, as he was defeated for reelection to the Tammany Democracy district leadership in that election. See William L. Riordan, *Plunkitt of Tammany Hall,* 34–35, 52–53.

p. 140   By night's end . . . : *New York Times,* November 8, 1905; Nasaw, *The Chief,* 199.

p. 141   "the dignity of" . . . : *New York Times,* November 9, 1905.

p. 141   The following day . . . : *New York Times,* November 10, 1905.

p. 141   An unusual voice . . . : *New York Times,* November 11 and 14, 1905; Woodward, *Origins of the New South,* 324; Harold C. Syrett, ed., *The Gentleman and the Tiger,* 227–28.

p. 142   On November 27 . . . : *New York Times,* November 28 and December 14, 27 and 28, 1905.

p. 143   Once again . . . : *New York Times,* May 29 and 30 and June 2, 25, 26, and 27, 1908. In his book, David Nasaw erroneously concludes "There was no recount" of the 1905 mayoral election. While it did not happen until the summer of 1908, a recount actually occurred. Nasaw was correct in noting that "Tammany Hall got away with robbery" in defrauding Hearst of the mayor's office in 1905. Nasaw, *The Chief,* 200.

p. 144   The price of a vote . . . : Genevieve B. Gist, "Progressive Reform in a Rural Community: The Adams County Vote-Fraud Case," *Mississippi Valley Historical*

Review (June 1961): 62–63; Jeremiah W. Jenks, "Money in Practical Politics," *The Century* 44 (October 1892), 940–945; A. Z. Blair, "Seventeen Hundred Rural Vote Sellers: How We Disfranchised a Quarter of the Voting Population of Adams County, Ohio," *McClure's Magazine* (November 1911), 35.

p. 144   Blair found . . . : Blair, "Seventeen Hundred Rural Vote Sellers," 38; Gist, "Progressive Reform in a Rural Community," 66–67; *Cincinnati Enquirer,* December 24, 1910.

p. 145   "It has been" . . . : *Cincinnati Enquirer,* December 26, 30, and 31, 1910.

p. 146   "Many people sold their vote" . . . : *Literary Digest,* February 4, 1911; Theodore Roosevelt, "Applied Good Citizenship," *Outlook,* November 11, 1911; *Cincinnati Enquirer,* January 4, 1911. In 1913, the Ohio legislature passed a bill restoring the franchise to those in Adams County who had lost it during the vote-fraud trials. Governor James B. Cox (the Democratic nominee for president in 1920) vetoed the bill, saying that only the chief executive had the constitutional right to grant pardons. Gist, "Progressive Reform in a Rural Community," 77.

p. 147   Writing for the Court . . . : *U.S. v. Moseley* 238 U.S. 383 (1915); Donn M. Roberts to A. O. Stanley, June 20, 1915, box 3, A.O. Stanley Papers, Special Collections, University of Kentucky; *New York Times,* January 2, 6 and 13, and March 10, 1915.

p. 148   Roberts allegedly . . . : *New York Times,* March 11, 12, and 21, and April 2, 4, 7, 13, and 20, 1915; Frank S. Roby to Stanley, May 26, 1915, Stanley Papers.

p. 149   In November 1923 . . . : *New York Times,* January 20, 1924.

p. 152   Literacy tests, poll taxes, . . . : Keyssar, *The Right to Vote,* 128–29.

p. 152   In the early 1900s . . . : Carrie Chapman Catt and Nettie Rogers Shuler, *Woman Suffrage and Politics,* 170–73, 186–87; Keyssar, *The Right to Vote,* 194.

p. 152   In a Texas . . . : Sara Hunter Graham, *Woman Suffrage and the New Democracy,* 71–72, 133–34.

p. 153   In Florida . . . : Ortiz, *Emancipation Betrayed,* 191–228. For a portrait of the ways white supremacists fought to curtail the black vote in Detroit, see Kevin Boyle's magnificent *Arc of Justice,* 250–53.

p. 154   Between 1789 . . . : Rowell, *A Historical and Legal Digest,* 510–1901; Neil MacNeil, *Forge of Democracy,* 135–36; George B. Galloway, *History of the House of Representatives,* 32–33; *New York Times,* February 27, 1921.

p. 154   Senate contests . . . : Losing candidates usually contested a House or Senate election only when the margins were close. While these contests provide the historian with some remarkable evidence about election fraud at the ground level, contested elections should not be used as an accurate barometer to analyze the full extent of fraud in a given era. As the historian Mark Summers notes, "Contested elections may underestimate the number of cases in which fraud played a role in defeating one candidate. As long as one side won handily, the other was discouraged from bringing formal charges that might sully but could not change the overall result." Summers, *Party Games,* 114–15.

p. 155   One of he most famous . . . : *New York Times*, December 16, 1926; Anne M.
           Butler and Wendy Wolff, *United States Senate Election, Expulsion, and Censure
           Cases*, 323–25.

p. 156   In several Philadelphia wards . . . : Samuel J. Astorino, "The Contested Senate
           Election of William Scott Vare," *Pennsylvania History* 28 (April 1961): 192–93;
           Maynard C. Krueger, "Election Frauds in Philadelphia," *National Municipal
           Review* (May 1928): 295–97; McCaffery, *When Bosses Ruled Philadelphia*, 137–39.

p. 156   The committee stated . . . : Butler and Wolff, *United States Senate Election,
           Expulsion, and Censure Cases*, 328–29. Following the Senate vote on Vare and
           Wilson, Governor Fisher appointed Joseph R. Grundy to fill the vacancy.

p. 157   In 1924 . . . : Butler and Wolff, *United States Senate Election, Expulsion, and Cen-
           sure Cases*, 312–14.

p. 158   In a 1930 Democratic primary . . . : Butler and Wolff, *United States Senate Elec-
           tion, Expulsion, and Censure Cases*, 342–45. The Heflin and Bankhead case was
           highlighted in the Senate's dismissal of Coke Stevenson's contest against
           Lyndon Johnson in the 1948 Texas Democratic primary runoff race.

CHAPTER SEVEN

p. 161   Democrats claimed . . . : Elliot M. Rudwick, *Race Riot in East St. Louis*, 4, 7–15,
           184–89. Rudwick notes that white St. Louisans ignored their own role in elec-
           tion fraud, so that by 1917 "race and vote fraud appeared synonomous" (10).

p. 161   In a 1922 . . . : *New York Times*, January 13, 1924.

p. 162   The overwhelming problem . . . : St. Louis *Post-Dispatch*, August 16, 1935.

p. 163   "not liable . . . :" Franklin Roosevelt to Bernard Dickmann, February 19, 1934,
           Box 48, Jefferson National Expansion Memorial Archives, St. Louis (here-
           inafter JNEMA).

p. 163   In July 1934 . . . : W. C. Bernard, "A Comprehensive Program for Reclamation
           of the St. Louis Riverfront, to be Effected By the Construction and Operation
           of a Riverview Freeway, 1934," Bernard F. Dickmann Papers, Box 2, Western
           Historical Manuscript Collection, Univ. of Missouri, Columbia.

p. 164   As the city leaders saw it . . . : St. Louis *Post-Dispatch*, August 16, 1935; St.
           Louis *Star-Times*, May 13, 1935. Members of the Memorial Commission in St.
           Louis were representative of the city's financial elite: the presidents of three
           major banks, the manager of the Railway Exchange Building, and a former St.
           Louis mayor. St. Louis *Star-Times*, May 16, 1935.

p. 165   "You are familiar". . . : Wade T. Childress to Russell Murphy, July 26, 1935, Box
           3, JNEMA.

p. 165   "also a real estate". . . : St. Louis *Post-Dispatch*, August 9 and 16, 1935.

p. 166   One group . . . : St. Louis *Post-Dispatch*, September 5 and 6, 1935; Paul W.
           Ward, "Washington Weekly," *Nation*, March 4, 1936; Taxpayers Defense Asso-
           ciation Pamphlet, Clifford Greve Papers, Missouri Historical Society, St. Louis.

p. 167   "The Shylocks of finance . . .": News Release from W. C. D'Arcy, n.d., Jefferson
           National Memorial Files, Special Collections, St. Louis Public Library.

p. 167   "take charge"..."property owners": Bertha K. Passure to Luther Ely Smith, June
          29, 1935, JNEMA; "Excerpts of Minutes of Board of Directors of Chamber of
          Commerce, June 4, 1935," JNEMA; St. Louis *Post-Dispatch*, August 23, 1935.

p. 167   "wreck home owners . . .": St. Louis *Post-Dispatch*, September 9, 1936.

p. 158   A pamphlet . . . : Joseph Harris et al. to JNEMA, n.d., JNEMA; *St. Louis Argus*,
          August 30, 1935. Labor support for the bond issue can be seen in the endorse-
          ment of the *St. Louis Union Labor Advocate*, September 2, 1935.

p. 168   "We will know . . .": St. Louis *Post-Dispatch*, September 8, 1935; St. Louis
          Globe-Democrat, August 29, 1935.

p. 169   The Chamber of Commerce . . . : St. Louis Chamber of Commerce, "Down-
          town Riverfront Occupancy Survey, August 1935," in *Balter v. Ickes*, JNEMA;
          John G. Marr to Russell Murphy, April 9, 1935, Box 3, JNEMA; *Bond Issue
          News*, n.d., scrapbook one, Paul O. Peters Collection, box 21, Special Collec-
          tions, Andrews Library, College of Wooster, Wooster, Ohio; St. Louis *Post-
          Dispatch*, September 4 and 9, 1935; April Lee Hamel, "The Jefferson National
          Expansion Memorial: A Depression Relief Project" (Ph.D. dissertation, St.
          Louis University, 1983), 56. Political scientist Lana Stein concluded that Dick-
          mann merely "successfully urged city voters to pass the bond referendum," the
          usual description of the electoral politics. Stein, *St. Louis Politics*, 32–34. See also
          St. Louis *Star-Times*, September 10, 1936.

p. 170   A crucial moment . . . : St. Louis *Post-Dispatch*, September 10 and 11, 1935; St.
          Louis *Globe-Democrat*, September 11, 1935.

p. 170   The relative calm . . . : St. Louis *Post-Dispatch*, September 11 and 12, 1935.

p. 171   One such precinct . . . "more valuable": Mrs. Charles Carnali to Russell Murphy,
          September 13, 1935, JNEMA; William D'Arcy to E. Lansing Ray, September
          13, 1935, box 71, JNEMA.

p. 171   The Citizens' Non-Partisan . . . : Paul O. Peters to Franklin D. Roosevelt, Sep-
          tember 24, 1936, box 21, Peters Collection; "Public Necessity or Just Plain
          Pork?," scrapbook 2, Peters Collection; St. Louis *Post-Dispatch*, July 22, Sep-
          tember 8, 9 and 11, 1936. Roosevelt turned the matter over to the Justice
          Department, where Assistant Attorney General Joseph B. Keenan responded
          that he referred it to the "investigating division of the Federal Emergency
          Administration."

p. 172   In one barbershop . . . : St. Louis *Post-Dispatch*, July 23 and 28, 1936.

p. 173   "Ward and precinct" . . . : St. Louis *Post-Dispatch*, July 23, 1936.

p. 174   "Irregularity seemed". . . : St. Louis *Post-Dispatch*, July 24 and September 12,
          1936.

p. 175   Not surprisingly . . . : St. Louis *Post-Dispatch*, July 25, 26, and 27, 1936.

p. 175   By the end of July . . . : St. Louis *Post-Dispatch*, July 31, 1936.

p. 176   The details of the . . . : St. Louis *Post-Dispatch*, September 10, 1936.

p. 176   "One of the Democratic". . . "number of votes": St. Louis *Post-Dispatch*, August
          4 and September 10, 1936.

p. 177   To Chairman Waechter . . . : St. Louis *Post-Dispatch*, August 6, 14, 15, and 20 and September 9 and 18, 1936; *Washington Post*, September 22, 1936.

p. 178   Yet the grand jury . . . : St. Louis *Post-Dispatch*, December 12, 17, and 23, 1936, and September 17, 1937; St. Louis *Star-Times*, September 10, 1936; Hamel, "The Jefferson National Expansion Memorial," 94.

p. 179   The project stalled . . . : Sharon A. Brown, "Making a Memorial: Developing the Jefferson National Expansion Memorial National Historic Site, 1933–1980" (Ph.D. dissertation, St. Louis University, 1983), 24–26; Dickson Terry, "A Monument to Thirty Years of Patience, Perseverance, and Determination," *Cherry Diamond, Missouri Athletic Club* (Sept. 1964), in JNEMA Vertical Files; Harold L. Ickes, *The Secret Diary of Harold L. Ickes*, 489; Cary M. Schneider, "St. Louis and the Gateway Arch: A Case History of an Urban Icon" (Honors Paper, Cornell College, 1970), 18. St. Louis *Post-Dispatch*, December 4, 1936; Hamel, "The Jefferson National Expansion Memorial," 98.

p. 180   The supporters of the memorial . . . "affect the result": Paul O. Peters to Luther Ely Smith, November 26, 1936, December 9, 1936, Greve Papers; Luther Ely Smith to William Allen White, June 16, 1937, Greve Papers; St. Louis *Post-Dispatch*, January 14, 1937.

p. 181   Peters's attempt . . . : *New York Times*, April 10, August 18, 1936; *Balter v. Ickes*, no. 6827, U.S. Court of Appeals, Washington, D.C., in JNEMA.

p. 182   The court declared . . . : *St. Louis Post-Dispatch*, March 29, 1937.

p. 182   In May 1938 . . . : *St. Louis Post-Dispatch*, May 21, 22, and 23, 1938.

p. 183   Most substantial group . . . : "Property Holdings of Opponents to the Jefferson National Expansion Memorial, Including Owners, Lessees, and Tenants," June 1, 1934, Greve Papers.

p. 183   One member of Congress . . . : *Congressional Record*, vol. 81, 75th Congress, 1st Session, 1937, 4518, 8117–18; Appendix, 1806; St. Louis *Globe-Democrat*, April 19, 1939; St. Louis *Star-Times*, September 10, 1936; Brown, "Making a Memorial," 61–62; James Neal Primm, *Lion of the Valley*, 452–54. Rep. Lambertson called for an investigation of the entire Jefferson National Expansion Memorial, but the House did not even take action on it. He then suggested that if the memorial was built, a special room should be also constructed "to exhibit all the historical documents and evidences of fraud and corruption."

p. 184   In order to understand . . . : "Meeting of the St. Louis Real Estate Board and Jefferson National Expansion Memorial Association, January 21, 1935," JNEMA; "St. Louis Real Estate Exchange, September 5, 1935 Resolution," Box 71, JNEMA.

p. 185   Real estate companies owned . . . : Ralph W. Coale, Assessor, "Combined Assessments on Ground and Improvements on Real Estate Located Between Eads Bridge, Poplar Street, Third Street, and the Mississippi River, June 1, 1934," Greve Papers; Legal Committee Memo, n.d., JNEMA.

p. 186   "Real estate men". . . : St. Louis *Globe-Democrat,* August 29, 1935.

p. 186   "Whereas the city . . .": "St. Louis Real Estate Exchange, January 23, 1936, Resolution," JNEMA; *St. Louis Post-Dispatch,* February 10 and June 1, 19 and 22, 1939; *St. Louis Star-Times,* February 14, 1939. The appraisers of the property were appointed by the federal courts, and were composed primarily of attorneys and real estate agents. The Interior Department eventually purchased the property for $5,970,000, which was 11.2 percent greater than the assessed value. The final price for the condemned property was a source of considerable debate between the warring factions in the bond issue. Paul Peters claimed the property would cost a staggering $27.5 million, while supporters were more accurate, saying in 1935 the property was worth $5.7 million. "Bulletin to Members of Special Committee," August 29, 1935, Greve Papers; St. Louis *Star-Times,* August 24, 1935.

p. 187   Despite the claims . . . : *St. Louis Commerce,* January 10, 1940; Hamel, "The Jefferson National Expansion Memorial," 129–30.

p. 187   One was A. W. Albrecht . . . : *Congressional Record,* vol. 81, 75th Congress, 1st Session, 1937, 8118; *Nation,* March 4, 1936.

p. 188   Mrs. Elsa Pappas . . . : *St. Louis Post-Dispatch,* June 21, 1939.

p. 188   After World War II . . . : *New York Times,* June 15, 1941, and October 24 and 29, 1965.

p. 189   Once again . . . : *St. Louis Globe-Democrat,* November 9, 1966, March 8, 9, 1967.

CHAPTER EIGHT

p. 193   When Jim died . . . : Rudolph H. Hartmann, *The Kansas City Investigations,* 11–13, 58–59; Maurice M. Milligan, *Missouri Waltz,* 169–203; see also John Gunther, *Inside U.S.A.,* 344–48.

p. 194   Like all big city bosses . . . : *St. Louis Post-Dispatch,* July 26, 1936; Alonzo L. Hamby, *Man of the People,* 102–03; Roy Ellis, "A Civic History of Kansas City, Missouri" (Ph.D. dissertation, Columbia University, 1930), 231–33; Lyle W. Dorsett, *The Pendergast Machine,* 59–61.

p. 194   Truman's victory . . . : Robert H. Ferrell, *Truman and Pendergast,* 26–30; David McCullough, *Truman,* 211–12; Richard S. Kirkendall, *A History of Missouri,* 176; Hamby, *Man of the People,* 195–96.

p. 195   The details . . . : *Kansas City Star,* March 6, 7, 27, and 28, 1934; Arkansas City (Kansas) *Traveler,* March 31, 1934; Milligan, *Missouri Waltz,* 138–44. Due to extensive criticism of his inability to protect city voters during the election, Kansas City police chief Eugene Rippert resigned in late March 1934; *St. Louis Post-Dispatch,* September 3 and 4, 1936.

p. 196   In the general election . . . : Ferrell, *Truman and Pendergast,* 40–43; *St. Louis Post-Dispatch,* December 17, 1936 and February 17 and 24, 1937. As senator, Truman also worked unsuccessfully to block Milligan's appointment as U.S. District Attorney; Milligan, *Missouri Waltz,* 160. In *Man of the People,* Alonzo Hamby finds it "realistic to observe that the percentages had some connection to the respect and esteem that Truman and Cochran had achieved in their home bailwicks. (196)" To describe Cochran winning 98.9 percent of the Kansas city vote takes the notion of "respect and esteem" to new heights.

p. 197 In a 1946 . . . : *Kansas City Star,* September 29 and 30 and October 1, 7, and 12, 1946; "The Kansas City, Missouri Primary Election of 1946," Tom C. Clark Papers, Harry S. Truman Presidential Library, Independence, Missouri.

p. 198 His brother, . . . : *Hearings Before the Special Committee of Campaign Expenditures,* United States Senate, 72nd Congress, 2nd Session (hereinafter referred to as the *Overton Hearings*), 792–800; Robert Sherrill, *Gothic Politics in the Deep South,* 20; Glen Jeansonne, *Leander Perez,* 71–72.

p. 199 Long's support . . . : Jeansonne, *Leander Perez,* xvi, 69–74, 99–100.

p. 199 As a freshman senator, . . . : Butler and Wolff, *United States Senate Election, Expulsion, and Censure Cases,* 351–52; T. Harry Williams, *Huey Long,* 604–05.

p. 199 Broussard's specific charges . . . : *Overton Hearings,* 16–17, 138, 967; Butler and Wolff, *United States Senate Election, Expulsion, and Censure Cases,* 353; Williams, *Huey Long,* 607–09.

p. 201 In November 1932, . . . : *Overton Hearings,* 2710–28; Williams, *Huey Long,* 654–55.

p. 201 The Louisiana Attorney General . . . : *Overton Hearings,* 2726–28; Williams, *Huey Long,* 655–57.

p. 202 When the jury . . . : Warren O. Coleman to R. Whitley, August 27, 1934; George Guion to Warren O. Coleman, August 25, 1934, in Huey P. Long FBI File, Special Collections, LSU; *Overton Hearings,* 2728; Williams, *Huey Long,* 657–58.

p. 202 Meanwhile, a new grand jury . . . : Washington *Herald,* December 7, 1933; Williams, *Huey Long,* 658–59.

p. 204 By the end of 1934 . . . : J. Edgar Hoover to Marvin H. McIntyre, September 12, 1934, Huey Long FBI File, LSU; Williams, *Huey Long,* 660.

p. 204 The Honest Election League's . . . : Pamela Tyler, *Silk Stockings and Ballot Boxes,* 83–87, 127–33; Adam Fairclough, *Race and Democracy,* 35.

p. 205 In 1934 . . . "away from the polls": Greg Mitchell, *The Campaign of the Century,* 329, 333–34; *New York Times,* August 29, 1934.

p. 205 United for California . . . : Greg Mitchell, *The Campaign of the Century,* 366, 407, 427, 476–77; *New York Times,* October 25, November 4, 7, 8, 1934.

p. 206 As the Depression . . . : Louisville *Courier-Journal,* December 9, 1927; *Lexington Leader,* November 5, 6 and 8, 1920; James C. Klotter and Lowell H. Harrison, *A New History of Kentucky,* 352; Ronald D. Eller, *Miners, Millhands, and Mountaineers,* 5–85.

In a 1925 election for sheriff in Harlan County, four precincts in Lynch made the crucial difference, delivering a vote of 2,483 to 61 for the winning candidate, the margin necessary for victory. A local circuit judge concluded that "About every election law upon the statute books was violated in the holding of the election in the Lynch precincts." *Green v. Ball* 288 S.W. 309.

p. 207　When the National Guard . . . : Louisville *Courier-Journal,* August 5, 6 and 8, 1933.

p. 208　Three months later . . . : *Gross v. Ball* 81 S.W. 2d 409; Louisville *Courier-Journal,* November 8 and 9, 1933.

p. 208　The National Guard . . . : *Middleton v. Poer* 121 S.W. 2d 28; Louisville *Courier-Journal,* November 3, 1937, and November 9, 1938.

p. 209　"If you fail". . . : *Harlan* (Ky.) *Daily Enterprise,* November 2 and 10, 1942; William D. Forester, *Harlan County Goes to War,* 118–19.

p. 210　"Harlan County sends". . . : *Harlan Daily Enterprise,* November 15, 1942.

p. 210　The details of Chandler's popularity . . . : *Harlan Daily Enterprise,* November 4 and 10, 1942; Louisville *Courier-Journal,* May 10 and June 20, 1943.

p. 210　Federal District Judge . . . : Louisville *Courier-Journal,* January 7, 1944; *U.S. v. Saylor* 322 U.S. 385 (1944). In a dissenting opinion, Justice William O. Douglas, joined by Justices Hugo Black and Stanley Reed, said that ballot-box stuffing was a crime under Kentucky law, and that the federal government had once written election fraud into law during Reconstruction, but had subsequently repealed the measure and allowed states to govern fraud. In a statement that revealed how little Douglas understood about the history of election fraud, he wrote:

> "Let the states of this great Union understand that the elections are in their own hands, and if there be fraud, coercion, or force used they will be the first to feel it. Responding to a universal sentiment throughout the country for greater purity in elections, many of our States have enacted laws to protect the voter and to purify the ballot. These, under the guidance of State officers, have worked efficiently, satisfactorily, and beneficently; and if these federal statutes are repealed that sentiment will receive an impetus which, if the cause still exists, will carry such enactments in every State of the Union."

p. 211　Among the ninety-nine . . . : *Harlan Daily Enterprise,* June 6, 1943, and February 8, 1945.

p. 211　By the summer of 1945 . . . : Louisville *Courier-Journal,* July 28 and 29, 1945; *Harlan Daily Enterprise,* July 29, 1945.

p. 211　C. C. Ramey . . . : *United States of America v. Clinton C. Ball, et al.* case 11145, grand jury report, U.S. District Court, London Division, Eastern District of Kentucky, records in National Archives, Southeast Region, East Point, Georgia; Louisville *Courier-Journal,* July 28, 1945.

p. 212　One month after . . . : *Harlan Daily Enterprise,* August 5, 1945; Louisville *Courier-Journal,* August 3, 1947.

CHAPTER NINE

p. 215　In 1942, . . . : John Egerton, *Speak Now Against the Day,* 373–79. In the 1877 Georgia constitution, governors were limited to two successive terms of two years each. After serving these terms, a former governor could not run again until four years after the end of the second term. In 1941, the constitution was changed to allow governors to serve one four-year term, and could not be eligible to run again until four years after the end of the previous term. Talmadge had been first elected in 1932, and then reelected in 1934. After the required interim, he was elected again in 1940, but was defeated by Arnall in 1942, who could serve only one term.

p. 216   White Southerners . . . : *Smith v. Allwright* 321 U.S. 649 (1944); the Smith case came on the heels of another crucial case involving primary elections and election fraud. In *U.S. v. Classic* 313 U.S. 299 (1941), the Court ruled that voters in a Louisiana primary race had a right to have their ballots counted. Lawson, *Black Ballots*, 100; Keyssar, *The Right to Vote*, 248–49; Egerton, *Speak Now Against the Day*, 380.

p. 216   Gene Talmadge . . . : William Anderson, *The Wild Man From Sugar Creek*, 215–33; Egerton, *Speak Now Against the Day*, 382–88.

p. 218   "There was no finesse". . . : Sherrill, *Gothic Politics in the Deep South*, 38–39.

p. 219   The race for governor . . . : Egerton, *Speak Now Against the Day*, 388–89.

p. 219   The source . . . : *Atlanta Journal*, March 2 and 3, 1947. For his work in uncovering the frauds in Telfair County, Goodwin was awarded a Pulitzer Prize the following year.

p. 220   "mad because". . ."may be held": *Atlanta Journal*, March 3 and 4, 1947.

p. 220   Senator E. F. Griffith . . . : *Atlanta Journal*, March 5, 1947.

p. 221   Two weeks later . . . : *Atlanta Journal*, March 19, 1947; Egerton, *Speak Now Against the Day*, 483; Sherrill, *Gothic Politics in the Deep South*, 49.

p. 221   A bomb went off . . . : Sherrill, *Gothic Politics in the Deep South*, 42, 54–55; *Atlanta Constitution*, June 29 and 30 and July 2, 1950. In DeKalb County, a member of the county League of Women Voters, Madeleine Brenner, charged eighteen members of the county Democratic executive committee with election fraud. Since her complaint involved federal elections, the FBI was asked to investigate. Brenner said she witnessed ballots being removed from the boxes before the polls were closed. See *Atlanta Constitution*, July 1, 1950; *New York Times*, July 1, 1950.

p. 223   "forcefully [believes]" . . . : Herman E. Talmadge, *You and Segregation*, 78–79.

p. 223   South Texas . . . : Mary Kahl, *Ballot Box 13*, 80–91. For a background on the Parr family, see Evan Anders, *Boss Rule in South Texas*, 171–93; Robert Dallek, *Lone Star Rising*, 330.

p. 224   "Parr was the Godfather . . .": Dahl, *Ballot Box 13*, 88–89.

p. 224   But Johnson broke . . . : For the background of the 1941 Texas election, see Robert A. Caro, *The Path to Power*; Ronnie Dugger, *The Politician*, 235, 323.

p. 225   In 1948 . . . : *Dallas Morning News*, August 22, 1948; Robert A. Caro, *Means of Ascent*, 172–76; *Dallek*, Lone Star Rising, 315–16.

p. 225   On primary day . . . : Caro, *Means of Ascent*, 264–66, 303–08; Dallek, *Lone Star Rising*, 318; Kahl, *Ballot Box 13*, 93; *Dallas Morning News*, August 29, 1948.

p. 226   Soon after the polls closed . . . : *Dallas Morning News*, August 29, 1948; *Austin Statesman*, August 30, 1948.

p. 227   "We didn't rush" . . . : Caro, *Means of Ascent*, 308–12; Dallek, *Lone Star Rising*, 327.

p. 227   After some Houston precincts . . . : *Dallas Morning News*, August 30 and 31, 1948; *Austin Statesman*, August 30 and September 1, 1948; Caro, *Means of Ascent*, 313–15; Kahl, *Ballot Box 13*, 128.

p. 228   Then Parr had . . . : *Dallas Morning News*, September 2, 5, 7 and 8, 1948; *Austin Statesman*, September 3 and 7, 1948; Kahl, *Ballot Box 13*, 100–05; Caro, *Means of Ascent*, 316–17.

p. 228   "I was beaten" . . . : Caro, *Means of Ascent*, 318–20.

p. 228   E. H. Shomette . . . :*Austin Statesman*, September 9, 1948.

p. 229   Stevenson took his case . . . : Dallek, *Lone Star Rising*, 330–34; *Dallas Morning News*, September 12, 1948.

p. 229   While the legal battle . . . : *Dallas Morning News*, September 14 and 22, 1948; *Austin Statesman*, September 13 and 14, 1948; Caro, *Means of Ascent*, 346–48; Kahl, *Ballot Box 13*, 143.

p. 230   By that one vote . . . : *Austin Statesman*, September 24 and 28, 1948; Dallek, *Lone Star Rising*, 336–43; Kahl, *Ballot Box 13*, 210–11; *Dallas Morning News*, September 25 and 30 and October 6, 1948; Laura Kalman, *Abe Fortas*, 201–02.

p. 231   Stevenson also asked . . . : Tom C. Clark to LBJ, February 1, 1949, in Tom C. Clark Papers, Truman Library; "Memorandum With Respect to the Texas Second or 'Run-Off' Primary," Clark Papers. Clark and Johnson remained close friends, and President Johnson later appointed Clark's son, Ramsey, attorney general in 1967.

p. 232   The Texas Journalist . . . : Dugger, *The Politician*, 341.

p. 232   Russell Long . . . : Robert Mann, *Legacy to Power*, 91–93, 141–42.

p. 234   While Johnson and Russell . . . : For background on the Ed Prichard case, see Tracy Campbell, *Short of the Glory*, 7–130, 133–40, 166.

p. 236   By the early 1960s, . . . : *Baker v. Carr* 369 U.S. 186 (1962); *Gray v. Sanders* 372 U.S. 368 (1963); *Reynolds v. Sims* 377 U.S. 533 (1964); Keyssar, *The Right to Vote*, 284–87; Jimmy Carter, *Turning Point*, 26–41.

One of the counties in Carter's district, Terrell, was known by civil rights workers as "Terrible Terrell" because of the vast disparity between white and black voting rights in the county. In 1958, 64.4 percent of the county's 4,700 white citizens could vote, whereas only 1.7 percent of the county's 8,500 black citizens possessed the right to vote. The county was well known as one where whites intimidated and defrauded black voters, and where white election officials purposefully prohibited blacks who had graduated from college from passing the literacy tests. See Lawson, *Black Ballots*, 206–07.

p. 237   Early on Election Day . . . : *Atlanta Journal*, October 23 and 26, 1962; Carter, *Turning Point*, 83–89; Peter G. Bourne, *Jimmy Carter*, 115–19.

p. 238   Due to the . . . : *Atlanta Journal*, October 26 and November 1, 4 and 5, 1962; Bourne, *Jimmy Carter*, 121–26; Carter, *Turning Point*, 100–02, 118, 155–56.

p. 239   On November 1, . . . : *Atlanta Journal,* November 7, 1962; Bourne, *Jimmy Carter,*
          128–30.

p. 240   In remembering the case . . . : Pennington also felt that his role was indispen-
          sable in saving Carter's career. In 1980, John Pennington was dying of cancer
          when he was visited by President Jimmy Carter. According to Carter, Pen-
          nington's last wish was to ride back to Washington on Air Force One, for, as he
          told Carter, it would be "payment for helping you get to be president." Carter,
          Turning Point, 198.

p. 241   "Give us the ballot" . . . : King quoted in Keyssar, *The Right to Vote,* 258; Lawson,
          Black Ballots, 155–64.

CHAPTER TEN

p. 242   An example is . . . : Two early works are Theodore H. White, *The Making of the
          President, 1960,* 13–36; and Schlesinger, *A Thousand Days,* 74–78. A recent
          examination is Robert Dallek, *An Unfinished Life,* 295–96.

p. 243   In order to win . . . : Dallek, *An Unfinished Life,* 257–58; Dan B. Fleming,
          Kennedy vs. Humphrey, West Virginia, 1960, 107–18.

p. 243   In Logan County . . . : F. Keith Davis, *West Virginia Tough Boys,* 138–41,
          152–54; Raymond Chafin and Topper Sherwood, *Just Good Politics,* 130–50;
          Harry W. Ernst, *The Primary That Made a President,* 16–17. Some of Chafin's
          opponents dismiss his claims, saying Chafin would never have spent that much
          money on a county campaign and would have kept the money himself. Others
          say the figure exceeded $35,000.

p. 244   "utterly flabbergasted" . . . : Barry M. Goldwater, *With No Apologies,* 105–07.
          Goldwater and the agent, Walter Holloway, assumed the report was simply "too
          hot to handle" for Rogers and Nixon. Rogers ordered an FBI investigation of the
          West Virginia primary, but in June 1960 concluded no evidence of fraud could be
          found. Federal law at the time did not specifically prohibit vote-buying. Chap-
          manville mayor Clyde Freeman was indignant at the Justice Department's con-
          clusions, saying "all sorts of irregularities" took place in Logan County alone.
          New York Times, June 13, 1960; Fleming, *Kennedy vs. Humphrey,* 111–14.

          One can only surmise how much evidence Hoover's FBI collected on the
          Kennedys and the 1960 election, since his secretary, Helen Gandy, destroyed
          especially sensitive files such as Kennedy's upon Hoover's death. See Athan G.
          Theoharis and John Stuart Cox, *The Boss,* 325–32.

p. 244   As Election Day approached . . . : News release, November 3, 1960, Republican
          National Committee, November 1960 Scrapbook, Thruston B. Morton Papers,
          Special Collections, University of Kentucky; *Houston Chronicle,* November 24,
          1960; *New York Times,* June 13, 1960.

p. 245   "That guy . . .": *Nation,* September 3, 1960.

p. 245   The *Daily News* . . . : Adam Cohen and Elizabeth Taylor, *American Pharaoh,*
          263–64; *Chicago Daily News,* October 6, 1960; see also John Landesco, "Election
          Fraud," in John A. Gardiner and David J. Olson, eds., *Theft of the City,* 51–59.

p. 246   Benjamin Adamowski . . . : Edmund F. Kallina, Jr., *Courthouse Over White House,*
22, 46–47. Kallina's account of the 1960 election is an exhaustive examination
of how fraud played a crucial role in Chicago elections, and understands that
1960 should not be seen as either an aberration in Chicago political history or
dismissed as an irrelevancy where fraud was minimized. Kallina's book is one
that should be seen as a corrective to the vast amount of literature, particularly
from Kennedy insiders, who discount or dismiss fraud as a critical player in the
1960 election. See also George C. Edwards III, *Why the Electoral College is Bad
for America,* 123–24.

p. 246   As the polls closed . . . : Nixon wrote in 1962 that many supporters wished he
had asked the Justice Department to have U.S. marshals police the polls in
Chicago, as well as have the ballot boxes impounded following the election.
Richard Nixon, *Six Crises,* 419.

p. 247   Late on election night . . . : *Washington Evening Star,* November 10 and 19,
1960; *New York Times,* November 12, 1960; *Washington Post,* November 12,
1960; *Los Angeles Times,* November 10, 2000; David Greenberg, *Nixon's Shadow,*
188–89; Theodore White, *The Making of the President, 1960,* 35; Len
O'Connor, *Clout,* 156–62. In his comments after Election Day, Nixon carefully
avoided conceding and instead said: "If the present trend continues, Senator
Kennedy will be the next president of the United States." Nixon, *Six Crises,* 389.

p. 249   When an official ballot . . . : News release, November 29, 1960, Republican
National Committee, Morton Papers; Mike Royko, *Boss,* 118–19; "Report on
Election Procedures in the 39th Ward, 25th Precinct, Located at 3801 W.
Lawrence Avenue, Chicago, Illinois, on November 8, 1960," Morton Papers.

p. 249   Meanwhile, the charges . . . : *Houston Chronicle,* November 19, 22, 24 and 26,
1960; O. Douglas Weeks, *Texas in the 1960 Presidential Election,* 61–64.

p. 251   On November 24 . . . : *Houston Chronicle,* November 24 and 29, 1960.

p. 252   By December 1 . . . : *New York Herald Tribune,* December 5 and 6, 1960; *Chicago
Daily Tribune,* November 30, 1960; *New York Daily News,* December 2, 1960;
New York Times, November 25, 1960; Nashville *Tennessean,* December 2, 1960;
Kallina, *Courthouse Over White House,* 118; Albert Fay to Thruston B. Morton,
December 5, 1960, Morton Papers.

p. 253   "The Republican actions" . . . : *Chicago Daily Tribune,* December 2, 1960;
Chicago's American, December 3, 1960; *Chicago Sun-Times,* December 3, 1960;
Cohen and Taylor, *American Pharaoh,* 268.

p. 254   "preserve the sanctity" . . . : *Chicago Daily Tribune,* December 3, 1960; Interview
with Thruston B. Morton, conducted by Charles Atcher, October 1, 1974,
Thruston B. Morton Oral History Project, Special Collections, University of
Kentucky. In his account of the 1960 election, Edmund F. Kallina, Jr. accepts
Nixon at his word and calls the vice president's "refusal" to contest the election
"in the best tradition of American politics." See *From Courthouse to White House,*
103–04. Nixon was as experienced as anyone on the American political scene in

1960 and understood the difficulty of the task before him in challenging the election, as well as the stain it would produce if his campaign was successful and Nixon had been inaugurated. He certainly distanced himself in public from Morton and the recount effort, and subsequent historians have accepted this version at face value. Yet Morton's own words indicate that Nixon took a larger role in the recount effort than has been acknowledged. David Greenberg, "Life After Certification," *Slate*, November 18, 2000; *Chicago Evening Star*, November 19, 1960; *New York Times*, December 15, 18 and 23, 1960.

p. 255 Lawyers for the Texas GOP . . . : *New York Herald Tribune*, December 5, 1960; *Houston Chronicle*, December 8, 1960. For the Republican challenge in Nevada, see *Las Vegas Sun*, November 30, 1960 and *Las Vegas Review-Journal*, November 24, 1960. Kennedy won Nevada by just 2,493 votes, and the GOP centered its recount contest in Clark County, where JFK won by nearly 6,000 votes.

p. 256 By December 7 . . . : *Washington Post*, December 8, 1960.

p. 256 On Sunday . . . : *Chicago Tribune*, December 4 and 8, 1960.

p. 256 Despite the pessimism . . . : *Chicago Tribune*, December 8, 1960; Cohen and Taylor, *American Pharaoh*, 268–69.

p. 257 judges in both Texas and Illinois . . . : *Chicago Daily Tribune*, December 13, 1960; *Chicago Daily News*, December 16, 1960; *Houston Chronicle*, December 13, 1960; *New York Times*, December 13, 1960.

p. 258 The recount covered . . . : Kallina, *From Courthouse to White House*, 146–56. Adamowski referred to the recount as "justice by bankruptcy" (158).

p. 258 On December 16 . . . : Morris J. Wexler, "Report to the Honorable Richard B. Austin, Chief Justice of the Criminal Court of Cook County," April 13, 1961; Cohen and Taylor, *American Pharaoh*, 277. In January 1962, the Board of Election Commissioners issued a report that stated that no fraud had occurred in the 1960 election, with the lone exception of ninety election judges whom the BEC termed had a "lack of understanding." Kallina, *FromCourthouse to White House*, 220.

p. 259 "We won" . . . : "Excerpts from Address by Sen. Thruston B. Morton, January 26, 1961, at Chicago, Illinois," General Correspondence, Box 533, Richard M. Nixon Pre-Presidential Papers, National Archives, Pacific Region, Laguna Niguel, California; Greenberg, *Nixon's Shadow*, 189.

p. 260 There were also suggestions . . . : Richard M. Nixon to Chuck Lichtenstein and Agnes Waldron, September 12, 1961, "Six Crises Manuscript," Folder 258, Nixon Pre-Presidential Papers. The charges of Joe Kennedy's influence with Giancana and the Chicago syndicate in the 1960 election are highlighted in Seymour Hersh, *The Dark Side of Camelot*, 131–53.

p. 260 Nixon picked up . . . : Kallina, *From Courthouse to White House*, 163–66.

p. 261 As usual . . . : *Houston Chronicle*, November 28, 1960. Mundt's plan had some self-serving aspects. In a state such as South Dakota with a single congressional district, his plan would still be a "winner-take-all" system, thus skewing the power of small states in the Electoral College even further.

p. 262   In order to verify . . . : *Chicago Tribune*, March 23, 1972.

p. 262   But the Tribune reporters . . . : *Chicago Tribune*, March 23 and 24, 1972.

p. 265   Over the succeeding days . . . : *Chicago Tribune*, March 25 and 29, September 11, 12 and 15, 1972.

p. 266   "Vote fraud is a way of life" . . . : *Chicago Tribune*, September 13, 1972.

p. 266   In September 1972 . . . : *Chicago Tribune*, September 16, 1972; F. Richard Ciccone, "Making Votes Count," *Chicago History* (Winter 2002): 13. The demise of Daley's methods did not completely alter Chicago elections. In a 1979 mayor's race, when asked how many votes had been cast in his precinct, one officer responded: "We won't know how many votes we got until we find out how many we need."

p. 267   In 1976 . . . : *New York Times*, November 5, 1976; *Chicago Tribune*, November 2 and 4, 1976; Cohen and Taylor, *American Pharaoh*, 554–55. Carter beat Ford in Chicago by 425,000 votes, 50,000 fewer than Kennedy's margin in 1960. The Republican candidate, Jim Thompson, won a landslide victory for governor in the same election, and a number of Daley allies suffered defeats.

          In the 1976 Democratic primary in California, Jimmy Carter's campaign came under fire for its use of "street money." Several prominent African-American ministers in Oakland were given between $1,000 and $5,000 for "routine campaign expenses" from the Carter campaign. The money did Carter little good in the Golden State, considering that he lost both the California primary to Jerry Brown and the state to Gerald Ford in November. In the summer of 1976, the Carter campaign estimated it had spent over $200,000 in "street money," or "walking-around money," that could be a payment to a local ward boss, a "contribution" to a local neighborhood club, or even food and drink to voters. *Los Angeles Times*, August 8, 1976. Like 1960, the 1976 election was a very close one, and had Gerald Ford won Ohio and Hawaii, which he lost by less than 15,000 total votes, he would have remained in the White House.

CHAPTER ELEVEN

p. 269   Southern demagogues . . . : Dan T. Carter, *From George Wallace to Newt Gingrich*, 1–31; J. Todd Moye, *Let the People Decide*, 40–86.

p. 269   In 1957, . . . : Robert A. Caro, *Master of the Senate*, 165–202; Keyssar, *The Right to Vote*, 259.

p. 269   In 1963, . . . : Lawson, *Black Ballots*, 284–86; John Dittmer, *Local People*, 215–302; Moye, *Let the People Decide*, 114–147. For the FBI's role in the Voting Rights Act, see Kenneth O'Reilly, *Racial Matters*, 49–77.

p. 270   "bore a strong resemblance" . . . : Keyssar, *The Right to Vote*, 263–64.

p. 270   Since the 1960s . . . : Lizabeth Cohen, *A Consumers' Republic*, 331–44; Callahan, *The Cheating Culture*, 1–97.

p. 271   Challenges along First Amendment . . . : *Burson v. Freeman* 504 U.S. 191 (1992). In his dissent, Justice John Paul Stevens (joined by Sandra Day O'Connor and David Souter) wrote that "Even under the most sanguine scenario of participatory democracy, it is difficult to imagine voter turnout so complete as to require the clearing of hundreds of thousands of square feet simply to ensure that the path to the polling place door remains open and that the curtain that protects the secrecy of the ballot box remains closed." See also Robert Brett Dunham, "Defoliating the Grassroots: Election Day Restrictions on Political Speech," *Georgetown Law Journal* 77 (August 1989): 2137–2200. The Wisconsin zone of five hundred feet was later ruled unconstitutional, since even private property owners within the zone could not place a campaign sign in their yards. An appellate court ruled that this constituted an "impermissible infringement on free speech." *Calchera v. Procarione* 805 F. Supp. 716 (1992). The Wisconsin legislature later redrew the zone to the one-hundred-foot mark. For the Kentucky case, see *Anderson v. Spear* 189 F. Supp. 2d. 644 (2002). In January 2004, the panel from the U.S. Sixth Circuit ruled that while the state provided "ample evidence of Kentucky's history of election fraud and corrupt elections practices, glaringly thin is its evidence as to why the legislature . . . ultimately arrived at a distance of 500 feet." The three-judge panel agreed that "this overbroad restriction significantly impinges on protected speech." *Louisville Courier-Journal,* January 17 and 22, 2004. According to a county clerk in a mountain county of Kentucky, as the buffer zone around the polls increased, the jobs of vote buyers and thugs was made increasingly harder. "Distance is important in preventing corruption and intimidation," he said. "Access is everything."

In 1986, when Justice William Rehnquist was nominated to be Chief Justice, witnesses testified at his Senate confirmation hearing that in the mid-1960s, Rehnquist had harassed African-American and Latino voters at Arizona polling sites. The witnesses claimed that Rehnquist, a Republican activist, demanded to know if the minority voters were "qualified" to vote, a charge Rehnquist denied.

In the *Burson* ruling, the Court noted that even in elections not involving local, state, or national political representation, limits on polling place electioneering are recognized. The National Labor Relations Board, for example, limits electioneering activities near the polling place in union elections.

p. 272 Louisiana enacted . . . : *New York Times,* January 9 and 24, February 13 and 16, April 12, May 5 and 13, June 4, and July 2, 1977; Adam Fairclough, *Race and Democracy,* 474. Jeansonne, *Leander Perez.* For vote-buying during the gubernatorial campaigns of Edwin Edwards, see John Maginnis, *The Last Hayride,* 131–32, 297–98.

p. 273 In 1974, . . . : Jeansonne, *Leander Perez,* 74–82; Fairclough, *Race and Democracy,* 465–66. When Perez appeared on William F. Buckley's "Firing Line" in 1968, the host commented on elections in the area and mentioned to Perez, "I understand in one of these elections Zazu Pitts, Charlie Chaplin, and Babe Ruth voted for you?" Perez retorted: "No, that was not in my parish. That was in St. Bernard." *The Ends of the Earth: Plaquemines Parish, Louisiana,* video produced by Louis Alvarez and Andrew Kolker, The Center for New American Media, 1982.

p. 275   A similar pattern . . . : Leslie County, Kentucky was (and remains) a Republican
          stronghold. After leaving the White House, former president Richard Nixon
          made his first public appearance in Leslie County. Muncy spearheaded the drive
          to bring Nixon to the county. After his election-fraud conviction, Muncy
          blamed his ties to Nixon for his political and legal problems. Muncy's story was
          the subject of the film *Big Lever: Party Politics in Leslie County, Kentucky*, dir. by
          Francis Morton, Appalshop Productions, 1982.

p. 277   "Now who do you want". . . : Louisville *Courier-Journal*, October 11, 1987.

p. 277   "basically stole the election". . . : Louisville *Courier-Journal*, October 11, 1987.

p. 278   "To get 50 percent". . . : Louisville *Courier-Journal*, October 12 and 13, 1987.
          For a recent case in which a prominent eastern Kentucky financier was con-
          victed of vote-buying, see *New York Times*, August 29, 2004, *Lexington Herald-
          Leader*, September 16, 2004.

p. 278   In a memo . . . : Louisville *Courier-Journal*, October 13, 1987.

p. 279   "by allowing corruption". . . : "Attorney General's Task Force on Election Fraud:
          Report to Fred Cowan, Attorney General, Commonwealth of Kentucky"
          (1988), 11.

p. 279   "People not involved". . . : Louisville *Courier-Journal*, October 12, 1987; Lex-
          ington *Herald-Leader*, June 19 and 20, 2003.

p. 280   In a 1998 primary election . . . : Lexington *Herald-Leader*, April 20, 2000, and
          September 27 and October 1, 2003; Louisville *Courier-Journal*, August 16 and
          September 24, 2003.

p. 281   "Absentee vote fraud". . . : "Election Reform Agenda," 2001, Kentucky Secretary
          of State's Office. A variety of reforms proposed by the Secretary of State (who
          was John Y. Brown III, the former governor's son) aimed at curbing election
          fraud, especially absentee fraud, was rejected by the Kentucky General Assembly
          in 2002. See also Jewell and Cunningham, *Kentucky Politics*, 16–18, 65.

p. 281   In a May 2002 primary . . . : *Lexington Herald-Leader*, May 9, 22, 29, and 30,
          and June 4, 2002; *New York Times*, June 2, 2002; Louisville *Courier-Journal*, June
          3, 2002. The highest percentage of absentee balloting in the 2002 primary in
          Kentucky occurred in Owsley County, where 9.35 percent of the eligible elec-
          torate voted absentee. For a defense of absentee-voting methods from a
          Southern perspective, see Marlin Hawkins, with Dr. C. Fred Williams, *How I
          Stole Elections*.

p. 282   In Dodge County . . . : U.S. v. McCranie 169 F. 3rd 723 (1999).

p. 282   One of the most remarkable aspects . . . : *Curry v. Baker* 802 F. 2nd 1302 (1986);
          New York Times, June 26 and 29, August 2, 16, and 23, September 4 and 18,
          October 2, and November 5, 1986.

p. 283   In the fall of 1990 . . . : *St. Louis Post-Dispatch*, September 9, 1990. In 2005, five
          Democratic officials in east St. Louis were convicted of vote-buying in the 2004
          election. *St. Louis Post-Dispatch*, June 30, 2005.

p. 284   The twentieth century . . . : Keyssar, *The Right to Vote*, 311–15. See also Piven and Cloward, *Why Americans Still Don't Vote*. Piven and Cloward's earlier book, *Why Americans Don't Vote*, was instrumental in initiating a national discussion that helped create the motor voter bill.

In 2002, the Republican National Committee conducted an investigation and discovered that in eleven states, over 140,000 people were registered to vote in at least two jurisdictions. This was probably a result of people moving to new residences and obtaining new registrations while not alerting their old county clerks' offices of their new residencies. While this explanation could explain the dual registrations as innocent oversights, the RNC also discovered that of these people, 689 had voted twice in the differing locales in 2000. *Washington Post*, June 13, 2002. For a critique of the motor-voter law, see John Fund, *Stealing Elections*, 23–25.

p. 285   In Texas . . . : Caltech-MIT Voting Technology Project, *Voting: What Is, What Could Be*, also available at www.vote.caltech.edu/.

p. 285   No state had gone as far . . . : "Oregon Election, 2000," Report Prepared by Del Information Services, January 2001.

p. 285   In March 2000 . . . : *New York Times*, October 14, 2002; California Secretary of State Bill Jones, California Internet Voting Task Force, "A Report on the Feasibility of Internet Voting," January 2000. For an analysis of the possibilities of internet voting, see R. Michael Alvarez and Thad E. Hall, *Point, Click, and Vote*. There have even been questions about the ethics of some political figures' financial stakes in the industry that records votes. Senator Chuck Hagel (R Neb.), for example, owned stock in a company that installed and ran the voting machines in his home state. See Thom Hartmann, "If You Want To Win an Election, Just Control the Voting Machines," *Common Dreams Newscenter*, February 6, 2003.

p. 286   Two bitter rivals . . . : *Miami Herald*, November 5 and 6, 1997. For some historical examples of the realities of Florida politics and voting methods, see Tracy E. Danese, *Claude Pepper and Ed Ball*.

p. 287   When investigators uncovered . . . : *Miami Herald*, November 10, 1997. The absentee fraud in Miami stands in stark contrast to predictions from earlier liberal academics, who saw no threats of fraudulent elections arising from the use of absentee ballots. In 1960, James MacGregor Burns and Jack Walter Peltason wrote: "In order to prevent fraud," they concluded, "absentee voting has been made so difficult and cumbersome that often only the most zealous citizen will go to the trouble of sending in an absentee ballot." Thirty years later, no one could describe the process of obtaining an absentee ballot as "cumbersome." Burns and Peltason, *Government By the People*, 343.

p. 288   "I thought he was gathering". . ."Oh, my God": *Miami Herald*, November 11, 12, 13, and 16, 1997.

p. 288   "buried under a small mountain" . . . : *Miami Herald*, November 14, 15, and 16, 1997. The 1984 case was *Bolden v. Potter* 452 So. 2d 564 (Fla., 1984).

p. 289   "thieves who steal democracy". . . : *Miami Herald,* February 3, 1998.

p. 289   Carollo's civil suit . . . : *Miami Herald,* February 11, 1998.

p. 289   Handwriting experts . . . : *Miami Herald,* March 5, 1998. In his ruling, Judge Wilson relied primarily on a Florida Supreme Court case of *Boardman v. Esteva* 323 So. 2d. 259 (1975). In that case, Chief Justice James Adkins ruled that "in developing a rule regarding how far irregularities in absentee ballots will affect the result of the election, a fundamental inquiry should be whether or not the irregularity complained of has prevented a full, fair, and free expression of the popular will." Chief Justice Adkins then made a pronouncement on the nature of election fraud and its real victims: "The real parties in interest here, not in the legal sense but in realistic terms, are the voters. They are possessed of the ultimate interest and it is they whom we must give primary consideration."

p. 290   A three-judge panel . . . : *In re Protest of Election Returns and Absentee Ballots* 707 So. 2d. 1170, Florida 3rd District Court of Appeals (1998). The Appeals Court relied heavily on *Bolden v. Potter* 452 So. 2d. 564 (Fla., 1984), which the Florida Supreme Court stated "When substantial fraudulent vote-buying practices are clearly shown to have been involved, the election must be declared void. Failure to do so will cause the electorate to lose confidence in the electoral process." *Miami Herald,* March 12, 1998. Although the court recognized that Mayor Suarez was not implicated in the fraud, that made no difference. "The evil to be avoided," the Court ruled, "is the same, irrespective of the source. As long as the fraud, from whatever source, is such that the true result of the election cannot be ascertained with reasonable certainty, the ballots should be invalidated."

p. 291   "You mean I'm sick" . . . : *Miami Herald,* March 12, 1998. The absentee voters in the Miami election suit claimed that having their legal votes thrown out violated their Constitutional rights, especially the equal protection clause of the Fourteenth Amendment. The court disagreed and concluded that the problems in the Miami election were merely "episodic" in nature and did not "demonstrate that the entire process is fundamentally unfair." *Scheer v. City of Miami* 15 F. Supp. 2d. 1338 (1998).

p. 291   In California . . . : Caltech-MIT Voting Technology Project, *Voting: What Is, What Could Be* also available at www.vote.caltech.edu; the absentee levels on California history are provided on the California Secretary of State's Web site, at www.ss.ca.gov.

    In a University of Miami law review article published in the spring of 2000, the journal undertook to find a remedy for any future abuses of the Florida absentee ballot. The journal proposed that "Courts should explicitly determine where, by reasonable inference, the fault for the voter lies and then connect the remedy to the results of that determination." If, for example, Candidate A wins the machine vote but Candidate B eventually was declared the winner due to problematic absentee ballots, "it would then be proper to invalidate all the absentee votes and declare A the winner." Not realizing how the upcoming presidential contest in Florida would boil down to very similar circumstances, the journal concluded that "Candidate B should be held accountable for the actions of his or her supporters where they have sought to subvert the political processes so important to a healthy democracy." "Florida Absentee Voter Fraud: Fashioning an Appropriate Judicial Remedy," *University of Miami Law Review* 54 (April 2000): 661–62. For an assessment of a 1996 California congressional election contest between Democrat Loretta Sanchez and Republican Robert Dornan, see Lori Mennite and David Callahan, "Securing the Vote: An Analysis of Election Fraud," at www.demos-usa.org, 40–43.

CHAPTER TWELVE

p. 292   The 2000 . . . : For a mainstream account, see Robert P. Watson, "The State of Elections: People, Politics, and Problems," in Robert P. Watson, ed., *Counting Votes.*

p. 293   On primary day . . . : *Greenville* (S.C.) *News,* February 20, 22, and 24, 2000; Columbia (S.C.) *State,* February 20, 2000. In South Carolina, the parties are responsible for holding their own primaries. In responding to the court order, the Republican party had told the Justice Department it could open 1,425 of 1,752 polling sites in the state, which was twice as many as the 1996 primary. The 2000 primary saw a turnout surge from 276,000 voters in 1996 to 565,000 in 2000. The county Republican chair replied that "no precincts were closed," rather that they were "consolidated" and that "in no case was a voter required to go further than to an adjoining precinct." See Greenville *News,* November 23, 2000.

p. 293   In St. Louis . . . : *Report by Matt Blunt, Secretary of State,* "Mandate for Reform: Election Turmoil in St. Louis, November 7, 2000," 30–33; *St. Louis Post-Dispatch,* November 8 and 9, 2000.

p. 296   The GOP held . . . : *Nation,* July 15, 2001. Two civil cases against the GOP absentee-ballot drive centered on Jeb Bush's letter, which was superimposed on the state seal, a violation of state law. The Bush administration in Tallahassee stated that they had not used a seal, but that the printer had on his own commandeered an outdated one from the Internet. *Nation,* July 15, 2001.

p. 297   "These days" . . . : *Tallahassee Democrat,* November 6, 2000; *Miami Herald,* November 6, 2000.

p. 297   The crush of voters . . . : *Miami Herald,* November 10, 2000; *Palm Beach Post,* November 9, 2000.

p. 298   Statewide, Buchanan . . . : *Palm Beach Post,* November 10, 2000; *Miami Herald,* November 10, 2000. Shortly after the election, researchers went to Canada to test how confusing the butterfly ballot actually was. When a psychologist substituted the names of Canadian officials into the ballot and asked random shoppers to vote with the ballot, four of 116 "voters" botched their choice in the same fashion as the Gore–Buchanan model in Miami-Dade County. This was statistically similar to the "mistaken" votes for Gore that actually went to Buchanan. See *Miami Herald,* December 1, 2000.

p. 299   Perhaps the luckiest . . . : The structural advantage of having a candidate's name placed first on a ballot is analyzed in Jon A. Krosnick, Joanne M. Miller, and Michael P. Tichy, "An Unrecognized Need for Ballot Reform: The Effects of Candidate Name Order on Election Outcomes," in Ann N. Crigler, Marion R. Just, and Edward J. McCaffery, eds., *Rethinking the Vote,* 51–74.

p. 299   Under Florida law . . . : *Palm Beach Post,* November 9 and 10, 2000; *Thirty-Six Days: The Complete Chronicle of the 2000 Presidential Election Crisis by Correspondents of the New York Times,* 10–11; Martin Merzer and the Staff of the *Miami Herald, The Miami Herald Report,* 2–71.

p. 300   In Duval County, . . . : *Miami Herald,* December 2, 2000.

p. 300   First-time Creole-speaking voters . . . : *Miami Herald,* November 9 and 10, 2000; Orlando *Sentinel,* November 8, 2000.

p. 302   Yet because of . . . : The inflated totals for Bush centered on a problem in the Earl Brown Park precinct in Volusia County. A computer memory card malfunctioned and erroneously deducted 16,022 votes from Gore. The error was corrected in the early hours of Wednesday morning, November 8. See Daytona Beach *News-Journal,* November 10, 2000.

p. 303   On November 8 . . . : *Orlando Sentinel,* November 10, 2000; *Thirty-Six Days,* 14–17.

p. 304   Yet Bush's official "lead" . . . : The Florida Secretary of State's Web site's address is http://election.dos.state.fl.us/. The official results are interesting, compared to preliminary results released by Harris's office in the days after the election. The week following the election, for example, Harris stated that Bush held a lead of 300 votes statewide. On November 19, Bush's lead ballooned to 930 when 630 overseas absentee ballots were added. *Palm Beach Post,* November 15 and 19, 2000.

p. 304   There were problems . . . : *New York Times,* July 15, 2001; Kosuke Imai and Gary King, "Did Illegal Overseas Ballots Decide the 2000 U.S. Presidential Election?," *Perspectives on Politics* 2 (Sept. 2004).

p. 305   Considering that Bush . . . : In her book, published in 2002, Harris claimed that contrary to liberal prognosticators, "Al Gore *never* [italics in original] led Florida on election night! Despite his loss of thousands of votes in the heavily Republican precincts of the western panhandle, George W. Bush continued to lead the entire evening." Harris's evidence concerning "thousands" of lost Republican votes comes from the anecdotal estimate of a Democratic TV personality. Katherine Harris, *Center of the Storm,* 3, 17.

p. 305   The GOP had also mailed . . . : *Miami Herald,* November 17, 2000; *Palm Beach Post,* November 17, 2000; *Nation,* July 15, 2001. According to Florida law, military personnel could claim Florida as their residence, even if they had never lived in the state. All that was necessary was the intent to live in the state at some time in the future.

p. 305   On November 18, . . . : *Miami Herald,* November 18 and 19, 2000; *Orlando Sentinel,* November 11 and 19, 2000; Jeffrey Toobin, *Too Close to Call,* 130.

p. 306   "We're getting kicked around". . . : *Orlando Sentinel,* November 20, 2000; *Palm Beach Post,* November 20, 2000; Toobin, *Too Close to Call,* 131. Just as Democrats found themselves dealing with sometimes contradictory statutes, the GOP did as well concerning the postmarks on the absentee ballots. While state law required postmarks, a federal law stated that ballots sent by overseas military personnel "shall be carried expeditiously and free of postage."

p. 307   On November 21, . . . : The Political Staff of the Washington *Post, Deadlock,* 113–14; *Thirty-Six Days,* 125–28; *Orlando Sentinel,* November 18, 2000; *Miami Herald,* November 27, 2000; *New York Times,* July 15, 2001.

p. 308   Jason Unger . . . : *New York Times,* July 15, 2001; *Miami Herald,* November 28, 2000.

p. 309   "The GOP's legal" . . . : *Miami Herald,* November 28 and 30, 2000. The number of absentee votes Bush picked up when the overseas absentee votes were reconsidered was actually 124. *Palm Beach Post,* November 27, 2000.

p. 309   Since the votes . . . : *New York Times,* July 15, 2001.

p. 310   Political commentators weighed in . . . : *Miami Herald,* November 12, 2000. For a valuable lesson on the substantial roadblocks one state encountered in amending its electoral vote, the historian Peter H. Argersinger warns that a case from the 1890s should alert us to the limits of electoral reform. In Michigan, the "Miner" law changed the state's electoral vote to congressional districts rather than winner-take-all. Democrats favored the plan while Republicans, led by President Benjamin Harrison, opposed it. Although the law survived various legal challenges, it was quickly repealed after Republicans regained power in the state. Argersinger correctly notes "Then, as now, those with effective political power over the electoral system used it ruthlessly to promote their own interests without regard to the rights of their opponents, their own expressed ideology, or the claims of democracy." Argersinger, "Electoral Reform and Partisan Jugglery," *Political Science Quarterly* 119 (Fall 2004): 499–520.

p. 311   One study found . . . : *Miami Herald,* December 1, 2000; *New York Times,* July 17, 2001; Caltech-MIT Voting Technology Project, *Voting: What Is, What Could Be,* July 2001, also available at www.vote.caltech.edu. In May 2002, the Bush administration's Justice Department filed five lawsuits concerning the 2000 election, and three of the suits involved Florida counties. The suits centered on discriminatory treatment of minority voters as well as the purging of the voter rolls in an attempt to correct problems before the 2002 election. Skeptical Democratic senators, alarmed at the paucity of administration efforts regarding civil rights, questioned the timing of the suits, and the N.A.A.C.P. asked why the suits were aimed at the county level, rather than the state, where more structural changes could occur. *New York Times,* May 22, 2002.

   As Dennis F. Thompson points out, the very definition of voting, according to the 1965 Voting Rights Act, means more than simply casting a ballot. An essential component of the Act states that an equally important device is "having such ballot counted properly and included in the appropriate totals of votes cast." See Dennis F. Thompson, *Just Elections,* 53.

p. 311 While approximately eleven percent . . . : U.S. Commission on Civil Rights, "Voting Irregularities in Florida During the 2000 Presidential Election," June 2001.

p. 312 Gadsden County is one of Florida's most Democratic counties. Of registered voters in the county, 22, 016 were Democrats, compared to 2,593 Republicans. African-Americans comprised 12,803 of the registered Democrats. Gadsden was the only Florida county to vote Democratic when Ronald Reagan won the state in 1984. It is also one of the poorest counties in the state, with 25.9 percent of its population living in poverty. See *Miami Herald,* December 3, 2000.

p. 312 African-American voters . . . : *Orlando Sentinel,* November 10, 2000; Ron Formisano, "State Won't Escape Racist Voting Antics," *Gainesville Sun,* February 3, 2001; U.S. Commission on Civil Rights, "Voting Irregularities." The *Miami Herald* examined the extent that convicted felons had voted in the 2000 election. In partial returns from twelve counties, the *Herald* found that 445 votes had been illegally cast by felons. Nearly 75 percent of the ballots were for Gore, giving Republicans ammunition that fraud had played a role in Gore's totals. Of these votes, 45 were cast by convicted murderers, sixteen rapists, and at least two people listed on the state's registry of sexual offenders. One of these was Clarence E. Williams, who also had Alzheimer's disease. Some on this list saw the issue in terms of disfranchisement. Theron McDaniel, a 42–year-old deacon in his church, had been convicted of dealing in stolen property in 1977. "They're still holding that over me?" McDaniel asked. A later examination of twenty-two counties revealed that 764 felons had voted. *Miami Herald,* December 1 and 10, 2000. Greg Palast, "Ex-Con Game: How Florida's 'Felon' Voter-Purge Was Itself Felonious," *Harper's* (March 2002): 48–49. Palast writes that 2,873 names were removed from the voter rolls in Florida on constitutionally dubious grounds. Since 35 states allow felons to vote, removing those who had once lived in one of these states violated the Constitution's "full faith and credit" clause in revoking the civil rights that someone would have received in another state. The Florida Supreme Court had actually stated this just weeks before the election, but the directive from Governor Jeb Bush's clemency office authorized the purge. See also Greg Palast, *The Best Democracy Money Can Buy,* 11–71.

In Florida, some counties employed the felon list while others ignored it. Guy Stuart has concluded that if the entire state had used the felon purge, Republicans would have benefited. But since only two counties conducted a complete purge, the felon list "may have ended up favoring the Democrats because in counties that did not use the list, it is likely that some ineligible voters voted, and those ineligible voters were more likely to be Democrats." "Databases, Felons, and Voting: Bias and Partisanship of the Florida Felons List in the 2000 Elections," *Political Science Quarterly* 119 (Fall 2004): 473.

p. 313   the Commission's report . . . : U.S. Commission on Civil Rights, "Voter Irregularities."

p. 314   Although rumors were rampant . . . : *Tallahassee Democrat*, November 8, 2000; *Miami Herald*, November 8, 2000.

p. 315   While one can make . . . : *St. Petersburg Times*, November 19, 2000.

p. 315   In Seminole County, . . . : *Orlando Sentinel*, November 13 and 29, 2000; *Thirty-Six Days*, 98–99, 162. *Thirty-Six Days*, 308–09; *Jacobs v. Seminole County Canvassing Board; Taylor v. Martin County Canvassing Board.* See also Alan M. Dershowitz, *Supreme Injustice*, 38–39.

p. 316   On election night . . . : *Thirty-Six Days*, 173–74. In the recount, only ten counties reported lower figures from the original tallies, and these were usually one or two votes, not 218 as in Nassau.

p. 317   Hordes of interested partisans . . . : *Orlando Sentinel*, November 13, 2000; *Miami Herald*, November 13, 2000.

p. 318   On November 22, . . . : *Thirty-Six Days*, 134–35; Dershowitz, *Supreme Injustice*, 36–37.

p. 318   Supervisor David Leahy . . . : *Orlando Sentinel*, November 14, 2000; *Miami Herald*, November 23 and 26, 2000; *Thirty-Six Days*, 134–35; Toobin, *Too Close to Call*, 154–57. In the *Wall Street Journal*, columnist Paul Gigot wrote glowingly of the "semi-spontaneous combustion" in Miami-Dade County that produced a "bourgeois riot" that "could end up saving the presidency for George W. Bush." Quoted in Dershowitz, *Supreme Injustice*, 37.

p. 319   On November 26, . . . : *Thirty-Six Days*, 164–65. In her "official" tally, Harris ruled that Palm Beach's recount was not complete and state law required that counties "manually recount *all* ballots" [italics mine]. Democratic lawyers contended that Harris was cherry-picking, since she had counted the results in three counties where there had been sample manual recounts. Harris's tally also did not include an additional 157 votes for Gore produced by the partial recount in Miami-Dade County that was halted by the mob on November 22. If those partial counts had been included, Bush's official majority would have stood at 188 votes.

       The following year, several organizations published their own findings concerning the recount. Assuming that the Supreme Court had not intervened and the recount could have proceeded, a study conducted by the National Opinion Research Center at the University of Chicago found that the answer depends on the standard used to measure voter intent. Ironically, if the count had proceeded along the lines demanded by the Gore team, Bush would have won by a margin ranging from 225 to 493 votes. These recounts of "undervotes" in four predominantly Democratic counties would have not been enough to overtake Bush. On the other hand, had a statewide recount of both "undervotes" and "overvotes" taken place, Gore would have won by margins of 42 to 171 votes, depending on how restrictive the definition of a legal vote could be established. Louisville *Courier-Journal*, November 12, 2001.

p. 320   Senator John Sherman . . . : Richard H. Pildes, "Disputing Elections," in Arthur
J. Jacobson and Michel Rosenfeld, *The Longest Night,* 81–82.

p. 321   "This is terrible" . . . : Dershowitz, *Supreme Injustice,* 156–57, 164.

p. 321   On separate occasions . . . : Alexander Keyssar, "The Right to Vote and Election
2000," in Jack N. Rakove, ed., *The Unfinished Election of 2000,* 77; *Gore v. Harris*
772 So 2d. 1243 (Fla., 2000); *Orlando Sentinel,* November 23, 2000; *Miami
Herald,* December 12, 2000; Michel Rosenfeld, "*Bush v. Gore:* Three Strikes for
the Constitution, the Court, and Democracy, but There is Always Next Season,"
in Jacobson and Rosenfeld, *The Longest Night,* 111.

p. 321   The high court interceded . . . : *Boardman v. Esteva* 323 So 2d. 259 (Fla. 1975);
Bush v. Gore 531 U.S. 98 (2000); *Bush v. Gore* 121 S. Ct., 512.

p. 322   The manner in which . . . : Larry D. Kramer, "The Supreme Court in Politics,"
and Pamela S. Karlan, "Equal Protection: *Bush v. Gore* and the Making of a
Precedent," in Rakove, *The Unfinished Election of 2000*; Dershowitz, *Supreme
Injustice,* 55–57.

p. 322   Yet to Republicans . . . : Adherents of the "tie" theory conveniently ignore Gore's
half-million popular-vote majority, or the latent problems in Florida's voting
procedures. See, for example, Steven G. Calabresi, "A Political Question," in
Bruce Ackerman, ed., *Bush v. Gore,* 129–44. An adviser to George W. Bush's
campaign, Calabresi nonetheless concluded that "*Bush v. Gore* improperly
resolved a political question" (141).

p. 322   "Our consideration" . . . : *Bush v. Gore* 531 U.S. 98 (2000).

p. 323   On January 20, . . . : *New York Times,* January 21, 2001.

p. 323   The one, commissioned . . . : *Miami Herald,* April 4 and 8, 2001. Walter R.
Mebane, Jr., has concluded that if "precinct-tabulated optical scan ballots" had
been available throughout Florida—the best available voting machines that
could have detected thousands of overvotes in time for the voter to correct
them—Gore would have won by over 30,000 votes. See "The Wrong Man is
President! Overvotes in the 2000 Presidential Election in Florida," *Perspectives
in Politics* 2 (Sept. 2004): 525–35.

p. 324   A year after the election . . . : *New York Times,* November 12, 2001.

p. 324   "the counters" . . . : In addition to Boss Tweed, another noteworthy political boss
has also been attributed with saying "The people who cast the votes decide
nothing. The people who count the votes decide everything"—Joseph Stalin.

CONCLUSION

p. 326   For added measure . . . : *Los Angeles Times,* March 15, 2004; *New York Times,*
October 30, 2002, and March 16, 2004. The same month that HAVA became
law, Attorney General John Ashcroft announced the Voting Access and
Integrity Initiative, which targeted election fraud by assigning federal prosecu-
tors to monitor alleged election crimes. Critics of the initiative noted that the
Justice Department seemed more interested in protecting the "integrity" of the

ballot rather than ensuring "access." More to the point is the assertion that having prosecutors on alert for stories of fraud would more likely intimidate minority voters, most of whom vote for the party that opposed Ashcroft. See Jeffrey Toobin, "Poll Position," the *New Yorker,* September 20, 2004.

Another form of violence threatened American elections after 9/11. The threat of possible terrorist attacks worried American election officials in the summer of 2004, and some proposed a rather draconian solution. A commission established under HAVA suggested to congressional leaders that a process should be established to reschedule a presidential election in case of a terrorist attack. DeForest B. Soaries, chair of the U.S. Election Assistance Commission, had earlier alerted Homeland Security Secretary Tom Ridge that some plan for altering or even *canceling* a presidential election should be considered. Such a plan presented numerous constitutional challenges, and posed the possibility of terrorist threats if the possibility of postponing or canceling an election loomed. National Security Adviser Condoleezza Rice dismissed the suggestion, noting: "We've had elections in this country when we were at war, even when we were at civil war." *New York Times,* July 12, 2004.

p. 326   "You know why" . . . : Quoted in Keyssar, "The Right to Vote and Election 2000," 90.

p. 326   Similar to the ways . . . : *Los Angeles Times,* March 15, 2004; *New York Times,* October 30, 2002, and March 16, 2004. In national elections in India in 2004, party officials used various tactics to intimidate opponents, including detonating small bombs outside polling places, and a device called "booth capturing," where thugs would steal ballot boxes and brazenly stuff them with ballots. From the standpoint of the *New York Times,* this was "the same old fraud" that characterized so many other Indian elections. Despite new electronic machines, party officials still practiced tricks that displayed how little democracy millions of Indians enjoyed. When similar cases in American history are uncovered, our collective response refuses to apply the same terminology. *New York Times,* April 27, 2004.

p. 327   The new Florida . . . : Christopher Hitchens, "Ohio's Odd Numbers," *Vanity Fair* (March 2005). Hitchens notes that in examining the myriad of complaints emerging from Ohio, "in practically every case where lines were too long or machines too few the foul-up was in a Democratic county or precinct, and in practically every case where machines produced impossible or improbable outcomes it was the challenger who suffered and the actual or potential Democratic voters who were shortchanged, discouraged, or held up to ridicule as chronic undervoters or as sudden converts to fringe-party losers."

In addition to areas where long lines caused some voters to wait seven hours, most of the major problems in Ohio were located in the major metropolitan areas. In Cuyahoga County, 93,000 more ballots were cast than registered voters. In Fairview Park, there were 18,472 votes cast where only 13,342 voters were reg-

istered. Election officials speculated that absentee ballots were mistakenly placed
in the count for particular areas, making it appear as though more votes were cast
than were registered. In the final tally, the officials claimed, the problem was corrected. *Salon.com,* November 10, 2004. See the Cuyahoga results at boe.cuya-
hogacounty.us/boe/. In Columbus, a computer error mistakenly added nearly
3,900 votes for Bush, an indication that some electronic malfunctions could still
occur. *Nation,* November 29, 2004. One of the strangest moments occurred in
Warren County, Ohio, where county commissioners ordered "a complete security
lockdown" in vote counting, citing FBI warnings of a possible terrorist threat.
The FBI denied issuing any such warning. In Warren County, Bush received 72
percent of the vote, not far from his performance four years earlier. *Cincinnati
Enquirer,* November 5 and 12, 2004. Dick Morris, a former adviser to President
Clinton, suggested that "foul play" may explain the exit-polling discrepancy,
adding that "exit polls are almost never wrong." Therefore, the possibility loomed
that Democrats had "deliberately manipulated" the exit polling in order to "chill
the Bush turnout." See "Those Faulty Exit Polls Were Sabotage," *thehill.com,*
November 4, 2004; *New York Times,* December 29, 2004.

The Election Incident Reporting System, as compiled by *verifiedvoting.org,*
received over 34,000 claims in the 2004 election, and over 1,200 in Cuyahoga
County alone. The Web site, established by David Dill of Stanford, concluded
in mid-November that the evidence did not indicate that the election was
stolen. "We do not believe that there is any more reason to look for problems in
this election than in previous elections." Statement, November 15, 2004, at
verifiedvoting.org. Making yet another appearance in the 2004 election were
"undervotes," where no vote was recorded for president. In Ohio, predominantly
African-American precincts that still relied on punchcards saw 1 in 31 votes
"lost," while that rate was 1 in 75 in predominantly white areas. *New York Times,*
December 24, 2004. Shortly before President Bush's inauguration, Senator
Kerry said "thousands of people were suppressed in the effort to vote." *New York
Times,* January 17, 2005.

Nearly four months after the election, an Illinois company, Danaher Controls, announced it had identified an error in one laptop computer that mistakenly attributed thousands of extra votes to President Bush in a Columbus
suburb. In the first count, Bush received 4,258 votes, according to the laptop,
but when it was noted the precinct had only 638 cast votes, an audit concluded
Bush actually received only 365 votes, a difference of 3,893 votes. The company
noted "the laptop was busy completing another task just as numbers from that
precinct were being fed into it." Such benign conclusions beg the question of
how many other computers encountered such problems in a rather simple
counting procedure. *Akron Beacon Journal,* February 12, 2005.

p. 328   Some of the skeptics . . . : Greg Palast, for example, wrote that "Kerry Won" two days
after the election at *tompaine.com.* See also Kathy Dopp's widely cited statistical blog

at *residentbush.com/Aftermath-2004_Florida-results.htm* (Nov. 3, 2004), as well as Thom Hartmann's writings at *www.commondreams.org*. See also *Washington Post*, December 15, 2004. Dopp is a Utah mathematician who noted that some counties with high proportions of Democratic registrants had voted heavily for Bush. The electronic voting machines, the theory goes, reversed votes. Six Democratic members of Congress, in their request to the GAO for an investigation, used Dopp's findings as evidence that something was amiss. Considering the changing nature of Southern voters, such charges were quickly dismissed by political scientists as another example of conservatives leaving the Democratic party. These counties had seen strong Republican support in other elections. *New York Times*, November 12, 2004. See also Steven F. Freeman, of the University of Pennsylvania, "The Unexplained Exit Poll Discrepancy," at www.truthout.org/does_04/111404A.shtml. A team of Berkeley sociologists also suggested that President Bush may have received between 130,000 and 260,000 "excess votes" in Florida based on their multiple-regression analysis. Michael Hout, et al., "Working Paper: The Effect of Electronic Voting Machines on Change in Support for Bush in the 2004 Florida Elections," November 2004, at www.yuricareport.com/ElectionAftermath04/BerkeleyElection04_WP.pdf. A popular pre-election site was that of Princeton molecular biologist Sam Wang at http://synapse.princeton.edu/~sam/pollcalc.html; as of July 2005, it's still there and still interesting.

p. 328   The most striking contest . . . : *Seattle Times*, December 17, 22, 23, and 30, 2004, and February 22 and June 2, 3, and 7, 2005; *New York Times*, December 24, 2004, and May 24, 2005; John Fund, "Florida Northwest," *Wall Street Journal*, November 29, 2004. Washington State Republicans later claimed that over 1,100 felons had illegally voted in the governor's race, and 884 of them were in Democratic-leaning King County. What's more, by April 2005, officials in King County admitted that they had found 111 uncounted absentee ballots. Fund writes that reform efforts in Washington State to correct the problems within the 2004 election actually introduce further problems, such as expanding mail-in voting. *Wall Street Journal*, April 11, 2005.

p. 329   One element of the danger . . . : *New York Times*, November 9 and December 2, 2003. In late December 2003, officials with VoteHere Inc., a company manufacturing security technology for electronic voting machines, disclosed that a computer hacker had broken in to its computer network and may have copied various sensitive materials. VoteHere's chief executive stated that the hacker was probably trying to prove a point: "We think this is political. There have been break-ins around election companies over the last several months," but added that the break-in did not affect the integrity of electronic voting machine technology. When one Diebold technician complained of the faulty quality controls, one insider noted, "He was gone. They fired him. The attitude among the others there was 'I don't care how screwed up these things are, I'm going to keep quiet.'" In November 2003, a suit was filed against Diebold under a California "whistle-blower" statute, claiming that the company's poorly designed equipment exposed California elections to hackers. *San Francisco Chronicle,* July 11, 2004. In the 2004 Super Tuesday primary in California, more than six hundred Diebold machines froze or failed, with failure rates of 24 percent in Alameda County and 40 percent in San Diego County. For months, Diebold had been warned of serious problems in their software from state election officials, but they did nothing to change their systems. One California elections official stated: "Diebold may suffer from gross incompetence, gross negligence. I don't know whether there's any malevolence involved." California's Secretary of State Kevin Shelley was so troubled by the assortment of problems Diebold

machines produced that he called for a criminal investigation, claiming Diebold's "conduct was absolutely reprehensible." *Oakland Tribune,* April 20, 2004; *New York Times,* December 29, 2003; *Los Angeles Times,* May 1, 2004. Some informative websites for the voter-verified paper audit trails (VVPAT) are *verifiedvoting.org* and *wheresthepaper.org.*

p. 330   Another danger . . . : *New York Times,* December 2, 2003. In his book on recent election fraud, *Wall Street Journal* columnist John Fund dismissed criticisms of the Diebold systems as part of a general fear by liberals of a conspiracy to steal elections. Fund, *Stealing Elections,* 111–17. To this date, no case of a programmer attempting to fix an election has been prosecuted. In 2002, in another arena in which close contests can decide considerable fortunes, a programmer pleaded guilty conspiring to fix the $3 million "pick six" wager at the Breeders' Cup. In what was called the "Pick Six Fix," a computer programmer for the firm that oversaw the complex wagering system rigged the results so that some of his co-conspirators could share in the prize. *New York Times,* November 17 and 21, 2002; *Washington Post,* December 12, 2002.

In June 2005, the Houston-based Election Center, comprised of former election officials from fifteen states, issued a report claiming election practices should adjust to the "way America lives." The report called for precincts to be replaced by "vote centers" where citizens could vote over a period of weeks. These centers would allow counties to concentrate limited resources into better-equipped centers. The report also called for broadening the use of absentee ballots. *Washington Post,* June 7, 2005.

p. 331   At first glance . . . : *New York Times,* December 2 and 15, 2003, and March 2, 2004. One of the leading proponents of the paper receipt model is computer scientist Rebecca Mercuri. See *Harvard University Gazette,* October 28, 2004. In addition to the paper receipt model, computer scientists at MIT and Cal Tech have proposed a system utilizing "frogs" to protect the security of the ballot. This system would provide each voter with a small card called a "frog" that contains a small amount of memory and in which the contents cannot be changed or altered. The frog would act as a punchcard, of sorts. Once a voter had signed in to an election official and proven his or her identity, they would be given a frog to take to a "vote-generation" station. Here the voter would actually cast votes for candidates, which would be stored on the frog. Then, the frog would be taken to another "vote-casting" station where the frog would be read and the vote recorded. The frog would be dropped into a bin where it would serve as a backup in case of a recount. See Shuki Bruck, David Jefferson, and Ronald L. Rivest, "A Modular Voting Architecture ("Frogs"), August 2001 at http://theory.lcs.mit.edu/~rivest/pulications.html.

At a May 2004 meeting of the federal Election Assistance Commission, some California elections officials voiced reservations about paper receipts. A 37–inch paper ballot with tiny print, one official claimed, would only guarantee confusion among voters. Even the League of Women Voters opposed having electronic machines produce paper receipts. The League thought that some groups that have been previously excluded from voting, such as those who cannot read, would be driven away by the receipts. Meanwhile, a computer scientist from Johns Hopkins claimed that insiders would be the most likely culprit to sabotage the electronic machines—"The vendor is in a position to make the election come out however they like it and it would be undetectable." *Washington Post*, May 6, 2004; *New York Times*, June 11, 2004. Another suggestion is an audio version of the paper receipt called the Voter Verifiable Audio Audit Transcript Trail," or VVAATT. This system would involve voters placing headphones on while in the voting booth. A tape would play the choices before the voter and tell the voter for whom they were prepared to vote. Once satisfied, the voter would push a button marked "Vote." The vote would be recorded electronically both electronically and on tape, and no paper trails would be present. In case of a recount, the tape would allow officials to actually hear the votes of the individual voters. See Ted Selkor, "The Voter Verifiable Audio Audit Transcript Trail," Caltech-MIT Voting Technology Project, September 29, 2004.

p. 332   In a purge . . . : *New York Times*, February 6, April 18, and August 16, 20, and 23, 2004.

p. 333   Another form . . . : *Detroit Free Press*, February 8, 2004; *New York Times*, January 10, 2004.

p. 333   Supporters of absentee voting . . . : Caltech-MIT Voting Technology Project, *Voting: What Is, What Could Be*, July 2001; *New York Times*, August 22, 2004; Thompson, *Just Elections*, 34. The problems with mail-in votes are not limited to the United States. In Great Britain, "postal voting" presented some alarming problems preceding an election in 2005. In Birmingham, six Labour party officials were denied their seats in a local election due to mail-in fraud that a judge said would "disgrace a banana republic." In addition to illegally impersonating legal voters, party activists went door to door offering to complete a ballot, while some enterprising cheaters opened ballots and changed them with correcting fluid. *Economist*, April 9, 2005.

Support for extending the secret ballot is not universal, even among some modern political scientists. See Geoffrey Brennan and Philip Pettit, "Unveiling the Vote," *British Journal of Political Science* 20 (May 1997): 311–33. Brennan and Pettit's article is remarkably lacking in any understanding of how elections are conducted at the local level. They find that without secrecy, voters would be "publicly answerable for their electoral choices and will be encouraged to vote in a discursively defensible manner" (311).

p. 334 A series of municipal elections . . . : Dallas *Observer,* June 14, July 26 and August 30, 2001; National Public Radio, "All Things Considered," July 25, 2002. The Dallas elections were uncovered by Dallas *Observer* reporter Jim Schutze, who wrote "This kind of ballot chicanery takes place in Dallas elections on a whole-sale basis, with complete impunity and total arrogance. It has been [so] easy to get away with in the past that the people doing it don't even bother to hide." Schutze understood that the absentee ballot fraud was about more than partisan oneupsmanship. "This system is dominated by and operated for the benefit of the big money interests downtown." The brokering system in Dallas was "one in which poor people can never win." For some other recent local elections that involved absentee-ballot fraud, see *St. Louis Post-Dispatch,* September 28, 2002; *Connecticut Post,* October 18, 2002; *Chicago Sun-Times,* March 20, 2003.

p. 334 In 2004, the Pentagon . . . : *New York Times,* January 21, 2004. A national commission formed after the 2000 election (headed by former presidents Gerald Ford and Jimmy Carter) recommended that each state should appoint an individual responsible for supervising the practice of overseas absentee voting. Nothing was mentioned concerning other types of absentee ballots. *To Assure Pride and Confidence in the Electoral Process,* Report of the National Commission on Federal Election Reform, 7–8, 42–43. Carter later criticized Katherine Harris and her successor, Glenda Hood, for holding "strong political biases," and said that the way in which the Florida vote was counted in 2000 was especially objectionable to "us Americans, who have prided ourselves on setting a global example for pure democracy." *Washington Post,* September 26, 2004. Along with former Secretary of State James Baker, Carter led another federal election reform effort in 2005. For the first public hearings into some of the better-known problems in the 2004 presidential race, see *Washington Post,* April 19, 2005.

p. 336 Internet voting discriminates . . . : A constitutional amendment proposed by Rep. Jesse Jackson, Jr. (D-Ill.) in 2004 seeks to address systemic problems in voting, and would ensure that precincts would get equal numbers of voting machines that would decrease the long lines at the polls. Yet the amendment would not go very far at all in ensuring the integrity of elections. The amendment, for example, actually enhances the Electoral College yet supports same-day registration. The amendment also reads: "Each state shall administer public elections in the State in accordance with election performance standards established by the Congress. The Congress shall reconsider such election performance standards at least once every four years to determine if higher standards should be established to reflect improvements in methods and practices regarding the administration of elections."

p. 337   It would diminish . . . : See Robert A. Dahl, *How Democratic is the American Constitution?*, 86–87. For a defense of the Electoral College, see Judith Best, "Weighing the Alternatives: Reform or Deform?" in Jacobson and Rosenfeld, *The Longest Night*, 350.

Professor Keith E. Whittington has argued that the Electoral College actually reduces the likelihood of election fraud by containing any disputed counts to one state. "Rather than encourage candidates and their supporters to search for, or invent, election irregularities across the nation, the Electoral College concentrates the dispute and makes an appropriate and timely resolution more likely," he writes. "Vote fraud must be organized across several closely contested states in order to be effective in altering the results of the election under the Electoral College." This argument seems to fall on thin ice considering the events of 2000, but Whittington made these remarks in reaction to that election. Keith E. Whittington, "The Electoral College: A Modest Contribution," in Jacobson and Rosenfeld, *The Longest Night*, 389.

There have been numerous suggestions about how to reform the current electoral system in electing a president. Among these are a proportional system, whereby a candidate would receive a proportional number of electoral votes to correspond to their popular-vote margin in a given state; a system in which the winner of the national popular vote would receive a certain number of automatic electoral votes, as well as one that would guarantee that a state's electors honored the wishes of their state's voters. Another plan, implemented by Maine and Nebraska in 2000, provided that their electoral votes would be divvied up by providing one vote for winning a congressional district and two for winning the plurality of the state. All of these attempt to end the current "winner takes all" system to ensure a more accurate portrait of how their state voted. Of course, a plan that would be consistent with virtually every other election in the United States would simply end the Electoral College with a direct election of the president. Even this plan has several alternatives, including ones that provides for a runoff if a certain plurality was not achieved. See also Steven Hill, *Fixing Elections*, ix–xi, 20–25.

The Electoral College gave Russian president Vladimir Putin leverage against concerns that Russian elections for regional governors were becoming undemocratic. "In United States you first elect the electors," Putin commented, "and then the electors vote for the presidential candidates." To Putin, the American system "is exactly what we are doing with regards to bringing of governors in the Russian Federation to power." The U.S. presidential election of 2000 also represented to Putin how "the electoral system was not efficient, not effective." In a not-so-subtle response to President Bush, Putin added, "We are not going to poke our nose into your democratic system because it's up to the American people to say what is good or what is not." Putin was interviewed by Mike Wallace on CBS's *60 Minutes*, May 8, 2005. George C. Edwards III correctly notes: "Direct election would create a disincentive for fraud, because altering

an election outcome through fraud would require an organized effort of proportions never witnessed in the U.S." See his excellent work, *Why the Electoral
College is Bad for America*, 123–25.

p. 336   Yet new proposals . . . : *Miami Herald*, May 27, 2004; *New York Times*, September
13, 2004. As Gov. Bush defended the new law, investigations were proceeding in
a 2004 Orlando city election where absentee fraud was alleged. Without the
ability to verify witness signatures, many more suspicious elections would go
unchallenged. The new law concluded that "Absentee ballots make it easier for
senior citizens and military personnel to exercise their right to vote." In an East
Chicago, Indiana, mayoral race in 2003, the U.S. Justice Department investigated
charges of absentee-ballot fraud. In 2004, the Indiana State Supreme Court
voided the election due to "zealotry to promote absentee voting." One example of
the "zealotry" from East Chicago concerned Sheila Pierce, who testified that she
was facing eviction from her apartment and allowed a party operative from the
mayor's office to fill out her absentee ballot in return for $100.00. Pierce also
claimed that she was threatened if she testified.

          In February 2005, the proposed Count Every Vote Act, co-sponsored by
Senators Hillary Rodham Clinton (D-NY) and Barbara Boxer (D-CA),
included a provision allowing blanket "no-excuse" absentee balloting in all federal and state elections.

p. 336   For over two hundred . . . In 1969, a proposal to amend the Constitution and
abolish the Electoral College had considerable support from the U.S. House of
Representatives, winning 338–70. President Richard Nixon endorsed the
amendment, perhaps remembering the 1960 race. In the Senate, a filibuster led
by North Carolina's Sam Ervin and South Carolina's Strom Thurmond ended
the amendment's chances of going to the states. Alexander Keyssar has written
persuasively that the reason that this attempt failed was not necessarily because
of opposition from the small states; rather, the problem was in the power placed
in the Southern states and maintained by racial discrimination. After the 1965
Civil Rights Bill, what Keyssar terms the "five-fifths rule" was in place in the
South. Since the Southern states included African-Americans in their populations for electoral purposes yet disfranchised them, "the number of votes actually cast in the South between 1900 and 1960 was tiny in comparison to the size
of its electoral vote." *Boston Globe*, October 17, 2004.

p. 338   "Why bother?" . . . : See *Charleston* (W.V.) *Gazette*, May 11, 2004. The culture
of corruption is comparable to Amitai Etzioni's concept of "social norms."
According to Etzioni, environmental concerns can impact one's value systems,
so that "If people follow their community's do's and don'ts because they see the
social norms as costs or constraints, they will tend to violate the norms when the
benefits of abiding by them are lower than are the gains of violating them and
the risks of detection are low." "Social Norms: Internalization, Persuasion, and
History," *Law and Society Review* 34 (2000): 161.

p. 339   Just days after . . . : *New York Times*, November 22, 23, 25, and 27 and December 2, 3, 4, and 28, 2004; *New Yorker*, December 13, 2004.

p. 339   There was and is . . . during the Florida recount, some protestors in Delray Beach attended a rally on Nov. 10 for a revote in Palm Beach County. This was backed by the *Miami Herald's* Carl Hiaasen, who noted that "misspent ballots in Palm Beach could deliver Florida, and thus the U.S. presidency, to a candidate who wasn't the intended choice of a majority of the state's voters." *Miami Herald*, November 11, 12, 2000.

Selected Bibliography

ARCHIVAL COLLECTIONS

College of Wooster, Special Collections, Andrews Library, Wooster, Ohio
    Paul O. Peters Collection.

Federal Bureau of Investigation, Washington, D. C.
    J. Edgar Hoover Official and Confidential Files

Filson Historical Society, Louisville, Kentucky
    Robert W. Bingham Papers
    Helm Bruce Papers
    Bullitt Family Papers, Oxmoor Collection
    J. H. Haager Scrapbook
    Henry Clay Papers
    Louisville Police Records, Force Book 1904-21
    Hugh McCullough Scrapbook

Jefferson National Expansion Memorial Archives, St. Louis
    Jefferson National Expansion Memorial Records

Lyndon B. Johnson Presidential Library, Austin, Texas
    House of Representatives Files

Lyndon B. Johnson Papers

Library of Congress, Washington, D. C.
    Harold L. Ickes Manuscript Diary
    Joseph L. Rauh, Jr., Papers

Louisiana State University, Special Collections, Hill Memorial Library
    David French Boyd Papers
    Huey P. Long FBI File
    Edward Clifton Wharton Family Papers

Louisville Free Public Library, Louisville, Kentucky
    "Elections" files

Missouri Historical Society, St. Louis
    James K. Douglas Papers
    Clifford Greve Papers
    Jefferson National Expansion Memorial Papers
    Louis LaBeume Papers
    Luther Ely Smith Papers

National Archives, Pacific Region, Laguna Niguel, California
    Richard M. Nixon Pre-Presidential Papers

National Archives, Southeast Region, East Point, Georgia
    U.S. District Court, London Division, Eastern District of Kentucky
    United States of America v. Clinton C. Ball, et. al. case 11145, grand jury report

St. Louis Public Library
    Jefferson National Expansion Memorial Files

Harry S. Truman Presidential Library, Independence, Missouri
    Tom C. Clark Papers
    Harry S. Truman Papers

University of Kentucky, Special Collections
    Scholl v. Bell, no. 41519, and *Peter v. Wilson*, no. 41524, Jefferson Circuit Court
    Thruston B. Morton Oral History Project
    Thruston B. Morton Papers
    A. O. Stanley Papers

Western Historical Manuscript Collection, University of Missouri, Columbia
    Bernard F. Dickmann Papers

GOVERNMENT SOURCES

"Attorney General's Task Force on Election Fraud: Report to Fred Cowan, Attorney General, Commonwealth of Kentucky" (1988).

"Boles vs. Edwards," 42nd Congress, 2nd session, Report no. 10.

California Secretary of State Bill Jones, California Internet Voting Task Force, "A Report on the Feasibility of Internet Voting," January 2000.

City of Louisville, Board of Aldermen, *Annual Report for 1905*. Louisville: Globe Printing, 1906.

Congressional Record

"Election Fraud in Arkansas," 42nd Congress, 2nd session, Report no. 5.

Hearings Before the Special Committee of Campaign Expenditures, United States Senate, 72nd Congress, 2nd Session, Pursuant to S. Res. 174. Washington, D.C.: Government Printing Office, 1933.

"Investigation of Alleged Electoral Frauds in the Late Presidential Election," 45th Congress, 3rd Session, Report no. 140.

Iowa Constitutional Convention Proceedings (1857).

Louisville Election Contest Case. "Opinion of Chancellors Miller and Kirby, April 16, 1907."

Proceedings of the Kentucky Constitutional Convention (1849-50).

Maryland Constitutional Convention (1851).

Massachusetts Constitutional Convention, vol. I (1853).

Official Report of the Proceedings and Debates in the Convention, Assembled at Frankfort, on the Eighth Day of September, 1890, to Adopt, Amend, or Change the Constitution of the State of Kentucky.

Report by Matt Blunt, Secretary of State. "Mandate for Reform: Election Turmoil in St. Louis, November 7, 2000,"

Rowell, Chester H. *A Historical and Legal Digest of all the Contested Election Cases in the House of Representatives of the United States from the First to the Fifty-Sixth Congress, 1789-1901,* 56th Congress, 2d Session, Doc. 510, 1901.

"Special Committee Appointed to Investigate the Troubles in the Territory of Kansas," U.S. House of Representatives, 34th Congress, 1st Session, (Serial 869) no. 200.

Subcommittee on the Constitution of the Committee on the Judiciary, United States Senate, 98th Congress, 1st Session, "The Need for Further Federal Action in the Area of Criminal Vote Fraud." Washington, D. C.: Government Printing Office, 1984.

Supplemental Report of the Joint Committee of the General Assembly of Louisiana, "Conduct of the Late Elections and the Condition of Peace and Good Order" New Orleans: A. L. Lee, 1869.

"Testimony Taken by the Select Committee on Alleged Frauds in the Presidential Election of 1876," 45th Congress, 3rd Session, Misc. Doc. 31.

To Assure Pride and Confidence in the Electoral Process, Report of the National Commission on Federal Election Reform. Washington, D.C.: Brookings Institution Press, 2002.

U.S. Commission on Civil Rights, "Voting Irregularities in Florida During the 2000 Presidential Election." June 2001.

U.S. House of Representatives, 40th Congress, 3rd Session (1868), Miscellaneous Document no. 53.

U.S. House of Representatives, 40th Congress, 3rd Session, (1869) "Condition of Affairs in Georgia," Miscellaneous Document no. 52.

U.S. House Reports, "Condition of the South," 43rd Congress, 2nd Session, no. 261.

U.S. Senate Miscellaneous Documents, 44th Congress, 2nd Session, "Testimony as to the Denial of the Elective Franchise in Mississippi at the Election of 1875 and 1876," Misc. Document no. 45.

U.S. Senate Report, "Florida Election, 1876," 44th Congress, 2nd Session, Report no. 611.

Wexler, Morris J. "Report to the Honorable Richard B. Austin, Chief Justice of the Criminal Court of Cook County," April 13, 1961.

NEWSPAPERS AND MAGAZINES

Aberdeen (Miss.) *Examiner*
Akron (Ohio) *Beacon Journal*
Arkansas City (Kansas) *Traveler*
Atlanta Constitution
Atlanta Journal
Austin Statesman
Baltimore *Sun*
Bangor (Maine) *Daily Whig and Courier*
Baton Rouge *Daily Advocate*
Boston Globe
Charleston (W.V.) *Gazette*
Chicago *Daily News*
Chicago *Evening Star*
Chicago *Herald*
Chicago *Sun-Times*
Chicago Tribune
Chicago's American
Cincinnati *Daily Commercial*
Cincinnati *Enquirer*
Columbia (S.C.) *State*
The Critic
Daily Chicago Times
Dallas Morning News
Dallas Observer
Daytona Beach *News-Journal*
Detroit Free Press
The Economist
Gainesville Sun
Greenville (S.C.) *News*
Harlan (Ky.) *Daily Enterprise*
Harper's Weekly
Hartford Courant
Harvard *Gazette*
Houston Chronicle
Indianapolis *Daily Sentinel*
Kansas City Star
Kentucky Elk
Kentucky Irish-American
Las Vegas *Review Journal*
Las Vegas *Sun*

Lexington (Ky.) *Herald–Leader*
Literary Digest
Los Angeles Times
Louisville *Anzieger*
Louisville *Courier-Journal*
Louisville Daily Courier
Louisville *Evening Post*
Louisville *Herald*
Louisville *Herald-Post*
Louisville *Times*
Louisville Weekly Democrat
Madison (Wisc.) *Daily State Journal*
Miami Herald
Milwaukee *News*
Nashville *Tennessean*
Nation
National Economist
National Municipal Review
New Orleans *Bee*
New Orleans *Commercial Bulletin*
New Orleans *Daily Picayune*
New Orleans *Louisiana Courier*
New Orleans Republican
New York Daily News
New York Evening Post
New York Evening World
New York *Herald*
New York *Herald-Tribune*
New York *Morning Express*
New York Times
New Yorker
Newark *Advertiser*
North American Review
Oakland Tribune
Orlando *Sentinel*
Outlook
Palm Beach (Fla.) *Post*
Philadelphia *Daily News*
Philadelphia *Inquirer*
Providence *Journal*
Richmond (Va.) *Dispatch*
San Francisco Chronicle

Seattle Times
St. Louis Argus
St. Louis Commerce
St. Louis *Globe-Democrat*
St. Louis *Post-Dispatch*
St. Louis *Star-Times*
St. Louis Union Labor Advocate
St. Petersburg (Fla.) *Times*
Tallahassee Democrat
Vanity Fair
Wall Street Journal
Washington Daily National Intelligencer
Washington *Daily Union*
Washington *Evening-Star*
Washington *Herald*
Washington Post

BOOKS

Ackerman, Kenneth D. *Boss Tweed: The Rise and Fall of the Corrupt Pol Who Conceived the Soul of Modern New York.* New York: Carroll and Graf, 2005.

Adams, Henry. *Democracy: An American Novel.* New York: Farrar, Straus and Young, 1952; originally published by Henry Holt, 1880.

Allen, W. B. ed., *George Washington: A Collection.* Indianapolis: Liberty Classics, 1988.

Altschuler, Glenn C. and Stuart M. Blumin, *Rude Republic: Americans and Their Politics in the Nineteenth Century.* Princeton University Press, 2000.

Alvarez, R. Michael and Thad E. Hall, *Point, Click, and Vote: The Future of Internet Voting.* Washington, D.C., The Brookings Institution, 2004.

Anders, Evan. *Boss Rule in South Texas: The Progressive Era.* Austin: University of Texas Press, 1979.

Anderson, William. *The Wild Man From Sugar Creek: The Political Career of Eugene Talmadge.* Baton Rouge: Louisiana State University Press, 1975.

Avrich, Paul. *The Haymarket Tragedy.* Princeton: Princeton University Press, 1984.

Baker, Jean H. *Affairs of Party: The Political Culture of Northern Democrats in the Mid-Nineteenth Century*. Ithaca: Cornell University Press, 1983.

Basler, Roy P. ed., *The Collected Works of Abraham Lincoln, I*. New Brunswick: Rutgers University Press, 1953.

Bensel, Richard Franklin. *The American Ballot Box in the Mid-Nineteenth Century*. Cambridge: Cambridge University Press, 2004.

Benson, George C. S. *Political Corruption in America*. Lexington, Mass.: Lexington Books, 1978.

Benton, Josiah Henry. *Voting in the Field: A Forgotten Chapter of the Civil War*. Boston: Privately printed, 1915.

Bernstein, Iver. *The New York City Draft Riots: Their Significance for American Society and Politics in the Age of the Civil War*. New York: Oxford University Press, 1990.

Bissett, Jim. *Agrarian Socialism in America: Marx, Jefferson, and Jesus in the Oklahoma Countryside, 1904-1920*. Norman: University of Oklahoma Press, 1999.

Bourke, Paul and Donald DeBats, *Washington County: Politics and Community in Antebellum America*. Baltimore: Johns Hopkins University Press, 1995.

Bourne, Peter G. *Jimmy Carter: A Comprehensive Biography from Plains to the Presidency*. New York: Scribners, 1997.

Bowers, Claude G. *The Tragic Era: The Revolution After Lincoln*. Cambridge: The Riverside Press, 1929.

Boyer, Richard O. *The Legend of John Brown: A Biography and History*. New York: Alfred A. Knopf, 1973.

Boyle, Kevin. *Arc of Justice: A Saga of Race, Civil Rights, and Murder in the Jazz Age*. New York: Henry Holt, 2004.

Brightley, Frederick C. *A Collection of Leading Cases on the Law of Elections in the United States*. Philadelphia: Kay and Bro., 1871.

Brown, Robert E. *Middle-Class Democracy and the Revolution in Massachusetts, 1691-1780*. New York: Russell and Russell, 1955.

Bryce, James. *The American Commonwealth,* vol. II. (London: Macmillan Co., 1901.

Burns, James MacGregor and Jack Walter Peltason. *Government By the People: The Dynamics of American National Government.* Englewood Cliffs: Prentice-Hall, 1960.

Burrows, Edwin G. and Mike Wallace, *Gotham: A History of New York City to 1898.* New York: Oxford University Press, 1999.

Butler, Anne M. and Wendy Wolff, *United States Senate Election, Expulsion, and Censure Cases, 1793-1990.* Washington, D.C.: Government Printing Office, 1995.

Callahan, David. *The Cheating Culture: Why More Americans Are Doing Wrong to Get Ahead.* New York: Harcourt, 2004.

Callow, Alexander B. Jr., *The Tweed Ring.* New York: Oxford University Press, 1966.

Campbell, James E. *The American Campaign: U.S. Presidential Campaigns and the National Vote.* College Station: Texas A & M Press, 2000.

Campbell, Tracy. *Short of the Glory: The Fall and Redemption of Edward F. Prichard, Jr.* Lexington: University Press of Kentucky, 1998.

Cantrell, Gregg. *Kenneth and John B. Rayner and the Limits of Southern Dissent.* Urbana: University of Illinois Press, 1993.

Caro, Robert A. *Master of the Senate: The Years of Lyndon Johnson.* New York: Alfred A. Knopf, 2002.

——————. *Means of Ascent: The Years of Lyndon Johnson.* New York: Knopf, 1990.

——————. *The Path to Power: The Years of Lyndon Johnson.* New York: Knopf, 1982.

Carter, Dan T. *From George Wallace to Newt Gingrich: Race in the Conservative Counterrevolution, 1963-1994.* Baton Rouge: Louisiana State University Press, 1996.

Carter, Jimmy. *Turning Point: A Candidate, A State, and a Nation Come of Age.* New York: Times Books, 1992.

Catt, Carrie Chapman and Nettie Rogers Shuler. *Woman Suffrage and Politics: The Inner Story of the Suffrage Movement.* New York: Charles Scribner's Sons, 1926.

Caudill, Harry M. *Slender is the Thread: Tales From a Country Law Office.* Lexington: University Press of Kentucky, 1987.

Cecelski, David S. and Timothy B. Tyson, *Democracy Betrayed: The Wilmington Race Riot of 1898 and its Legacy.* Chapel Hill: University of North Carolina Press, 1998.

Chafin, Raymond and Topper Sherwood, *Just Good Politics: The Life of Raymond Chafin, Appalachian Boss.* Pittsburgh: University of Pittsburgh Press, 1994.

Clanton, Gene. *Populism: The Humane Preference in America, 1890-1900.* Boston: Twayne Publishers, 1991.

Clark, Thomas D. *Helm Bruce, Public Defender: Breaking Louisville's Gothic Political Ring, 1905.* Louisville: The Filson Club, 1973.

Cohen, Adam and Elizabeth Taylor. *American Pharaoh: Mayor Richard Daley, His Battle for Chicago and the Nation.* Boston: Little, Brown, 2000.

Cohen, Lizabeth. *A Consumers' Republic: The Politics of Mass Consumption in Postwar America.* New York: Vintage, 2003.

Coleman, Charles H. *The Election of 1868: The Democratic Effort to Regain Control.* New York: Columbia University Press, 1933.

Conley, Patricia Heidotting. *Presidential Mandates: How Elections Shape the National Agenda.* Chicago: University of Chicago Press, 2001.

Connor, R. D. W. and Clarence Poe. *The Life and Speeches of Charles Brantley Aycock.* Garden City: Doubleday, 1912.

Cresswell, Stephen. *Multi-Party Politics in Mississippi, 1877-1902.* Jackson: University Press of Mississippi, 1995.

Dahl, Robert A. *Who Governs?: Democracy and Power in an American City.* New Haven: Yale University Press, 1961.

Dallek, Robert. *An Unfinished Life: John F. Kennedy, 1917-1963.* Boston: Little, Brown, 2003.

—————. *Lone Star Rising: Lyndon Johnson and his Times, 1908-1960.* New York: Oxford University Press, 1991.

Danese, Tracy E. *Claude Pepper and Ed Ball: Politics, Purpose, and Power.* Gainesville: University Press of Florida, 2000.

Davenport, John I. *The Election Frauds of New York City and Their Prevention.* New York: Privately printed, 1881.

Davis, F. Keith. *West Virginia Tough Boys: Vote Buying, Fist Fighting, and a President Named JFK.* Chapmanville, WV: Woodland Press, 2003.

Dawson, Joseph G. III, *Army Generals and Reconstruction: Louisiana, 1862-1877.* Baton Rouge: Louisiana State University Press, 1982.

Dershowitz, Alan M. *Supreme Injustice: How the High Court Hijacked Election 2000.* New York: Oxford University Press, 2001.

Dinkin, Robert J. *Voting in Provincial America: A Study of Elections in the Thirteen Colonies, 1689-1776.* Westport: Greenwood Press, 1977).

Dittmer, John. *Local People: The Struggle for Civil Rights in Mississippi.* Urbana: University of Illinois Press, 1994.

Donald, David Herbert. *Lincoln.* New York: Simon and Schuster, 1995.

Dorsett, Lyle W. *The Pendergast Machine.* New York: Oxford University Press, 1968.

Dugger, Ronnie. *The Politician: The Life and Times of Lyndon Johnson.* Old Saybrook: Konecky and Konecky, 1982.

Edwards, George C. III. *Why the Electoral College is Bad for America.* New Haven: Yale University Press, 2004.

Eller, Ronald D. *Miners, Millhands, and Mountaineers: Industrialization of the Appalachian South.* Knoxville: University of Tennessee Press, 1982.

Egerton, John. *Speak Now Against the Day: The Generation Before the Civil Rights Movement in the South.* New York: Knopf, 1994.

Ellis, William E. *Robert Worth Bingham and the Southern Mystique: From the Old South to the New South and Beyond.* Kent: The Kent State University Press, 1997.

Ernst, Harry W. *The Primary That Made a President: West Virginia 1960.* Eagleton Institute: Issues in Practical Politics, 1962.

Ethington, Philip J. *The Public City: The Political Construction of Urban Life in San Francisco, 1850-1890.* Cambridge: Cambridge University Press, 1994.

Fairclough, Adam. *Race and Democracy: The Civil Rights Struggle in Louisiana, 1915-1972.* Athens: University of Georgia Press, 1995.

Feldman, Glenn. *The Disfranchisement Myth: Poor Whites and Suffrage Restriction in Alabama.* Athens: University of Georgia Press, 2004.

Felknor, Bruce L. *Political Mischief: Smear, Sabotage, and Reform in U. S. Elections.* New York: Praeger, 1992.

Ferrell, Robert H. *Truman and Pendergast.* Columbia: University of Missouri Press, 1999.

Fitzgerald, Michael W. *Urban Emancipation: Popular Politics in Reconstruction Mobile, 1860-1890.* Baton Rouge: Louisiana State University Press, 2002.

Fleming, Dan B. *Kennedy vs. Humphrey, West Virginia, 1960: The Pivotal Battle for the Democratic Presidential Nomination.* Jefferson, N.C.: McFarland, 1992.

Flick, Alexander C. *Samuel Jones Tilden: A Study in Political Sagacity.* New York: Dodd, Mead, Co., 1937.

Fogelson, Robert M. *Big-City Police.* Cambridge: Harvard University Press, 1977.

Foner, Eric. *Free Soil, Free Labor, Free Men: The Ideology of the Republican Party Before the Civil War.* New York: Oxford University Press, 1970.

————. *Reconstruction: America's Unfinished Revolution, 1863-1877.* New York: Harper and Row, 1988.

————. *Tom Paine and Revolutionary America.* New York: Oxford University Press, 1976.

Ford, Worthington Chauncey, ed. *The Writings of George Washington,* vol. II. New York: G.P. Putnam's Sons, 1889.

Forester, William D. *Flatland Election Thieves and Mountain Bushwackers.* Privately published, 1999.

————. *Harlan County Goes to War.* William Forester, 1990.

Frank, Joseph Allen. *With Ballot and Bayonet: The Political Socialization of American Civil War Soldiers.* Athens: University of Georgia Press, 1998.

Fredman, L.E. *The Australian Ballot: The Story of an American Reform.* Lansing: Michigan State University Press, 1968.

Freehling, William W. *The Road to Disunion: Secessionists at Bay, 1776-1854.* New York: Oxford University Press, 1990.

Freeman, Joanne B. *Affairs of Honor: National Politics in the New Republic.* New Haven: Yale University Press, 2001.

Fund, John. *Stealing Elections: How Voter Fraud Threatens Our Democracy.* San Francisco: Encounter Books, 2004.

Galloway, George B. *History of the House of Representatives.* New York: Thomas Y. Crowell, 1976.

Garrity, John A. *Henry Cabot Lodge: A Biography.* New York: Alfred A. Knopf, 1953.

Gaventa, John. *Power and Powerlessness: Quiescence and Rebellion in an Appalachian Valley.* Urbana: University of Illinois Press, 1980.

Godkin, E. L. *Problems of Modern Democracy: Political and Economic Essays.* New York: Scribner's, 1896.

—————-. *The Triumph of Reform: A History of the Great Political Revolution, Nov. 6, 1894.* New York: Souvenir, 1895.

Goldwater, Barry M. *With No Apologies: The Personal and Political Memiors of United States Senator Barry M. Goldwater.* New York: William Morrow, 1979.

Goodwyn, Lawrence. *Democratic Promise: The Populist Moment in America.* New York: Oxford University Press, 1976.

Graham, Sara Hunter. *Woman Suffrage and the New Democracy.* New Haven: Yale University Press. 1996.

Greenberg, David. *Nixon's Shadow: The History of an Image.* New York: W.W. Norton, 2003.

Gronowicz, Anthony. *Race and Class Politics in New York City Before the Civil War.* Boston: Northeastern University Press, 1998.

Gunther, John. *Inside U.S.A.* New York: Harper Bros., 1947.

Hahn, Steven. *A Nation Under Our Feet: Black Political Struggles in the Rural South From Slavery to the Great Migration.* Cambridge: Harvard University Press, 2003.

Hair, William Ivy. *Bourbonism and Agrarian Protest: Louisiana Politics, 1877-1900.* Baton Rouge: Louisiana State University Press, 1969.

Hamby, Alonzo L. *Man of the People: A Life of Harry Truman.* New York: Oxford University Press, 1995.

Harris, Joseph P. *Registration of Voters in the United States.* Washington, D.C.: The Brookings Institution, 1929.

Harris, Katherine. *Center of the Storm: Practicing Principled Leadership in Times of Crisis.* Nashville: WND Books, 2002.

Harrison, Lowell H. and James C. Klotter, *A New History of Kentucky.* Lexington: University Press of Kentucky, 1997.

Hartmann, Rudolph H. *The Kansas City Investigations: Pendergast's Downfall, 1938-1939.* Columbia: University of Missouri Press, 1999.

Hawkins, Marlin with Dr. C. Fred Williams. *How I Stole Elections: The Autobiography of Sheriff Marlin Hawkins.* Privately printed, 1991.

Haworth, Paul Leland. *The Hayes-Tilden Disputed Presidential Election of 1876.* Cleveland: Burrows Bros., 1906.

Hersh, Seymour. *The Dark Side of Camelot.* Boston: Little, Brown, 1997.

Hershkowitz, Leo. *Tweed's New York: Another Look.* Garden City: Anchor Press, 1977.

Hill, Steven. *Fixing Elections: The Failure of America's Winner Take All Politics.* New York: Routledge, 2002.

Holt, Michael F. *The Rise and Fall of the American Whig Party: Jacksonian Politics and the Onset of the Civil War.* New York: Oxford University Press, 1999.

Hughes, Rupert. *George Washington: The Human Being and the Hero, 1732-1762.* New York: William Morrow, 1926.

Huston, Reeve. *Land and Freedom: Rural Society, Popular Protest, and Party Politics in Antebellum New York.* New York: Oxford University Press, 2000.

Hyman, Michael R. *The Anti-Redeemers: Hill-Country Political Dissenters in the Lower South From Redemption to Populism.* Baton Rouge: Louisiana State University Press, 1990.

Ickes, Harold. *The Secret Diary of Harold Ickes, The First Thousand Days, 1933-1936.* New York: Simon and Schuster, 1953.

Ivins, William M. *Machine Politics and Money in Elections in New York City.* New York: Harpers, 1887.

Jeansonne, Glen. *Leander Perez: Boss of the Delta.* Baton Rouge: Louisiana State University Press, 1977.

Jensen, Richard. *The Winning of the Midwest: Social and Political Conflict, 1888-1896.* Chicago: University of Chicago Press, 1971.

Jewell, Malcolm E. and Everett W. Cunningham, *Kentucky Politics.* Lexington: University Press of Kentucky, 1968.

Josephson, Matthew. *The Politicos: 1865-1896.* New York: Harcourt Brace, 1938.

Kahl, Mary. *Ballot Box 13: How Lyndon Johnson Won His 1948 Senate Race by 87 Contested Votes.* Jefferson, N.C.: McFarland Co., 1983.

Kallina, Edmund F. Jr. *Courthouse Over White House: Chicago and the Presidential Election of 1960.* Orlando: University Presses of Florida, 1988.

Kalman, Laura. *Abe Fortas.* New Haven: Yale University Press, 1990.

Kantrowitz, Stephen. *Ben Tillman and the Reconstruction of White Supremacy.* Chapel Hill: University of North Carolina Press, 2000.

Kelly, Kate. *Election Day: An American Holiday, An American History.* New York: Facts on File, 1991.

Kent, Frank R. *The Great Game of Politics.* Garden City: Doubleday, 1930.

Kettner, James H. *The Development of American Citizenship, 1608-1870.* Chapel Hill: University of North Carolina Press, 1978.

Key, V.O. *Politics, Parties, and Pressure Groups.* New York: Thomas Y. Crowell, 1942.

——————. *Southern Politics in State and Nation.* New York: Vintage Books, 1949.

Keyssar, Alexander. *The Right to Vote: The Contested History of Democracy in the United States.* New York: Basic Books, 2000.

Kirkendall. Richard S. *A History of Missouri, vol. V: 1919 to 1953.* Columbia: University of Missouri Press, 1986.

Kleppner, Paul. *Continuity and Change in Electoral Politics, 1893-1928.* New York: Greenwood Press, 1987.

——————.*Who Voted?: The Dynamics of Electoral Turnout, 1870-1980.* New York: Praeger, 1982.

Klotter, James C. *William Goebel: The Politics of Wrath.* Lexington: University Press of Kentucky, 1977.

Kornbluh, Mark Lawrence. *Why America Stopped Voting: The Decline of Participatory Democracy and the Emergence of Modern American Politics.* New York: New York University Press, 2000.

Kousser, J. Morgan. *Colorblind Injustice: Minority Voting Rights and the Undoing of the Second Reconstruction.* Chapel Hill: University of North Carolina Press, 1999.

——————-.*The Shaping of Southern Politics: Suffrage Restriction and the Establishment of the One-Party South, 1880-1910.* New Haven: Yale University Press, 1974.

Krock, Arthur. *Myself When Young: Growing Up in the 1890s.* Boston: Little, Brown, Co., 1973.

Lawson, Steven F. *Black Ballots: Voting Rights in the South, 1944-1969.* New York: Columbia University Press, 1976.

Lewinson, Paul. *Race, Class, and Party: A History of Negro Suffrage and White Politics in the South.* New York: Oxford University Press, 1932.

MacNeil, Neil. *Forge of Democracy: The House of Representatives.* New York: David McKay, 1963.

Maginnis, John. *The Last Hayride.* Baton Rouge: Gris Gris, 1984.

Malone, Dumas. *Jefferson and His Time: Jefferson the Virginian,* vol. I. Boston: Little, Brown, and Co., 1948.

Mann, Robert. *Legacy to Power: Senator Russell Long of Louisiana.* New York: Paragon House, 1992.

McCaffery, Peter. *When Bosses Ruled Philadelphia: The Emergence of the Republican Machine, 1867-1933.* University Park: The Pennsylvania State University Press, 1993.

McCormick, Richard P. *The History of Voting in New Jersey: A Study of the Development of Election Machinery.* New Brunswick: Rutgers University Press, 1953.

McCrary, George W. *A Treatise on the American Law of Election.* Chicago: Callaghan, 1887.

McCullough, David. *John Adams.* New York: Simon and Schuster, 2001.

————. *Truman.* New York: Simon and Schuster, 1992.

McGerr, Michael E. *The Decline of Popular Politics: The American North, 1865-1928.* New York: Oxford University Press, 1986.

McKinley, Albert. *The Suffrage Franchise in the Thirteen English Colonies in America.* Philadelphia: Publications of the University of Pennsylvania, 1905.

McPherson, James M. *Battle Cry of Freedom: The Civil War Era.* New York: Oxford University Press, 1988.

Merzer, Martin and the Staff of the *Miami Herald. The Miami Herald Report: Democracy Held Hostage.* New York: St. Martin's Press, 2001.

Miller, Donald L. *City of the Century: The Epic of Chicago and the Making of America.* New York: Simon and Schuster, 1996.

Miller, Richard Lawrence. *Truman: The Rise to Power.* New York: McGraw-Hill, 1986.

Miller, William D. *Memphis During the Progressive Era, 1900-1917.* Memphis: Memphis State University Press, 1957.

————. *Mr. Crump of Memphis.* Baton Rouge: Louisiana State University Press, 1964.

Miller, Zane L. *Boss Cox's Cincinnati: Urban Politics in the Progressive Era.* New York: Oxford University Press, 1968.

Milligan, Maurice M. *"Missouri Waltz: The Inside Story of the Pendergast Machine by the Man Who Smashed It.* New York: Charles Scribner's Sons, 1948.

Mitchell, Greg. *The Campaign of the Century: Upton Sinclair's Race for Governor of California and the Birth of Media Politics.* New York: Random House, 1992.

Morris, Roy, Jr., *Fraud of the Century: Rutherford B. Hayes, Samuel Tilden, and the Stolen Election of 1876.* New York: Simon and Schuster, 2003.

Moye, J. Todd. *Let the People Decide: Black Freedom and White Resistance Movements in Sunflower County, Mississippi, 1945-1986.* Chapel Hill: University of North Carolina Press, 2004.

Mushkat, Jerome. *Tammany: The Evolution of a Political Machine, 1789-1865.* Syracuse: Syracuse University Press, 1971.

Myers, Gustavus. *The History of Tammany Hall.* New York: Burt Franklin, 1968.

Nasaw, David. *The Chief: The Life of William Randolph Hearst.* Boston: Houghton Mifflin, 2000.

Nash, Gary B. *The Unknown American Revolution: The Unruly Birth of Democracy and the Struggle to Create America.* New York: Viking, 2005.

—————. *The Urban Crucible: The Northern Seaports and the Origins of the American Revolution.* Cambridge: Harvard University Press, 1979.

Nelson, Bruce C. *Beyond the Martyrs: A Social History of Chicago's Anarchists.* New Brunswick: Rutgers University Press, 1988.

Nesbit, Robert C. *Wisconsin: A History.* Madison: University of Wisconsin Press, 1973.

Nevins, Allan. *Abram S. Hewitt: With Some Account of Peter Cooper.* New York: Harper, 1935.

—————. ed., *Selected Writings of Abram S. Hewitt.* New York: Columbia University Press, 1937.

Niebuhr, Reinhold. *The Children of Light and the Children of Darkness: A Vindication of Democracy and a Critique of Its Traditional Defences.* New York: Scribner's, 1944.

Nixon, Richard. *Six Crises.* Garden City: Doubleday, 1962.

O'Connor, Len. *Clout: Mayor Daley and His City.* Chicago: Regnery, 1975.

Older, Mrs. Fremont. *William Randolph Hearst, American.* New York: D. Appleton-Century Co., 1936.

O'Reilly, Kenneth. *Racial Matters: The FBI's Secret File on Black America, 1960-1972.* New York: The Free Press, 1989.

Ortiz, Paul. *Emancipation Betrayed: The Hidden History of Black Organizing and White Violence in Florida from Reconstruction to the Bloody Election of 1920.* Berkeley: University of California Press, 2005.

Palast, Greg. *The Best Democracy Money Can Buy: The Truth About Corporate Cons, Globalization, and High-Finance Fraudsters.* New York: Plume, 2003.

Piven, Frances Fox and Richard A. Cloward. *Why Americans Still Don't Vote: And Why Politicians Want it That Way.* Boston: Beacon Press, 2000.

Polakoff, Keith Ian. *The Politics of Inertia: The Election of 1876 and the End of Reconstruction.* Baton Rouge: Louisiana State University Press, 1973.

The Political Staff of the Washington *Post. Deadlock: The Inside Story of America's Closest Election.* New York: Public Affairs, 2001.

Potter, David M. *The Impending Crisis: 1848-1861.* New York: Harper and Row, 1976.

Primm, James Neal. *Lion of the Valley: St. Louis, Missouri, 1764-1980* 3rd.ed. St. Louis: Missouri Historical Society Press, 1998.

Rawley, James A. *Race and Politics: "Bleeding Kansas" and the Coming of the Civil War.* Philadelphia: J.B. Lippincott Co., 1969.

Riordan, William L. *Plunkitt of Tammany Hall: A Series of Very Plain Talk on Very Practical Politics,* Terrence J. McDonald, ed. Boston: Bedford/St. Martin's, 1994.

Remini, Robert V. *Henry Clay: Statesman for the Union.* New York: W. W. Norton, 1991.

Reynolds, John F. *Testing Democracy: Electoral Behavior and Progressive Reform in New Jersey, 1880-1910.* Chapel Hill: University of North Carolina Press, 1988.

Richards, Leonard L. *The Slave Power: The Free North and Southern Domination, 1780-1860.* Baton Rouge: Louisiana State University Press, 2000.

Richardson, Leon Burr. *William E. Chandler: Republican.* New York: Dodd, Mead, 1940.

Robinson, Lloyd. *The Stolen Election: Hayes Versus Tilden, 1876.* New York: Tom Doherty, 2001.

Rogers, William Warren. *The One-Gallused Rebellion: Agrarianism in Alabama, 1865-1896.* Baton Rouge: Louisiana State University Press, 1970.

Rosswurm, Steven. *Arms, Country, and Class: The Philadelphia Militia and the "Lower Sort" During the American Revolution, 1775-1783.* New Brunswick: Rutgers University Press, 1987.

Royko, Mike. *Boss: Richard J. Daley of Chicago.* New York: E. P. Dutton, 1971.

Rudwick, Elliot M. *Race Riot in East St. Louis: July 2, 1917.* Carbondale: Southern Illinois University Press, 1964.

Ryan, Mary P. *Civic Wars: Democracy and Public Life in the American City During the Nineteenth Century.* Berkeley: University of California Press, 1997.

Sabato, Larry J. and Glenn R. Simpson, *Dirty Little Secrets: The Persistence of Corruption in American Politics.* New York: Times Books, 1996.

Sacher, John M. *A Perfect War of Politics: Parties, Politicians, and Democracy in Louisiana, 1824-1861.* Baton Rouge: Louisiana State University Press, 2003.

Schlesinger, Arthur M. *The Birth of a Nation: A Portrait of the American People on the Eve of Independence.* Boston: Houghton Mifflin, 1968.

Schlesinger, Arthur M., Jr., ed. *History of American Presidential Elections, 1789-1968.* New York: McGraw Hill, 1971.

Schultz, Mark. *The Rural Face of White Supremacy: Beyond Jim Crow.* Urbana: University of Illinois Press, 2005.

Sellers, Charles. *James K. Polk: Continentalist, 1843-1846.* Princeton: Princeton University Press, 1966.

Seymour, Charles and Donald Paige Frary. *How the World Votes: The Story of Democratic Development in Elections.* Springfield, Mass.: C.A. Nichols, 1918.

Sherrill, Robert. *Gothic Politics in the Deep South: Stars of the New Confederacy.* New York: Grossman, 1968.

Silcox, Harry C. *Philadelphia Politics From the Bottom Up: The Life of Irishman William McMullen, 1824-1901*. Philadelphia: Balch Institute Press, 1989.

Silbey, Joel H. *The Partisan Imperative: The Dynamics of American Politics Before the Civil War*. New York: Oxford University Press, 1985.

Simkins, Francis Butler. *Pitchfork Ben Tillman: South Carolinian*. Baton Rouge: Louisiana State University Press, 1944.

Smith, J. Allen. *The Growth and Decadence of Constitutional Government*. New York: Henry Holt, 1930.

Soule, Leon Cyprian. *The Know Nothing Party in New Orleans*. Louisiana Historical Society, 1961.

Spann, Edward K. *The New Metropolis: New York City, 1840-1857*. New York: Columbia University Press, 1981.

Squires, James D. *The Secrets of the Hopewell Box: Stolen Elections, Southern Politics, and a City's Coming of Age*. New York: Times Books, 1996.

Stampp, Kenneth. *America in 1857: A Nation on the Brink*. New York: Oxford University Press, 1990.

Stein, Lana. *St. Louis Politics: The Triumph of Tradition*. St. Louis: Missouri Historical Society Press, 2002.

Steffens, Lincoln. *The Shame of the Cities*. New York: McClure, Phillips, 1904.

Summers, Mark Wahlgren. *The Era of Good Stealings* (New York: Oxford University Press, 1993.

——————. *The Gilded Age: Or, the Hazard of New Functions*. Upper Saddle River: Prentice Hall, 1997.

——————. *Party Games: Getting, Keeping, and Using Power in Gilded Age Politics*. Chapel Hill: University of North Carolina Press, 2004.

——————. *The Plundering Generation: Corruption and the Crisis of the Union, 1849-1861*. New York: Oxford University Press, 1987.

——————. *Rum, Romanism, & Rebellion: The Making of a President, 1884*. Chapel Hill: University of North Carolina Press, 2000.

Swanberg, W.A. *Citizen Hearst: A Biography of William Randolph Hearst.* New York: Charles Scribner's Sons, 1961.

Sydnor, Charles S. *Gentleman Freeholders: Political Practices in Washington's Virginia.* Chapel Hill: University of North Carolina Press, 1952.

Syrett, Harold C. ed., *The Gentleman and the Tiger: The Autobiography of George B. McClellan, Jr.* Philadelphia: J.B. Lippincott, 1956.

Taylor, Joe Gray. *Louisiana Reconstructed, 1863-1877.* Baton Rouge: Louisiana State University Press, 1974.

Thelen, David. *Paths of Resistance: Tradition and Dignity in Industrializing Missouri.* New York: Oxford University Press, 1986.

Theoharis, Athan G. and John Stuart Cox. *The Boss: J. Edgar Hoover and the Great American Inquisition.* Philadelphia: Temple University Press, 1988.

Thirty-Six Days: The Complete Chronicle of the 2000 Presidential Election Crisis by Correspondents of the New York Times. New York: Times Books, 2001.

Thompson, Dennis F. *Just Elections: Creating a Fair Electoral Process in the United States.* Chicago: University of Chicago Press, 2002.

Tocqueville, Alexis de, *Democracy in America,* vol. II. New York: Vintage, 1945.

Toobin, Jeffrey. *Too Close to Call: The Thirty-Six Day Battle to Decide the 2000 Election.* New York: Random House, 2001.

Trelease, Allen W. *White Terror: The Ku Klux Klan Conspiracy and Southern Reconstruction.* New York: Harper and Row, 1971.

Tunnell, Ted. *Crucible of Reconstruction: War, Radicalism, and Race in Louisiana, 1862-1877.* Baton Rouge: Louisiana State University Press, 1984.

Tuska, Benjamin. *Know-Nothingism in Baltimore, 1854-1860,* n.p.

Tyler, Pamela. *Silk Stockings and Ballot Boxes: Women and Politics in New Orleans, 1920-1963.* Athens: University of Georgia Press, 1996.

Tyson, Timothy B. *Blood Done Sign My Name: A True Story.* New York: Crown, 2004.

Warren, G. B. *Boston: 1689-1776*. Boston: Little, Brown, 1970.

Watson, Thomas E. *The People's Party Campaign Book, 1892: Not a Revolt; It is a Revolution*. rep. By Arno Press, 1975.

Weeks, O. Douglas. *Texas in the 1960 Presidential Election*. Austin: Institute of Public Affairs, University of Texas at Austin, 1961.

White, Leonard D. *The Jacksonians: A Study in Administrative History, 1829-1861*. New York: Macmillan, 1954.

White, Theodore H. *The Making of the President, 1960*. New York: Atheneum, 1961.

Williams, Charles Richard. *Diary and Letters of Rutherford Birchard Hayes*. Columbus: Ohio State University Press, 1924.

Williams, R.H. *With the Border Ruffians: Memories of the Far West, 1852-1868*. London: John Murray, 1907.

Williamson, Chilton. *American Suffrage: From Property to Democracy, 1760-1860*. Princeton: Princeton University Press, 1960.

Williams, T. Harry. *Huey Long*. New York: Alfred A. Knopf, 1969.

Williamson, Joel. *The Crucible of Race: Black-White Relations in the American South Since Emancipation*. New York: Oxford University Press, 1984.

Wills, Garry. *"Negro President": Jefferson and the Slave Power*. Boston: Houghton Mifflin, 2003.

Winkle, Kenneth J. *The Politics of Community: Migration and Politics in Antebellum Ohio*. Cambridge: Cambridge University Press, 1988.

Wood, Gordon. *The Creation of the American Republic, 1776-1787*. Chapel Hill: University of North Carolina Press, 1969.

Woodson, Urey. *The First New Dealer: William Goebel*. Louisville: The Standard Press, 1939.

Woodward, C. Vann. *Origins of the New South, 1877-1913*. Baton Rouge: LSU Press, 1951.

TRACY CAMPBELL / DELIVER THE VOTE

—————————. *Reunion and Reaction: The Compromise of 1877 and the End of Reconstruction.* Boston: Little, Brown, 1951.

—————————. *Tom Watson: Agrarian Rebel.* New York: Macmillan, 1938.

Wright, George C. *Life Behind a Veil: Blacks in Louisville, Kentucky, 1865-1930.* Baton Rouge: Louisiana State University Press, 1985.

Yater, George H. *Two Hundred Years at the Falls of the Ohio: A History of Louisville and Jefferson County.* Louisville: Filson Club, 1987.

ARTICLES AND PAMPHLETS

Allen, Howard W. and Kay Warren Allen. "Vote Fraud and Data Validity." Jerome M. Clubb, et. al., *Analyzing Electoral History: A Guide to the Study of American Voter Behavior.* Beverly Hills, Ca.,: Sage, 1981.

American Party of Kentucky, "Proceedings of the Grand Council of Kentucky," August 20, 1856.

Appleby, Joyce. "Presidents, Congress, and Courts: Partisan Passions in Motion." *Journal of American History* 88 (September 2001).

Argersinger, Peter. H. "'A Place on the Ballot': Fusion Politics and Antifusion Laws." *American Historical Review* 85 (April 1980).

—————————. "Electoral Reform and Partisan Jugglery." *Political Science Quarterly* 119 (Fall 2004).

—————————. "New Perspectives on Election Fraud in the Gilded Age." *Political Science Quarterly* 100 (Winter 1985-86).

—————————. "To Disfranchise the People: The Iowa Ballot Law and Election of 1897." *Mid-America* 63 (January 1981).

Astorino, Samuel J. "The Contested Senate Election of William Scott Vare." *Pennsylvania History* 28 (April 1961).

Baldwin, Thomas P. "George D. Prentice, the Louisville *Anzieger,* and the 1855 Bloody Monday Riots." *Filson Club History Quarterly* October 1993.

Barnes, Kenneth C. "Who Killed John M. Clayton?: Political Violence in Conway County, Arkansas, in the 1880s." *Arkansas Historical Quarterly* 52 (Winter 1993).

Bass, Herbert J. "The Politics of Ballot Reform in New York State, 1888-1890." *New York History* (July 1961).

Baumgardner, James L. "The 1888 Presidential Election: How Corrupt?" *Presidential Studies Quarterly* 14 (Summer 1984).

Bernheim, A.C. "The Ballot in New York." *Political Science Quarterly* 4 (March 1889).

Best, Judith. "Weighing the Alternatives: Reform or Deform?" in Arthur J. Jacobson and Michel Rosenfeld, *The Longest Night: Polemics and Perspectives on Election 2000.* Berkeley: University of California Press, 2002.

Blair, A.Z. "Seventeen Hundred Rural Vote Sellers: How We Disfranchised a Quarter of the Voting Population of Adams County, Ohio." *McClure's Magazine* (November 1911).

Brennan, Geoffrey and Philip Pettit, "Unveiling the Vote." *British Journal of Political Science* 20 (May 1997).

Bruce, Helm. "What Kind of City Do You Want?" September 26, 1917.

Buenker, John D. "The Politics of Resistance: The Rural-Based Yankee Republican Machines of Connecticut and Rhode Island." *New England Quarterly* (June 1974).

Burcher, William M. "A History of Soldier Voting in the State of New York." *New York History* 25 October 1944.

Burnham, Walter Dean. "The Changing Shape of the American Political Universe." *American Political Science Review* 59 (March 1965).

—————————. "Theory and Voting Research: Some Reflections on Converse's 'Change in the American Electorate.'" *American Political Science Review* 68 (September 1974.)

——————. "Those High Nineteenth-Century American Voting Turnouts: Fact or Fiction?" *Journal of Interdisciplinary History* (Spring 1986).

Calabresi, Steven G. "A Political Question." Bruce Ackerman, ed., *Bush v. Gore: The Question of Legitimacy.* New Haven: Yale University Press, 2002.

Caltech-MIT Voting Technology Project. *Voting: What Is, What Could Be* (July 2001).

Campbell, Tracy. "Machine Politics, Police Corruption, and the Persistence of Vote Fraud: The Case of the Louisville, Kentucky Election of 1905." *Journal of Policy History* 15 (Summer 2003).

Castleman, David R. "Louisville Election Frauds in Court and Out." *National Municipal Review*, December 1927.

Ciccone, F. Richard. "Making Votes Count." *Chicago History* (Winter 2002).

Cohen, Norman S. "The Philadelphia Election Riot of 1742." *Pennsylvania Magazine of History and Biography* (July 1968).

Converse, Philip E. "Change in the American Electorate." Angus Campbell and Philip E. Converse, eds. *The Human Meaning of Social Change*. New York: Russell Sage, 1972.

Cox, Gary and J. Morgan Kousser. "Turnout and Rural Corruption: New York as a Test Case." *American Journal of Political Science* 25 (November 1981).

Deusner, Charles E. "The Know Nothing Riots in Louisville." *Register of the Kentucky Historical Society* (April 1963).

Donsanto, Craig C. "Federal Jurisdiction Over Local Vote Fraud." *Baltimore Law Review* 13 (Fall 1983).

Dunham, Robert Brett. "Defoliating the Grassroots: Election Day Restrictions on Political Speech." *Georgetown Law Journal* 77 (August 1989).

Etzioni, Amitai. "Social Norms: Internalization, Persuasion, and History." *Law and Society Review* 34 (2000).

"Florida Absentee Voter Fraud: Fashioning an Appropriate Judicial Remedy." *University of Miami Law Review* 54 (April 2000).

Fund, John. "Florida Northwest." *Wall Street Journal*, November 29, 2004.

Gavins, Raymond. "Fear, Hope, and Struggle: Recasting Black North Carolina in the Age of Jim Crow." David S. Cecelski and Timothy B. Tyson, *Democracy Betrayed: The Wilmington Race Riot of 1898 and its Legacy*. Chapel Hill: University of North Carolina Press, 1998.

Gienapp, William E. "Politics Seem to Enter Into Everything: Political Culture In the North, 1840-1860." William E. Gienapp, et. al., *Essays on American Antebellum Politics, 1840-1860*. College Station: Texas A&M University Press, 1982.

Gilmore, Glenda E. "Murder, Memory, and the Flight of the Incubus." in David S. Cecelski and Timothy B. Tyson, *Democracy Betrayed: The Wilmington Race Riot of 1898 and its Legacy*. Chapel Hill: University of North Carolina Press, 1998.

Gist, Genevieve B. "Progressive Reform in a Rural Community: The Adams County Vote-Fraud Case." *Mississippi Valley Historical Review* (June 1961).

Gray, Karen R. and Sarah R. Yates. "Boss John Whallen: The Early Louisville Years (1876-1883)." *Journal of Kentucky Studies* (1984).

Greenberg, David. "Life After Certification." *Slate*, November 18, 2000.

Hasen, Richard L. "After the Storm: The Uses, Normative Implications, and Unintended Consequences of Voting Reform Research in Post—*Bush v. Gore* Equal Protection Challenges." Ann M. Crigler, Marion R. Just, and Edward J. McCaffery, eds., *Rethinking the Vote: The Politics and Prospects of American Election Reform.* New York: Oxford University Press, 2004.

Hartmann, Thom. "If You Want To Win an Election, Just Control the Voting Machines." *Common Dreams Newscenter,* February 6, 2003.

Heckelman, Jac C. "The Effect of the Secret Ballot on Voter Turnout Rates." *Public Choice* 82 (1995).

—————-. "Revisiting the Relationship Between Secret Ballots and Turnout: A New Test of Two Legal-Institutional Theories." *American Politics Quarterly* 28 (April 2000).

Hitchens, Christopher. "Ohio's Odd Numbers." *Vanity Fair,* March, 2005.

Imai, Kosuke and Gary King. "Did Illegal Overseas Ballots Decide the 2000 U.S. Presidential Election?" *Perspectives on Politics* 2 Sept. 2004.

"Importance of a Register Law to the Purity of Elective Franchise." Louisville: N. W. White, 1840.

Jacobs, James Henry. "The West Virginia Gubernatorial Election Contest, 1888-1890." *West Virginia History* 7 (April, 1946).

Jenks, Jeremiah W. "Money in Practical Politics." *The Century* 44 (October 1892).

Karlan, Pamela S. "Equal Protection: *Bush v. Gore* and the Making of a Precedent." Jack Rakove, ed., *The Unfinished Election of 2000.* New York: Basic Books, 2001.

Keyssar, Alexander. "Right to Vote." Kermit L. Hall, ed., *The Oxford Companion to the Supreme Court.* New York: Oxford University Press, 1992.

————————. "The Right to Vote and Election 2000." Jack N. Rakove, ed., *The Unfinished Election of 2000*. New York: Basic Books, 2001.

King, Ronald F. "Counting the Votes: South Carolina's Stolen Election of 1876." *Journal of Interdisciplinary History* 33 (Autumn, 2001).

Kramer, Larry D. "The Supreme Court in Politics." Jack N. Rakove, ed., *The Unfinished Election of 2000*. New York: Basic Books, 2001.

Krosnick, Jon A., Joanne M. Miller, and Michael P. Tichy. "An Unrecognized Need for Ballot Reform: The Effects of Candidate Name Order on Election Outcomes." Ann N. Crigler, Marion R. Just, and Edward J. McCaffery, eds. *Rethinking the Vote: The Politics and Prospects of American Election Reform*. New York: Oxford University Press, 2004.

Krueger, Maynard C. "Election Frauds in Philadelphia." *National Municipal Review* (May 1928).

Landesco, John. "Election Fraud." John A. Gardiner and David J. Olson, eds. *Theft of the City: Readings on Corruption in Urban America*. Bloomington: Indiana University Press, 1974.

"Louisville Election Contest Cases: Report of James P. Helm, Chairman of the Committee of One Hundred."

Maizlish, Stephen E. "The Meaning of Nativism and the Crisis of the Union: The Know-Nothing Movement in the Antebellum North." William Gienapp, et.al., *Essays on American Antebellum Politics,1840-1860*. College Station: Texas A&M University Press, 1982.

Manne, Henry G. "Some Theoretical Aspects of Share Voting." *Columbia Law Review* 64 (December 1964).

Mayfield, Loomis. "Voting Fraud in Early Twentieth Century Pittsburgh." *Journal of Interdisciplinary History* 24 (Summer 1993).

Mebane, Walter R. Jr. "The Wrong Man is President! Overvotes in the 2000 Presidential Election in Florida." *Perspectives in Politics* 2 (Sept. 2004).

Mennite, Lori and David Callahan. "Securing the Vote: An Analysis of Election Fraud." New York: Demos, 2003.

Morison, Samuel Eliot. "Struggle Over the Adoption of the Constitution of Massachusetts, 1780." *Massachusetts Historical Society Proceedings* L (May 1917).

Moreno, Paul. "The Sixteenth Amendment in New York State: Politics and Constitutional Change." *Mid-America* 77 (Winter 1995).

Morriss, Dick. "Those Faulty Exit Polls Were Sabotage." thehill.com, November 4, 2004.

O'Gorman, Frank. "Campaign Rituals and Ceremonies: The Social Meaning of Elections
in England, 1780-1860." *Past and Present* 135 (May 1992).

"Oregon Election, 2000." Report Prepared by Del Information Services, January 2001.

Palast, Greg. "Ex-Con Game: How Florida's 'Felon' Voter-Purge Was Itself Felonious."
Harper's, (March 2002).

Parsons, William T. "The Bloody Election of 1742." *Pennsylvania History* 36 (July 1969).

Pildes, Richard H. "Disputing Elections." Arthur J. Jacobson and Michel Rosenfeld, *The
Longest Night: Polemics and Perspectives on Election 2000.* Berkeley: University of California Press, 2002.

Raskin, Jamin B. "Legal Aliens, Local Citizens: The Historical, Constitutional, and Theoretical Meanings of Alien Suffrage." *University of Pennsylvania Law Review* 141
(April 1993).

Redard, Thomas F. "The Election of 1844 in Louisiana: A New Look at the Ethno-Cultural Approach." *Louisiana* History 22 (Fall 1981).

Reynolds, John F.. "'The Silent Dollar': Vote Buying in New Jersey." *New Jersey History*
(Fall-Winter 1980).

——————-. and Richard L. McCormick. "Outlawing 'Treachery': Split Tickets and
Ballot Laws in New York and New Jersey, 1880-1910." *Journal of American History*
(March 1986).

Robinson, Cyril D. "The Mayor and the Police—the Political Role of the Police in
Society." George L. Mosse, ed., *Police Forces in History.* London: Sage Publications,
1975).

Rosenfeld, Michel. "*Bush v. Gore:* Three Strikes for the Constitution, the Court, and
Democracy, but There is Always Next Season." Arthur Jacobson and Michel Rosen-

feld, *The Longest Night: Polemics and Perspectives on Election 2000.* Berkeley: University of California Press, 2002.

Rusk, Jerrold G. "The American Electoral Universe: Speculation and Evidence." *American Political Science Review* 68 (September 1974).

————-. "The Effect of the Australian Ballot Reform on Split Ticket Voting: 1876-1908." *American Political Science Review* 64 (December 1970).

Sarvis, Will. "The Irrepressible Urge to Manipulate Election Fraud in Rural Missouri, 1940-1970." *Journal of the West* 39 (Fall 2000).

Schouler, James "Evolution of the American Voter." *American Historical* Review 2 (July 1897).

Sellers, Charles, "Election of 1844." Arthur M. Schlesinger, Jr. and Fred L. Israel, eds., *History of American Presidential Elections, 1789-1968,* vol. I, New York: McGraw-Hill, 1971.

Shofner, Jerrell H. "Florida in the Balance: The Electoral Count of 1876." *Florida Historical Quarterly* (October 1968).

Steffens, Lincoln. "Rhode Island: A State for Sale." *McClure's Magazine,* February 1905.

————-. "Fraud and Intimidation in the Florida Election of 1876." *Florida Historical Quarterly* (April 1964).

Stuart, Guy. "Databases, Felons, and Voting: Bias and Partisanship of the Florida Felons List in the 2000 Elections." *Political Science Quarterly* 119 (Fall 2004).

Talmadge, Herman E. "You and Segregation." Birmingham: Vulcan Press, 1955.

Testi, Arnaldo. "The Tribulations of an Old Democracy." *Journal of American History* 88 (September 2001).

Tunnell, T. B., Jr. "The Negro, the Republican Party, and the Election of 1876 in Louisiana." *Louisiana History* (Spring 1966).

Vandal, Gilles. "The Policy of Violence in Caddo Parish, 1865-1884." *Louisiana History* 32 (Spring 1991).

————-. "Politics and Violence in Bourbon Louisiana: The Loreauville Riot of 1884 as a Case Study." *Louisiana History* 30 (Winter 1989).

Vinson, John Chalmers. "Electioneering in North Carolina, 1800-1835." *North Carolina Historical Review* (April 1952).

Ware, Alan. "Anti-Partism and Party Control of Political Reform in the United States: The Case of the Australian Ballot." *British Journal of Political Science* 30 (January 2000).

Watson, Robert P. "The State of Elections: People, Politics, and Problems." Robert P. Watson, ed., *Counting Votes: Lessons From the 2000 Presidential Election in Florida.* Gainesville: University Press of Florida, 2004.

Winther, Oscar Osburn. "The Soldier Vote in the Election of 1864." *New York History* 25 (October 1944).

Woodruff, Clinton Rogers. "Election Methods and Reforms in Philadelphia." *Annals of the American Academy of Political and Social Science* (March 1901).

Wright, George C. "The Billy Club and the Ballot: Police Intimidation of Blacks in Louisville, Kentucky, 1880-1930." *Southern Studies* 23 (1984).

DOCUMENTARIES

"Big Lever: Party Politics in Leslie County, Kentucky." Directed by Francis Morton, Appalshop Productions, 1982.

"The Ends of the Earth: Plaquemines Parish, Louisiana." Produced by Louis Alvarez and Andrew Kolker, The Center for New American Media, 1982.

LEGAL CASES

Anderson v. Spear 189 F. Supp. 2d. 644 (2002)
Baker v. Carr 369 U.S. 186 (1962)
Balter v. Ickes 301 U.S. 709
Boardman v. Esteva 323 So.2d. 259 (1975)
Bolden v. Potter 452 So.2d 564 (Fla., 1984)
Burson v. Freeman 504 U.S. 191 (1992)
Bush v. Gore 531 U.S. 98 (2000)
Bush v. Gore 121 S. Ct., 512.
Calchera v. Procarione 805 F.Supp. 716 (1992)
Capen v. Foster 12 Pickering 485

Curry v. Baker 802 F.2nd 1302 (1986)

Ex Parte Yarbrough, et. al. 110 U.S. 651 (1884)

Gore v. Harris 772 So2d. 1243 (Fla., 2000)

Gray v. Sanders 372 U.S. 368 (1963)

Green v. Ball 288 S.W. 309.

Gross v. Ball 81 S.W. 2d 409.

In re Protest of Election Returns and Absentee Ballots 707 So2d. 1170, Florida 3rd District Court of Appeals (1998)

Jacobs v. Seminole County Canvassing Board 773 So. 2d 519 (2000)

James v. Bowman 190 U.S. 127 (1903).

McGuire v. State of Tennessee 7 Humph. 54

Middleton v. Poer 121 S.W.2d 28.

Orr et. al. v. Kevil, et. al., 100 S.W. 314.

People v. Harris 29 Cal. 678

Reynolds v. Sims 377 U.S. 533 (1964)

Scheer v. City of Miami 15 F.Supp.2d. 1338 (1998)

Smith v. Allwright 321 U.S. 649 (1944)

Taylor v. Martin County Canvassing Board 773 So. 2d 517 (2000)

U.S. v. Classic 313 U.S.299 (1941)

U.S. v. McCranie 169 F.3rd 723 (1999)

U.S. v. Moseley 238 U.S. 383 (1915)

U.S. v. Reese 92 U.S. 214 (1876)

U.S. v. Saylor 322 U.S. 385 (1944)

Williams v. Mississippi 170 U.S. 213 (1898)

THESES AND DISSERTATIONS

Brown, Sharon A. "Making a Memorial: Developing the Jefferson National Expansion Memorial National Historic Site, 1933-1980." Ph.D. dissertation., St. Louis University, 1983.

Cohen, Murray. "The Crusade Against Election Fraud by the Post-Dispatch and Star-Times of St. Louis in 1936." M.A. Thesis, University of Missouri, 1953.

Collins, Ernest. "The Political Behavior of the Negroes in Cincinnati, Ohio and Louisville, Kentucky." Ph.D. dissertation, University of Kentucky, 1950.

Cornell, Charlene M. "Louisville in Transition: 1870-1890." M.A. Thesis, University of Louisville, 1970.

Cusick, Robert I. Jr., "The History of the Louisville Division of Police From the Founding of the City to 1955." M.A. Thesis, University of Louisville, 1964.

Ellis, Roy. "A Civic History of Kansas City, Missouri." Ph.D. dissertation, Columbia University, 1930.

Fram, Steven Jeffrey. "Purifying the Ballot?: The Politics of Electoral Procedure in New York State, 1821-71." M.A. Thesis, Cornell University, 1983.

Gillette, Howard Frank. "Corrupt and Contented: Philadelphia's Political Machine, 1865-1877." Ph.D. dissertation, Yale University, 1970.

Hamel, April Lee. "The Jefferson National Expansion Memorial: A Depression Relief Project." Ph.D. dissertation, St. Louis University, 1983.

Henry, Sarah M. "Progressivism and Democracy: Electoral Reform in the United States, 1888-1919." Ph.D. dissertation, Columbia University, 1995.

Key, Valdimer Orlando, Jr. "The Techniques of Political Graft in the United States." Ph.D. dissertation, University of Chicago, 1934.

Kurtzman, David Harold. "Methods of Controlling Votes in Philadelphia." Ph.D. dissertation, University of Pennsylvania, 1935.

McClellan, Jimmie Rex. "Two Party Monopoly to Third Party Participation in American Politics," Ph.D. dissertation, Union for Experimenting Colleges and Universities, 1984.

McConville, Sister Mary St. Patrick. "Political Nativism in the State of Maryland, 1830-1860," Ph.D. dissertation, Catholic University of America, 1928.

Schneider, Cary M. "St. Louis and the Gateway Arch: A Case History of an Urban Icon." Honors Paper, Cornell College, 1970.

Wills, James T. "Louisville Politics, 1891-1897." M.A. Thesis, University of Louisville, 1966.

Acknowledgments

I n research that has spanned nearly a decade, my accumulated debts to a host of scholars, librarians, friends, and family members has grown exponentially. I am especially grateful to the staffs at the following libraries and archival collections: the William T. Young Library, University of Kentucky; the St. Louis Public Library; the Jefferson National Expansion Memorial Archives; the Missouri Historical Society; the Western Historical Manuscripts Collection at the University of Missouri; the National Archives in Laguna Niguel, California; the National Archives, Southeast Region, East Point, Georgia; the Harry S. Truman Presidential Library; the Lyndon B. Johnson Presidential Library; Hill Memorial Library, LSU; the Kansas City Public Library; and the special collections staff at the College of Wooster in Ohio. My thanks as well to the editors of the *Journal of Policy History* and the *Chronicle of Higher Education* for permission to reprint material originally published in those journals.

The staff at the Filson Historical Society in Louisville was very helpful, and I profited to no end from a grant that allowed me to spend time at the Filson exploring the hidden interiors of the 1905 Louisville election. Thanks especially to Shirley Harmon, Jim Holmberg, and director Mark Wetherington. The staff at the InterLibrary Loan department at the University of Kentucky processed an untold number of requests with their usual diligence. As always, Terry Birdwhistell and Jeff Suchanek in Special Collections at UK were exceptional. The chapter on Louisville simply could not have been written without their help. Terry, my co-director at the Ford Public Policy Research Center at UK, provided the kind of encouragement, good humor, and wise counsel that was indispensable and much appreciated.

I am fortunate to work with colleagues and friends who are as knowledgeable and supportive as those in the History Department at the University of Kentucky. Ron Formisano, Bill Freehling, David Hamilton, Phil Harling, Joanne Melish, Karen Petrone, and Jeremy Popkin all offered helpful suggestions on some early research concerning the St. Louis election of 1935. Dan Smith, Ron Eller, and Kathi Kern kindly tolerated my occasional absences from inter-departmental meetings so I could finish the manuscript. Tina Hagee and Carol O'Reilly each performed a dozen miracles on my behalf, making my work an easier task. I have also benefited from numerous conversations and seminars with graduate and undergraduate students at UK. I learned much from them. George Herring has been an exceptional colleague and friend. George is the premier historian of the Vietnam War, and he certainly helped me better understand the diplomacy of departmental and university politics in ways so I could avoid my own quagmires. We also shared a few beers and many enjoyable moments along the way watching the Kentucky basketball team, an organization with its own culture of corruption, some might say.

It is my singular good fortune to work with Mark Wahlgren Summers. Throughout the years of researching and writing this book,

Mark was more than generous with his time and knowledge, and he managed to convince me I was not as foolhardy to attempt this book as I thought. When I faced certain research challenges or dead end streets, all I had to do was walk to the other end of the hall to find Mark. I never left disappointed. He gave the manuscript as careful a reading as anyone, and I hope he did not suffer too much from a chronic bout of "Crook Fatigue" brought on by my labored prose. Lastly, many of the cartoons featured in this book came from Mark's extensive collection. His professional advice has been crucial, but pales in comparison to what his friendship has meant to me.

I am also fortunate to have John W. Wright as my agent, who was a champion of this book and its author through thick and thin. His tenacity and patience helped guide the manuscript through the labyrinth of the publishing process. Through it all, John believed in me in times when I am not sure I did. I am also glad that John's literary talents surpass his considerable prognostication capacities in the equine arts. My editor, Philip Turner, gave this book the care and attention most writers only dream about. From the outset, he quickly grasped what I wanted to do, and his democratic instincts pushed me to refine my arguments and bring life to the prose. Keith Wallman did wonders getting the book into production, and Phil Gaskill was a marvelous copy editor.

Richard Scher of the University of Florida first pointed me toward the Florida Secretary of State's website about the 2000 election. Old friends Chuck Bolton and Jim Bissett provided thoughtful editorial suggestions as well as some fascinating leads in stolen elections. Nell Goodwyn and her significant other supplied lodging, hospitality, good food and drink, and much-needed support and advice. They came to my personal and professional rescue on several occasions and went the extra mile helping me cut and retool a bloated manuscript. A number of people who asked to be, or should remain, anonymous, provided plenty of memorable stories and, at times, confessions of what they had witnessed, or done themselves, to win an election. Although I did not include these accounts in this book, each of them gave me a deeper understanding of how elections work.

I always benefited from the sound counsel and encouragement of Thomas D. Clark, a singular historian and public scholar who passed away just weeks before this book went to press. After his 101st birthday, Dr. Clark and I had several memorable discussions about the history of election fraud, and I especially enjoyed seeing the passion and intensity he displayed describing his own future writing projects. His was a life well-lived, and a career that remains the standard for all committed writers of the past to emulate.

Participating on a panel in 2002 with Alex Keyssar and Nancy Unger helped change the structure of this project in numerous ways. Alex later read the manuscript and offered excellent suggestions, while Nancy's infectious support meant so much when I badly needed it. Don Ritchie also read the manuscript with his usual careful eye and with amazing speed. He is truly "the machine." Susan Ferber offered some penetrating critiques early on and helped me conceive how to approach the research. Thanks also to Tim Tyson, whose own brilliant work convinced me to quit hiding behind the footnotes, and his suggestions on cutting the manuscript was much needed and appreciated.

The University of Kentucky was very helpful in giving me time and resources to finish the book. I want to especially thank Vice President Wendy Baldwin and the Office of Research and Support at UK for a summer research grant, as well as Dean Steven Hoch and the College of Arts and Sciences for much-needed travel and sabbatical research funds. My thanks as well to Dean Carol Pitts Diedrichs for her support of the Ford Center and helping carve out a role for me to play in the public policy arena.

Many politicians have provided me a unique education about how real politics works, but none more so than the late Kentucky Governor Edward T. "Ned" Breathitt. Although I suspected he never told me quite everything he knew about the art of delivering votes, he gave me my best primer about power politics. He also opened countless doors for me that made so many things possible. At every occasion I saw him over the years, he asked me about my progress and how much he looked forward to reading it. I am saddened he did not live to see it in print, and I dearly miss his stories and heartfelt kindness.

My son, Alex, grew into an impressive young man during the writing of this book, and he often allowed me to think and write while playing his guitar as softly, and expertly, as possible. His pointed questions about the structure of democratic societies have informed this book in significant ways. My youngest son, Drew, was born midway through, and he certainly had some interesting questions of his own, even if they had little to do with elections. Research and writing is often a lonely process, and my beloved sons made it a much easier task. As they grow older, I hope on every Election Day they will vote early, and just once.

Of course, no one did more to see this book come to fruition than my wife and best friend, Leslie. Not only did she take the kids on at least five hundred trips in order to give me time to write, she also read the entire manuscript and proved a demanding and critical editor. She did not let me get by with even one sloppy word or phrase, and pushed me to dig even deeper into the meaning of voting and democracy. I hate to disagree with Faulkner, but when he wrote, "You don't love because; you love despite," he did not know Leslie. I love her because.

Index

About the Author

TRACY CAMPBELL is the author of *The Politics of Despair: Power and Resistance in the Tobacco Wars*, and *Short of the Glory: The Fall and Redemption of Edward F. Prichard, Jr.*, which tells the story of a brilliant politician's demise due to ballot-box stuffing. *Short of the Glory* was nominated for a Pulitzer Prize. Campbell is Associate Professor of History and Co-Director of the Wendell H. Ford Public Policy Research Center at the University of Kentucky in Lexington.